PSYCHOLOGY AND THE CONDUCT OF EVERYDAY LIFE

Psychology and the Conduct of Everyday Life moves psychological theory and research practice out of the laboratory and into the everyday world. Drawing on recent developments across the social and human sciences, it examines how people live as active subjects within the contexts of their everyday lives, using this as an analytical basis for understanding the dilemmas and contradictions people face in contemporary society.

Early chapters gather the latest empirical research to explore the significance of context as a cross-disciplinary critical tool; they include a study of homeless Māori men reaffirming their cultural identity via gardening, and a look at how the dilemmas faced by children in difficult situations can provide insights into social conflict at school. Later chapters examine the interplay between everyday life around the world and contemporary global phenomena such as the rise of the debt economy, the hegemony of the labor market, and the increased reliance on digital technology in educational settings. The book concludes with a consideration of how social psychology can deepen our understanding of how we conduct our lives, and offer possibilities for collective work on the resolution of social conflict.

Ernst Schraube is Associate Professor of Social Psychology of Technology in Everyday Life in the Department of Psychology and Educational Studies at Roskilde University in Denmark.

Charlotte Højholt is Professor of Social Psychology of Everyday Life in the Department of Psychology and Educational S Denmark.

PSYCHOLOGY AND THE CONDUCT OF EVERYDAY LIFE

Edited by Ernst Schraube and Charlotte Højholt

LONDON AND NEW YORK

First published 2016
by Routledge
27 Church Road, Hove, East Sussex BN3 2FA

and by Routledge
711 Third Avenue, New York, NY 10017

Routledge is an imprint of the Taylor & Francis Group, an informa business

© 2016 Ernst Schraube and Charlotte Højholt

The right of Ernst Schraube and Charlotte Højholt to be identified as the authors of the editorial material, and of the authors for their individual chapters, has been asserted in accordance with sections 77 and 78 of the Copyright, Designs and Patents Act 1988.

All rights reserved. No part of this book may be reprinted or reproduced or utilised in any form or by any electronic, mechanical, or other means, now known or hereafter invented, including photocopying and recording, or in any information storage or retrieval system, without permission in writing from the publishers.

Trademark notice: Product or corporate names may be trademarks or registered trademarks, and are used only for identification and explanation without intent to infringe.

British Library Cataloguing in Publication Data
A catalogue record for this book is available from the British Library

Library of Congress Cataloguing in Publication data
Psychology and the conduct of everyday life / [edited by] Ernst Schraube and Charlotte Højholt.
    pages   cm
1. Human behavior. 2. Conduct of life–Psychological aspects. 3. Social psychology. I. Schraube, Ernst. II. Højholt, Charlotte.
HM1033.P84 2015
302–dc23   2015005700

ISBN: 978-1-138-81511-7 (hbk)
ISBN: 978-1-138-81512-4 (pbk)
ISBN: 978-1-315-74689-0 (ebk)

Typeset in Bembo
by Out of House Publishing

CONTENTS

List of Contributors   vii

Introduction: Toward a Psychology of Everyday Living   1
Charlotte Højholt and Ernst Schraube

1   Conduct of Everyday Life: Implications for Critical Psychology   15
   Ole Dreier

2   Conduct of Everyday Life in Subject-Oriented
   Sociology: Concept and Empirical Research   34
   Karin Jurczyk, G. Günter Voß and Margit Weihrich

3   Conduct of Everyday Life as a Basic Concept of
   Critical Psychology   65
   Klaus Holzkamp

4   The Maze and the Labyrinth: Walking, Imagining and the
   Education of Attention   99
   Tim Ingold

5   Embodying the Conduct of Everyday Life: From Subjective
   Reasons to Privilege   111
   Thomas Teo

6 The Ordinary in the Extra Ordinary: Everyday Living Textured by Homelessness 124
Darrin Hodgetts, Mohi Rua, Pita King and Tiniwai Te Whetu

7 Situated Inequality and the Conflictuality of Children's Conduct of Life 145
Charlotte Højholt

8 "There is No Right Life in the Wrong One": Recognizing this Dilemma is the First Step Out of it 164
Ute Osterkamp

9 Everyday Life in the Shadow of the Debt Economy 176
C. George Caffentzis

10 From Crisis to Commons: Reproductive Work, Affective Labor and Technology in the Transformation of Everyday Life 192
Silvia Federici

11 Frozen Fluidity: Digital Technologies and the Transformation of Students' Learning and Conduct of Everyday Life 205
Ernst Schraube and Athanasios Marvakis

12 The Politics of Hope: Memory-Work as a Method to Study the Conduct of Everyday Life 226
Frigga Haug

13 Collaborative Research with Children: Exploring Contradictory Conditions of the Conduct of Everyday Life 241
Dorte Kousholt

Index 259

CONTRIBUTORS

Ole Dreier, Department of Psychology, University of Copenhagen, Denmark and Lillehammer University College, Norway.

Silvia Federici, Hofstra University, United States.

Frigga Haug, Berlin Institute of Critical Theory, Germany.

Darrin Hodgetts, School of Psychology, Massey University, Auckland, New Zealand.

Charlotte Højholt, Department of Psychology and Educational Studies, Roskilde University, Denmark.

Klaus Holzkamp (1927–1995), Department of Psychology, Free University Berlin, Germany.

Tim Ingold, Department of Anthropology, University of Aberdeen, Scotland.

Karin Jurczyk, German Youth Institute, Department of Family and Family Policies, Munich, Germany.

Pita King, School of Psychology, Massey University, Auckland, New Zealand.

Dorte Kousholt, Department of Education, Aarhus University, Denmark.

Athanasios Marvakis, Department of Education, University of Thessaloniki, Greece.

Ute Osterkamp, Department of Psychology, Free University Berlin, Germany.

Mohi Rua, School of Psychology, University of Waikato, Hamilton, New Zealand.

Ernst Schraube, Department of Psychology and Educational Studies, Roskilde University, Denmark.

Thomas Teo, Department of Psychology, York University, Toronto, Canada.

G. Günter Voß, Department of Sociology, Chemnitz University of Technology, Germany.

Margit Weihrich, Department of Philosophy and Social Science, Augsburg University, Germany.

Tiniwai Te Whetu, School of Psychology, University of Waikato, Hamilton, New Zealand.

INTRODUCTION

Toward a Psychology of Everyday Living

Charlotte Højholt and Ernst Schraube

This book is about the psychological study of the conduct of everyday life in contemporary society. Presenting a body of critical and interdisciplinary work, it takes psychological theory and research practice out of the laboratory and into the real world. With its focus on the question of how human beings as active sensuous subjects live their everyday lives, it explores the conduct of life as a basis for understanding the dilemmas and contradictions we are confronted with in our daily lives.

From the earliest days of its formation as an independent discipline, psychology has been concerned with human experience, activity and self-reflection, but the question of how to conduct one's life has not received much attention. The growing awareness of this discrepancy over recent years has turned discussions within psychology toward the practice of everyday living and the concept of conduct of everyday life is getting incorporated into psychological theory and research practice. The importance of the conduct of everyday life for psychology lies in its conceptual relevance in exploring and understanding the everyday activities of individual subjects to organize, integrate and make sense of the multiplicity of social relations and contradictory demands in and across the different contexts in which they are engaged in their daily life. The concept takes into account how people collaboratively produce and reproduce their life through daily activities, habits, routines and personal arrangements of things and social relations. It directs attention to the social conditions in and with which people act, participate and live their everyday life and includes the question of how people are subjected to socio-material dispositions of power, knowledge and discourse. Furthermore, it facilitates an exploration of emerging new ways of everyday living and how these contribute to remaking the social world. Hence, working with the "conduct of everyday life" and refining this concept can support an understanding of psychological phenomena as they unfold in the reality of everyday living, and promote a fundamental renewal of psychological theory, methodology and practice.

In the following we will first indicate how the study of the *conduct of everyday life* builds on the study of *everyday life*, as well as how a turn toward a psychology of everyday living relates to the scientific self-understanding of conventional psychology and what kind of theoretical challenges it raises. Then we describe in more detail the practice of everyday living, including its conflictuality and collective coordination, and finally present an outline of the different chapters of this volume.

Formation and Challenges of a Psychology of Everyday Living

Since the mid 20th century, when scholars came to recognize the central significance of *everyday life* in understanding human affairs, the study of everyday life has become a major concern within the social and human sciences. Rather than everyday life merely consisting of trivial and banal day-to-day activities, scholars have realized that it constitutes the nucleus of human life and the space in which our social relations are produced and reproduced. Everyday life comprises all human activities situated in and across a multiplicity of spaces and contexts (home, work, educational institutions, shopping venues, recreational arenas, digital spaces, etc.). As Henri Lefebvre explains in his seminal work, *Critique of Everyday Life* (1947/1991):

> Everyday life is profoundly related to *all* activities, and encompasses them with all their differences and their conflicts; it is their meeting place, their bond and their common ground. And it is in everyday life that the sum total of relations which make the human – and every human being – a whole takes its shape and its form.
>
> (p. 97)

During the twentieth century, starting from the actualities of people's lives, the study of everyday life emerged as a distinct subject of research across a variety of disciplines (e.g., history, sociology, philosophy, anthropology) as well as interdisciplinary programs (e.g., cultural studies, media studies), developing a detailed vocabulary to explore the everyday world in its complex and problematic socio-historical relations (de Certeau, 1984; Ferguson, 2009; Gardiner, 2000; Goffman, 1959; Highmore, 2010; Pink, 2012; Sheringham, 2006; Smith, 1987, and many others).

The study of the *conduct of everyday life* builds on this substantial body of work and expands it with a new focus. Drawing on a "turn to the subject" and elaborated conceptualizations of subjectivity and the human being (e.g., Blackmann et al., 2008; Butler, 1989; Holzkamp, 2013; Walkerdine, 2002), it concentrates even more on human *activity* and systematically centers on the lived experience, agency and efforts of how human subjects *live* their *everyday life*. This entails a shift of focus toward the study of *everyday living from the perspectives and standpoints of the human subjects*. By structuring research through the experiences and involvement of human subjects, the complexity and problematic nature of everyday life can be dealt with more consistently. As a result, it becomes possible to explore what the world means for human life through everyday living and consider how this can be transformed for the better.

Why did it take psychology such a long time to engage in the conduct of everyday life as a major topic of research? Here, one reason can be found in conventional psychology's particular epistemology and scientific self-understanding. In conventional empirical research, the production of knowledge is situated in a specific setting. To investigate psychological phenomena, the researcher constructs an artificial situation – usually an experiment in a university laboratory. This construction establishes a dichotomy between this *experimental reality* and the *everyday reality*. Hence, while the experimental reality's artificial arrangement reduces the research matter's complexity to fit into the controlled and manipulable laboratory setting, this leaves open the question of how far knowledge of psychological phenomena produced in this duplicated reality can be transferred to and generalized in the reality of everyday life (Holzkamp, 2015, chap. 3 in this volume, p. 74f).

Such psychological research practice can be seen as a basis for the conspicuously *abstract* psychological knowledge and theory-building, since it confronts us with the dilemma of not knowing what the studied phenomena and problems are part of and connected with. Here, the interest in everyday life turns the endeavor of isolating "factors" and "variables" upside down, pointing instead to the need to explore how psychological phenomena and problems are endowed with content and significances precisely out of the contexts they are part of. For instance, personal ways of being involved in and experiencing dilemmas are connected to particular practices, relations, concerns and social structures. The concept of the conduct of everyday life might then open a route to overcome the abstract individualism of psychology (and its accompanying wordlessness) that encloses subjects in isolated psychological special functions and to contribute to a psychological epistemology grasping the richness, complexity and connectedness of psychological phenomena as well as the interrelations between human subjects and the world. Working with this concern implies situating empirical research and the production of psychological knowledge in the everyday reality in which psychological phenomena actually unfold.

Psychologists became increasingly aware of these epistemological dilemmas in psychological research practices during the 1970s, in particular through the discussion on the crisis of social psychology (Parker, 1989). The historical roots of this discussion can be traced back to the early work of Wilhelm Dilthey, Lev Vygotsky, Wilhelm Stern, Kurt Lewin and many others. But in the 1970s it induced new beginnings and a variety of alternative psychological approaches emerged, ranging from feminist psychology, phenomenology, discursive psychology and social constructionism to cultural historical activity theory and critical psychologies, taking psychological research out of the duplicated reality of the classical experimental setting into the reality of everyday life (e.g., Argyle, 1992; Brinkmann, 2012; Burkitt, 2004; Gergen, 2009; Hodgetts et al., 2010; Scheibe, 2000; Shotter, 1993; Stephenson & Papadopoulos, 2006). Within this broad movement and inspired by subject-oriented sociologists (Jurczyk & Rerrich, 1993; Voß, 1991; Jurczyk et al., 2015, chap. 2 in this volume), a group of critical psychologists paid increasing attention to the significance of the conduct of everyday life for psychology, and systematically started to explore its formation. As Klaus Holzkamp explains: "The conduct of everyday life is ... the elementary form of human existence" (2013, p. 314), and he suggests defining the constitutive subject matter of psychology not as the individual, nor the individual subject in societal relations, but "the subject within the context of her/his conduct of everyday life" (ibid., p. 314).

The concept of the conduct of everyday life offers an approach to overcoming a variety of psychology's fundamental internal challenges, discussed from different angles and theoretical backgrounds in the chapters of this book. In this discussion, some of the central challenges that emerge concern psychological knowledge's continuing individualism as well as the question of its general societal relevance.

Although Wilhelm Wundt, one of the founding fathers of academic psychology, emphasized that psychology deals with the human subject's experiences and activities in relation to others and the world (1897, p. 3), the conventional explanatory models in the history of psychology have consistently favored a radical individualism. As James Wertsch notes: within contemporary psychology "research is often based on the assumption that it is possible, even desirable, to study the individual ... in isolation" (1991, p. 2); despite "criticism" over decades, the "individualistic orientation is characteristic of the discipline in general" (ibid., p. 3). Furthermore, he explains:

> We can answer detailed questions about neuronal activity or neonatal reflexes, but we have very little to say about what it means to be human in the modern world ... Psychology has become increasingly less capable of providing insights into the major social issues of the day.
>
> (Ibid., p. 1f.)

Developing a concept of the conduct of everyday life addresses this challenge by opening up a specific approach to understanding the relationship between the individual and society. Since the conduct of life refers to the subject's integrative and constructive activity, it goes beyond a deterministic perspective merely conceptualizing the individual as a set of dependent variables of societal structures. On the one hand, the question of the conduct of life cannot be limited to how people adjust to some given conditions, since living one's life implies *arranging* conditions, together with others, revising plans and pursuing perceived interests. On the other hand, this concept goes beyond the voluntaristic perspective of autonomous individuals and recognizes that individual life is not just determined as each person would like, but is co-created through the fabric of the societal world. The conduct of everyday life represents a mediating category between the individual subjects and societal structures, articulating in particular the subjects' experiences and the scope of action as they grapple with these structures through collective and structuring actions. As Ole Dreier notes, a shift toward the conduct of everyday life enables us to bring our "analyses closer to what it means and takes to be a subject living in a society" (2015, chap. 1 in this volume, p. 17; see also Dreier, 2008).

The interest in the study of the conduct of everyday life is related to current transformations in society. Globalization, financial and environmental crisis, debt, migration, war and large-scale conflicts influence and change the patterns of social and individual life all over the world (e.g., Caffentzis, 2015, chap. 9 in this volume; Federici, 2015, chap. 10 in this volume). As a result of these changes, psychological theory, research and practice is confronting new complex problems and challenges. Psychologists are now dealing with people whose social realities and forms of life are undergoing changes toward increasing individualism, as well as greater social and cultural heterogeneity and complexity. This sets the stage for new complex problems to emerge through advances in technologies, digitalization, new forms of work and modes of production, unemployment and poverty, increasing individual mobility, lifelong education and a readiness for change, etc. In this context, there is a growing need for psychology to move out of the laboratory to investigate and understand how people confront and experience local changes in relation to social systems, institutions, technologies and daily life practices in the course of their everyday life. Psychological theory and research, in turn, thus have to relate their understanding of human sensuous activities and experiences to the social practices and structures in which people live and experience their problems. Here, the theories developed on how people conduct their lives need to be sensitive to complex movements, trajectories and shifts as well as to the historical, cultural, local and global conditions of life. In addition, this requires reflecting on the new methodologies and research practices facilitating the empirical investigations of the everyday realities and problems in people's lives.

The Practice of Everyday Living

Conceptualizing the conduct of everyday life involves three essential dimensions. Human activities often come to be seen as "everyday" when they are processes involving a daily repetition such as, for example, getting up in the morning, making breakfast, discussing who is going to buy the food for dinner, taking the children to nursery school, going to work, etc. This elementary *cyclical organization of everyday living*, which includes rhythms, routines and habits, constitutes a fundamental dimension of the conduct of everyday life. However, these rhythms and routines of daily life are not just mechanisms and do not happen automatically, but are active achievements of an individual subject. Since they include not only arranging and resolving practical daily tasks and demands, but also coordinating and integrating these in an overall arrangement, Karin Jurczyk, G. Günter Voß and Margit Weihrich have described the conduct of life as the "arrangement of the individual arrangements" (2015, chap. 2 in this volume, p. 46). The rhythms and routines relieve us of the need to constantly observe, negotiate and justify what we do or do not do, and provide a basic foundation for our lives.

However, the conduct of everyday life involves more than just the ordinary repetitiveness and cyclical structure of everyday living. The practice of everyday living requires not only a reproductive dimension, but also a productive one, where we transcend ordinary routines and cycles either deliberately or through necessity. The productive dimension allows us to organize and come to terms with the different, contradictory and often unforeseeable demands, disruptions and challenges we are confronted with in the various arenas of our daily life. Therefore, the conduct of everyday life also always involves a dimension of *transcendence and extra-ordinary experience and activity*, situations in everyday living where we enter unknown territory, engage in serious challenges and struggles, experience exceptional moments of happiness, joy or insight (or the opposite) in which we may sometimes even have the impression that these extra-ordinary moments are precisely where life "really" happens.

Both the ordinary cyclical and the extra-ordinary transcending aspects of everyday living are integrated in a third central dimension of the conduct of everyday life. Living one's life includes what we could call the subject's specific *integrative sensibility and way of sense-making* without which the conduct of life would not be possible. Hence, the conduct of life does not just refer to the day-to-day organization and integration of the various demands, it is also connected to the subject's conception of his/her history as well as future. It is related (and we might not always be aware of it) to a broader imagination of how we see the world and what we want with our life, and out of this broader imagination of our life and the anticipation of action possibilities, the concrete ordinary and extra-ordinary everyday activities and arrangements become meaningful and accomplishable. The personal experience of cohesion in life is also related to social conflicts, for instance between contradictory demands in life, and how such conflicts develop and are unlocked or reach an impasse. In the following, we discuss in more detail how personal sense-making is interlaced with the social conflictuality of the conduct of everyday life.

All the different approaches presented in this book discuss the conduct of everyday life as a fundamentally collective process. The concept of conduct of life is applied and developed in analyzing how subjects conduct their lives in collaboration with other subjects and in relation to different matters in their lives. Such conceptualizations seek to capture the inherently social dimension of our lives as human beings and, in this way, set the subject in the plural. This focus points to *social coordination and conflicts* as the central problems of the personal conduct of life (Axel, 2011; Chimirri, 2014). Shifting the notion of the conduct of life from single persons' lives to the processes of arranging different but interwoven lives changes our understanding of routines in everyday life. Developing routines is not just an individual project. Our routines are created, maintained and negotiated in the context of coordination with others' conducts of life, which may also entail conflict or struggles with them. Those involved in each other's everyday lives – whether as family members, colleagues, neighbors or friends – cooperate and disagree over how to establish preferences, make plans, prioritize and carry out simple everyday routines as well as more comprehensive alterations, rebuildings and diversions.

In today's Western countries people live their everyday lives in a plurality of contexts. In these different contexts, the lives of participants are connected with each other in fundamentally different ways, and their activities are structured in relation to different purposes and conditions. In these interconnected practices, problems at one place (e.g., in the family) are often related to conflicts *between diverse contexts* (e.g., school and home, or different workplaces) where those involved take part. Thus, in the trajectory across everyday contexts, very different issues and concerns have to be taken into account and related to one another. Therefore, when people conduct their everyday lives they are taking part in reproducing, negotiating and changing social structures, and arranging lives involves exploring *structural possibilities*, connections and restrictions in everyday life. In this way we may investigate social structures through the personal ways subjects relate and ascribe meanings to these in everyday living – as expressed in their personal participation and experiences as well as in their dilemmas and conflicts.

Analyzing such aspects of everyday living builds on theoretical insights from research highlighting the historical and conflictual nature of social processes (e.g., Chaiklin, Hedegaard & Jensen, 1999; Holland & Lave, 2001; Juul Jensen, 1999; Lave, 2008, 2011). Such an approach points to the nature of everyday living as fundamentally conflictual, rather than conflict as an intermittent experience linked to disturbances or errors. Since conflict is regarded as an inherent part of social practices, this *general* conflictuality may be seen as an analytical background for understanding the *specific* dilemmas of the conduct of everyday life.

Focusing on the conduct of everyday life opens up personal as well as social and political perspectives and concerns. The growing individualization of core institutions (such as family, education and work) and of the ways to organize social life places new demands on our conduct of everyday life. Against this background, a scholarly interest in the concept may then itself tend to gravitate toward individualistic discourses of human life where knowledge of the conduct of everyday life appears to offer the potential to monitor, discipline and regulate the lives of others. However, it is precisely the knowledge of how people experience these ideologies and social changes in the conduct of their everyday lives, and how people work on transforming them, which could also reveal the forces of individualization and governing others.

A point of reference in the common life that subjects live in a shared world illustrates how interests and perspectives are not just different, but also connected and related through joint yet multifaceted issues, concerns and problems. The participants' conflicts are an expression of that shared engagement, and provide an opportunity to expand our understanding of common problems (Busch-Jensen, 2015). In this way, a concept of the conduct of everyday life can potentially derive knowledge from different people's experiences of dilemmas in their everyday life – not as knowledge about "other persons" but as knowledge about societal problems seen from these persons' perspectives (elaborated in Kousholt, 2015, chap. 13 in this volume, p. 245f). By inquiring into the meanings, reasons and conflicts involved in everyday living, psychology can gain a new relevance in exploring, understanding and transforming social problems. We need to connect the different aspects of multifaceted concerns instead of reducing their complexity to dichotomies between "social interests" and "individual interests." In this way, the concept of everyday life may offer options for solidarity and a democratic research methodology where common problems are explored through the way they are experienced in everyday living and from different locations and positions. Here, the contributions in this book set out to advance this approach further by engaging in critical dialogues on how people actively seek to create and conduct their lives in and across the complex realities of today's everyday life, and also to consider the related theoretical discussions and conceptualizations.

In various ways, the following chapters illustrate a move toward a situated, social and contextual understanding of psychological processes. Several chapters, for instance, underline the implication here of a need for methodological practices where researchers participate in everyday practices and cooperate with those outside academia as "co-researchers" in a shared exploration of social problems (instead of positioning the "other" as the object of research). Such methodologies conceptualize flexible ways of "fitting into daily life" through varies modes of participation, enriching the researchers with a situated insight from mundane and often unnoticed or even neglected perspectives. In the words of Darrin Hodgetts, Mohi Rua, Pita King and Tiniwai Te Whetu:

> The style of research in which we engaged in our project operates in a more flexible manner where we try harder to fit into everyday events ... A case-based methodology characterized by closer and more engaged relations between researchers and participants than is typically evident in psychology.
> (2015, chap. 6 in this volume, pp. 141–142)

In this vein, this volume attempts to substantiate a variety of critically situated approaches to the experiences and actions of the conduct of life in today's social and technological world, and to debate how the study of subjects in the context of their conduct of everyday life can contribute to the renewal of psychological theory, methodology and practice. How can we develop knowledge about and research into the active efforts of subjects to engage in everyday activities, tasks and participations across time and space? What kind of new forms of doing and thinking in everyday life are emerging and how do they contribute to the remaking of the social world? How can we reconceptualize subjectivity, agency and possibilities of social and political change? The 13 chapters in this volume are written by distinguished scholars working in psychology and other social and human sciences who are engaged in developing this field of research and, through their theoretical, methodological as well as empirical work, contributing to the study of the conduct of life in and across the different arenas of everyday life.

Explorations in Everyday Living

In the first chapter of this volume Ole Dreier highlights the power of the concept of the conduct of everyday life to reform the psychological gaze. He focuses especially on the implications of the concept for critical psychology and explains how it can enable a shift in the approach of critical psychology from studying subjects in their immediate life situation vis-à-vis an overall social structure to studying how they conduct their lives in structures of everyday social practice. Such a shift, he argues, will change how we comprehend the psychological functioning of persons, their experiences, concerns, stances and self-understanding. It also changes how we comprehend the significance of an overall social structure for subjects by considering it from the standpoint and perspective of persons conducting their lives in structures of social practice.

In Chapter 2, Karin Jurczyk, G. Günter Voß and Margit Weihrich introduce a sociological approach to the study of the conduct of everyday life. They describe the development of their body of research over the years, conceptualizing the conduct of life as the discrete effort made by the individual in order to meet the different – and sometimes conflicting – demands that arise in the various spheres of everyday life, and to arrange them into a livable whole. Society can therefore be understood through the everyday lives of the individuals performing these actions. In the presentation of their extensive empirical research on the forms, methods, resources and strains of the conduct of everyday life under a variety of living conditions they illuminate how conducting one's life in the process of social modernization is becoming an ever-increasing challenge.

Chapter 3 presents an unfinished manuscript by Klaus Holzkamp on the conduct of everyday life on which he was working before his death in 1995 (the text was published in German in the journal *Das Argument*; there exists a second unfinished manuscript by Holzkamp on the conduct of life published in English in 2013). During his research on learning Holzkamp became aware of the importance of everyday living for psychology. He realized that in the entire history of psychology the conduct of everyday life has not been to any extent systematically and comprehensively analyzed or conceptualized as a theoretical problem in its own right. Building on the work of the group of subject-oriented sociologists around Jurczyk, Voß and Weihrich, he began to delve into an exploration of the conduct of everyday life. This chapter presents some first insights on this route, including a discussion of the sociological approach, an analysis of why the concept has not so far been investigated within psychology, as well as reflections on how to study the conduct of life from the standpoint of the subjects.

In Chapter 4 the anthropologist Tim Ingold focuses on the importance of a specific practice of everyday living: walking and the practice of exposure as an alternative model of education. He argues for an educational practice that, rather than instilling knowledge into the minds of novices, leads them out into the real world. He compares these alternatives to the difference between the maze and the labyrinth. The maze, which presents a series of choices but predetermines the moves predicated on each, puts all the emphasis on the traveler's intentions. In the labyrinth, by contrast, choice is not an issue, but holding to the trail calls for continual attention. Education along the lines of the labyrinth does not provide novices with standpoints or positions, but continually pulls them from any positions they might adopt. It is a practice of exposure. The attention required by such a practice is one that waits upon things, and that is present at their appearance. To "appear things" is tantamount to their imagination, on the plane of immanent life. Human life is temporally stretched between imagination and perception, and education (in the original sense of the Greek *scholè*) fills the gap between them. He concludes that such a "poor pedagogy" provided by a mode of education that has no content to transmit, and no methods for doing so, nevertheless offers an understanding of the way to truth.

In Chapter 5, Thomas Teo discusses Holzkamp's approach to the conduct of everyday life in the context of critical psychology as an international progressive research program that can assimilate and accommodate critical traditions from inside and outside the West. He argues that Holzkamp provides a first-order solution to the relationship between society and the individual and a partial solution to the problem of how critical psychology should conceptualize the mediation between social structure and the conduct of everyday life. Drawing on the work of Pierre Bourdieu, Judith Butler and Peggy McIntosh, he suggests that the study of the conduct of life needs to include concepts such as *habitus*, *performativity* and *privilege* that are grounded in critical theories of embodiment and not in a philosophy of consciousness.

Everyday living is often conceptualized in terms of the mundane or ordinary. Yet, for increasing numbers of people disruption and the extra-ordinary have become normative. In Chapter 6, Darrin Hodgetts, Mohi Rua, Pita King and Tiniwai Te Whetu explore how the ordinary re-emerges within the extra-ordinary lives of a group of older homeless Māori men when they spend Tuesdays and Thursdays at a Marae garden (a traditional Māori meeting place for the conduct of daily life). The chapter illustrates and reflects on how to carry out empirical research on everyday living and presents insights on how gardening provides homeless Māori men with an opportunity to reaffirm culturally patterned relationships, heritage and identities.

Based on empirical research on children's conduct of life, Charlotte Højholt focuses in Chapter 7 on conflicts in everyday life and their relatedness to social, political and structural conflicts. With the concept of *situated inequality*, she draws attention to the social distribution of possibilities for taking part in and influencing the social coordination of everyday contexts. Discussing examples from children's conduct of everyday life across institutional arrangements, where several parties have different kinds of responsibility and conflicting perspectives on the children, she argues that the social (and political) conflicts *about* children lead to personal problems *for* children. In this way, the concrete dilemmas of children can teach us something about the social conflicts in and about school. Finally she discusses the challenges of how to conceptualize meanings of the children's social backgrounds as well as how to conceptualize their personal agency.

The starting point of Ute Osterkamp's exploration of everyday living in Chapter 8 is Adorno's famous dictum "there is no right life in the wrong one," and she argues that recognizing this dilemma is the first step out of it. Osterkamp indicates that Adorno's expression is often rejected with the argument that it denies any possibility of change and people's responsibility for it. Such objections seem to proceed from a restricted notion of human agency and responsibility, reducing them to the best possible adjustment to given conditions and norms. In contrast, she discusses how, from the perspective of a psychology conceptualized from a generalized subject standpoint, both the "inhumanity" of such a limited view of human agency and subjectivity, and the subjective need to overcome inhumane conditions, become visible. However, to overcome such a restricted concept of human agency and subjectivity, it is necessary to become aware of the varied forms and ways in which we unwittingly support in our own thoughts and actions conditions that we want to overcome. This includes the need to recognize and resist the many pressures that lead us to ignore all contradictory information so as to keep up the semblance of being able to live our lives in the right way, in contrast to others.

In Chapter 9 the philosopher George Caffentzis examines everyday life in the shadow of the rise of the debt economy in the United States. Recognizing that major theorists of everyday life (from Marx to Lefebvre) did not attend to the impact of debt, in his investigation Caffentzis articulates the new structure of the satisfaction of needs the debt economy imposes that is quite different from the structure of needs in the previous wage-dominated economy. Furthermore, he analyzes four different kinds of debtor–creditor relationships with respect to class relations, and reflects on new forms of alienation that Marx and 20th-century theorists of everyday life had neglected. The chapter concludes with a historical sketch of the anti-debt movement in the United States that developed in the wake of the 2008 financial crisis and that potentially can challenge contemporary conduct of everyday life in the debt economy.

In Chapter 10, feminist activist and political philosopher Silvia Federici explores how the subsumption of everyday living to the needs of the labor market affects our social relations and subjectivity, as well as how we can re-appropriate our lives, our bodies, and overcome the reproductive crisis that we are facing. She discusses these questions by examining how the restructuring of the world economy has affected reproductive work and gender relations, the role that technology has played in this process, and the initiatives that women in particular are taking, worldwide, to construct more cooperative and equitable forms of reproduction. She argues that everyday living today must begin with a struggle against the ongoing, historic assault on the means of our reproduction and our social and ecological environment.

In Chapter 11 Ernst Schraube and Athanasios Marvakis investigate the contradictory significance of digital technology in students' learning. The digitization of higher education is radically transforming learning and teaching relations, including the content of learning and the students' conduct of life. The chapter analyzes the relevance of digital technology for learners and their learning activities focusing on the question of learning. What is learning? How to integrate learners into learning theory and reflections on digital technology? Why, how and to what end does learning take place, and what are the best possible conditions for learning? Building on situated and participatory learning theory the chapter shows how learning is not just a transfer or internalization of knowledge, but a basic human activity for appropriating and changing the world, rooted in our conduct of everyday life. It argues for conceptualizing learning from the standpoint of the learners and describes decisive elements and phases of the learning activity including the crucial role of the fluid, mutual entanglement of learning and teaching. Based on a refined concept of learning it shows how the digitalization of students' learning environment reconfigures the structures of participation and how it can catalyze but also freeze the fluidity of learning and teaching.

Drawing on Antonio Gramsci's thoughts on how theoretical concepts relate to common sense, Frigga Haug explores in Chapter 12 the relationship between theory and everyday understanding as a basic challenge in the study of the conduct of life. The chapter introduces memory-work as a possible approach to deal with this challenge and presents its individual steps, theoretical foundations and possibilities for an empirical inquiry into everyday living. Haug highlights how memory-work can contribute to empower individual subjects taking control of their own conduct of life and presents the political project *Four-in-One-Perspective*. This is a proposal to understand everyday living as taking place in four main areas (work-life, reproduction, self-development and politics) and addresses the challenges in bringing these four areas together in one conduct of life instead of spending one's whole life in only one or two areas, unhappily and subordinated. Finally the chapter illustrates how to substantiate such a political project in anticipatory memory-work and work with hope.

In Chapter 13 Dorte Kousholt expands the methodological discussion of how to empirically explore everyday living by focusing on the interconnections of subjective and structural aspects of persons conducting their everyday life in and across social practices. Kousholt discusses the possibilities for arranging participatory research collaboration that enables the development of knowledge about common problems and contradictory life conditions in their meanings to different persons. Based on examples from her own research, where she followed children's lives and transitions across their different life contexts, she demonstrates how to investigate practices from different positions and perspectives and how this provides knowledge about the complexity of social conflicts and possibilities for change.

References

Argyle, M. (1992). *The social psychology of everyday life*. London: Routledge.
Axel, E. (2011). Conflictual cooperation. *Nordic Psychology, 20*(4), 56–78.
Blackmann, L., Cromby, J., Hook, D., Papadopoulos, D. & Walkerdine, V. (2008). Creating subjectivities. *Subjectivity, 22*, 1–27.
Brinkmann, S. (2012). *Qualitative inquiry in everyday life*. London: Sage.
Burkitt, I. (2004). The time and space of everyday life. *Cultural Studies, 18*(2/3), 211–227.
Busch-Jensen, P. (2015). The production of power in organizational practice: Working with conflicts as heuristics. *Outlines: Critical Practice Studies, 16*.

Butler, J. (1989). *Gender trouble: Feminism and the subversion of identity.* New York: Routledge.
Chaiklin, S., Hedegaard, M. & Jensen, U. J. (Eds.). (1999). *Activity theory and social practice.* Aarhus: Aarhus University Press.
Chimirri, N. A. (2014). *Investigating media artifacts with children: Conceptualizing a collaborative exploration of the sociomaterial conduct of everyday life.* Roskilde: Roskilde University.
de Certeau, M. (1984). *The practice of everyday life* (S. Rendall, Trans.). Berkeley: University of California Press.
Dreier, O. (2008). *Psychotherapy in everyday life.* Cambridge: Cambridge University Press.
Ferguson, H. (2009). *Self-identity and everyday life.* London: Routledge.
Gardiner, M. E. (2000). *Critiques of everyday life.* London: Routledge.
Gergen, K. J. (2009). *Relational being: Beyond self and community.* New York: Oxford University Press.
Goffman, E. (1959). *The presentation of self in everyday life.* New York: Anchor.
Highmore, B. (2010). *Ordinary lives: Studies in the everyday.* London: Routledge.
Hodgetts, D., Drew, N., Sonn, C., Stolte, O., Nikora, L. & Curtis, C. (2010). *Social psychology and everyday life.* Basingstoke: Palgrave Macmillian.
Holland, D. & Lave, J. (2001). *History in person: Enduring struggles, contentious practice, intimate identities.* Santa Fe, NM: School of American Research Press.
Holzkamp, K. (2013). Psychology: Social self-understanding on the reasons for action in the conduct of everyday life. In E. Schraube & U. Osterkamp (Eds.), *Psychology from the standpoint of the subject: Selected writings of Klaus Holzkamp* (pp. 233–341) (A. Boreham & U. Osterkamp, Trans.). Basingstoke: Palgrave Macmillan.
Jurczyk, K. & Rerrich, M. S. (Eds.). (1993). *Die Arbeit des Alltags: Beiträge zu einer Soziologie der alltäglichen Lebensführung* [The work of everyday life: Contributions to a sociology of the conduct of everyday life]. Freiburg: Lambertus.
Juul Jensen, U. (1999). Categories in activity theory: Marx's philosophy just-in-time. In S. Chaiklin, M. Hedegaard & U. Juul Jensen (Eds.), *Activity theory and social practice: Cultural-historical approaches* (pp. 79–99). Aarhus: Aarhus University Press.
Lave, J. (2008). Situated learning and changing practice. In A. Amin & J. Roberts (Eds.), *Community, economic creativity, and organization* (pp. 283–296). Oxford: Oxford University Press.
Lave, J. (2011). *Apprenticeship in critical ethnographic practice.* Chicago, IL: Chicago University Press.
Lefebvre, H. (1991). *Critique of everyday life* (J. Moore, Trans.). London: Verso. (Original work published 1947)
Parker, I. (1989). *The crisis in modern social psychology – and how to end it.* London: Routledge.
Pink, S. (2012). *Situating everyday life: Practices and places.* London: Sage.
Scheibe, K. E. (2000). *The drama of everyday life.* Cambridge: Harvard University Press.
Sheringham, M. (2006). *Everyday life: Theories and practices from surrealism to the present.* Oxford: Oxford University Press.
Shotter, J. (1993). *Cultural politics of everyday life: Social constructionism, rhetoric and knowing of the third kind.* Toronto: University of Toronto Press.
Smith, D. E. (1987). *The everyday world as problematic.* Boston, MA: Northeastern University Press.
Stephenson, N. & Papadopoulos, D. (2006). *Analysing everyday experience: Social research and political change.* London: Palgrave Macmillan.
Voß, G. G. (1991). *Lebensführung als Arbeit. Über die Autonomie der Person im Alltag der Gesellschaft* [Conduct of life as work: On persons' autonomy in the everyday life of society]. Stuttgart: Enke.

Walkerdine, V. (Ed.) (2002). *Challenging subjects: Critical psychology for a new millennium*. Basingstoke: Palgrave Macmillan.
Wertsch, J. V. (1991). *Voices of the mind: A sociocultural approach to mediated action*. Cambridge: Harvard University Press.
Wundt, W. (1897). *Outlines of psychology* (C. H. Judd, Trans.). New York: Stechert.

1
CONDUCT OF EVERYDAY LIFE
Implications for Critical Psychology

Ole Dreier

The concept of conduct of everyday life was introduced in sociology about 100 years ago by Weber (1952, 1978) and taken up again about 20 years ago by an interdisciplinary research group of, mostly, sociologists (Jurczyk & Rerrich, 1995; Jurczyk et al., 2015, chap. 2 in this volume). But the concept of conduct of everyday life also holds important potential for psychology. Above all, it is a powerful tool for capturing human subjectivity from the standpoint of where and how subjects live their everyday lives in societal structures of practice. Such an approach may transform psychology into a truly concrete science of the subject that captures psychological phenomena based on the functions and qualities they obtain in and for the everyday lives of subjects. Moreover, the concept of conduct of everyday life is a powerful tool for critical psychology. Critique acquires a more firm and concrete grounding when it is couched from the standpoint of subjects' conduct of their everyday lives. Such an approach introduces new critical perspectives on the discipline of psychology, on its theories and practices and on the societal arrangements of scopes for living everyday lives and their impacts on subjects' well-being, functioning and troubles. It thus offers new insights for subjects to reflect critically on their practice and guide its conduct.

Holzkamp (2013, 2015, chap. 3 in this volume) introduced the concept of conduct of everyday life into the theoretical framework of critical psychology, which is the background of my work too. In this chapter I take up how the concept of conduct of everyday life is integrated into critical psychology and used to develop this framework. First, I present the key reasons for introducing the concept into critical psychology. Then I go into important dimensions of the concept and the important challenges it raises for critical psychology – and for psychology in general. As I do so, the concept of conduct of everyday life is also developed further in order to fulfill its potential for contributing to the development of the framework of critical psychology. Since the topic is immense, I must select some dimensions and challenges but set aside others. The reasons for these choices will be made clear on the way. The chapter is an overview, and not a complete review, centering on dimensions and challenges that emerged in my work and comparing it closely with work by others that I was involved in.

Introducing the Concept of Conduct of Everyday Life into Critical Psychology

Critical psychology (Holzkamp, 1983; Schraube & Osterkamp, 2013) theorizes human beings as social beings living in societies by taking part in re-producing and changing their social conditions of life. It argues that psychology must study human beings from the standpoint and perspective of individual subjects in their immediate situation within an overall social structure. The individual subject encounters and experiences the possibilities and restrictions of the social world in her first-person perspective in the situation where she is located. Her reasons for acting in one way or another are also given to her in her first-person perspective in relation to her situation, as are her mental states, observations, thoughts, memories, emotions and motivations. This is so when she seeks to comprehend the socio-structural mediation of her possibilities and conflicts in her immediate situation, as well as when she merely orients herself by their immediate appearances within it. According to critical psychology, we must grasp the psychological functioning of persons in the first-person perspective of situated subjects whose psychological processes serve as their resources in dealing with their situations. Psychology must be couched as a science of the subject from the standpoint and perspective of the subject.

Human subjectivity becomes more tangible and comprehensible by studying how subjects function and develop by involving themselves in the world they live in. Psychology becomes richer and worldlier by considering thoroughly and broadly what it means and takes to live in the world. Our understanding of subjectivity and world are then expanded together, as a nexus. By contrast, mainstream psychology tends to view the world and the psyche as separate entities. It is so keen on getting the world into the head – as represented and as the object of internal mechanisms – that it tends to bypass the fact that the head is in the body in the world with others, in situated activity. But it is odd to imagine that we gain a richer psychology by reducing, or abstracting from, the significance of the world subjects are in for their psychological functioning.

Critical psychology was already a very wide-ranging theoretical approach to psychology before the concept of conduct of everyday life was introduced into it. But it had to be expanded further. It became clear that the concept of situation is too abstract – pseudo-concrete, really – to provide a sufficiently solid, concrete grounding of a worldly approach to subjectivity. After all, subjects are not merely located in a situation. Their immediate situation is a particular part of their ongoing everyday life. The subjective meaning of a situation and how a subject engages in it depend on what part it forms of her ongoing everyday life. We must, therefore, grasp how a subject lives her everyday life and grasp a situation as belonging to it. The foundation for the formation of subjectivity and experience is her everyday life and not a situation. This insight expands our analytic gaze from an immediate situation to an everyday life that is going on from day to day in a particular, subjectively and socially grounded and arranged way. Furthermore, everyday life contains many different situations in different places and spheres of activity. So it is not adequate to analyze a subject's situation in the singular in general terms. Situations must be grasped in the plural as different across the diverse contexts of a subject's everyday life.

These insights are central in the concept of conduct of everyday life. But when we relate this concept to the discipline of psychology, we must take into account that psychology is not just meant to study the everyday life – or the style of life – of a culture or a population. How persons conduct their everyday life comes closer to the core issues of subjectivity where what it takes to live in a particular way must be of primary interest.

We can now see why the concept of conduct of everyday life must be added to the theoretical framework of critical psychology. It brings our analyses closer to what it means and takes to be a subject living in a society. We gain a richer and more adequate grasp of persons as social beings by analyzing how they conduct their everyday life. It also lets us inquire into how the abilities, experiences, reasons, understandings, concerns, etc. of persons are associated with their conduct of life and affected by it, as well as how socio-structural forces affect their conduct of life.

The inclusion of the concept of conduct of everyday life also raises challenges in developing the framework of critical psychology. Like previous challenges, they arise from aspiring to overcome reductions in the analysis of subjectivity. The concept of conduct of everyday life is built into an existing theoretical framework in order to develop it further. As we shall see, the meaning of the concept depends on its status in relation to other concepts in this framework. In the process of developing this framework, the concept must therefore also be expanded and modified.

When Holzkamp introduced the concept into critical psychology, inspired by Jurczyk and Rerrich (1995), he highlighted the following characteristics: First, in our societies everyday life stretches across several, diverse social spheres of life – such as family, work and school – which raise different demands and call for different abilities and activities. Second, persons must hence coordinate their various activities, tasks and relationships with their various co-participants across different times and places. Third, they must seek to integrate their pursuit of these diverse demands and engagements in a coherent conduct of their everyday life. Fourth, in doing so, they must seek to manage what is necessary and important for them to get done. Fifth, establishing routines assists them in managing this. Sixth, they must develop a self-understanding guiding their conduct of life. Seventh, conducting an everyday life is an active accomplishment that may succeed or fail in various ways. And, eighth, there are important social differences and inequalities between how persons may accomplish this.

This brief overview of key dimensions of the concept of conduct of everyday life serves as background for what will be addressed below. But these dimensions will only be taken up insofar as they were elaborated, revised and led to new challenges in my ongoing work on conduct of everyday life in relation to topics of personhood, psychotherapy, intervention, family life, development and learning.

In accordance with the concept of conduct of everyday life, I first spell out implications of the societal arrangement of everyday life for research on persons and their conduct of everyday life in critical psychology. Next, I take up issues about self-understanding that can then be grounded and discussed in relation to the conduct of life of persons in structural arrangements of everyday social practice. Afterwards I turn to issues about the relations between overall, societal structures and persons conducting their life in structures of everyday social practice, as seen from the standpoint and perspective of these persons in their conduct of everyday life. Finally, I briefly characterize the current state of research on conduct of everyday life in critical psychology and mention some challenges we are now facing.

The Societal Structuring of Everyday Life

In our societies, everyday life is arranged in such a way that members, in the course of their day and night, ordinarily take part in several social practices by moving into and across the contexts where these practices take place. The practices of family, work, school, leisure activities, sleep and so forth take place in different contexts and during different periods of time in the day and night. The basic sequence of the everyday movements of persons across places is, thus, socially arranged and this social ordering gives everyday life a rudimentary measure of ordinariness. On the basis thereof, persons establish and conduct an ordinary everyday life that also holds degrees of variation because they participate in some social practices/contexts on a daily basis, but in others only regularly, occasionally, during a particular period of time or just once.

When persons move into other contexts, they enter other practices. They take part in the arrangements and relations of these other practices, occupy other positions and face other co-participants, demands, responsibilities and possibilities for what they may do. So they take part in other ways, which call for other abilities and are grounded in and give rise to other subjective experiences, concerns and reasons. That is, for instance, evident when persons leave home and enter work, school, etc. This contextual functioning of persons introduces a many-sidedness and complexity into human personhood that is usually overlooked in psychological research (Dreier, 2008a, 2009, 2011b, 2015a).

Moreover, the social practices in different contexts are linked in a social structure of practices. Particular links are structurally arranged between the social practices in particular contexts. Their purposes overlap or must be pursued across several contexts. Particular relations of power exist and are exercised between them. Arrangements specify who has which access to them and across them. And persons taking part in linked social practices develop overlapping concerns and reasons for participating in each of them. As a result, what goes on in one context affects and interferes in the practices of other contexts.

Social practices of expertise are typically arranged in such a way. Take, for example, the practice of school in relation to family. Against the background of what goes on in school and in pursuit of the concerns of school, teachers and other experts associated with school affect, and may interfere in, the lives of families in an indirect and direct way. In doing so, they consider how to achieve such an impact on the lives of families of schoolchildren, or of particular children, so that these children do well in school and overcome various school-related difficulties and troubles. Likewise, parents consider their options for caring indirectly for their children in school, that is, how they may contribute from home to their children's learning, development and overcoming of troubles in school. They also consider how to care for their children by involving themselves directly in aspects of school practice. Besides, they watch out to forestall unwanted interferences from school in the life of their children and family. Children must find out how to do well and live well in each context, and how to balance the diverse demands on their participation in each in their conduct of everyday life. So, these links and concerns affect the conduct of life of individual family members differently as well as how they, together, conduct their joint family life. They also affect how teachers and other school-associated experts conduct their work. In fact, each party in this pursuit of concerns across contexts is affected differently. They take part in school practice and family practice and use the links between them in different ways, develop different positioned concerns and are caught in different conflicts (Dreier, 2008a, 2011c; Højholt, 2015, chap. 7 in this volume).

Many social practices are arranged so that they must be pursued across several diverse contexts. Thus, social practices of education involve pursuits of learning across a variety of contexts (Dreier, 2008b) as seen in, for example, studies on academy of music educations by Nielsen (1999) and Dahlberg (2013). Likewise, supplementary training courses are meant to affect everyday work practices elsewhere (Jurow & Pierce, 2011) and therapy sessions are meant to affect particular troubles in everyday life elsewhere (Dreier, 2000, 2008a, 2011a). Persons entering these social practices must find out how to pursue their concerns in the training courses or therapy sessions and in their various involved everyday social contexts so that they take advantage of the particular possibilities for doing so that these diverse contexts offer. To accomplish this, they must participate in particular situated ways in these diverse contexts. At the same time, their various situated pursuits must hang together in such a way that they may reach their desired outcomes and avoid unwanted outcomes. Moreover, they must integrate what they come to want to do differently into their ordinary conduct of everyday life within and across their home, work, school, etc. with diverse co-participants, arrangements, demands, positions, possibilities, concerns and stakes. This often involves changing their conduct of everyday life, too.

The contexts of training courses, therapy sessions and so forth become particular, temporary parts of the everyday life that persons conduct together with the more long-term contexts of their families, work practices, schools, etc. in which these expert practices are meant to work. But much else matters and must be accomplished in the complex everyday life of persons than the pursuits associated with their temporary participation in, for example, therapy sessions. In order to be sustained, these pursuits must, hence, be carried out in between much else that goes on and happens on the way. And persons must often change their conduct of everyday life to be able to carry out these pursuits and sustain them in the future.

Persons as Participants

The arguments above underline that individual persons live by taking part in social practices – not by their own efforts alone. Persons, literally, are participants in social practices. We must recognize this fact of life in theoretical terms by conceptualizing persons as participants in social practices. This fundamental, social character of personhood is seen in the partial and particular ways in which persons take part in social practices. Persons live by selecting and realizing some of the countless aspects and relations of social practices while setting aside and bypassing many others. In other words, the participatory character of personhood not only refers to how subjects relate to other subjects and exchange or negotiate perspectives on each other and on their joint practices. It also refers to how persons conduct their everyday life in relation to particular social practices with particular purposes, arrangements, technologies, positions and scopes for participation. Theorizing persons as participants is a necessary component of a critical psychology of persons and their conduct of everyday life (Dreier, 2008a). It permeates this chapter and must be pointed out before we can continue the line of argument.

Routines

The concept of participation lets us grasp how persons may live in social practices that are much more encompassing than any person can handle alone. Even so, the everyday life of persons as participants is very complex, rich and full of constraints. Persons must, therefore, establish routines in their conduct of everyday life to leave sufficient room to pursue their major personal concerns, economize the time and effort spent on certain activities, reduce the amount of attention for their execution and preclude elementary breakdowns. These characteristics of routines are usually stressed in research on conduct of everyday life while others are overlooked. Thus, routines mark certain familiar doings as belonging to the way I conduct my life and as something I am attached to and which may be involved in defining who I am. They also represent personal preferences for certain ways of doing things that I may change again later.

What is more, contrary to accounts in mainstream psychology, routines are hardly elementary building blocks of complex activities and abilities that provide a fixed foundation and scaffold for everyday life that is strictly adhered to and carried out in the same way every time. This becomes obvious by looking at how routines are involved in the personal conduct of everyday life where other aspects of routines stand out (Dreier, 2008a, 2011b, 2015a). Routines must be fitted in with the other activities and concerns in the conduct of everyday life that they should not get in the way of engaging in and pursuing. As a result, their execution is interrupted, postponed, changed or given up. Routines are also mixed with other activities in various kinds of intermingling or multitasking so that they are carried out in varying ways. Moreover, routines must leave room to pursue variety in everyday life and to seize unforeseen events and opportunities. This sets limits on the extent of routinization of everyday life that cannot be governed entirely by fixed procedures, timetables and weekly plans.

Rather than following fixed rules and procedures, most everyday routines are loose and sketchy with more or less specified standards for how and when they are to be picked up to avoid problems or breakdowns. These standards specify whether a routine is to be realized with fixed or flexible intervals on an everyday, regular or irregular basis. In addition, when a person establishes routines within a context, she must take her commitments in other contexts of her everyday life into account. Furthermore, routines are part of social practices. They must be negotiated, distributed and coordinated between co-participants defining who does which parts of what, how, when and in which order. And co-participants in a context may have different concerns about distributing and arranging its routines because these arrangements must fit their diverse personal commitments in different other contexts. Still, in spite of the complexity of embedding routines in the conduct of everyday life, they must remain so well-defined that they can create reliefs of time, effort and attention and assist in sustaining sufficient stability in personal and joint practices.

Personal and Joint Arrangements and Preferences

However, the concept of routine lacks distinct boundaries. It is used for a range of activities from simple, limited procedures to more encompassing ways of doing things in everyday life. But there are good reasons to reserve a special term for the latter. The term personal arrangement is proposed (Dreier, 2008a, 2011b, 2015a). Persons include simple routines in more extensive personal arrangements of their conduct of everyday life that they establish in relation to the societal arrangements of everyday social practice. Such personal arrangements may hold numerous routines on definite or indefinite points in their fixed or variable sequence of activities. That is, arrangements contain non-routinized activities as well as fixed or flexible routines.

Which arrangements persons make depend on their societal and cultural location and on their social positions in relation to class, gender and age. Some personal arrangements concern the conduct of everyday life within one context, for example, the course and conduct of (parts of) their morning or evening activities at home. These personal arrangements rest on the material structure and technical equipment of their home, the fit up and furnishing of its rooms and on pre-concerted agreements about life at home between the members of the household. They overlap with the personal arrangements of other members and must be negotiated with them. This includes the establishment of joint arrangements. The personal and joint arrangements in a context also depend on the significance of this context for the involved persons compared with the other contexts they take part in separately.

Other personal arrangements concern their everyday life across contexts. They regulate the personal priorities of their diverse responsibilities and engagements in different contexts, for example, by regulating the extent and timing of their co-presence in particular contexts. They also regulate their transitions between contexts, for example, as arrangements for re-entering, re-gathering and re-integrating with the other members at home after work/day care in the evening. These personal arrangements of everyday responsibilities and engagements across contexts must be negotiated with co-participants in different contexts in relation to the joint arrangements in these contexts.

Like routines, personal arrangements establish a certain order and stability in the conduct of everyday life. They economize the time and attention necessary for its conduct and assist in the coordination of activities, responsibilities, engagements and preferences. And like routines, personal arrangements are marked by degrees and kinds of fixedness or looseness delineating a range of desired and acceptable variations in their realization, beyond which troubles may arise.

Altogether, the personal arrangements of everyday life establish a more or less rudimentary and loose agenda and a rhythm of activities across the day that every person seeks to compose so that it suits her well. Persons develop individual preferences about which rhythms of activity, fixed or open arrangements and agendas and extent and kind of variation within and between days suit them best. These individual preferences also reflect their different responsibilities and priorities within and across contexts. Finally, persons change their preferences and personal and joint arrangements over time.

Coherence, Stances and Pursuits

Conducting a life across diverse social contexts is a complicated endeavor. Research usually stresses that being engaged and carrying responsibilities in diverse social contexts creates personal time binds and strains (e.g., the influential work by Hochschild, 2001). The concept of conduct of everyday life highlights other consequences. It focuses on a person's integration and accomplishment of what is necessary for her and what matters most to her into a manageable everyday life. An everyday life with diverse demands and commitments may fall apart if it is not conducted so that it hangs together. Diverse and conflicting demands and commitments may pull it apart if she does not maintain a sufficient measure of coherence. And she must establish a suitable balance between its parts, activities, concerns and commitments to have sufficient room to pursue what matters most to her. To do so, she must, to some degree, make up her mind about what she stands for. She must develop more or less articulate and sustained stances about what is important, what she commits herself to and against and what she wants preserved or changed in the complex social practices she takes part in (Dreier, 2008a). Finding out what she stands for helps sustain coherent directions in her ongoing life and reduces the risks of her life falling apart into disjointed or mutually defeating parts.

These characteristics of the conduct of everyday life are, for instance, evident when the members of a family enter joint family therapy. They have different perspectives on the troubles they want help to overcome; what they want changed or preserved in their joint family life; which changes in the arrangements and conduct of their family life they find acceptable and desirable; and, therefore, what it means for them to take part in their joint therapy sessions and what they want to pursue by doing so. But if they are to succeed in overcoming their troubles, they must seek to replace disjointed individual pursuits of change with more concerted ones. This involves making up their minds and reconsidering many times over what they stand for concerning their joint family life and its part in their different individual lives.

How a person conducts her everyday life and engages in its contexts reflects a mixture of necessities, preferences and stances. Her conduct of everyday life is also selective and partial because she can relate to only some of the countless demands and possibilities encountered in social practice. Moreover, she can only pursue a limited number of her activities and concerns in a particular period of time. Meanwhile, she must let herself drift along anyhow with what happens in social practice as to the many other demands and activities of her everyday life. At later points in time, she may then replace and reconfigure which concerns to pursue or just let drift along.

Self-understanding

We have seen that a person's experiences, concerns and stances are aspects of her conduct of everyday life in relation to the societal arrangements of everyday social practice. She comes to understand social practices and herself in and through her conduct of everyday life. A person's self-understanding is her understanding of herself as the one who conducts her life the way she does (Dreier, 2008a, 2011b, 2015a). It is based on perceiving herself as the person whose sequence of first-person experiences accompanies her activities in the structures of her everyday social practice. It is, therefore, also based on perceiving herself and her conduct of life differently from its diverse locations. Her self-understanding arises from her conduct of everyday life, remains grounded in it and guides its realization.

This notion of self-understanding is in accordance with Holzkamp's (2013, 2015, chap. 3 in this volume) work about it, and is in some respects different from it. He approaches the conduct of everyday life in connection with the fundamental question of how to build a critical science of the subject from a first-person perspective. To Holzkamp, the principal question in such a science concerns a subject's reasons for acting in a particular way. When he turns to the topic of a subject's conduct of everyday life, he, therefore, highlights her self-understanding and zooms in on her reasons for conducting her life in a particular way. According to him, subjects clarify their self-understandings in an intersubjective process where they exchange perspectives on their reasons for action while acknowledging that their respective reasons are grounded in their respective life situations. Indeed, Holzkamp proposes that a meta-subjective discourse about the clarification of subjective reasons between a researcher and her co-researching subject(s) should replace the methodologically privileged, isolated experimental set-up of mainstream psychology in a critical science of the subject from a first-person perspective.

Osterkamp (2001, 2014; Osterkamp & Schraube, 2013) continues this approach to subjects' conduct of everyday life. She emphasizes that complex and contradictory societal conditions make it problematic for individual subjects to be reasonably certain whether their decisions and actions are in line with, or at least do not contradict, their own life interests. "Clarifying the real groundedness of an individual's actions (then includes clarifying) the concrete constraints and compulsions underlying them" (Osterkamp & Schraube, 2013, p. 5). This can only be accomplished in a meta-subjective discourse where subjects assist each other in unraveling the compromises they entered against their interests. Subjective self-understandings thus really are social self-understandings. In this way Osterkamp underlines the participatory nature of subjects' lives and understandings and argues for cultivating a critical social practice of self-clarification that may lead to joint efforts to overcome pressures toward adaptation assisted by the analytic tools of critical psychology. She sees the meta-subjective understanding as a platform for the generalization of subjective reasons that acknowledges the subjectivity and groundedness of all human beings and, thus, excludes nobody.

This work on the conduct of everyday life focuses on self-understanding, more specifically, on subjects' reasons for conducting their everyday lives as they do and their critical reflections on these reasons in exchanges with others in a special dialogical situation. But this situation is only characterized by how subjects relate to each other. The impacts of the particular contexts and social practices, where these dialogues and critical reflections take place, are not considered. There is a risk of idealizing an abstract speech situation, existing nowhere in its pure form, and of turning it into an abstract norm of good understanding, as in the theory of communicative action by Habermas (1984, 1987). To avoid this, we need a broader frame of analysis. We must turn to a contextual view on dialogues, reflections and self-understanding in which general characteristics and concerns hang together with specific, contextual ones. Analyses of dialogues must include the situations in which subjects come to an understanding with each other as particular encounters in different, local contexts. That is, not only the persons – be they allies or opponents – and how they relate to each other, but also the social practices, the one in which their reflections take place as well as the other practices on which they reflect and for which their reflections are to matter. Situations in different contexts hold different positions, scopes for participation and expertise.

Participants have different concerns in relation to situations in different contexts that also have different statuses in their conduct of everyday life. So they have different meanings to them and they take part in them for different reasons. Situated circumstances and concerns affect all discourses and exchanges of perspectives, also between psychological researchers and their subjects. And a special practice in a particular context hangs together with and works with and against other practices, also when participants seek to use what they got out of it elsewhere. An analysis of the social practices of science that disregards all this is too abstract and general.

My research on the social practice of psychotherapy underlines this broader approach to self-understanding and critical reflections. It shows that a person develops her self-understanding by pursuing dialogues and reflections across diverse contexts/practices and by using her current understanding of her concerns and options in these different practices to direct her pursuits. Some social practices are institutionalized for such pursuits, for example, the practices of therapy and education that are temporarily added to, and take place intermittently beside, the ordinary everyday practices of the persons involved. Similar purposes may be pursued in other extraordinary contexts, for example, while being in hospital, on vacation or in other cultural and natural surroundings. So there are many different sources and places for cultivating self-understanding. Persons pursue an issue of self-understanding through different sources and places and combine what they get out of them in a particular way. Thus, while attending therapy, clients learn about their therapy-related issues of self-understanding from many sources in many places and not only in their therapy sessions (Dreier, 2008a; Mackrill, 2008a, 2008b).

We can now see that the general potential of a meta-subjective discourse is meshed with other concerns that matter in situated ways and are affected by the silent powers of societal relations and arrangements. We also see that we must go beyond the notion, cultivated in the tradition of the Enlightenment, that reflection and knowledge are gained at a distance in a retreat. It led to a downgrading or disregard for other situated practices of reflection, for reflections carried out in ongoing, situated activities and for combining various practices of reflection in pursuit of understanding. It also opened the door to a normative ranking of dialogues and self-understandings depending on where they were accomplished, with those carried out at a distance in a retreat at the top and those meshed with other concerns in ongoing everyday lives at the bottom.

However, it is not enough to situate analyses of dialogues and self-understandings. We must link self-understanding and reflection more closely with the conduct of everyday life in practice. That is, we must ask how self-understanding and reflection inform and guide a person's ongoing conduct of life, how a particular self-understanding is involved in conducting her life in practice, and how it challenges her conduct. But we must also ask how occurrences and issues in her conduct of life in practice affect and challenge her self-understanding. In fact, her self-understanding informs her conduct of life, but it is also infused and challenged by it. It arises from her practice, which feeds it. What is more, a person addresses issues of self-understanding and reflects intermittently in the ongoing activities of her conduct of everyday life (cf. Jensen, 2012).

Finally, because a person's self-understanding is about being the person conducting her life the way she does, her self-understanding is linked with the particular places, activities, relationships and co-participants of her everyday life. Smith (1987) emphasizes such close links between self-understanding and the situated lives of embodied subjects. According to her, a person's identity reflects her commitments to her concrete everyday life with specific others in rich, concrete social relationships, specific places and senses of place, specific activities and particular organizations of rhythms of life. Such a situated notion of self-understanding may show how a person understands herself by finding and rediscovering herself where she is located.

We have now spelled out implications of the societal arrangement of everyday social practice for the conduct of everyday life of persons, and for their experiences, concerns, pursuits, stances and self-understandings as subjective dimensions thereof. In the remaining part of the chapter we sketch a further major challenge in developing a critical psychology centered on the conduct of everyday life of persons. We must address the relations between overall social structures and the conduct of life of persons in structures of everyday social practice as seen from their everyday locations and perspectives. This also involves expanding what was said above about the subjective aspects of a person's conduct of everyday life, including her self-understanding.

Structural Arrangements

The conceptual move from life situation to conduct of everyday life highlights the structural arrangement of spheres of practice in everyday life. We must grasp the importance of this basic structure of everyday life for the personal conduct of everyday life so that we can move beyond the usual assumption in social theory of a life situation, or an everyday life world, without any structure subsumed within an overall social structure. But, in itself, the basic ordering of everyday life presents an oversimplified view of social structure. Social contexts and practices are also linked within an overall social structure. The arrangement of contextual social practices is part of the social structure too. Local social contexts are involved in the social structure in diverse, interrelated ways. So we must grasp how the societal arrangement of everyday life is linked with the social structure and grasp the situated presence and meaning of general structural issues in it.

This major challenge has not been met in a sufficiently robust manner and it will take sustained interdisciplinary efforts to do so. Social theory usually conceives individuals too narrowly and abstractly as subsumed under a structure of society. That leads to a poor theory of subjects in social practice. This traditional notion of social structure must be revised. We face a three-dimensional challenge of analyzing the structure of society, the arrangement of everyday social practice, and the everyday conduct of life, as well as how the three are linked in practice. Thus, situations and contexts are embedded in a personal conduct of everyday life, a social arrangement of everyday life and a social structure. We must ask questions on all three dimensions and on how they are linked.

Particularly little light has been shed on the links between structure of society and arrangements of everyday life. To illuminate this we need to move from functionalist notions of social structure to notions of structures of practice in space and time. The social practice theorist Schatzki (2002) analyzed concepts of social order, concluding that we comprehend social structure best as socio-material arrangement of and in social practices. Then we can analyze the separation of contextual practices in space and time; the arrangement of practices in particular contexts; which chains of activities are possible across which contexts; the technological mediations within and across contexts; and which conditions give which persons legitimate access to participate in particular contexts. We can also analyze how arrangements of social practices promote or inhibit the pursuit of particular concerns, how they do so in unequal ways for participants on different positions and how they promote or inhibit particular forms of divided or joint practices. These questions combine an analysis of power with a search for possibilities for action. They are being addressed in research projects in various fields of social practice. But much more work is needed, in order to become more precise about the following.

Overall Issues in Local Practices

Why must a science of the subject grasp overall structural issues as issues in everyday life? Because we must move beyond capturing them as general issues and ideas to analyzing them as concretely encountered issues for subjects, their experiences of them and their ways of dealing with them in their everyday social practice. A science of the subject cannot leave the standpoint of the subject in everyday life to theorize about overall issues. It must, precisely, analyze them where embodied subjects encounter them in their everyday lives. So we must fill the theoretical gap between social structure and everyday life from the location of persons in everyday life instead of from above. Fortunately, "overall" issues are literally to be found all over. Still, our task is not merely to identify overall issues – or encompassing issues of whatever scale – locally, but in the conduct of everyday life of persons in which they encounter them and in which they gain a particular meaning for them. A science of the subject must know much more about this.

According to Brecht, "The laws of motion are hardly conceivable from the standpoint of the ball" (1963, p. 301). This statement is evocative but misleading. Though human beings sometimes feel kicked around, they are not balls kicked around by Brecht as some Newtonian scientist from a different species than "us balls." And balls do not have standpoints. Brecht endorses a notion of knowledge as gained at a distance from the ball game. He misses the potentials for comprehension in the experiences persons gather by moving across contexts in their conduct of everyday life (Dreier, 2008b, 2015b). Moving into other places offers chances of recognizing overall issues through their other presences and meanings in other practices. Persons may then reconsider the contextual similarities and differences of their impacts and meanings. Re-encountering and reconsidering them offers chances of looking beyond the veil of local arrangements and realizing the widespread forces and arrangements they originate from. Indeed, persons must grasp how things hang together, their coherence, and there are other sources for learning about this besides reading or hearing about it from media, research or other persons.

When persons move across social contexts and practices, they also encounter a variety of ways in which other persons conduct their everyday life and they may learn how this is affected by encompassing social divisions of class, gender, ethnicity and age with associated issues such as exclusion and poverty.

On this background, it may become clearer to them how they, in their conduct of everyday life, are part in re-producing or changing overall issues. They may come to see how they may address and affect such issues, among other things, by finding out from where it is best to pick them up and by establishing suitable trajectories for pursuing them across times and places. But persons can only participate in encompassing, political activities if their conduct of everyday life does not prevent it or break down in the meantime. Such dilemmas may make them see their conduct of everyday life in a new light and rearrange it.

Persons experience and address overall issues in the nexus of their conduct of everyday life. How they experience and address them hence depends on their status and meaning in and for their conduct of everyday life. The way they arranged their conduct of everyday life affects how they experience them and what they do about them. It also lets them avoid seeing, play down, get around and postpone certain issues. After all, persons handle experiences and issues in a complex and composed conduct of everyday life, which is highly selective and does not relate to everything around them. However, a person's understanding of social relations, which her life is inextricably involved in, and of what she may do in relation hereto, also makes her raise many issues of self-understanding.

In one respect Brecht was right in his statement above. Having no command over something tends to limit a person's understanding of it. Increasing her hold on something, conversely, makes her more certain to have understood it. That is why she may learn about something by contributing to change it. It then ceases to lie beyond her grasp in both senses of the term. Conversely, the more she merely focuses on what seems to go on in her immediate situation, the more events and forces from elsewhere seem to strike down into her everyday life and affect it beyond her expectations and anticipations. Events then appear to occur more arbitrarily and incidentally – like short cuts in postmodern art. Her conditions of life seem to a higher degree to be subject to chance, to good or bad luck distributed blindly among us. This too has implications for her self-understanding.

Control/Dependence

Because persons live by taking part with others in social practices, they cannot control their life on their own. They can only increase their determination over it by taking part in determining joint life conditions and arrangements together with others. Autonomy, conceived as an individual's complete control over her life choices and conditions, is not possible. In conducting their everyday life, persons both depend on others – in the sense that they rely on and benefit from what others do – and are in a state of dependence in relation to powerful others and to relations of power affecting them. In other words, to conduct one's life does not presuppose complete control over the conditions of its conduct. It rests on a mixture of conducting and depending, in the dual sense of depend on and dependence. And it is characterized by various degrees and kinds of having some aspects of your life in your grip and dependences in other respects. Whereas a person has a grip on some aspects of her life and its coherence, she must drift along with other aspects while taking care that it does not disrupt and collapse. The concrete mix of control and dependence in the conduct of life of persons reflects concrete social relations of power. Differences in social conditions of life also imply different options for getting around disturbing events and warding off their impacts on one's everyday life and self-understanding. Furthermore, in pursuing changes to her conduct of everyday life, a person must find out whom to involve as allies among the other persons who are involved due to existing ties, commitments and obligations. She must negotiate changes of her conduct of everyday life with them and the outcome of these negotiations affect whether and how the changes she pursues may come about.

The neoliberal arrangements of societal contradictions also affect the conduct of everyday life. Though persons live by taking part, and not as autonomous agents, they face the contradiction of being held individually responsible for their life and, at the same time, controlled from above, of being left to themselves and being controlled. This contradiction between control, responsibility and self-determination infuses their doings and self-understandings. Haug (1977) identified it as an "as if-quality" in how individual persons experience their responsibility and self-determination. This contradiction also affects the relations of clients to institutional expertise and interventions.

Stability, Complexity and Contradictions

A completely stable conduct of everyday life is not possible without complete control. The conduct of life is, therefore, marked by instabilities. Persons may attempt to exclude contradictions from their agenda, get around them and live by other selected conditions, and there are distinct social differences between their scopes for doing so. But it is not possible without restricting compromises. Nor is it true that adaptation to the current conditions involves no drawbacks, restrictions and conflicts, or that risks and conflicts only arise in trying to change the given situation. So, temporary compromises are crucial to what conduct of life is about and is caught up in as a way to keep contradictions at bay and affect their meanings and impacts without being able to resolve and eliminate them. Some contradictions are then displaced as conflicts between people with different stances on how to deal with them, or they appear as dilemmas leading to shifts and instabilities in their conduct of everyday life. Others return because they are unresolved and disrupt the achieved level of stability anew. Most likely, something will turn up to challenge the achieved stability when its grounding is selective and holds persisting contradictions. When the conduct of everyday life, and its changes, involves difficult and unresolvable issues, it becomes problematic and marked by struggles. More often than not in a contradictory nexus, when a person extends her conduct of life in one respect, it is subjected to restrictions in other respects. Contradictions in the nexus of her conduct of everyday life may even make her real life interests appear to her as a heavy duty.

The fact that any individual person's powers over her life conditions are incomplete is mirrored in her incomplete knowledge and in the partial opacity of her self-understanding. The last three sections on issues of social structure in relation to conduct of everyday life made it clear that a person's self-understanding must be affected by the challenges of living in a contradictory nexus. Its stability must be called into question by being torn between diverse and conflicting interpretations of issues, and by lacunas of opacity, precariousness and doubts. A person must find out how to deal with these matters; that is, whether to assert, hold on to or change her self-understanding in relevant respects. Such processes of self-clarification will be called for over and over again and they may lead her to face "the concrete constraints and compulsions" in the real groundedness of her actions (Osterkamp & Schraube, 2013, p. 5).

Current Status and Future Work

We have now presented the current status and challenges concerning the concept of conduct of everyday life in critical psychology. We went through the major steps in introducing, working with and expanding this concept so far. First we took up the shift from studying subjects in their immediate life situation in relation to an overall social structure to studying subjects conducting their lives in the structural arrangements of everyday life. Then we added the relation to overall structural issues as seen from subjects' conduct of everyday life in the structural arrangements of everyday life. In each shift we conceived the subjective dimensions of personal functioning as implications of a new view on the social world.

The concept of conduct of everyday life has the potential to reform the psychological gaze on what it means and takes to be a person and on many dimensions and problems of personhood. It fosters a worldly, down-to-earth conception of persons in the nexus in which they develop and address these dimensions and problems in their conduct of everyday life. It comprises new insights into these dimensions and problems. And it changes the foundation and approach of a critical psychology that does not set aside everyday life as the rest of life outside the important social institutions, but recognizes it as the way practices are given – and in part arranged – for persons and as the way they experience and handle them. Furthermore, the concept of conduct of everyday life leads to new conceptual and empirical insights into everyday life. But the topic of conduct of everyday life is immense and there is much more work to do conceptually.

The conceptual developments presented in this chapter were used in or emerged from empirical studies. But the fields and topics of these studies were not presented. They are about issues in education and learning, work, healthcare, rehabilitation, chronic illness, counseling, therapy and childcare. Children, parents, patients/clients and their next of kin, various employees and professionals and various institutions involved in these practices were in focus. The occurrence of events and troubles were studied, as well as how persons struggle to regain a grip on their life by re-establishing or changing their conduct of life. But, given the extraordinary scope of the concept, there is much more to go into in these and many other fields of practice. What is more, we must expand the scope of empirical research by examining other forms of conduct of everyday life as contrasting exemplars. Thus, the conduct of life of homeless persons shows other patterns of movement, situatedness, stability, access and power (Kristensen & Schraube, 2014). Here stability and (lack of) control are rooted in patterns of movement across places in which persons cannot rely on being settled in a particular place, such as a home, where they can meet, keep their things, retreat, etc.

The concept of conduct of everyday life also leads to a different grasp of institutions. Institutional practices are analyzed as everyday practices linked with other everyday practices elsewhere. We highlight how institutional purposes reach beyond their boundaries and become part of the conduct of life of their users elsewhere, how access and participation are arranged and how users link their participation in them with their lives in other contexts. Institutions are, at one and the same time, part of more encompassing institutional arrangements of social order and of the conduct of everyday (work) life of their managers, employees, professionals – for example, psychological practitioners – and users. We can ground the reasons why participating in institutions has different meanings and implications for persons in different positions who are involved in different other contexts. These insights into work practices offer critical correctives on professional regimes of power and self-understanding. They can be used critically and constructively to change and improve those practices in accordance with their purposes of serving the lives of their users.

As stated above, we are re-addressing and filling the gap between social structure and everyday life in social theory from the location of persons in their everyday lives rather than by subsuming them under an abstract notion of structure (Dreier, 2006). Regardless of whether overall relations and powers are present all over or in a locally scattered manner, we address their meaning for persons as they encounter them in their conduct of everyday life. Such an approach is important for considering issues of culture too. It would be a mistake to subsume concrete everyday ways of life under an abstract notion of a culture. Instead, we must address sociocultural variations and diversities in structural arrangements of everyday life and in the conduct of everyday life. Doing so will raise many challenges, empirically as well as conceptually. It will, most likely, lead to changes and expansions in the conception of conduct of everyday life, but it will also open up studies of cultural forms of life constructively and productively. Though the concept was developed and deployed in the sociocultural nexus of Western modernity, it does not necessarily blindly affirm this nexus or must be strictly limited hereto. In critiques of the concept, it is important to distinguish between conceptual issues and empirical bases, as well as between constructive potentials and critical limits.

References

Brecht, B. (1963). *Schriften zum Theater. Band. 7*. Frankfurt/M.: Suhrkamp.
Dahlberg, M. (2013). *Learning across contexts: Music performance students' construction of learning trajectories*. Unpublished doctoral dissertation, Norwegian Academy of Music, Oslo.
Dreier, O. (2000). Psychotherapy in clients' trajectories across contexts. In C. Mattingly & L. C. Garro (Eds.), *Narrative and the cultural construction of illness and healing* (pp. 237–258). Berkeley, CA: University of California Press.
Dreier, O. (2006). Wider die Strukturabstraktion. *Forum Kritische Psychologie, 50*, 72–83.
Dreier, O. (2008a). *Psychotherapy in everyday life*. New York: Cambridge University Press.
Dreier, O. (2008b). Learning in structures of social practice. In K. Nielsen, S. Brinkmann, C. Elmholdt, L. Tanggaard, P. Musaeus & G. Kraft (Eds.), *A qualitative stance: Essays in honor of Steinar Kvale* (pp. 85–96). Aarhus: Aarhus University Press.
Dreier, O. (2009). Persons in structures of social practice. *Theory & Psychology, 19*, 93–112.
Dreier, O. (2011a). Intervention, evidence-based research and everyday life. In P. Stenner, J. Cromby, J. Motzkau, J. Yen & Y. Haosheng (Eds.), *Theoretical psychology: Global transformations and challenges* (pp. 260–269). Concord, Ont.: Captus Press.
Dreier, O. (2011b). Personality and the conduct of everyday life. *Nordic Psychology, 63*, 4–23.
Dreier, O. (2011c). Livet i familien og udenfor. In S. Straand (Ed.), *Samhandling som omsorg: Tværfaglig psykososialt arbeid med barn og unge* (pp. 43–61). Oslo: Kommuneforlaget.
Dreier, O. (2015a). The person and her conduct of everyday life. In J. Straub, E. Sorensen, P. Chakkarath & G. Rebane (Eds.), *Cultural psychology in interdisciplinary dialogue: Hans Kilian lectures in social and cultural psychology and integrative anthropology*. Gießen: Psychosozial.
Dreier, O. (2015b). Learning and conduct of everyday life. In A. Larraín, A. Haye, J. Cresswell, G. Sullivan & M. Morgan (Eds.), *Dialogue and debate in the making of theoretical psychology*. Concord, Ont.: Captus Press.
Habermas, J. (1984). *The theory of communicative action: Vol. 1. Reason and the rationalization of society*. Boston, MA: Beacon Press.
Habermas, J. (1987). *The theory of communicative action: Vol. 2. Lifeworld and system: A critique of functionalist reason*. Boston, MA: Beacon Press.
Haug, F. (1977). *Erziehung und gesellschaftliche Produktion: Kritik des Rollenspiels*. Frankfurt/M.: Campus.
Hochschild, A. R. (2001). *The time bind: When work becomes home and home becomes work*. New York: Henry Holt.
Holzkamp, K. (1983). *Grundlegung der Psychologie*. Frankfurt/M.: Campus.

Holzkamp, K. (2013). Psychology: Social self-understanding on the reasons for action in the conduct of everyday life. In E. Schraube & U. Osterkamp (Eds.), *Psychology from the standpoint of the subject: Selected writings of Klaus Holzkamp* (pp. 233–341). Basingstoke: Palgrave Macmillan.

Jensen, L. M. (2012). Reflecting on life, not on the mind: The concept of self-reflection without stability. In L. M. Jensen, *Interactions between persons and situations in daily life: A study in personality psychology* (pp. 81–119). Doctoral dissertation, Copenhagen: University of Copenhagen, Department of Psychology.

Jurczyk, K. & Rerrich, M. S. (Eds.). (1995). *Die Arbeit des Alltags: Beiträge zu einer Soziologie der alltäglichen Lebensführung*. Munich: Lambertus.

Jurow, A. S. & Pierce, D. (2011). Exploring the relations between "soul" and "role": Learning from the courage to lead. *Mind, Culture, and Activity, 18*, 26–42.

Kristensen, K. & Schraube, E. (2014). Conduct of everyday life. In T. Teo (Ed.), *Encyclopedia of critical psychology* (pp. 291–293). New York: Springer.

Lave, J. & Wenger, E. (1991). *Situated learning: Legitimate peripheral participation*. Cambridge: Cambridge University Press.

Mackrill, T. (2008a). Pre-treatment change in psychotherapy with adult children of problem drinkers: The significance of leaving home. *Counselling & Psychotherapy Research, 8*, 160–165.

Mackrill, T. (2008b). Exploring psychotherapy clients' independent strategies for change while in therapy. *British Journal of Guidance and Counselling, 36*, 441–453.

Nielsen, K. N. (1999). *Musical apprenticeship: Learning at the Academy of Music as socially situated*. Doctoral dissertation, Aarhus University, Department of Psychology.

Osterkamp, U. (2001). Lebensführung als Problematik der Subjektwissenschaft. *Forum Kritische Psychologie, 43*, 4–35.

Osterkamp U. (2014). Subject matter of psychology. In T. Teo (Ed.), *Encyclopedia of critical psychology* (pp. 1870–1876). New York: Springer.

Osterkamp, U. & Schraube, E. (2013). Introduction: Klaus Holzkamp and the development of psychology from the standpoint of the subject. In E. Schraube & U. Osterkamp (Eds.), *Psychology from the standpoint of the subject: Selected writings of Klaus Holzkamp* (pp. 1–15). Basingstoke: Palgrave Macmillan.

Schatzki, T. R. (2002). *The site of the social: A philosophical account of the constitution of social life and change*. University Park, PA: Pennsylvania State University Press.

Schraube, E. & Osterkamp, U. (Eds.). (2013). *Psychology from the standpoint of the subject: Selected writings of Klaus Holzkamp*. Basingstoke: Palgrave Macmillan.

Smith, D. E. (1987). *The everyday world as problematic*. Boston, MA: Northeastern University Press.

Weber, M. (1952). *The Protestant ethic and the spirit of capitalism*. New York: Scribner.

Weber, M. (1978). *Economy and society*. Berkeley, CA: University of California Press.

2
CONDUCT OF EVERYDAY LIFE IN SUBJECT-ORIENTED SOCIOLOGY
Concept and Empirical Research

Karin Jurczyk, G. Günter Voß and Margit Weihrich[1]

Introduction

The sociological concept of the *conduct of everyday life* attempts to grasp society from the everyday lives of people performing actions in the various areas of their lives. This re-contouring of the sociological view toward the relationship between subject and society is very similar to the understanding of the critical psychologist Klaus Holzkamp (2015, chap. 3 in this volume). The basic premise of the concept is that people have to tackle all of the different – and in some cases contradictory – demands that they encounter in the various spheres of everyday life. This *work of everyday life* (Jurczyk & Rerrich, 1993) does not occur of its own accord; however, it is a discrete effort made by the person that is becoming increasingly challenging.

It is no coincidence that this analytical approach developed in the early 1980s, when a renewed surge of modernization in Western industrial societies could no longer be ignored. The terminology with which this surge was described was different: as a "second," as a "reflexive" or "new," or as a "late" or "fluid" modernity (Bauman, 2000; Beck, 1992; Giddens, 1986, 1991). In each of these cases was an erosion of the structures and values that had established themselves alongside developed industrialized society and that had become entrenched in the 1960s as a Fordist mode of organization of "working and living."[2] The increasingly globalized service and information society, new traffic and information technologies and individualized and emancipatory value frameworks formed the background to this transformation. The boundaries within relationships relating to occupation, gender and family, whose arrangement according to the dichotomy of private and public had until then been a central pillar of industrialized society, were consequently blurred and became more flexible. The internal differentiation between "working and living," as well as their relationship to one another, therefore became negotiable to an entirely unprecedented degree. This was because these erosions, processes of blurring and uncertainties had direct effects on the concrete everyday lives of people, on many details of their life conduct, their personal plans for the future and their perception of life. There was no suitable theoretical or empirical framework within which to fully understand and analyze these processes, or with which to categorize them from the point of view of social theory, however.

The aim of filling these gaps was the starting point for the work of a research team that was formed in 1986 within the framework of Collaborative Research Center (Sonderforschungsbereich) 333 at the University of Munich on the development perspectives of work (cf. Lutz, 2001).[3] This undertaking was based on the results of the previous Collaborative Research Center 101, which had pursued three lines of research independently of one another: work in the form of occupations, the occupational and familial work of women, and work within the framework of state administration (Bolte, 1995, p. 16). It became clear, however, that this segmented view could no longer provide sufficient answers to the pressing contemporary problems of "working and living" in the context of late modernity. The team therefore searched for integrating approaches and possible perspectives on the "whole." The idea of making everyday life the subject of research presented itself. This is where "everything comes together": living, loving and working; resources and restrictions; new degrees of freedom and new compulsions (Jurczyk & Rerrich, 1993). The concept of a "division of labor of the person" (Jurczyk et al., 1985; Treutner & Voß, 1982), which conceived of the individual as an entity that integrates various fields of work, constituted the starting point. The question that then presented itself was: How are people able to organize their everyday lives and to assemble all of the things that have to be done in the various spheres of everyday life into a livable whole under open and uncertain conditions?

It became apparent, however, that there was a lack of the conceptual framework necessary for the corresponding empirical research, while the development of such a framework was necessarily dependent upon empirical input in order to develop the dimensions of an altered everyday life, to more clearly define categories and to differentiate between analytical levels. The research team therefore took a consistent inductive-deductive approach, linking empirical results and historical-analytical theories with conceptual work in a spiral-shaped and mutual process. Despite the fact that the focal point of the project was initially empirical, the development of a corresponding new concept proved to be essential, and later showed itself to be very fruitful indeed. Drawing on the central category of *life conduct* ("Lebensführung") by Max Weber (cf. in particular Weber, 1905/1950), the term *conduct of everyday life* was attributed to this concept.

The project was inspired by the research perspective of *subject-oriented sociology*, which had already been developed in previous years in the same Munich research context (Bolte, 1983; Voß & Pongratz, 1997). This focused on a conception of the relationship between the individual and society that – similarly to the structuration theory of Giddens (1986), for example – was understood as a bidirectional constitutive process. Here the focus is on the aspects of social and personal action that provide and communicate structure, rather than the dichotomy of structure and subject. This made it possible to grasp conceptually the fact that people were, on the one hand, exposed to new requirements and excessive demands to perform particular actions by conditions created by uncertain, blurred frameworks; and that, on the other hand, they created new living and working arrangements that were not merely reactions to the former, but were instead discrete creative efforts. Alongside a theoretical conjunction of action and structure, or individual and society, the conduct of everyday life – as the concept eventually became known – focused on the ambivalent way in which the demands and opportunities of "fluid" modernity were tackled (Bauman, 2000).

This chapter is structured as follows. It starts with a description of the central empirical results of the main piece of research carried out by the project group *The Conduct of Everyday Life*, and of the indications of the widespread interest with which this research program continues to be met to this day. We begin with the empirical results not only because the description and explanation of concrete social transformation was the occasion and aim of our research, but also because the development of the concept was significantly shaped by our empirical experiences, and the urgent need to explore theoretical questions became apparent only in the course of carrying out the research. This resulted in a course of action that alternated between the empirical and the theoretical. The central pillars of the theoretical concept of the conduct of everyday life are therefore discussed following the empirical section. The section that follows sketches out important theoretical and conceptual as well as other methodological developments. The current time-diagnostic potential of the concept is elucidated in the conclusion.

Conduct of Everyday Life in the Process of Modernization: The Main Empirical Study

In this chapter, we will introduce the study conducted by the Munich project group, which laid the foundation for the sociology of the conduct of everyday life. The research was carried out in the late 1980s and early 1990s. The empirical results and time-diagnostic evaluations have lost none of their relevance since then.

Methodology and Case Selection

In its empirical study – and thus in the selection of its interviewees – the project group *The Conduct of Everyday Life* took its cue primarily from two social transformation processes: the increasing flexibility of working hours since the mid-1980s and the deregulation of employment conditions on the one hand, and the changes in the life perceptions and life plans of women in particular, which expressed themselves in a redefinition of traditional gender roles, on the other hand. Both developments, it was assumed, present particular demands on the organization of everyday life. Between 1986 and 1991 (including a preliminary assessment), approximately 100 narrative-generating guided interviews were conducted with women and men who had children to look after and who worked in fields affected in different ways by the processes of transformation outlined above: journalists, industrial workers, sales assistants, providers of care for the elderly, employees of a conglomerate and service providers for data-processing. The contrasting of urban and rural areas constituted another criterion: The industrial workers and sales assistants were in a rural environment, whereas the other groups studied lived in either city or town environments.

The qualitative data-collection process was open, but simultaneously concentrated on particular subjects: Questions were asked about the actions carried out in the course of a typical day, and about the ways in which these actions were performed, as well as about coordination with others, resources and strains, and about life perceptions, biographical experiences and plans for the future (on this subject, see Projektgruppe "Alltägliche Lebensführung", 1995).

After Reunification, eastern Germany was integrated into the research on the conduct of everyday life. The reason for this was twofold: The first aim was to be able to research the conduct of everyday life in a situation of upheaval that affected all of society, and the second was to gain a retrospective insight into the conduct of everyday life in the German Democratic Republic. In cooperation with a newly founded sister project at the University of Leipzig, the project group conducted approximately 70 interviews with members of the occupation groups previously examined in western Germany: journalism, care for the elderly, retail and industrial work. However, people who had previously been employed as journalists had, in the course of the upheaval, become freelance entrepreneurs; many industrial workers had become so-called "zero-hour reduced-working-hours" employees and were thus in actual fact unemployed; providers of care for the elderly worked in institutions that functioned quite differently from the ones they were used to; and even the working conditions of the sales assistants in the department store that had been absorbed by a West German chain had undergone radical change. This made it possible to achieve a deep insight into the role of life conduct in a rapidly progressing social process of transformation (on this subject, see also Hofmann & Dietzsch, 1995; Kudera, 1997; Weihrich, 1998). The empirical material therefore also provides a historically valuable view of work and life in Germany from the late 1980s to the early 1990s.

In the discussion that follows, we will provide empirical insights into the life-conduct patterns of the West German groups that were studied. We will discuss two of these groups in greater detail as examples: the journalists and the industrial shift workers. We will juxtapose these with a number of particularities from two further groups that were studied: the sales assistants and the providers of care for the elderly. We will then introduce the time-diagnostic assessments of the time at which the research was carried out, and finally provide a brief overview of the results of the East German study.[4]

Life-Conduct Patterns between Tradition and Modernity: Empirical Insights

The central challenge of the *conduct of everyday life of journalists* is the way in which they deal with openness:[5] with irregular working hours that are subject to external prescriptions to only a negligible degree, expectations of mobility, insecure income conditions, a high intrinsic motivation to work without the guarantee of a return, expectations of equality in gender roles, and challenges to traditional family forms. Openness here refers, first, to the professional situation and perspective; second, to time management; third, to areas of responsibility within the family; and fourth, to social integration. These factors feature considerable room for maneuvering, as well as constraints within which decisions have to be made under conditions of insecurity. The life conduct of the journalists interviewed as the most modern of the groups included in the sample is therefore confronted in a particular way by the challenge of securing continuity through permanent balancing acts and of achieving feats of adaptation. Both of these elements are central functions of life conduct. It comes as no surprise that these balancing acts are in some cases very complex and in some cases very fragile. The methods and points of orientation of life conduct proved to be essential to the production of balances of this type. Four subtypes were reconstructed, which were, furthermore, gendered.

The *"Control"* type, which functions according to the motto "Rules, Rituals, Territories," is realized primarily by men. Here an attempt is made to establish rules and temporal structures that are as clear as possible, and to maintain them for as long as possible; to disambiguate points of orientation; and to prevent ambivalences from rising to the surface. Openness is shut down again in this way. Everyday life is to a large extent organized in accordance with purposive rationality. This is, however, generally only possible by falling back on the "social resource of women," who, when required to do so, pick up the slack for the men without voicing too much dissent. The *"Discipline"* type, in contrast, plans only that which needs to be planned, and otherwise strives for as much freedom as possible. "Planning" here refers mainly to planning a framework. The aim is to allow variability and flexibility in the execution of the details. This less rigid, more female pattern makes it possible to achieve a certain amount of predictability and continuity, but it pays greater heed to familial considerations. The points of orientation center primarily on balance: on a successful combination of family and work. For women this disposition over their professional time has the apparently paradoxical effect that they have to defend their paid work against the demands of the family. In some cases they therefore long for a firmer structural framework. The *"Acrobatics"* type is, by comparison, much more significantly shaped by ambivalence and indecision, which can rapidly turn into feelings of internal and external conflict. The opportunity to design one's everyday schedule without external constraints is experienced both as a freedom and as a strain. Rigorous control and situational actions alternate without leading to the attainment of a successful balance. This life conduct, which is practiced by women in particular, oscillates between the art of living and chaos. And, last but not least, the *"Trust"* type responds to open parameters with an almost total absence of planning and regularities, as well as a rejection of traditional values. Life conduct is regulated primarily through self-confidence, trust in one's partner and trust in the world. Situational elements in life conduct are not experienced as threatening or chaotic; routines are practiced but can change over time. This also applies to the gender-specific division of labor, the details of which are repeatedly negotiated discursively. Both partners trust that they will get what is due to them when the need arises. This is, however, also the reason why this type is practiced most often by men. Life and work areas are not segmented, but in some cases purposefully mixed. Openness – though on the basis of access to ample resources – becomes the name of the game.

As a whole, this shows that only active and reflexive navigation of life conduct on the basis of central resources (most importantly: networks, skills and material security) can prevent openness in work and living conditions from turning into insecurity, and the risks from outweighing the opportunities.

The life conduct of *shift workers in a rural industrial enterprise* provides a contrast to this in many respects. The corresponding company acquires its workforce systematically based on temporal availability. As a result of this, this partial sample features only men who practice an essentially traditional division of labor from the point of view of gender. In addition, the rural environment strengthens this alignment with traditional models as well as recourse to routines. This evenness and "closedness" in life conduct is, on the one hand, an appropriate method for coping with the extremely changeable work rhythms in night, evening and day shifts, which are, furthermore, dictated by others. On the other hand, it also corresponds to a mentality that in some cases verges on fatalism. The motto "Taking Things as They Come" can also be seen as a successful strategy for adapting to circumstances that are largely out of one's control and to difficult previous biographical experiences. Work is the natural purpose of life, and the family is the putty of life conduct. A number of surprises can be found beneath this apparently entirely traditional surface, however. One of these is that the high value attributed to mutual support in the rural environment applies not only to networks between neighbors and relatives, but also to the division of labor within the family. Communality as a value also governs the cooperation between women and men with reference to housework. On balance it means that, despite their clearer role assignment, the male shift workers help their wives almost as much as do the male journalists with their more modern attitudes. The decisive difference lies in the fact that, unlike in the lives of the journalists, there are no conversations or negotiations here. The shift workers simply help in pragmatic terms whenever it is necessary and possible for them to do so. This also reveals the degree to which the establishment of routines and adherence to tradition can relieve the strains of life conduct. Seen from another angle, the stresses of modernity with the value it attaches to individuality and self-realization as well as to a broad range of options become all the more obvious. In this group, too, nonetheless, it is clear that life conduct is not simply "there," but must be actively established and maintained as a response to contrary working-hour rhythms. Only the methods are specific to this group: The establishment of boundaries and segmentation here serve to reduce complexity, and habits and rituals dominate behavior.

Both of the groups discussed below – sales assistants and providers of care for the elderly – are considered to be lines of work typically carried out by women. This raises issues concerning the organization of everyday life that appear to be typical of women's living situations. The life conduct of *female sales assistants*, even when it takes place in a rural environment, is governed by entirely different factors than that of the shift workers. In the case of the female sales assistants, the everyday task of providing care for others is central. They therefore typically work part-time, which they hope will allow them to combine work and family. In principle, the fact that the work schedule must, or can, be determined anew each and every week means that it is possible to react with flexibility to familial demands. In reality, this leads to endless sequences of coordination, both among colleagues and with family members and other people who help. These women structure their everyday lives to a large extent around the needs of the people for whom they feel responsible. If they are to retain some degree of autonomy to act, they have to find substitutes for the work they do as carers. In general, these substitutes in turn are also all female: sprightly grandmothers, neighbors and aunts. Care for others is a "regime of co-operations between various groups and generations of women" (Rerrich, 1995, p. 190). And yet these women also focus on their paid work. This is because for them, freedom means (also) being able to carry out paid work. They practice the corresponding balancing acts according to the "*skillful balance*" or "*resigned perseverance*" type, as well as the "*reflexive re-arrangement*" type.

The life conduct of the *providers of care for the elderly*, however, is characterized by the requirement to integrate this specific occupation, with its considerable physical and psychological strains and boundary-less working hours that go beyond "normal working hours," into everyday life. This, too, is an occupation carried out primarily by women, although it is also characterized by generation-specific elements. In terms of method, emotion and cognition, these life-conduct patterns can be divided into several types: With the "*nun*" type, life conduct presents itself as an ideological and practical unit; in "*job-centered routinization*" life is subordinated to paid work; in "*family-centered routinization*" the ethos of work and duty, which initially applies to the family, is expanded to apply to paid work. Whereas these three types are to be found mainly among older generations of carers, the following are more characteristic of a younger generation: The "*experience-oriented situativity*" type makes a conscious effort to establish a balance between duties and inclinations. The "*value-oriented planning*" type gives even greater emphasis to self-realization as a guiding principle for life conduct (Dunkel, 1995, p. 243). In a service-related occupation that continues to rely on "undivided dedication" to others, the conditions under which the younger generation was socialized also leads to an implementation of more modern values, whose realization requires particular efforts to achieve integration in life conduct, however.[6]

Time-Analytical Classification and Ideal Types

The descriptions of the groups studied form the material from which the research group developed time-analytical assessments of the development of the conduct of everyday life against the background of the discussion about the modernization of society. To this end, the initial modernization theory hypotheses of the project were re-examined in the light of the empirical results. This highlighted numerous paradoxical consequences of modernization, ambiguities and asynchronies.[7]

The first hypothesized tendency of modernization focuses on an increasing *rationalization* of life conduct. The empirical results show that old and new forms of mastering everyday life are being combined. On the one hand, individual actions and spheres of action are arranged consciously and with the aim of promoting efficiency. Furthermore, life conduct as a whole is increasingly becoming an object of purposeful navigation. On the other hand, this does not necessarily take place in a mode of life conduct characterized by methodical purposive rationality. Instead, life-conduct patterns that can be characterized in terms of ideal types are combined as necessary.

We differentiate between the ideal types of traditional, strategic and situational life conduct. *Traditional life conduct* refers to the functioning of life conduct on the basis of traditions that govern unchallenged: One lives in the same way that one has always lived *because* this is how it has always been. Stability and habits are at the heart of life conduct. Dealing with change – which was a necessity under the conditions examined – proves to be a problem. *Strategic life conduct*, in contrast, contains elements of reflexivity. It is focused on efficiency: One's course of action is governed by planning and control, everyday life is organized from start to finish and the individual areas of life are segmented. This ideal type, which comes closest to Max Weber's concept of "methodical life conduct" (cf. particularly Weber, 1905/1950), reaches its limits when it is confronted with occurrences or parameters that are difficult to plan or control. This is a very common phenomenon of late modernity. *Situational life conduct*, too, is reflexive and rational. Here, everyday actions take place in the form of reactive or desired adaptations to changing situations, and decisions are made depending on the situation encountered. This "muddling through" has improvisational elements and allows openness and flexibility, though it can also lead to instability, indecision and chaos.

In each of the life-conduct types, routines are shown to be decisive mechanisms to achieve continuity and to reduce the number of decisions that constantly have to be made. The variation lies only in the degree of routinization. In addition, an unexpected category presented itself. It appears – if only at first glance – to contradict rational action: Trust reveals itself to be a central coping strategy of a modernity in which boundaries have been dissolved. It plays a decisive role in coping with uncertainty. Most importantly, it makes it possible to eschew direct and total control of all activities, and to simultaneously maintain everyday life conduct.

The second hypothesized tendency of modernization focuses on an increasing *individualization* of life conduct. Modernity is based on the foundation of the program of individual self-realization and autonomous decision-making. Even if there is an increase in the scope for action in some areas, this is essentially a compulsion to make decisions with limited decision-making authority. The active structuring of everyday life means an inevitably new requirement, though it does not necessarily signify individual self-determination in the sense of freedom. Self-control and self-sociation are becoming increasingly important social mechanisms. Personality-related factors such as personal stability, the readiness to take risks and self-confidence prove to be more important than previously assumed in this context. The new significance of the actor is undercut by prevailing mechanisms of social injustice, however. These develop alongside the categories of sex, social stratum and ethnicity, and result from the options accessible and resources (income, education, social networks) available to the individual, and from the constraints and risks that these entail.

The third hypothesized tendency of modernization focuses on the increasing *equalization of gender relations* as the dismantling of gender-specific hierarchies in life conduct. This, too, is expressed in an ambivalent and contradictory way: The old inequalities have not been abolished. In some respects they have been reduced, but above all else, they present themselves in new guises. The dichotomies between male and female life conduct through the attribution of familial work as women's "natural" responsibility continue to exist regardless of all of the rhetoric about equality and despite women's increasing participation in the labor force. Contrary to the expectation that male partners will take over the reproductive work that arises as women's participation in the labor force increases, thus solving problems of double responsibilities, it is mainly female networks that carry out this work, whether without pay or for low pay. Men see themselves as helpers at most, and draw careful distinctions between temporal and actual responsibility for the everyday life of the family. Those men who play a more egalitarian role experience the same constraints as women in their life conduct, however. And yet the complexity of modernized relations between the sexes becomes apparent only when life conduct as a practical "doing" and as a meaningful system are differentiated from one another: Attitudes and practices can diverge sharply from one another not only in men, but also in women. The latter expect increased participation from their male partners without relinquishing their own spheres of control. The discrepancy between orienting oneself and acting can mean that a division of labor that is on the surface traditional is in fact the result of rational and consensual negotiations between partners who have egalitarian approaches.

The fourth hypothesized tendency of modernization focuses on the theory, popular in the 1980s, of a putative *"end of the work-oriented society."* Our results, in contrast, point to an increasing *"workification" of everyday life*. Social differentiation and the increase in options cause the complexity of everyday life to increase. As a result, the linking of the spheres of activity, each of which is governed by an internal logic and which are drifting apart socially, becomes more complex and more demanding. If the aim of life conduct is the creation of consistency, order, and coherence, then this aim becomes a demanding task through the erosion of traditions, values and structural benchmarks. Individuals have to compensate individually for that which no longer fits together structurally. They establish boundaries as a framework of everyday life, for example wherever working hours increasingly encroach on family life. "Workification processes" are also to be seen in frequent negotiations between the sexes, in the increased effort expended by all participants upon synchronization, coordination and planning. The participation of women in the labor force leads not only to more paid work, to work on the "self" and to overtaxing (of oneself), but also to the penetration of the logic of work into the world in which one lives. As life conduct becomes an effort that is both productive and reflexive, the concept of work paradoxically liberates itself from its reduction to gainful work in the course of the modernization of modernity.

Results Relating to the Conduct of Everyday Life in Eastern Germany

The empirical research initiated by the project group *The Conduct of Everyday Life* in eastern Germany after Reunification also led to results that were interesting from the point of view of modernization theory and conceptual aspects. On the one hand, on the basis of a qualitative panel examination of the conduct of everyday life in the East German process of transformation between 1991 and 1993 (Weihrich, 1993, 1998, 1999) – which was conducted beyond the framework of the Sonderforschungsbereich 333 – the particularities of the conduct of everyday life in the German Democratic Republic were retrospectively identified. There were the everyday confrontations with official models, self-evident definition via gainful employment of men and women alongside gender-specific divisions of labor in relation to housework and family work, as well as societal work and the politicization of private relationships. On the other hand, and most significantly, the conduct of everyday life in a situation of radical transformation affecting society as a whole, in which an existing system of institutions was replaced by a new one and nothing was safe, was examined. What happens to the conduct of everyday life in a situation of radical transformation affecting society as a whole, and which sweeps like a whirlwind through everyday life? The repeated questioning made it possible to show that the conduct of everyday life was by no means invalidated by the transformation of the entire social structure. Its form and logic could be reconstructed across time and societal systems. It could be shown that when people are confronted with new options and impositions, they use their conduct of everyday life to orient themselves as though it were a beacon. This is also true when the requirements for action with which they were confronted in the past no longer exist. The conduct of everyday life subsequently showed itself to be both a restriction and a resource when dealing with the new conditions. The decisive factor was orientation via established conduct of everyday life using contact points with the new system, rather than rational adaptation to the new structures. The conduct of everyday life seeks out places in which it can continue to function below the radar of the person concerned. In this way, it becomes a category relevant to inequality, alongside "hard" factors such as age, sex, qualification and occupation.

Hindsight shows that, by focusing on the early 1990s, the study examined a historically significant time period: a moratorium between a "No Longer" and a "Not

Yet" during which the role that many people in eastern Germany would play in the new system of institutions was determined. The adaptation to the new order's abstract logic of the market, which was politically expected, supported by the transformation research of the time and to some extent also prescribed to the actors, was counteracted by the people's practice of orienting themselves according to their conduct of everyday life – by something profoundly social that made possible stability in the midst of all the turbulence: the stability of the people and the stability of institutions.

The Theoretical Concept "Conduct of Everyday Life": Seven Basic Points[8]

Theoretical guiding principles for a concept that eventually came to be known as the conduct of everyday life developed with reference to the category of life conduct that had already been positioned at the heart of his theoretical construct by Max Weber (particularly in Weber, 1905/1950; see also Weber, 1920/1993, 1922/2013; on this subject cf. Abel & Cockerham, 1993; Hennis, 2000). This process, in which empirical research and theory informed one another, took place incrementally simultaneously with, and with material connections to, the work of the Munich project group in the late 1980s.

Against the background of the reception of theoretical approaches with a similarly broad interest in the "entirety" of people's lives, these were in separate pieces of theoretical work developed into an approach that also drew on system-theoretical terms (for a detailed discussion, see Voß, 1991). And yet this approach is, at its core, by no means aligned with a systems theory in the narrower sense. Instead the language reminiscent of systems theory used in some places serves to clarify aspects of the concept generally and with almost theoretical neutrality without being explicitly subjugated to a system-theoretical paradigm. It is therefore, for example, possible to use it to describe the consequences of the communication of actions of people in the various areas of their lives as emergent effects of their actions, which can take on lives of their own with regard to the person.

An unambiguous paradigmatic alignment would in any case not be possible because the subject examined behaves in a way that is almost entirely at odds with virtually all current concepts of sociology (and of other disciplines). If the concept features "elective affinities" (cf. Weber with his famous reference to Goethe, particularly in Weber, 1905/1950), then it does so most clearly with reference to the universal historical deliberations, and the action-theoretical considerations based upon them, of Max Weber. There are, however, simultaneously clear points of contact with the phenomenological concepts of sociology, and not least with a subject-theoretical reading of Karl Marx, particularly of his early writings (Marx, 1844/2007) and the philosophical anthropological passages that draw on them in the economic oeuvre (particularly Marx, 1867/2012, chap. 5).

This approach to the determination of the conduct of everyday life is outlined by the following thesis-like basic points.

a. Conduct of Everyday Life as the Interrelation of Action

The conduct of everyday life refers to the totality of actions in people's everyday lives, which thus constitute a person's life. Although structures of meaning and interpretations play an important regulative function here, life conduct is not defined (at least not primarily) as a construction of meaning (as, for example, in the phenomenological concepts of the *lifeworld* (e.g., Grathoff, 1989) or of *everyday life* (Schütz, 1978)), or indeed as a framework for the individual cultural stylization of life with the aim of social distinction, as is the case in lifestyle research (for an overview, see Müller, 1989, 1992; Müller & Weihrich, 1990). It is, instead, defined primarily as *practice*. Despite the fact that the activities of everyday life invariably follow one another and life conduct thus necessarily takes place in time, the concept of the conduct of everyday life does not focus primarily on the diachrony of life as is the case in biographical or life-course research (e.g., Kohli, 1984). The concept's interest is instead geared toward the interrelation of activities that have a formative influence on a person's life at a particular moment in time or for a particular period. The synchrony of life is therefore the subject; that which, day after day, constitutes the proverbial "treadmill of everyday life."

b. Conduct of Everyday Life as Interrelation and Form of Everyday Activities

Although the concept of the conduct of everyday life potentially examines all activities of everyday life, it is not the pure sum or the detailed sequence of what is, in the final analysis, a limitless number of different activities carried out by people (which is, for example, captured by time-budget research (Blass, 1980) and time geography (Deinet, 2009; Hägerstrand, 1975)). Life conduct is instead defined as the structure of the activities that are part of life on an everyday basis. The view of the concept is therefore not so much analytically dismantling but instead integrative: It is about the *interrelation* of practical everyday life and its *forms*, rather than about the abundance of elements. It is about the forms of the activities carried out by people on a day-to-day basis in the social spheres that are relevant to them (such as work, family, consumption, politics), which thus become the spheres of their lives.

The observation of such forms can be broken down into the dimensions of temporal, spatial, material, social, meaningful, media-technical, emotional and bodily aspects. The form of a person's life conduct is therefore contingent upon when and at which points in time and with which temporal logics, in which places and with which forms of mobility, the shape and manner of the content, in which social contexts and with reference to which social norms and interpretations of meaning, as well as with which technical means or media resources, and finally with which emotional states and bodily-corporal dispositions (including their gender orientations) a person typically carries out actions in the course of their everyday life.

The conduct of everyday life is thus characterized by the ways in which a person positions themselves in relation to the various social spheres to which they refer, and the ways in which they *arrange* themselves in the aforementioned dimensions. Furthermore, the conduct of everyday life is a way, a form in which these discrete social arrangements are connected to constitute a functioning overall arrangement. It is the arrangement of the individual arrangements of a particular person.

c. Conduct of Everyday Life as the Individual's System of Action

This character of the interrelation of everyday activities can be understood in terms of a *system of action*, which establishes a conceptual focus on particular aspects. The basal function of this system is the integrative communication of various activities. Individuals, according to the central hypothesis, refer to their environments not through isolated discrete activities, but via activities within the framework of a functionally differentiated and integrated everyday system of action, the system of the conduct of everyday life. In this way the discrete activities achieve a higher degree of effectiveness (e.g., through effects relating to specialization, synergy and emergence), and life as a whole thus achieves potentially increased levels of freedom in relation to the demands of the social environment to which the individual must respond. The conduct of everyday life is a system on the level of the individual, or, more specifically, a *system of the individual*, a system of action that belongs to the individual, to which they are bound and which they support. One could even see life conduct as the system of action of the individual, namely as the basal form of communication and integration of the person's entire spectrum of everyday activities, through which the individual positions themselves in relation to the social systems of relevance to them and through which they respond to their demands.

d. Conduct of Everyday Life as the Individual's Active Construction and Effort

This personal system of action does not exist of its own accord. One does not simply *have* a life conduct, and it is not a passive reflex reaction to social conditions or opportunities (as the concept of "circumstances" would argue), either. The emphasis here is instead on the fact that the system of life conduct is invariably *actively constructed*, *practiced* on an everyday level and *maintained*, as well as adapted, when necessary, to changing conditions by every person with reference to their individual social situation or position. It must, in other words, be modified as the circumstances require. Whether or not the people concerned are aware of it: They "conduct" their lives.

This construction effort, too, can be broken down into various dimensions, so that it is possible to explore with which temporal, spatial, material and other *methods* a person's life conduct is produced (or maintained or changed). It is also possible to examine the temporal, spatial, material and other resources (including the universal resource of money) that are drawn upon in order to do so, as well as the social spheres in which they originate, and how they were acquired – and in some cases even actively created – there.

The emphasis on the elements of construction and effort in life conduct finally opens up a perspective upon a consistently dynamic view of the ways in which everyday life is set up. This should be understood as a flexible form of the continuous process of everyday negotiation of social demands and opportunities. "The conduct of everyday life" therefore does not refer to a fixed framework, but to a structured (and structuring) procedure with which everyday actions are every day coordinated and integrated, and which leads to relatively stable (temporal, spatial, etc.) regulations of an individual's actions in the spheres of their everyday life.

e. The Self-Contained Logic of the System of the Conduct of Everyday Life

Although life conduct is a (dynamic) product of the individual, one should not assume that, in accordance with voluntaristic subjectivism, it is dependent on the individual's will alone. The degree to which life conduct is the result of conscious design is always limited. It is always also (if not primarily) the consequence of situational decisions and pragmatic ad hoc arrangements, which come into being with limited reflexivity. Regardless of the fact that it is the product of an individual, life conduct gains both a functional and a structural *autonomy* in relation to its producer. This results from the fact that a life conduct, once it has been set up as an action-structuring modus for everyday life, can no longer be changed at will by the individual because it is based upon numerous binding arrangements with social reference areas and actors, and these cannot be revoked without further ado. As the individual can therefore no longer drop out of their life conduct without some effort, and can no longer modify it as they please, they and their actions are – whether they like it or not – always subject to the regime of the system of the activity regulation that they themselves have set up. The flow of activities of everyday life occurs to a large extent within this framework. Although it is possible to modify it to a certain degree, doing so also serves to constantly reinforce it. An established life conduct is no longer freely available to the individual. One might say that it no longer really belongs to them, and that it gains a sort of independent existence in relation to them, an independent existence upon which the individual in turn becomes more or less dependent. In this way the system of life conduct upholds its own logic "behind the back" (cf. Karl Marx) of the individual.

f. The Non-Deterministic Sociation of the Conduct of Everyday Life

Voluntaristic subjectivism is furthermore eliminated by the fact that the concept of the conduct of everyday life (sociologically evidently) implies that its object, though personally constructed and borne, is systematically shaped by social conditions. No matter how much emphasis is placed on the personal responsibility and constructivity of life conduct, this does not conceal the fact that one does not live one's life alone, but that one is instead integrated into manifold social contexts, and that life conduct is therefore invariably and in a systematic manner *sociated*. Three aspects are of particular significance:

First, objective social conditions in the social spheres of the individual present more or less inflexible constraints and demands (but also opportunities and resources) for the individual's life conduct. Second, manifold sociocultural influences also have an effect on life conduct: patterns of interpretation, normative standards and cultural models for what life conduct should or could look like in the individual's particular circumstances. Objective conditions and sociocultural influences are, however, not seen as determining conditions. They are, instead, actively appropriated through life conduct. And, finally, it is obvious that one generally practices life conduct not in isolation, but together with others in various forms of immediate social cohabitation (such as families, partnerships and networks). These are social modes of an active interlacing and cooperative production and maintenance of individual life conducts, which are therefore always also joint (e.g., familial) life conducts.

g. Conduct of Everyday Life as a System sui generis

The concept emphasizes the element of personal construction and effort involved in life conduct, while simultaneously highlighting the fact that it should not be equated with the psycho-physical individual. It instead represents a dynamic emergence of subjects that take on lives of their own in relation to them and can thus in turn have an effect on them. The social conditionality and forming of life conduct is simultaneously recognized while emphasizing that life conduct is not a social system or social entity. Life conduct is instead – according to this theory – a system *sui generis*, which with its own form and logic inserts itself between the individual and society, and fulfills important functions. Where the individual is concerned, requirements can be mastered more successfully, and resources can be used more effectively, so that the individual life gains an increase in relative autonomy in relation to society. Where society is concerned, the conduct of everyday life makes an important contribution to the solution to the problem of *social integration*. The constant efforts made by members of society to achieve a functioning everyday life help to connect and unify what is socially separated. The daily routine also produces an important chunk of continuity in the case of a crisis in an individual's intimate social circle or in their living environment, during organizational changes in companies and during structural change in labor markets.

Everyday life conduct should therefore be seen as a decisive element in the communication of the individual and society, which is systematically differentiated from other oft-cited entities (such as habitus, role/norm, environment/subculture, institution/organization). The concept emphasizes that people do not position themselves in relation to social spheres through isolated individual activities and that the specific manner in which they position themselves also shapes and changes these social spheres, but that they do so within the framework of a system of everyday-life arrangement. By regulating their activities in the spheres of life that are of relevance to them, and because they coordinate this regulation in arrangements of the conduct of everyday life, people form an integrated interrelation for their social actions that constitutes a bridge between them and the social spheres relevant to them. Life conduct is thus an entity through which the person communicates with social spheres and thus with society as a whole. Life conduct can simultaneously, through its clustering to form typical patterns, have social repercussions. In this way it can (co-)construct society and therefore has a potentially transformative dimension. In return, the person experiences society only as communicated by its system of the conduct of everyday life. How the individual and society bilaterally relate to each other is thus to a considerable degree shaped by the nature of this connection: through the individual forms and logics of everyday life conduct.

This state of affairs describes a systematic blind spot in the prevalent formation of theories and empirical research in sociology, not only at the time during which the concept was developed, but also to this day. Holzkamp recognized this with great clarity and forcefulness, and named an analogous problem of similar urgency for psychology (in particular in Holzkamp, 2015, chap. 3 in this volume; see also Holzkamp, 2013). This blind spot raises the issue of more than just a secondary research gap of some shape or other. The concept of the conduct of everyday life assumes, with considerable self-confidence and a degree of risk, that the conduct of everyday life, as suggested above, constitutes an absolutely fundamental (though it has previously been largely overlooked by research) "link" in the mutually constitutive relationship of "living" individuals (cf. Karl Marx, for example repeatedly in 1867/2012) in their concrete historical everyday lives, and the various equally concretely historical social relations (Karl Marx).

Everyday life conduct is thus a veritable missing link in sociology and, as Holzkamp attempts to show with great emphasis, also in psychology. It is also Holzkamp who with impressive empathy describes monumental scholarly astonishment like that experienced by the members of the conduct of life research group (2015, chap. 3 in this volume): The experience that the real, practical everyday lives of people, which constitute the "real" lives of the members of a society, are largely ignored by research. One might even say that they are denied or, if one wishes to see it in psychological terms, suppressed. There has for many years been a varied and very stimulating body of research into "everyday life" that is, in the broadest sense, sociological (such as that in, among many others, Garfinkel, 1984; Goffmann, 1959; Schütz, 1978, 2011; see also de Certeau, 2011; Heller, 1987; and Lefebvre, 2008). And yet we share Holzkamp's impression that a fragmentary approach is taken here (whereby this is also of great importance), or a very distant perspective is applied, whereas the concrete and – most importantly – the "entirety" of people's lives in in its polymorphic breadth and immediate everyday practice (and thus also in its apparent banality) simply does not feature. And yet it is precisely this that constitutes people's lives (if one asks them): not more, but not less, either.

In order to work on this blind spot, the research group *The Conduct of Everyday Life* not only accepted the risk of postulating with great chutzpah a new sociological subject and of claiming to work on a remarkable desideratum in the social sciences; these theoretical deliberations and this empirical work also approach the very fringes of what is, or should be, in the mainstream of our subject area (of sociology). The concept positions itself (not only in this respect) in a no-man's-land between numerous hotly contested fronts and finds itself caught in the crossfire by virtually abandoning society in its clear focus on the subject as the pillar of the analysis without, however, engaging in something like psychology (as Holzkamp quite rightly points out).

What takes place in the research into the conduct of everyday life is a sociological conceptualization of subjectivity and even of individuality from a sociological point of view and as a genuine subject of sociology. And it is simultaneously – as Holzkamp, too, remarks – more than a form of sociology that pays marginal attention to people but that in the final analysis does in fact engage in conventional sociology. It is not up to us to decide whether this constitutes an offer to psychology to examine society with its instrumentarium from a subject-theoretical point of view (as is in fact attempted by the life-conduct project with its subject-oriented perspective, though with sociological instruments). Holzkamp appeared to be heading in this direction.

Conduct of Everyday Life: A Flourishing Research Program

Numerous other pieces of research have been inspired by the empirical evidence and concept of the conduct of everyday life. The first part of the following section is dedicated to a number of important empirical follow-up studies. The second part explores the conceptual and methodical developments, such as the shift from the individual to the familial life conduct, and reconstructs the connection between the conduct of everyday life and the figure of the *entreployee* and of the *working customer*.

Further Research

The selected empirical follow-up studies described below draw from the concept and original design to a significant extent, but always also extend the concept, so that one now speaks of a discrete *sociology of the conduct of everyday life*. To illustrate this, we will discuss four research areas in more detail.

The first research area consists of the work on the conduct of everyday life of members of particular occupational groups. These pieces of work present conceptual innovations beyond the establishment of types. Norbert Huchler's research (2012) into the personal and professional everyday life of airline pilots in commercial air traffic serves as one example. Pilots work under conditions that blur boundaries (in particular in terms of space and time), and have to react to the accelerated change to which they find themselves exposed. Huchler categorizes the arrangements developed and adds a fourth ideal type of the conduct of everyday life to the ones previously constructed: *collective life conduct*. The time-diagnostic punchline lies in the fact that the pressure that is exerted upon the life conduct of pilots can be viewed as a paradigm for life under conditions in which numerous boundaries of personal and professional life are blurred in the fluid work-oriented society of our times: We are all becoming pilots.[9]

In a second area, the focus is on the family as the milieu in which life conduct takes place. Here Jurczyk, Schier, Szymenderski, Lange and Voß (2009) also explore the increasingly flexible spatial and temporal conditions of work and of life, while systematically concentrating their examination of life conduct on family and on gender relations. Against the background of an empirical examination of the conduct of everyday life of mothers and fathers in the film business and in retail, they speak of a "twofold blurring of boundaries" of family and work. Under these conditions joint familial life conduct becomes a *production effort* – and it also becomes a precarious undertaking. Parents are frequently so exhausted that they merely contribute to pragmatic compatibility management, but not to the construction of togetherness. Both self-care and care for others – increasingly also by fathers – are often practiced at the boundaries of the possible.

Third, Alma Demszky von der Hagen (2006) sets another accent by researching everyday sociation, thus pursuing the sociologically highly relevant question of how society develops "from the bottom," and thus from the individual actions performed by people. To this end, she studied the "small societies" that are the family, friends and relatives in their contexts in the workplace and the dwelling place, specifically in a housing estate in Budapest, which provides an additional insight into the particularities of a post-communist society. The author understands the conduct of everyday life as a modus of sociation and emphasizes the active construction efforts of people that have been superimposed on the former more or less passive sociation.

Finally, we would like to note that fictitious people, too, have a conduct of everyday life. Weihrich and Voß (2004) have studied how investigators in contemporary detective novels combine work and life, and have reconstructed the conduct of everyday life of Guido Brunetti from the novels of Donna Leon, of Kurt Wallander from the novels of Henning Mankell, and of Vic Warshawski from the novels of Sara Paretsky. Readers find out as much about the everyday lives of the investigators, and the associated organizational problems, as they do about their investigative work. This makes it possible to reconstruct not only the various conducts of everyday life, but also – because these are serial crime stories – their stability over time. In the organization of their everyday lives, fictitious actors use their conduct of everyday life to orient themselves. Here, too, these patterns correspond to their various social framework conditions. Fictitious worlds are also social worlds, in which the corresponding social mechanisms are at work.

For further examples from the research program, for the integration of the concept into other research contexts and for conceptual further developments, see Voß and Weihrich (2001) and Weihrich and Voß (2002).

Theoretical, Methodical and Time-Diagnostic Connections

a. The Conduct of Everyday Life and Action Theory

G. Günter Voß has revealed the relationship between the concept of the conduct of everyday life and approaches that also examine "life as a whole," before presenting a system-theory-inspired version of the concept of the conduct of everyday life (1991). Margit Weihrich (1998) applies a different theoretical focus: She provides an action-theoretical foundation for the concept of the conduct of everyday life and connects it to the current socio-theoretical discussion about the micro-foundation of processes and structures. An individual actor, according to this model, establishes their conduct of everyday life in relation to all of the different action situations in which decisions about actions have to be taken on an everyday basis. The result is that the conduct of everyday life can be understood as a bundle of decision-making rules for everyday situations, which the actor uses as a point of reference when making everyday decisions. This conception can also be used to criticize the model of rational choice in decision-making: Everyday challenges are unclear, unpredictable and contradictory, so that decisions about actions cannot be made on the basis of subjective expected utility focused on the future that is applied to an individual situation. In the face of decision-making demands such as these it makes much more sense to commit oneself, and to use one's conduct of everyday life, and thus the past, as a guideline.

A conception of the conduct of everyday life such as this can also be connected to the socio-theoretical discussion about "social mechanisms" that is currently in progress within the framework of an explanatory sociology if one places the conduct of everyday life in "Coleman's bathtub" (Weihrich, 2001). This macro-micro-macro model shares a lot of common ground with the conception of subject-oriented sociology as proposed by Karl Martin Bolte (1983). Here, too, the idea of the actor is the starting point, and one's efforts are focused on the explanation of social systems of which one assumes that they result from the actions of individuals without it being possible to reduce the former to the latter. Our actor must engage with these systems, nevertheless, in order to make a decision about an action. When inserting the conduct of everyday life into this macro-micro-macro model, it becomes apparent that the conduct of everyday life functions as an instrument for perception when it comes to the *definition of the situation*; that it functions as a rule for decision-making when it comes to making *choices about actions*; and that, finally, it also determines the *aggregation logic*. The conduct of everyday life is consolidated, and perhaps it is in this way that the very conditions under which the established life conduct can be applied without difficulty can be reproduced. Of course this is not necessarily the case, as the author's research into the conduct of everyday life in the East German transformation process has shown (Weihrich, 1998): The conduct of everyday life can prove to be a resource, but also a restriction. It is always true that an actor must also engage with their conduct of everyday life, however. Like other restrictions and resources, too, it confronts the actor as a situational demand.

b. Familial Conduct of Everyday Life

Although the conduct of everyday life was from the beginning conceived as socially integrated and as entangled with other people, and the empirical research, too, concentrated on members of the labor force in the active family phase, the single individual was the conceptual and methodological focal point. And yet it is necessary to distinguish between the quotidianally pragmatic individual linking of socially disparate spheres of activity within the framework of life conduct (as an *intra*personal connection) and the *inter*personal intertwining of life conduct in private life forms in the sense of a "shared life conduct" (on this subject see also the concept of "linked lives" by Elder, 1994). The systematic expansion of the concept from an individual toward a familial life conduct can therefore to this day be viewed as a theoretical desideratum despite the fact that the first steps have been taken (as will be discussed below), and these are currently being developed further in combination with a methodological twist.

In the immediate context of the main study by the project group, Maria S. Rerrich (1994) in particular already explored how women actively "combine what diverges socially" with reference to a group of female sales assistants in the countryside. She describes the irreconcilable demands that result from the process of separation of social spheres such as paid work, family, public services and education, as well as the efforts made to achieve their reintegration in order to make it possible to care for others within the family. In her research Rerrich highlights the fact that the efforts at agreement and coordination necessary to achieve this can by no means be limited to the sphere of the nuclear family. Instead, the many unpaid and paid helpers, ranging from the grandmother to the cleaning lady (each of whom has her own life conduct), are an indispensable component of familial life conduct (Rerrich, 2006).

Kerstin Jürgens describes in more detail the processes of the everyday concurrence and of the intertwining of individual life conducts within the family in research closely aligned with the Munich project group that examines the familial conduct of everyday life of industrial workers (Jürgens, 2001; Jürgens & Reinecke, 1998). She conceives familial conduct of everday life as an interaction between that which is "own" and that which is "shared" and delves into this in more detail with reference to the coordination of activities and interests on a material, spatial, temporal, emotional and social level (Jürgens, 2001, pp. 40ff.) The gendered division of resources as well as power and decision-making authority is of particular significance to the forms and processes of familial conduct of everday life.

A number of other authors (see, for example, Rönkä & Korvela, 2009), too, have in the meantime turned their attention to the question of how people act and coordinate individual life conducts on the basis of their integration into the family, and how they are merged into a joint frame of reference for action within a family and *as* a family. Studies on familial everyday life by Kousholt (2011) in particular stress that family is a "conflictual community" and that processes of coordination (can) cause friction.

At present a research group at the German Youth Institute[10] is pursuing the aim of developing a better understanding of the connecting of the conduct of everyday life in families, and of conceiving more clearly and empirically researching the corresponding practices in greater depth and on a broader basis (Keddi, 2014). In recent years, a praxeological shift in family research has become apparent (Daly, 2003; Lüscher, 2012; Morgan, 2011). It was made necessary by the growing demands on private life under the conditions of late modernity with its twofold blurring of boundaries (Hochschild, 1997; Jurczyk et al., 2009). As a result of "de-traditionalization," individualization and the blurring of boundaries, family is no longer self-evident. It is no longer a pre-existing resource with a fixed form, but must be actively "produced" as a joint life-connection in processes of "doing family" (Jurczyk, Lange & Thiessen, 2014). This becomes particularly clear in research into step-families, adoptive families, foster families and same-sex families. This effort to produce family in the context of and *through* familial life conduct here differentiates the levels of primarily organizational compatibility management, the production of "we-ness" and the act of "displaying family" as outward stagings or inward reassurements of belonging together (Finch, 2007; Galvin, 2006; Schier & Jurczyk, 2007). The targeted examination of shared routines and rituals and of "doing boundary" in relation to other family members, as well as to spheres external to the family such as paid work, constitutes an important focal point (Jurczyk et al., 2009).

Empirical research into this area is in its early stages, however, and a number of fundamental questions remain unanswered: Is there such a thing as joint familial life conduct, or is it not always a case of mere intersections and commonalities as each individual person is integrated into other social spheres? And is the sum of the individual life conducts of people who live together as a family under one roof (automatically) familial life conduct? The interim conclusion is that corresponding efforts at intertwining must always be understood on two levels: as a connection with social spheres of action and with other people. In addition, the distinction must be made on two levels with reference to family: the level of community (as an interrelation of action when it comes to the question of co-presence and joint activities, for example) and that of togetherness (as an ideational interrelation with respect to shared convictions and values, for example). These many and varied aspects make the expansion of the concept from individual to familial life conduct into a persistent, and simultaneously highly interesting, challenge.

The research group is also pursuing the ambitious aim of researching familial life conduct with the help of quantitative methods, thus making it possible to describe distributions of actions and patterns of action in connection with orientations and existing parameters for larger groups of the population. To this end, an attempt was made to implement the concept of familial life conduct in the DJI survey "AID:A" (*Growing up in Germany: Everyday Worlds*). At present the possibilities and boundaries of a "translation" of a qualitatively generated concept into a quantitatively operationable concept are being explored. On the one hand, this brings forth very interesting representative detailed results, for example with respect to shared activities, inter-familial divisions of the labor of care and approaches to multi-locality

(Schier, 2013; Zerle & Keddi, 2011). On the other hand, it has proved remarkably difficult to quantitatively operationalize life-conduct arrangements as interrelations of actions and not as single activities. This is all the more complicated because families, as opposed to individuals, are the subject.

c. New Forms of Labor

Soon after the completion of the work carried out by the project group *The Conduct of Everyday Life* it was suspected that the flexibilization and deregulation of gainful work that has taken place increasingly since the 1980s would result in the fact that workers and employees would have to take an increasingly entrepreneurial approach in the future. With the discussion about the structural transformation of gainful work that is taking place in the sociology of work and industry, this has developed into a theory with a time-diagnostic approach with regard to a self-entrepreneurial workforce ("Entreployee") (first Voß & Pongratz, 1998; see also Pongratz & Voß, 2003a, 2003b; Voß, 1998; among others). The description and explanation of a historically new social model for the workforce is at its heart. According to this view, the previously dominant type of the "vocational employee" (as a historical successor to the "proletarian worker") – who is, in a manner concisely defined in terms of labor legislation, dependent on a salary, based in a specific occupation, socially protected and geared toward the execution of work in a manner that is primarily directly dependent on direction – is, in the transition to a post-Fordist capitalism, gradually being replaced by the entreployee. The latter is characterized by three features:

If in the course of the flexibilization of work there is a tendency toward direct managerial control of the employee being reduced and replaced by indirect forms of direction, workers have to formulate their concrete work tasks more autonomously than in the past ("self-control"). A new quality of exploitation of human labor potential (particularly through "self-exploitation"), accompanied by the danger of a trend toward total access to people's potential, is the drawback.

As a consequence, the employees' relationships with their own abilities as economic "commodities" (Karl Marx) undergo a transformation. Owners of labor potential who in the past only rarely acted economically, and who generally did so passively, must increasingly become actors who behave strategically and who systematically develop their labor potential toward a progressively market-driven economic use, and they must utilize it actively ("self-commercialization").

One notable consequence is that the entire interrelation of the lives of working people is undergoing structural change. A relatively stable way of life primarily oriented toward recreation and divided into "work" and "free time" in a traditional manner is turning into a total organization of an increasingly blurred framework for life ("self-rationalization") that makes use of all individual resources. Life conduct is becoming more and more similar to an economically oriented and rationally organized business; in other words, it is assuming the "character of a business organization" already suggested by Max Weber in his work on occidental rationalism (Weber, 1905/1950).

When developed further, ideas that arose shortly afterwards in a research context that is at first glance entirely unconnected similarly showed themselves to be continuations of the work on life conduct. Empirical research on structural change in service activities related to individuals (e.g., Dunkel & Voß, 2004) showed that customers are increasingly and purposefully integrated as "quasi-employees" who can be used productively in the provision of services. In conscious analogy to the theory of the entreployee this developed into a theory that focused on the sphere of consumption in relation to a possible structural change in the socially dominant type of consumer (first Voß & Rieder, 2006; see also Rieder & Voß, 2013, among others). The primarily "buying customer" (as a successor to the pre-industrial consumer, who appeared primarily as a "self-producer") typical of Fordism is now becoming, according to this theory, a "working customer," who is characterized by the following features:

The consumer is now no longer a mere buyer or passive user or consumer of commodities and services. The consumer's labor is instead systematically used by companies in a productive manner, albeit very differently from the path of formal wage-dependent employment. Private activities are in this way systematically subsumed by the regime of company utilization in the production of goods and services.

Customers are in this context increasingly (and generally without receiving economic compensation) becoming explicit sources of company value. Individuals are no longer the source of additional value for companies only in their roles as working people, but also in their roles as consumers. People's consumptive productivity is thus subjected to business "economicization" of an entirely new quality.

Consumers are in the final analysis effectively transformed in a wide variety of ways into company employees by virtue of the fact that they use the resources of the companies (such as vending machines, software tools) and submit to organizational rules in relation to their contribution to the generation of the companies' gains. Their private productivity as an element of individual consumption in the framework of the conduct of everyday life in this way becomes subject to a purposeful organizational control and connection.

Customers and clients interact with many different companies that provide services, compiling services from a variety of different offers, to which end they use their private resources, professionalize themselves and carry out the "interactive work" necessary for the creation of services along with the employees. Looking at the work carried out by customers and clients in the service society, it is possible to speak of a "customer/client life conduct" in which these services are brought together (Hoffmann & Weihrich, 2013).

Conduct of Everyday Life: Current Challenges and Opportunities

In the research streams described above it is possible to see the conceptual relevance, the time-diagnostic acuteness and the invariably surprising timeliness of the research on the conduct of everyday life. The concept reveals that historical developments in the sphere of gainful work are closely connected to complementary changes in the private sphere and in that of consumption. Most importantly, however, it draws attention to the fact that these changes come together in the person's everyday life, and must be concretely appropriated and tackled through practical action.

This achievement has become no easier to accomplish. Looking back over the trends identified by the project group *The Conduct of Everyday Life* it becomes clear that nothing has eased off since then, and that much has in fact become more drastic – and that life conduct can ultimately also fail when one simply no longer manages to "get all one's ducks in a row."

The *rationalization of life conduct* is thus increasing and gains (not least through the opportunities provided by new personalized communication technologies) an entirely new quality. In the course of complex social processes in which boundaries are blurred, the boundaries between work and life are dissolved (Gottschall & Voß, 2003; Voß, 1998), while social access to the individual in the sense of a "subjectification" primarily – though not exclusively – in the sphere of gainful work reaches a new historical level (Huchler, Voß & Weihrich, 2007; Kleemann, Matuschek & Voß, 2003). Against this background it is increasingly the task of individuals to give structure to their lives; the efficient optimization of the conduct of everyday life has become the goal. Not only is life progressively becoming work – this "work of life" must now also be organized in a business-like manner. As an entrepreneur of the self one works at the "businessification" of life conduct.

The early realization that the *individualization of life conduct* has little to do with autonomous design, but that instead constraints with limited powers to make decisions about such a design are coming to the fore – this, too, applies to life conduct in a particular manner nowadays. Society is undergoing a significant shift toward individuals handling things themselves: being responsible and accountable for things themselves as people in gainful work, as citizens, patients, consumers and so on. As a result, the individuals concerned (and there are few to whom this does not apply) are sucked to an unprecedented degree into the maelstrom of self-expenditure and self-use.

The *equalization of gender relations*, too, proceeds apace in the familiar paradoxical manner. The integration of women into paid work is increasing, and the demands on the compatibility of work and life are increasing, too (also among a growing number of men). And yet the reality continues to be quite different: The organization of paid work still stands in opposition to compatibility, so that it is no surprise when a traditional gender-specific division of labor proves to be the "more relaxed" solution in comparison to the time pressure that arises when both partners work virtually full-time (or, even more significantly, the strains experienced by single parents). Gender-specific differences in income therefore continue to exist, and housework and the coordination of the family continue to be largely the responsibility of women across the various constellations (on this subject, see Heiden & Jürgens, 2013).

An "*end to the work-oriented society*" is therefore less likely to come about than it ever has been. While the demands on self-organization in paid work rise, a complementary radical "workification of everyday life" can be observed: The act of joining together the spheres of activity, each of which is governed by its own logic and which are drifting apart socially, is becoming an elaborate and demanding task. Individuals have to take an even more active role in taking charge of their working and living conditions, and are now, more than ever, forced to mobilize and employ their entire personal potential. In order to meet the demands of the world of modern work and life they must dispose of a wide skill set.

One of these skills is the ability to care for oneself. According to Voß and Weiß (2013), depression, anxiety disorders and burn-out can be interpreted as significant social illnesses in the transition to the 21st century. They can simultaneously be read as crises of life conduct in a society in which the boundaries are increasingly blurred, in which integration is no longer successful. Voß and Weiß describe a dangerous mixture of self-development and excessive demands on the self as being at work: Individuals want to take advantage of the new liberties, to experience satisfaction in their work and life, to enjoy their work – and therefore exert themselves fully and exhibit a high degree of intrinsic motivation. But this also leads people to experience considerable pressure. They no longer know how to establish boundaries to contain the excessive demands and strains, and interpret every failure as self-induced, to which they react by exerting ever-greater efforts.

As a result the "self-reproduction of the person" (Heiden & Jürgens, 2013) is under threat – a demand that is added to the reproductive efforts that people must make every day and over the course of time in order to maintain their performance in the workplace and their social integration. The resources for "care" – as physical and emotional assistance given to oneself and others – are depleted under the conditions of increasing strain and exhaustion (Jurczyk, 2010). Without this kind of caring everyday practice, both the individual's quality of life and the social relationship of reproduction and gainful work are called into question, however. A "crisis of reproduction" can then be diagnosed (Jürgens, 2010), as can a "wearied society" (Voß, 2010; Voß & Weiß, 2013), an extension of the idea of the "wearied self" (Ehrenberg, 2009).

The question of "successful life conduct" arises against this background. If self-care means being able to establish boundaries, an established conduct of everyday life could prove to be a practice that makes the establishing of boundaries possible. The conduct of everyday life could provide shelter from the impositions of optimization described above as a relatively stable system of action, as a guiding principle for making everyday decisions, or as a self-constructed framework that in the final analysis holds the individual together. The main aim would then not be to choose and realize one's own concept of the good life; it would be to ensure that the practices that have been developed with consideration for all of the various and always already contradictory demands from the different areas of life can be maintained. In this case the conduct of everyday life itself also requires protection, however. This could take the form of thinking about ways in which "space for willful reproduction practices to unfold" can be created that would tolerate the "singularities of individual everyday routines and life practices" (Heiden & Jürgens, 2010, p. 267). This in no way means a strategic optimization of the conduct of everyday life. To the contrary: The aim would be to retain the self-contained logic of the established conduct of everyday life. The fact that life conduct has the tendency to take on a life of its own in relation to the person, and is not at all easy to change, would provide a good basis for this.

And yet the limits of the conduct of everyday life are reached if the demands of everyday life continue to develop in the manner described above, so that integration cannot succeed. The arrangement that the person has worked to achieve can then be shattered by the effects of the social organization of work and life. This results in disastrous effects not only for the person, but also for society.

Notes

1 We would like to thank Wolfgang Dunkel for his support and Jane Michael for her outstanding translation of a challenging paper.
2 Use of the phrase "work and life" should here be understood as a quotation of a commonly used formula. We are fully aware of the contraction that it implies. For the research project and the theoretical concept of the conduct of everyday life that is at its heart, the idea that one "lives" in the sphere of "work" (which refers to paid work) and that one "works" in a wide variety of different ways in "life" (which refers to all areas of life with the exception of gainful "work") is systematically constitutive. This also points to the fact that the academic and social debate about the definition of "work" (for a detailed discussion, cf. Voß, 2010), which continues to this day, represents an important factor underpinning research into the conduct of everyday life, and to the fact that a systematically "broad" definition of work is at its core, encompassing all socially relevant forms of work-related activity.
3 Luise Behringer, Wolfgang Dunkel, Karin Jurczyk, Werner Kudera, Maria S. Rerrich and G. Günter Voß (and in the early stages Elisabeth Redler and Ortrud Zettel) were involved with the project group *The Conduct of Everyday Life*; they were later joined by Sylvia Dietmaier-Jebara and Margit Weihrich. Karl Martin Bolte was in charge of the project as a whole.
4 For further important follow-up studies that grew directly out of the project group's work, see Behringer (1998), Dietmaier-Jebara (2005) and Dunkel (1994), among others.
5 As most of the journalists we studied were freelance journalists, insecurity was particularly pronounced here.
6 It would be beyond the scope of an chapter of this length to discuss the two other groups studied in western Germany. They comprised skilled workers and employees of a conglomerate, who organize their lives under comparatively stable employment conditions and with a degree of flexibility (flexitime; cf. Voß, 1995a) on the one hand; and on the other hand young data-processing operators who work on an international level and who, under difficult conditions, as far as working hours are concerned (round-the-clock shift work), and with good pay, enter arrangements that can function for only a limited amount of time (cf. Dietmaier, 1995).
7 The following discussions summarize Jurczyk and Voß (1995) and Kudera (1995).
8 This section is based on a revision by Voß (1995b).

9 For further work on the conduct of everyday life among individual occupation groups and work forms, see Egbringhoff (2007) and Morgenroth and Schindler (2012), among others.
10 The group includes Christine Entleitner, Karin Jurczyk, Michaela Schier and Claudia Zerle-Elsäßer.

References

Abel, T. & Cockerham, W. C. (1993). Lifestyle or Lebensführung? Critical remarks on the mistranslation of Weber's "Class, status, party." *The Sociological Quarterly*, *34*(3), 551–556.

AID:A (2015). Growing up in Germany: Everyday Worlds. Retrived from www.dji.de/index.php?id=1419

Bauman, Z. (2000). *Liquid modernity*. Cambridge: Polity Press.

Beck, U. (1992). *Risk society: Towards a new modernity*. London: Sage.

Behringer, L. (1998). *Lebensführung als Identitätsarbeit: Der Mensch im Chaos des modernen Alltags*. Frankfurt/M.: Campus.

Blass, W. (1980). *Zeitbudget-Forschung: Eine kritische Einführung in Grundlagen und Methoden*. Frankfurt/M.: Campus.

Bolte, K. M. (1983). Subjektorientierte Soziologie: Plädoyer für eine Forschungsperspektive. In K. M. Bolte & E. Treutner (Eds.), *Subjektorientierte Arbeits- und Berufssoziologie* (pp. 12–36). Frankfurt/M.: Campus.

Bolte, K. M. (1995). Zur Entstehungsgeschichte des Projekts im Rahmen einer "subjektorientierten" Forschungsperspektive. In "Projektgruppe "Alltägliche Lebensführung" (Eds.), *Alltägliche Lebensführung: Arrangements zwischen Traditionalität und Modernisierung* (pp. 15–22). Opladen: Leske & Budrich.

Daly, K. (2003). Family theory versus the theories families live by. *Journal of Marriage and Family*, *65*(4), 771–784.

de Certeau, M. (2011). *Practice of everday life*. Berkeley, CA: University of California Press.

Deinet, U. (Ed.). (2009). *Methodenbuch Sozialraum*. Wiesbaden: VS Verlag für Sozialwissenschaften.

Demszky von der Hagen, A.-M. (2006). *Alltägliche Gesellschaft: Netzwerke alltäglicher Lebensführung in einer großstädtischen Wohnsiedlung*. Munich: Rainer Hampp.

Dietmaier, S. (1995). Ein Arrangement auf Zeit. Die Lebensführung von EDV-OperatorInnen. In Projektgruppe "Alltägliche Lebensführung" (Eds.), *Alltägliche Lebensführung: Arrangements zwischen Traditionalität und Modernisierung* (pp. 303–328). Opladen: Leske & Budrich.

Dietmaier-Jebara, S. (2005). *Gesellschaftsbild und Lebensführung: Gesellschaftspolitische Ordnungsvorstellungen im ostdeutschen Transformationsprozess*. Munich: Rainer Hampp.

Dunkel, W. (1994). *Pflegearbeit – Alltagsarbeit: Eine Untersuchung der Lebensführung von AltenpflegerInnen*. Freiburg: Lambertus.

Dunkel, W. (1995). Zur Integration des Berufs in das Alltagsleben: Das Beispiel der Altenpflegekräfte. In Projektgruppe "Alltägliche Lebensführung" (Eds.), *Alltägliche Lebensführung: Arrangements zwischen Traditionalität und Modernisierung* (pp. 213–251). Opladen: Leske & Budrich.

Dunkel, W. & Voß, G. G. (Eds.). (2004). *Dienstleistung als Interaktion: Beiträge aus einem Forschungsprojekt – Altenpflege, Deutsche Bahn, Call Center*. Munich: Rainer Hampp.

Egbringhoff, J. (2007). *Ständig selbst: Eine Untersuchung der alltäglichen Lebensführung von Ein-Personen-Selbständigen*. Munich: Rainer Hampp.

Ehrenberg, A. (2009). *The weariness of the self: Diagnosing the history of depression in the contemporary age*. Montreal: McGill Queens University Press.
Elder, G. H., Jr. (1994). Time, human agency and social change: Perspectives on the life course. *Social Psychology Quarterly, 57*(1), 4–15.
Finch, J. (2007). Displaying families. *Sociology, 41*(1), 65–81.
Galvin, K. M. (2006). Diversity's impact on defining the family: Discourse-dependence and identity. In L. H. Turner & R. West (Eds.), *The family communication sourcebook* (pp. 3–20). Thousand Oaks, CA: Sage.
Garfinkel, H. (1984). *Studies in ethnomethodology*. Chichester: Wiley-Blackwell.
Giddens, A. (1986). *The constitution of society: Outline of the theory of structuration*. Chichester: Wiley-Blackwell.
Giddens, A. (1991). *The consequences of modernity*. Cambridge: Polity Press.
Goffman, E. (1959). *The presentation of self in everyday life*. New York: Anchor.
Gottschall, K. & Voß, G. G. (Eds.). (2003). *Entgrenzung von Arbeit und Leben: Zum Wandel der Beziehung von Erwerbstätigkeit und Privatsphäre im Alltag*. Munich: Rainer Hampp.
Grathoff, R. (1989). *Milieu und Lebenswelt: Einführung in die phänomenologische Soziologie und sozialphänomenologische Forschung*. Frankfurt/M.: Suhrkamp.
Hägerstrand, T. (1975). Space, time and human conditions. In A. Karlqvist, L. Lundqvist & F. Snickars (Eds.), *Dynamic allocation of urban space* (pp. 3–14). Lexington, MA: Saxon House.
Heiden, M. & Jürgens, K. (2013). *Kräftemessen: Betriebe und Beschäftigte im Reproduktionskonflikt*. Berlin: Edition Sigma.
Heller, A. (1987). *Everyday life*. London: Routledge.
Hennis, W. (2000). *Max Weber's question*. Newbury: Threshold Press.
Hochschild, A. R. (1997). *Time bind: When work becomes home and home becomes work*. New York: Henry Holt.
Hoffmann, A. & Weihrich, M. (2013). Interactions in service relationships: The customer's point of view. In W. Dunkel & F. Kleemann (Eds.), *Customers at work: New perspectives on interactive service work* (pp. 100–123). Houndmills: Palgrave Macmillan.
Hofmann, M. & Dietzsch, I. (1995). Zwischen Lähmung und Karriere: Alltägliche Lebensführung bei Industriearbeitern und Berufsumsteigern in Ostdeutschland. In B. Lutz & H. Schröder (Eds.), *Entwicklungsperspektiven von Arbeit im Transformationsprozeß* (pp. 65–95). Munich: Hampp.
Holzkamp, K. (2013). Psychology: Social self-understanding on the reasons for action in the conduct of everyday life. In E. Schraube & U. Osterkamp (Eds.), *Psychology from the standpoint of the subject: Selected writings of Klaus Holzkamp* (pp. 233–341). Basingstoke: Palgrave Macmillan.
Huchler, N. (2012). *Wir Piloten: Navigation durch die fluide Arbeitswelt*. Berlin: edition sigma.
Huchler, N., Voß, G. G. & Weihrich, M. (2007). *Soziale Mechanismen im Betrieb: Theoretische und empirische Analysen zur Entgrenzung und Subjektivierung von Arbeit*. Munich: Hampp.
Jurczyk, K. (2010). Care in der Krise? Neue Fragen zu familialer Arbeit. In U. Apitzsch & M. Schmidbaur (Eds.), *Care und Migration: Die Ent-Sorgung menschlicher Reproduktionsarbeit entlang von Geschlechter- und Armutsgrenzen* (pp. 59–76). Opladen: Budrich.
Jurczyk, K., Lange, A. & Thiessen, B. (Eds.). (2014). *Doing family: Familienalltag heute. Warum Familienleben nicht mehr selbstverständlich ist*. Weinheim: Beltz/Juventa.
Jurczyk, K. & Rerrich, M. S. (1993). Einführung: Alltägliche Lebensführung: der Ort, wo "alles zusammenkommt." In K. Jurczyk & M. S. Rerrich (Eds.), *Die Arbeit des Alltags: Beiträge zu einer Soziologie der alltäglichen Lebensführung* (pp. 11–45). Freiburg: Lambertus.
Jurczyk, K., Schier, M., Szymenderski, P., Lange, A. & Voß, G. G. (2009). *Entgrenzte Arbeit – entgrenzte Familie: Grenzmanagement im Alltag als neue Herausforderung*. Berlin: edition sigma.

Jurczyk, K., Treutner, E., Voß, G. G. & Zettel, O. (1985). "Die Zeiten ändern sich": Arbeitszeitpolitische Strategien und die Arbeitsteilung der Personen. In S. Hradil (Ed.), *Sozialstruktur im Umbruch: Karl Martin Bolte zum 60. Geburtstag* (pp. 147–164). Opladen: Leske & Budrich.

Jurczyk, K. & Voß, G. G. (1995). Zur gesellschaftsdiagnostischen Relevanz der Untersuchung von alltäglicher Lebensführung. In Projektgruppe "Alltägliche Lebensführung" (Eds.), *Alltägliche Lebensführung: Arrangements zwischen Traditionalität und Modernisierung. Opladen* (pp. 371–407). Opladen: Leske & Budrich.

Jürgens, K. (2001). Familiale Lebensführung. In G. G. Voß & M. Weihrich (Eds.), *Tagaus tagein: Neue Beiträge zur Soziologie alltäglicher Lebensführung 1* (pp. 33–60). Munich: Hampp.

Jürgens, K. (2010). Deutschland in der Reproduktionskrise. *Leviathan, 38*(4), 559–587.

Jürgens, K. & Reinecke, K. (1998). *Zwischen Volks- und Kinderwagen: Auswirkungen der 28,8-Stunden-Woche bei der VW AG auf die familiale Lebensführung von Industriearbeitern*. Berlin: edition sigma.

Keddi, B. (2014). Familiale Lebensführung als alltägliche Herausforderung – von der mikrosoziologischen Nahaufnahme zur praxeologischen Repräsentativstudie. In K. Jurczyk, A. Lange & B. Thiessen (Eds.), *Doing family: Familienalltag heute. Warum Familienleben nicht mehr selbstverständlich ist*. Weinheim: Beltz/Juventa.

Kleemann, F., Matuschek, I. & Voß, G. G. (2003). Subjektivierung von Arbeit: Ein Überblick zum Stand der soziologischen Diskussion. In M. Moldaschl & G. G. Voß (Eds.), *Subjektivierung von Arbeit* (pp. 57–114). Munich: Hampp.

Kohli, M. (Ed.). (1984). *Soziologie des Lebenslaufs*. Darmstadt: Luchterhand.

Kousholt, D. (2011). Researching family through the everyday lives of children across home and day care in Denmark. *Ethos, Journal of the Society for Psychological Anthropology, 39*(1), 98–114.

Kudera, W. (1995). Zusammenfassung der Ergebnisse. In Projektgruppe "Alltägliche Lebensführung" (Eds.), *Alltägliche Lebensführung: Arrangements zwischen Traditionalität und Modernisierung* (pp. 331–370). Opladen: Leske & Budrich.

Kudera, W. (1997). Die Lebensführung von Arbeitern – ein gesamtdeutsches Phänomen. In G. G. Voß & H. J. Pongratz (Eds.), *Subjektorientierte Soziologie* (pp. 183–200). Opladen: Leske & Budrich.

Lefebvre, H. (2008). *Critique of everyday life*. London: Verso.

Lüscher, K. (2012). Ambivalence and practice as emerging topics of contemporary family studies. In E. Scabini & G. Rossi (Eds.), *Family transitions and families in transition* (pp. 93–108). Milan: Vita e Pensiero.

Lutz, B. (Ed.). (2001). *Entwicklungsperspektiven von Arbeit. Ergebnisse aus dem Sonderforschungsbereich 333 der Universität München*. Oldenburg: Akademie-Verlag.

Marx, K. (2007). *Economic and philosophic manuscripts of 1844*. New York: Dover. (Original work published 1844)

Marx, K. (2012). *Capital: A critique of political economy* (Vol. 1). London: Penguin. (Original work published 1867)

Morgan, D. H. J. (2011). *Rethinking family practices*. Basingstoke: Palgrave Macmillan.

Morgenroth, S. & Schindler, S. (2012). *Feuerwehralltag: Eine soziologische Untersuchung zur Lebensführung von Feuerwehrmännern im 24-Stunden-Wachalltag*. Munich: Rainer Hampp.

Müller, H. P. (1989). Lebensstile: Ein neues Paradigma der Differenzierungs- und Ungleichheitsforschung? *Kölner Zeitschrift für Soziologie und Sozialpsychologie, 41*(1), 53–71.

Müller, H. P. (1992). *Sozialstruktur und Lebensstile: Der neue theoretische Diskurs über soziale Ungleichheit*. Frankfurt/M.: Suhrkamp.

Müller, H. & Weihrich, M. (1990). *Lebensweise – Lebensführung – Lebensstile: Eine kommentierte Bibliographie*. Neubiberg: Forschungsberichte der Fakultät für Pädagogik der Universität der Bundeswehr München.
Pongratz, H. J. & Voß, G. G. (2003a). From employee to "entreployee": Towards a "self-entrepreneurial" work force? *Concepts and Transformation, 8*(3), 239–254.
Pongratz, H. J. & Voß, G. G. (2003b). *Arbeitskraftunternehmer: Erwerbsorientierungen in entgrenzten Arbeitsformen*. Berlin: edition sigma.
Projektgruppe "Alltägliche Lebensführung" (Eds.). (1995). *Alltägliche Lebensführung. Arrangements zwischen Traditionalität und Modernisierung*. Opladen: Leske & Budrich.
Rerrich, M. S. (1994). Zusammenfügen, was auseinanderstrebt: Zur familialen Lebensführung von Berufstätigen. In U. Beck & E. Beck-Gernsheim (Eds.), *Riskante Freiheiten* (pp. 201–218). Frankfurt/M.: Suhrkamp.
Rerrich, M. S. (1995). Die Alltagsaufgabe der Sorge für andere: zur Lebensführung von Verkäuferinnen. In Projektgruppe "Alltägliche Lebensführung" (Eds.), *Alltägliche Lebensführung: Arrangements zwischen Traditionalität und Modernisierung* (pp. 171–211). Opladen: Leske & Budrich.
Rerrich, M. S. (2006). *Die ganze Welt zu Hause: Cosmobile Putzfrauen in privaten Haushalten*. Hamburg: Hamburger Edition.
Rieder, K. & Voß, G. G. (2013). Customers at work: A fundamental change in service work. In W. Dunkel & F. Kleemann (Eds.), *Customers at work: New perspectives on interactive service work* (pp. 177–196). Basingstoke: Palgrave Macmillan.
Rönkä, A. & Korvela, P. (2009). Everyday family life: Dimensions, approaches, and current challenges. *Journal of Family Theory and Review, 1*(2), 87–102.
Schier, M. (2013). Räumliche Entgrenzungen – Multilokales Familienleben: Spezifische Anforderungen einer mehrörtigen Alltagsgestaltung und die Rolle von Medien. In U. Wagner (Ed.), *Familienleben: Entgrenzt und vernetzt?! Interdisziplinäre Diskurse 7* (pp. 39–55). Munich: Kopaed.
Schier, M. & Jurczyk, K. (2007). Familie als Herstellungsleistung in Zeiten der Entgrenzung. *Aus Politik und Zeitgeschichte, 34*, 10–17.
Schütz, A. (1978). *Alfred Schütz und die Idee des Alltags in den Sozialwissenschaften: Hrsg. von Walter Sprondel und Richard Grathoff*. Stuttgart: Enke.
Schütz, A. (2011). *Collected papers* (Vol. 1). Heidelberg: Springer.
Treutner, E. & Voß, G. G. (1982). Arbeitsmuster – Ein theoretisches Konzept zum Zusammenhang von gesellschaftlicher Arbeitsteilung und der Verteilung von Arbeiten auf Ebene der Subjekte. München. Überarbeitete Fassung. In W. Kudera & G. G. Voß (Eds.) (2000), *Lebensführung und Gesellschaft. Beiträge zu Konzept und Empirie alltäglicher Lebensführung* (pp. 29–37). Opladen: Leske & Budrich.
Voß, G. G. (1991). *Lebensführung als Arbeit: Über die Autonomie der Person im Alltag der Gesellschaft*. Stuttgart: Enke.
Voß, G. G. (1995a). Große Sicherheiten, kleine Karrieren: zur alltäglichen Lebensführung von FacharbeiterInnen und Angestellten eines Großkonzerns. In Projektgruppe "Alltägliche Lebensführung" (Eds.), *Alltägliche Lebensführung: Arrangements zwischen Traditionalität und Modernisierung* (pp. 253–301). Opladen: Leske & Budrich.
Voß, G. G. (1995b). Entwicklung und Eckpunkte des theoretischen Konzepts. In Projektgruppe "Alltägliche Lebensführung" (Eds.), *Alltägliche Lebensführung: Arrangements zwischen Traditionalität und Modernisierung* (pp. 232–243). Opladen: Leske & Budrich.
Voß, G. G. (1998). Die Entgrenzung von Arbeit und Arbeitskraft: Eine subjektorientierte Interpretation des Wandels der Arbeit. *Mitteilungen aus der Arbeitsmarkt- und Berufsforschung, 31*(3), 473–487.

Voß, G. G. (2010). Auf dem Weg zu einer neuen Verelendung? Psychosoziale Folgen der Entgrenzung und Subjektivierung der Arbeit. *Vorgänge, 49*(3), 15–22.

Voß, G. G. & Pongratz, H. J. (Eds.). (1997). *Subjektorientierte Soziologie*. Opladen: Leske & Budrich.

Voß, G. G. & Pongratz, H. J. (1998). Der Arbeitskraftunternehmer: Eine neue Grundform der "Ware Arbeitskraft"? *Kölner Zeitschrift für Soziologie und Sozialpsychologie, 50*(1), 131–158.

Voß, G. G. & Rieder, K. (2006). *Der arbeitende Kunde: Wenn Konsumenten zu unbezahlten Mitarbeitern werden*. Frankfurt/M.: Campus.

Voß, G. G. & Weihrich, M. (Eds.). (2001). *Tagaus – tagein: Neue Beiträge zur Soziologie Alltäglicher Lebensführung 1*. Munich: Rainer Hampp.

Voß, G. G. & Weiß, C. (2013). Burnout und Depression – Leiterkrankungen des subjektivierten Kapitalismus oder: Woran leidet der Arbeitskraftunternehmer? In S. Neckel & G. Wagner (Eds.), *Leistung und Erschöpfung: Burnout in der Wettbewerbsgesellschaft* (pp. 29–57). Berlin: Suhrkamp.

Weber, M. (1950). *The Protestant ethic and the spirit of capitalism*. London: Butler & Tanner. (Original work published 1905)

Weber, M. (1993). *The sociology of religion*. Boston, MA: Beacon Press. (Original work published 1920)

Weber, M. (2013). *Economy and society. An outline of interpretive sociology*. New York: McGraw Hill. (Original work published 1922)

Weihrich, M. (1993). Lebensführung im Wartestand: Veränderung und Stabilität im ostdeutschen Alltag. In K. Jurczyk & M. S. Rerrich (Eds.), *Die Arbeit des Alltags: Beiträge zu einer Soziologie der alltäglichen Lebensführung* (pp. 210–234). Freiburg: Lambertus.

Weihrich, M. (1998). *Kursbestimmungen: Eine qualitative Paneluntersuchung der alltäglichen Lebensführung im ostdeutschen Transformationsprozeß*. Pfaffenweiler: Centaurus.

Weihrich, M. (1999). Alltägliche Lebensführung im ostdeutschen Transformationsprozeß. Aus Politik und Zeitgeschichte. *Beilage zur Wochenzeitung Das Parlament, B 12*(99), 15–26.

Weihrich, M. (2001). Alltägliche Lebensführung und institutionelle Selektion oder: Welche Vorteile hat es, die Alltägliche Lebensführung in die Colemansche Badewanne zu stecken? In G. G. Voß & M. Weihrich (Eds.), *Tagaus – tagein. Neue Beiträge zur Soziologie alltäglicher Lebensführung 1* (pp. 219–236). Munich: Rainer Hampp.

Weihrich, M. & Voß, G. G. (Eds.). (2002). *Tag für tag: Alltag als Problem – Lebensführung als Lösung? Neue Beiträge zur Soziologie Alltäglicher Lebensführung 2*. Munich: Rainer Hampp.

Weihrich, M. & Voß, G. G. (2004). Alltägliche Lebensführung und soziale Ordnung im Kriminalroman. In T. Kron & U. Schimank (Eds.), *Die Gesellschaft der Literatur* (pp. 313–340). Opladen: Barbara Budrich.

Zerle, C. & Keddi, B. (2011). "Doing care" im Alltag Vollzeit erwerbstätiger Mütter und Väter. Aktuelle Befunde aus AID:A. *Gender, 3*(3), 55–72.

3
CONDUCT OF EVERYDAY LIFE AS A BASIC CONCEPT OF CRITICAL PSYCHOLOGY

Klaus Holzkamp

Background

Why have I suddenly and without prior notice begun to concern myself with what has been termed the *conduct of life*? Not only may other people who have seen this happening be surprised, I myself am in a sense astonished that I have suddenly ended up looking into the "conduct of life" – despite the fact that I actually had other plans for my further research – and that it in fact looks as though I shall be staying with this subject for the next few years. So that both I and other people can be clearer about my reasons for being interested in this research topic, I shall start by saying a bit more about what led up to this choice.

1. In my work with students in seminars and projects and while preparing for examinations, I gradually began to see more and more clearly something that was actually self-evident, which was that the conventional idea that students' learning processes result mainly from the *relationship between the conditions of learning at university and the students' personal willingness to learn* is somehow too simple (perhaps this conclusion is a form of the *teaching–learning short circuit* to which I drew attention elsewhere in 1993). I had realized that in fact these learning processes are also decisively *mediated* by the students' life situations and activities outside of the university, or, to be more exact, their entire *conduct of everyday life* (this was the expression that spontaneously came to me) of which their life at the university is only one aspect or segment. I saw that the extent to which the students are able to organize their lives in such a way that learning at university is a central organizational principle that structures their daily lives as a whole would seem to be decisively dependent on whether they can actually be physically and mentally *present* at the lectures and other learning events at the university and whether they can take advantage of the opportunities for learning that are offered there (be it by accepting them on a simple level or with critical distance).

Having clarified for myself the fact that learning at university is mediated by the students' organization of their lives it was only a small step to the insight that neither the teaching staff nor the university administration "officially" takes note of this and that it is also rarely addressed systematically in discussions with the teaching staff during their consultation hours or in seminars. While the students do, of course, talk to each other about how they organize their lives, for the teaching staff this is more or less uncharted territory, which is also usually not even acknowledged as an "uncharted" dimension. In my experience one is most likely to encounter indirect indications of it in working groups and particularly in projects that are carried out in longer-term collaborative groups. Here we do hear such things as "I can't come in the evenings this week, it's my turn to look after Silke," or, "If possible not on Friday, I've promised to help Maria move into her new apartment on that day," or "I'd rather do the transcription of the tapes next week, because then three of my room-mates will be on holiday."

When I began to think more deeply about this point I realized that the "depublicization" of how the students organize or conduct their everyday lives at university not only leads to administrative and didactic shortcomings, but must also be reflected in the implicit or even scientific *theory building on student learning processes*, for instance, where differing success rates of students having attended the same courses are (unthinkingly) summarily attributed to differences in the "motivation to learn," differences in "ability" etc. of the individual students (which are then considered to be due to differences in "aptitude" or "socialization"). It became clear to me that, on the one hand, such personalizing attributions close off further questioning as to possible disruptions and contradictions in the way students organize their lives that arise from shortages of specific resources but also from many other more or less unknown circumstances. On the other hand, it is precisely because of this that the fiction of the individual accountability and "assessability" of students' performance, on which the administrative and "educational" organization of student careers at university is based, can be sustained. From all of this I concluded that there is a need to make the connection between students' performance and their organization of their everyday lives a subject of discussion with the students themselves. However, before doing so I considered it necessary to clarify the concept *conduct of everyday life* theoretically, for example in the context of a project on "Learning at University."

2. Once I had realized that *students'* learning activities may be linked to how they conduct their lives on a daily basis, I could connect this with certain chance observations that I was able to make of what one might call "*full-fledged*" *academic workers* at university. *Their* academic work, too, can – as I began to see – only be adequately understood if one assumes that in doing it *they always in some way have to "reconcile" its demands with the demands in other areas of their lives.* Thus, some colleagues' commitment to their academic work is evidently systematically limited by the fact that they regularly have to "take care of their families" in the evenings and at weekends. Where colleagues left their families and moved into an apartment of their own, the most obvious reason no longer seemed to me to be that they had a girlfriend they wanted to live with. Perhaps those colleagues also wanted to create the conditions necessary

to really be able to devote themselves to their academic work without being interrupted. The fact that I had not previously hit on the doubtlessly even greater problems faced in this area by women in academia was presumably only because there are very few of them among the professors in my circle of colleagues. In this context I realized that I could also see my own numerous attempts to escape from my family commitments in a different light if I looked at them from this point of view, and that in the process a kind of living evolved whereby commitment to a life partner and commitment to academic work were no longer in conflict with each other.

From there I arrived at the (admittedly speculative) thought that the problem of how to reconcile one's professional work with one's family life as an average male academic might even be reflected in the *nature of the organization of academic activities and publishing in the psychological "scientific community."* Therefore, both the practice of leading psychological journals, particularly in the United States, of accepting only short articles on experimental studies and dispensing with more detailed theoretical discussions and the move away from longer monographs toward collections of papers that are frequently based on lectures given at conferences, are (among other things) quite "family friendly." One can no doubt quite easily produce such "morsels" in the gaps between fulfilling one's domestic duties, effectively precluding the risk of being caught up in and carried away by issues of science to such an extent that one's "ordered" family-based conduct of life would suffer. An average academic career – four experimental publications in standard journals per year – would thus be easily achievable without having to neglect one's wife and children. One could even go further and suppose that the dominant epistemology of psychology – i.e., the marginalization and devaluation of reflections on the basic theoretical principles and methodological problems of the discipline and their replacement by mini-theories and their experimental "testing" – is probably not totally unaffected by the integration demands of the conduct of everyday life of those who pursue a science thus conceived. American middle-class ideology, with its conservatism and family-orientedness, and academic psychology, which is fundamentally conservatively organized, would thus in some respects live in each other's pockets. Thus seen, scientific self-doubt, critiquing and attempts to embark on a fundamentally new orientation are both "speculative" and unscientific and anything from "untidy" to immoral, because they are detrimental to a "normal," i.e., family-centered lifestyle. Consequently, within the typology of scientists operative among psychology researchers, the "tough-minded scientist" – as distinguished from the "tender-minded philosopher" – is a successful scientist who does not neglect his family.

The reader will perhaps by now have begun to understand that, having taken cognizance of such impressions and considerations, which I had previously seen more as side issues, I gradually came to adopt the view that I must – in order to be able to test and substantiate these impressions and considerations – address myself to the concept of the "conduct of life" on a more fundamental level and in more detail. I realized – and this strengthened my resolve decisively – that to date the "conduct of life" has evidently *been greatly neglected in traditional psychology*. Although we do find, in specific contexts, other concepts that can be seen as more or less closely related to the concept of "conduct of life" – for instance, in developmental psychology, personality research, educational psychology, occupational and organizational psychology, etc. – nowhere in the entire history of psychology as a discipline since Wundt has *everyday living* been to any extent systematically and comprehensively analyzed or conceptualized *as a theoretical problem in its own right*. I became – to the extent that I began to get a sense of the central psychological importance of the concept of the conduct of life – more and more curious to discover why that is so. Nevertheless, in order to begin investigating this question I first had to, at least to a certain degree, translate my own previous understanding of conduct of life into a scientific understanding – preferably not merely intuitively, but taking into account contributions to the subject from *outside psychology*.

Conduct of Everyday Life in Subject-Oriented Sociology

However, my initial explorations into sociology and philosophy were not particularly fruitful. I did sometimes find the phrase *"conduct of life,"* but in connection with other concepts that were not clearly distinguished from it, especially the concept of "lifestyle," which has remained very popular to this day, and relatively unclear differentiations between it and approaches of life history research, which is now very widespread in the (non-psychological) social sciences. Even in recent publications whose titles actually contain the phrase *"conduct of life"* (Vetter, 1991), again I found relative overlaps or equations of "conduct of life" with "lifestyle," "life situation," "life context," "lifeworld," etc. I can only imagine that it is this broadening of the concept that led Vetter to describe the concept of "conduct of life" in his introduction as a catch-all term (ibid.). I also found it frustrating that in all such conceptualizations what I was trying to get to grips with in the thought process described above failed to emerge in a clear and tangible way.

I was thus bracing myself for a rather lengthy preliminary historical analysis of the concept (which hardly added to my enthusiasm for the subject) when, following up on a tip from a colleague at my institute, I came across a research group that in my view had not only already made the necessary historical clarifications and distinctions and defined the concept of the "conduct of life" more precisely, but had also presented their own concept of the "conduct of everyday life" that they had developed theoretically and proved empirically. This was sufficiently differentiated and developed for me to be able to build directly on to it with my own ideas. I am referring to a research project entitled *Flexibilized Employment and the Organization of the Conduct of Life in Individuals*. This project was part of Collaborative Research Center 333 of Munich University, the members of which were Karl Martin Bolte, Luise Behringer, Wolfgang Dunkel, Karin Jurczyk, Werner Kudera, Maria S. Rerrich and Gerd Günter Voß [Editors' note: for a detailed presentation of this research approach, see Jurczyk et al., 2015, chap. 2 in this volume]. Some representative papers of the project have been (in addition to some individual publications) published in a collection of articles entitled *The Work of Daily Living: Contributions to a Sociology of the Conduct of Everyday Life* (Jurczyk & Rerrich, 1993a), which includes publications by many of the members of the project. There is also a monograph by Gerd Günter Voß on the subject entitled *The Conduct of Life as Work: On the Autonomy of the Person in the Daily Life of Society* (1991), in which the basic theoretical and methodological positions of the project are further articulated and contrasted with other approaches. In my view, anyone who is seriously interested in working on the "conduct of everyday life" must read the work of this project. In what follows I will therefore briefly outline its main positions only as far as is necessary to render understandable my own discussion of the reasons for the exclusion of the concept of the "conduct of everyday life" from psychology and the analyses I have conducted on the basis of the science from the standpoint of the subject[1] (which are intended to remedy this deficiency). I shall then present certain points in more detail later – where necessary.

Perhaps the concept *conduct of life* (in this section of the chapter this always refers to the concept as understood by the above-mentioned project of Collaborative Research Center 333) is most easily accessible if we seek to understand the difference between the "*conduct* of everyday life" and "the *course* of a life" (in the sense of a life history or the biographical dimension of "life"). While *conduct of life* is, of course, in *reality* an aspect of one's life history and thus also subject to all its changes (from birth to death), *functionally* the "conduct of everyday life" must be considered to be a separate process that is distinct from a person's life history. In a sense this results from the specific givenness of "everyday life" that is organized by the individual's "*conduct of life*" or mode of leading his/her life. An individual's activities become everyday through the daily *repetition* of processes such as, for example (standard sequence): getting up in the morning at 7 o'clock, having breakfast, reading the newspaper, going to work at 8.30, coming home at 5 p.m., having supper, watching television and going to bed. The *routinization* of such a sequence is in a certain sense essential, i.e., indispensable to life, it arranges things so that "life goes on." As "everydayness," the everyday character of the conduct of life has so-to-speak its own *reproductive or self-reproductive system quality* that cannot be reduced to developments and changes over the course of one's life history. Voß (1991, pp. 99ff.) correspondingly emphasizes the *synchrony* of the activities of everyday living as something distinct from the *diachronic plan* of the life history.

If one wishes to capture the system quality of the "conduct of everyday life" more exactly, one must realize above all that – despite the routinization of daily life – it does not take place all by itself, but is always an *active achievement of the individual*. This applies not only where there is a broader scope for personal design, but also to activities that are rigidly "prescribed" from outside: while I *have to* get up at 7 a.m. if I am to get to work or school on time, it is *I* who must get up and I *could* in fact stay in bed. That is, the individual and her or his "conduct of life" always has certain "*degrees of freedom*" (as Voß puts it), that is, s/he always has a relative "autonomy" in relation to her/his life circumstances, which may be small, but – because the *conduct of life* would then cancel itself out – could never tend to zero. This includes the fact that the routinization of the processes of living that is necessary for the conduct of everyday life and aimed for can never be a finally achieved "stationary state," but is a *dynamic equilibrium* that must constantly be re-established and protected against disturbances of various kinds.

This becomes quite clear when we realize that we do not lead our everyday lives in a one-dimensional process that is without contradiction, but that we encounter different kinds of *"external demands"* that emanate from different *"domains of life"* (such domains of life are, according to Voß (1991, p. 261), for example, one's "occupation," one's "family," one's "circle of friends," etc.), for which and with whom one must make certain *"arrangements"* such that the overall organization of one's everyday life can be described as the *"arrangement of arrangements"* (ibid., p. 262). The active effort that we have to make to lead our everyday lives can thus be characterized as an active integration of various "demands" from the respective domains of daily life that is manifested in different ways at different levels of demand. This is true at the "level of the *organization of time in everyday life*" in the form of activities of synchronization, coordination and planning; on the "level of the *functional division of labor organization of everyday life*," in the form of activities of coordination and negotiation of individual options such as the distribution of tasks and resources; and on the "level of the *social organization of daily life*" in the form of activities of negotiation and coordination to regulate relationships and social contacts (Jurczyk & Rerrich, 1993b, p. 27). The general background to the need for such constant integration efforts to handle different kinds of "demands" is the experience that the potentials that can be lived out are limited due to the *"scarcity"* of resources, i.e., the scarcity of material goods, the scarcity of capacities for care and attention and – in the last analysis – the *shortness of our lifetimes*, which ultimately has its roots in the personal experience of the finiteness of our lives. It is only because of such scarcities that we cannot simply fulfill the "demands" of life one after the other, but must develop, as we integrate them, an "economy" of the *conduct of life* with which we set priorities, make compromises, neutralize contradictions and resolve conflicts (or at least put them on hold). Hence, the way we lead our lives as an integrative processing, i.e., also an *"interpretation"* of the demands emanating from the different life domains in keeping with their relevance for the maintenance of our "everyday lives," has (as Voß, in particular, stresses in various contexts) its own *"self-contained logic"* vis-à-vis the given circumstances, which alone allows us to stand our ground in the face of the circumstances and thus to "'get everything together' that we have to do every day" (Jurczyk & Rerrich, 1993b, p. 12).

The concept of *conduct of everyday life* developed by the Munich research group adopts a fundamental theoretical stance in regard to the basic sociological problem of the *relationship between the individual and society* that goes beyond the internal differentiations alluded to above. Viewing the *"conduct of life"* as an active integrative (or, as it is occasionally put even more pointedly, *"constructive"*) activity of the subject, the group *critically distanced itself* from established sociological modes of thought in which the individuals are always in some way seen as *merely* a *dependent variable of the "societal structure"* or the like. On the one hand, the authors acknowledge that the conduct of an individual life is "by no means something that is and can be shaped in any way that the person alone would like, but is itself co-created by societal structures and mechanisms" (Kudera & Voß, 1990, p. 157) and thus they do not support the "ideological construction" according to which "every man ... forges his own destiny" (Jurczyk & Rerrich, 1993b, p. 37). On the other hand, they emphasize that "even those who have only bad alternatives to choose from are challenged to clear a way through the thicket of options." They see the conduct of life "as a *mediating category* between the subject and societal structures and focus particularly on the *scope for action that subjects have as they grapple with these structures*" (ibid., p. 37; emphasis added). This points toward a fundamental conceptual concern of the research approach of the Munich group, which we frequently find characterized as an "*orientation toward the subject*" — and which within *theoretical sociology* itself represents a critical or alternative position (see, for instance, Voß, 1991, p. 10f.; Bolte, 1983), although it can also be found in the area of overlap between sociology and psychology.

From the "subject orientation" approach we can now also understand the way in which the concept of the conduct of everyday life adhered to by the authors is specified in contrast to other sociological conceptualizations that appear to be similar. This is examined in depth in a monograph by Voß (1991). I shall present a brief outline of this discussion, taking the (as I mentioned above) now widespread and popular concept of "*lifestyle*" as an example. Voß (ibid., pp. 180ff.) devotes a detailed analysis to the history and meaning of the construct and comes to the conclusion that while one could in principle use the term "lifestyle" to accentuate a *certain aspect of the "conduct of life"* — i.e., its "expressive" or "aesthetic demonstrative" side — the way the word is in fact used more or less prohibits it. Thus, for example, he points out that in his elaboration of the concept as a means of "stylizing" our own lives or our own group affiliations symbolically and culturally, Pierre Bourdieu (to whose work on the subject the current prevalence of and popularity of the "lifestyle" concept is mainly attributable; cf. Mörth & Fröhlich, 1994) developed a terminology that might be used to express — as in the concept of the "habitus" — individuals' active, subject-related capacities for shaping their lives. However, Voß adds that on closer scrutiny we find that Bourdieu never abandoned the conventional basic sociological position that *the individual is determined by the structure of society* and that he thus conceived of the "habitus" and "lifestyle" as dependent dimensions of mass- and class-specific structural properties of society. In Voß's view, since it is so widely understood in this way "lifestyle" cannot be considered to be a specification of "conduct of life." Rather the concept of the conduct of everyday life should be seen as a theoretical alternative to the lifestyle concept:

> In contrast to Bourdieu, the authors offer a *construction of the person* as a transmitter according to which the person actively relates to society, appropriates through work the conditions that s/he finds in society and organizes them, while also tending to change society, and in fact (together with others) to create it.
>
> (Voß, 1991, p. 170)

The critical and alternative position assumed by the Munich project with its concept of the conduct of life is articulated pointedly at certain junctures in the statement that the conduct of everyday life has been a *systematic "blind spot"* in sociology – and this *despite* the relative popularity of compounds containing the word "life," although (as I mentioned above with reference to Vetter, 1991) the term "conduct of life" is used interchangeably with other similar concepts. Voß gave voice to this criticism right at the beginning of his book, under the heading "The Individual and Society: Tertium Non Datur? Everyday Life as the 'Missing Link' of Sociology" (1991, p. 7). He went on to define in various contexts what he meant by this, i.e., the tendency to situate individual "lives" either (as we saw with the example of "lifestyle") on the side of "society" or (as in the concept of "identity") on the side of the individuals; that is, to neglect the level of the *mediation* between social conditions and individual life activities by active integration and construction efforts on the part of the subject. This is further explained elsewhere (Kudera & Voß, 1990) by pointing out that "in the social sciences a view of human life practice exists that breaks it up conceptually, further processes it based on the division of labor and blanks out the *subjects as the actors who constitute this practice*" (ibid., p. 156f.; emphasis added). The authors suggest that this is also reflected in the way in which sociology deals with the dichotomizations of "work and leisure" and "work and reproduction" that are characteristic of the prevailing societal conditions:

> There are a whole series of assumptions as to how these spheres are mediated, which are all similar in that the subject him-/herself as an agency that integrates his/her own life practice is sacrificed to a functional view of the meaning that each of these spheres has for the others.
>
> (Ibid., p. 157)

Up to this point I have restricted myself to developing the theory of the "conduct of life" of the Munich research group *systematically*, leaving out its knowledge interests and concrete research practice. I shall come back to them, but believe that I have already prepared myself sufficiently to discuss the question I posed above as to why the "conduct of life" is hardly addressed at all in theoretical psychology and thus constitutes a "blind spot" that may go far and away beyond the "blind spot" mentioned by the Munich Project in sociology. At the same time this should also make clear the starting point for conceptualizing "conduct of life" systematically from the standpoint of the subject as a perspective for our further analyses.

The Denial of/Defense against the Conduct of Everyday Life in Traditional Psychology and Psychoanalysis

In view of the fact that in the course of the division of labor that has developed since the last century sociology has assumed the role of an empirical science of "society," it should not surprise us that individual "life" has, in the process, come to have the position of a dependent variable of societal structure, be it as a process of "socialization" or as a "lifestyle" or the like, or precisely as the "conduct of life." It is thus understandable that approaches such as the Munich concept of the "conduct of life," which puts the spotlight on the subject's relative autonomy vis-à-vis society and his/her potential for sharing in the shaping of his/her own social circumstances, should have fallen into an oppositional stance toward traditional sociology. At the same time, one may be tempted (if one does not look too closely) to suppose that in such a "swimming against the tide" within *sociology* there is a movement toward a *convergence with psychology*, since psychology has, in the above-mentioned division of labor between the sciences, assumed the counterpart role of an empirical science of the *individual*. One might accordingly also suppose that the concept of the "conduct of life" of the individual as understood by the Munich researchers, which must, in sociology, first assert itself against resistance due to the traditional sociological understanding of its subject matter, would long have had a "right of domicile" in psychology where it would be among those basic concepts that are broadly discussed. How, then, are we to explain the fact that quite the opposite is the case, that there is an even greater silence surrounding the subject of the "conduct of life" in the discussion of fundamental issues in psychology than in traditional sociology? In order to find an answer to this question one must (as I see it) account above all for the dominant form of psychology's peculiar way of understanding "scientificity" and "rigorous" scientific research in the course of the development of the division of labor between the sciences that still characterizes or stigmatizes it today (whichever way you like to look at it) and which has isolated it from the other social sciences to such an extent that it no longer even wishes to call itself a social science. Due to complex borrowings from disciplines of the "natural" or "exact" sciences external to psychology, such as physiology, physics, mathematics and, recently, computer science, for psychology "scientific" procedure has finally come to be synonymous with *conceptualizing and realizing conditions under which human behavior is "predictable."* Thus, methodologically complex everyday life situations have been forced into second place as a topic of research, while priority is given to a *designated standard situation* in which the goal is to represent the relationship between the conditions introduced and the behaviors to be "predicted" ("independent" and "dependent" variables) in as pure a form as possible. This is considered to be the only way to demonstrate clearly whether the "behavior" in question is in fact attributable to the theoretical "conditions" and not to interfering factors of some kind: *the psychological experiment* as the "royal road" to acquiring knowledge in psychology. Since in the practice of research pure *experimental* control of conditions has its limits (a fact that is usually attributed to the complexity of the subject matter of psychology), a procedure with which the conditions could also be controlled statistically, i.e., *inferential statistics*, was developed in conjunction with psychology's focusing on the "experiment." This made it possible, although the experimental effects of side effects can only seldom be isolated to a sufficient degree, nonetheless to assess at least the degree of *probability* with which the "predicted" behavior can be attributed to the effects of the conditions established by the experimenter. In what follows it is this implied complementary relationship that is meant when the term *basic experimental statistical model* of traditional psychology is used.

With the construction of a dichotomy between a highly complex, difficult to capture "everyday reality" and an "experimental reality" established and controlled by the researcher as the designated locus of the acquisition of scientific knowledge, traditional psychology has landed itself with the problem of the relationship between the two "realities" and of the *transferability of experimental findings to everyday reality*, which is fundamentally insoluble. Since the "decontaminated" complex of conditions from which the experimental findings are extracted does not, by definition, occur in "everyday reality," these findings cannot, also by definition, be applied to them. For the same reason, the alternative claim that it is possible to do so to the extent that there are structural similarities between "experimental reality" and "everyday reality" does not get us any further (because it is, by definition, not possible to know or say anything about the structure of "everyday reality"). Due to the insight implied in this (which has also repeatedly been admitted by representatives of traditional psychology), i.e., that it is not possible to learn anything substantial about extra-experimental life situations from experimental results (e.g., about learning in school from learning experiments), in many fields there has been a shift to carrying out one's own empirical studies in the respective life situations, effectively reinvestigating the problems already examined by the "pure" experimental research. Nevertheless, these studies usually follow the same logic of "analysis of conditions" as experimental research itself, only with reduced stringency criteria – for example, using "*quasi-experimental*" designs instead of experimental designs, with which it is still supposed to be possible somehow to achieve statistical, experimental control of the conditions also in everyday situations. Obviously this does not, however, solve the above-mentioned problem of application, but merely displaces it. What it does is simply once again designate in the everyday situations an experimental and/or statistically "adjusted" reality as the locus of knowledge acquisition, and while the view that the findings made in such "quasi-experimental realities" are "closer" to everyday reality than findings of pure experimental research is intuitively plausible, it is not really justifiable (except perhaps for situations that are in themselves similar to the structure of the "experimental reality," such as the school class, cf. Holzkamp, 1993, p. 444). This can doubtlessly only be remedied by leaving the said conditions, the variable model and the associated construction of the two "realities," completely behind us and opting for different models. Simply to refer to "qualitative methods" is obviously not enough, since the variable model of psychology (in an altered and attenuated form) can still exert an effect even under these conditions. It is difficult to ascertain to what extent there are in fact (already) fields of research in psychology that go beyond thinking in terms of variables; however, this is not the topic of our discussion. At all events, to date such developments have not had any effect on psychology's main conception of itself (the reasons why psychology's "experimental-statistical" identity continues to be sustained would in fact seem to be rooted not only in the philosophy of science, but also in the sociology of science and/or to be of an ideological nature). The construction of a designated situation of scientific insight is characteristic not only of traditional *academic* psychology with its emphasis on "experimental reality" as opposed to "everyday reality." A construction that is similar (in this respect), with a corresponding duplication of reality, is also found in a discipline that, despite not usually being considered to belong to psychology (in Germany), nonetheless has a strong influence on it and on public awareness, and that is psychoanalysis, with its emphasis on the *"therapeutic setting"* as the preferred, if not sole, locus of the generation of psychoanalytic insight. In its classical form, this setting, which is also referred to as the "therapeutic situation," is already clearly qualified by a special *seating arrangement* that Freud himself introduced: the patient lies on a couch and the therapist is seated in an armchair behind it. This arrangement is not simply a matter of secondary importance or dispensable if need be, but a constitutive aspect of the therapeutic situation. Freud accordingly gave analysts clear instructions:

> A particularly large number of patients object to being asked to lie down, while the doctor sits out of sight behind them. They ask to be allowed to go through the treatment in some other position, for the most part because they are anxious not to be deprived of a view of the doctor. Permission is regularly refused.
> (Freud, 1955a/1973, p. 139)

Freud also added further instructions regarding the mental state into which the parties should put themselves within the setting, recommending that the therapist

> surrender himself to his own unconscious mental activity, in a state of *evenly suspended attention*, to avoid so far as possible reflection and the construction of conscious expectations, not to try to fix anything that he had heard particularly in his memory and by these means to catch the drift of the patient's unconscious with his own unconscious.
> (Freud, 1955/1973, p. 239)

Freud also had requirements for *patients* wishing to enter treatment with him:

> We instruct the patient to put himself into a state of quiet, unreflecting observation, and to report to us whatever internal perceptions he is able to make – feelings, thoughts, memories, in the order in which they occur to him. At the same time we warn him expressly against giving way to any motive which would lead him to make a selection among these associations or to exclude any of them, whether on the ground that it is too *disagreeable* or too *indiscreet* to say, or that it is too *unimportant* or *irrelevant*, or that it is nonsensical and need not be said.
> (Freud, 1963/1973, p. 287)

Furthermore, Freud gave his patients instructions as to how to behave in their everyday lives outside the therapy sessions so that they would not interfere with them but support and substantiate their healing function. Thus he demanded that the "*analytic treatment should be carried through, as far as is possible, under privation – in a state of abstinence*" (Freud, 1955b/1973, p. 162). This rule of abstinence is intended to ensure that the patient's motivation to continue the treatment will be sustained after the initial successes and not diminished by premature gratifications of various kinds. Freud even required the patient to "promise not to take any important decisions affecting his life during the time of his treatment – for instance, not to choose any profession or definitive love-object – but to postpone all such plans until after his recovery" (Freud, 1958b/1973, p. 153). Here the patient's everyday life was as far as possible to be virtually "suspended" in the interests of an undisturbed treatment. Freud also developed and conceptualized clear ideas about the special "mechanisms" that characterized the further course of the treatment process thus shaped by the psychoanalytic setting (in its spatial and mental prerequisites). The decisive driving force of the therapy is therefore – aside from the patient's "resistance," which is produced by the therapy, and its analysis by the therapist – the mechanism of "*transference*," i.e., of a kind of "false" falling in love with the therapist, through which Freud saw the patient as in fact "transferring" her instinctual infantile wishes on to the therapist, although she felt her loving feelings to be genuine. The therapist was to both make use of this state and hold it in a sense in abeyance, so that it did not develop into a real love relationship between him and the patient, which included the demand that the therapist manage and monitor his own "*countertransference*." Freud believed that through the "transference" as a phenomenon that was specific to the psychoanalytic situation "we regularly succeed in giving all the symptoms of the illness a new transference meaning and in replacing [the patient's] ordinary neurosis by a 'transference-neurosis' of which he can be cured by the therapeutic work" (Freud, 1958b/1973, p. 154).

The arrangements of the classical psychoanalytic setting – particularly the spatial ones – have been largely modified in some of the more recent versions of psychoanalysis. However, in my view Lorenzer (1974, p. 105) puts the problem in a nutshell when he writes:

> And even if the setting was no longer enforced as psychoanalytic practice progressed, the mere circumstance that up to the full development of the current state of the art in psychoanalytic theory-building it has been structured as it is and not otherwise clearly demonstrates that this institution has remained commensurate with the procedure and the object of the exercise to the present day.

In other words, the psychoanalytic setting must not be reduced to a mere arrangement used to facilitate the practice of psychotherapy, but must be considered as (that is, it aspires to be) a *special place where therapeutic practice and scientific acquisition of insight genuinely coincide*, and without which – because it is *only here* that the above-mentioned conditions for the constitution of the therapeutic process are realizable – the basic psychoanalytic concepts could not have been developed in the first place. Therefore – as Lorenzer (1974) convincingly showed – according to the basic psychoanalytic approach, analysts by no means need to abandon the analytic setting in order to conduct their investigations. On the contrary, in Lorenzer's view it is here, and only here, that genuine psychoanalytic research takes place. Thus, from the immanent standpoint, the fact that Freud had, for instance, never seen "Little Hans," whose "case" had a pronounced influence on psychoanalytic theory building, and that he obtained his knowledge of him only from therapy sessions with his father, was not a deficit, but a direct consequence of the logic of psychoanalytic knowledge acquisition. It is thus in line with this thinking that Lorenzer pushes direct experiences out of the setting quite radically to the margins of the psychoanalytic knowledge acquisition process, for instance when, in reference to psychoanalytic research on children, he writes: "There is in fact a rich field of direct observation, particularly in infant research. It does, of course, at most function as an appendage of psychoanalysis" (1974, p. 284). It is not my intention here to investigate to what extent the designation of the therapeutic situation as a means of gaining knowledge or insight is also characteristic of psychological models of therapy outside of psychoanalysis or whether in those cases it is also considered to constitute an independent "therapeutic" process of gaining insight (Meehl, 1954; Cronbach & Meel, 1955). At all events, the model function of psychoanalytic thought would also seem to me to be evident in many areas of non-analytic clinical psychology.

In sum, we can say that in traditional psychology in the broader sense, i.e., including psychoanalysis, the procedure of acquiring knowledge must basically be considered to be essentially bound to *designated standard situations created by the researcher*, the *"experiment"* or the *"therapeutic setting,"* including *a division of reality into two different kinds*, an *"experimental"* or *"therapeutic reality"* in which the actual empirical research takes place, and an *"everyday reality"* whose scientific status and predictive power are inferior. Thus, the methodological planning of psychological knowledge acquisition is essentially oriented toward separating the two "realities" from each other as cleanly as possible, i.e., ensuring that the "purely" scientific research conditions in the "experiment" or "setting" are not contaminated by an infiltration of everyday reality. The above-mentioned lack of clarity regarding the relationship between "scientific" and "everyday" reality and the transferability of insights gained in experiments and the setting to the everyday lives of the individuals are, therefore, since they are included in the "duplication of reality" that has developed in the course of the history of psychology, in a sense *constitutive* of the definition of the subject matter of psychology as a whole; that is, they are quasi a "congenital defect" that has, from the start, placed it at a epistemological disadvantage in comparison to neighboring disciplines such as sociology and social anthropology. This unclear relationship is inherently incurable and can only be obscured or explained away by means that are ultimately ineffective. I do not wish to enter into a detailed discussion of this here – since that would go beyond the scope of my topic – but simply to draw attention to what is a symptom (but in my view a very illuminating one) of how psychology and psychoanalysis obfuscate and repress processes that are inherent in the system. In other words, my intention is to highlight the above-mentioned *deliberate blindness of psychology and psychoanalysis about the existence and the scientific conceptualization of their subjects' or patients' conduct of everyday life.*

One could consider this blindness to be sufficiently explained by the fact that psychology has to – as the flipside, so-to-speak, of its designation of insight-providing "standard situations" – devalue and marginalize its experimental subjects' or clients' everyday lives, and thus also their *conduct* of their everyday lives. Nonetheless, I believe that we will only get to the root of the problem if we turn this argument round and realize that – if we were officially to recognize the "conduct of everyday life" as a basic scientific problem – the above-mentioned "standard situations", i.e., the experiment and the setting, would themselves inevitably lose their *uniqueness as loci of insight*. I shall now explain this point in more detail.

If we were to understand the "conduct of life" (as did the Munich research group) as an active integrative and constructive effort of the subject through which she or he "comes to arrangements" with the demands of various areas of life and coordinates these arrangements in an overall arrangement ("arrangement of the arrangements"), we would also have to regard the "experiment" and the "setting" as subject to such arrangements. However, this would mean admitting that the significance attached to the experiment/setting in the individual's overall arrangement of his or her conduct of everyday life is not determined by the experimenter or the therapist. We would also have to see that it is not the experimenter/therapist who has the monopoly on the interpretation of the function and significance of the experiment or setting – as the latter believes as a result of his/her theoretical bias – but the experimental subjects or clients. Thus, the subjects and clients have their own ways of making sense of the experiment/setting based on the contexts of their own everyday lives, and they can also reinterpret the *instructions/statements of the experimenters/therapists*, which the latter believe assure *their "loci of knowledge acquisition" a special epistemological status*, in ways that fit the *contexts of their everyday lives*. That is, one could say that they can keep "catching up." This fact, which is actually obvious but has been repressed for ideological reasons, has (as is well known) led to the establishment of an entire subdiscipline of experimental psychology, i.e., the *"social psychology of the experiment,"* in which the wayward responses to the instructions of the subjects, who have their own ideas about what is happening in the experimental situation and can and do surreptitiously/latently act accordingly, is, on the one hand, accepted as fact and, on the other, is nonetheless in turn supposed to be subjected to experimental control (cf. for example Markard, 1984, p. 142f.). In psychoanalysis (and perhaps also in other areas of clinical psychology) there has been little interest in examining the question as to how clients perceive and/or interpret the therapeutic session and the function of the therapist *from a standpoint outside of the therapy session* or what consequences this has for their behavior inside therapy (only in a large research project inaugurated by Ole Dreier in Copenhagen, the results of which are soon to be published [Editors' note: Dreier, 2008], has the fact been systematically taken into account that not only is the family spoken about in the therapeutic dialogue, but therapists are also made the subject of discussion at clients' families' dining tables and that "readings" are thus developed of which therapists usually have no inkling). For example, Freud's instruction to therapists to require patients not only to observe the rule of "abstinence," but also more or less to put their lives on hold for the duration of the therapy (which, since they can hardly comply with this instruction – or wish to comply with it – opens up a new source of therapeutically utilizable guilt feelings) would seem to me to be an attempt to prevent patients from escaping the therapist's grasp by creating refuges in their everyday lives. One can thus arguably still see this instruction as symptomatic for psychoanalysis's stance toward the practices of everyday life today.

Conduct of Life Conceptualized from the Standpoint of the Subject

The standard situations of the experimental and psychoanalytical setting are, according to the basic methodological and theoretical principles of psychology and psychoanalysis, the context in which the experimental subjects' and clients' life situations are interpreted, but *they themselves* appear to provide a *context-free*, absolute standard for everything; that is, they have a special role as a *"privileged non-context"* (to use an apt term coined by Lave, Smith & Butler, 1989). They cannot therefore permit the use of a theoretical concept of the "conduct of everyday life" that would relegate the experiment or setting to being only *one context-dependent everyday situation of life among others*, which is integrated by the individual. Thus, not only have psychology and psychoanalysis neglected to concern themselves with a concept of the "conduct of everyday life" that would overcome its confinement to special areas of psychology and validate its basic character as an overarching dimension that structures *all* areas of everyday life (including experiments and the therapeutic setting) from the perspective of the subject, they have also regarded it quasi as a *threat to their own basic methodological demands* that must be *actively excluded or marginalized*. Accordingly, psychology and psychoanalysis must also systematically deny those "sides" of subjectivity that make the individual the agent of his or her own conduct of life, his or her capacity actively to respond relatively autonomously and in accordance with the "self-contained logic" of the way she or he leads her/his life, to the conditions in her/his environment and, where necessary or appropriate, to exert an influence on them. Where would we be if subjects could also take the liberty to respond actively to the "scientific" conditions of living established for them in accordance with the self-contained logic of their *own* ways of conducting their lives and thus, in their special role as a primary insight-constituting agents, to doubt the "logic" of the experiment or setting?

In all this lies – seen from a generalized standpoint – at least one of the main reasons why in the basic psychological and psychoanalytic concepts, even where the intention is to place the "subject" squarely in the center as the subject matter of research, the subject's ability also to catch up with and integrate the scientific endeavor with his/her interpretative activities *is not part of the agenda.* The "external view/standpoint" of science, which, even though it may perhaps only be in the final instance, is supposed to be the only standpoint from which objective research is conceivable, is considered to be the superordinate standpoint that is not reachable – or, to be more accurate, *may* not be reachable by the subjects who are the object of the exercise, because otherwise the science of psychology, in the only form in which it appears to be imaginable, could not take place.

It is doubtlessly not difficult to see that – if we were to continue this argument – our thoughts would inevitably lead us into the fundamental controversies that we have been carrying on for many years about the problem of "subject science" versus "control science," or "theories *about* people" versus "theories *for* people," which we shall not recapitulate in their entirety here.

However, it should by now have become clear that the "blindness" of psychology to the theoretical implications and consequences (of the concept) of the "conduct of everyday life" to which we have drawn attention cannot be overcome within the frameworks of traditional psychology or psychoanalysis because, in view of the special epistemological status of the experiment or setting to which they lay claim and all the arrangements derived from them that they feel obliged to make in order to reduce the subject or client to the "subject matter" of the research, they are unable to respond to how the clients have incorporated *science/the scientist into their conduct of everyday life*. In my view it is only possible to escape from this dilemma if the researchers quasi pull the experimental subjects, clients, etc., *over to their side*; that is, liberate them from their fictive role as subject matter of the research and make them into "co-researchers" – as in the methodology of science from the standpoint of the subject. Only by analyzing together in this way how people lead their everyday lives can we also investigate the processes of scientific investigation themselves as an area of the "conduct of everyday life" from the standpoint of the generalized subject without violating the principles of psychological knowledge acquisition. It has thus become clear that while a psychological conceptualization of the "conduct of life" cannot be developed from the position of traditional psychology due to its "blindness," it *can* be addressed from the position of psychology as a science from the standpoint of the subject. In what follows I therefore address the task of elaborating the above-mentioned sociological approach of the "conduct of everyday life," as developed by the Munich research group, psychologically in the terms of the science from the standpoint of the subject. Nevertheless, this brings us to a point where we cannot avoid including a discussion of the approach of the science from the standpoint of the subject as a whole, even if it be restricted to a specific focus.

A Reinterpretation of the Munich Concept of the "Conduct of Everyday Life" from the Perspective of the Science from the Standpoint of the Subject

The Knowledge Interest of Sociologists and the Science from the Standpoint of the Subject in the Conduct of Life: "Diagnosis of the Times" and "Self-understanding"

What does it mean to elaborate the Munich concept of the conduct of life from the standpoint of the subject? Why is it not possible in a psychology conceived as a science from the standpoint of the subject to leave it as it is and simply to work with it, particularly since it is already explicitly "subject-oriented"? In order to find an answer to this question, we will begin with the very general aspect of "knowledge interest" and first compare the knowledge interest of the science from the standpoint of the subject (as understood by Critical Psychology) with that of the Munich project.

Although the concept of the "conduct of life" as formulated by the Collaborative Research Center 333 at Munich University is conceived as being *subject-oriented*, one would be greatly mistaken if one were to take this to mean that it refers to some kind of convergence with *psychological* viewpoints and research questions. On the contrary, it is an approach that positions itself decidedly and exclusively within the context of *sociology*, as a contribution to the *empirical analysis of social structure*. Accordingly, historically its concept of the conduct of life is seen as deriving from classical sociology, i.e., from Max Weber, in whose work *The Protestant Ethic and the Spirit of Capitalism* attention was emphatically drawn to the connection between the development of modern capitalism and the puritan or pietistic demand that life be conducted ascetically:

> One of the fundamental elements of the spirit of modern capitalism, and not only of that but of all modern culture: rational conduct on the basis of the idea of the calling, was born – that is what this discussion has sought to demonstrate – from the spirit of Christian asceticism.
> (1958/2003, p. 180)

Thus, when Jurczyk and Rerrich (1993b, p. 33) position the Munich research on the conduct of life "in the broader context of the discussion within the social sciences on the development of the Federal Republic of Germany as a modern society," in my view they are situating the general knowledge interest of their project squarely within the general tradition of Weberian thought and research on the modern conduct of life (but with different historical and theoretical reference points).

Jurczyk and Rerrich (1993b) draw attention to the dimensions of societal development in, for example, the Federal Republic of Germany under the headings *"modernization," "rationalization"* and *"individualization"* (e.g., pp. 35ff., emphasis added) in many different contexts. Voß (1991, p. 359f.) characterizes the associated "transformation" of societal conditions as a "transformation of *attitudes and orientations*," "transformation of *forms of co-existence*" and "transformation of the *labor and employment conditions*" (emphasis added).

To begin with it follows from this view, which is decidedly historical and a diagnosis of the times, that even the *evolution* of the "conduct of life" as an independent problem or concept of the social sciences must be historicized.

> In our view in its literal, emphatic sense of "conducting" one's own life, i.e. giving it direction, the conduct of life only became a meaningful category during the *transition to modernity*. While people also "conducted" their lives in premodern societies and were never merely passively at the mercy of power structures, as a rule the restrictions of societal structures were greater and above all there was more acceptance of their being fixed rather than opportunities to go a step beyond established boundaries – e.g. the slave system or the estates of the realm.
>
> (Jurczyk & Rerrich, 1993b, p. 35; emphasis added)

Second, we understand that the "conduct of life" is considered mainly from the perspective of its *accentuation and differentiation* under the pressure of the new demands on individuals that were arising from modernization, including the rationalization and individualization of society, to organize their everyday lives independently. Even in their title, Kudera and Voß (1990) qualified the "conduct of life" as the "distribution of labor of persons under *pressure to change*" (emphasis added), and Voß (1991) developed out of the previously diagnosed societal modernization process in its various different dimensions research questions for analyzing the resulting changes in the conduct of life under the heading of "An increase in complexity, differentiation and autonomy of the conduct of life? Possible reactions on the level of the conduct of life" (ibid., pp. 363ff.). Voß also historicized the relative degree of autonomy of the conduct of life from the social conditions of living that he (as mentioned above) considered to be a *general* defining characteristic (qua "degrees of freedom"), that is, a "reaction" to the process of progressive modernization, which he summarized in the following "thesis": "The forms of the 'conduct of life' can become increasingly independent of the social conditions. This can result in an increase in problems or new kinds of problems between the two spheres (thesis of increasing autonomy)" (ibid., p. 369).

The decidedly *sociological overarching empirical research question* of the Munich Working Group also resulted from their interest in gaining insight into social structures and establishing a "diagnosis of the times." They wanted to demonstrate in as differentiated a manner as possible how the way in which individuals conduct their lives under the "pressure of modernization" is connected to various characteristics of social structure. To do so they used the classical sociological procedure of carrying out "surveys" in individuals with varying demographic characteristics. Jurczyk and Rerrich describe this as follows:

The participants were middle-aged and in couple relationships with at least one child. Both partners were required to be working. ... We considered this important because the increase in the percentage of women in gainful occupations and the increasingly clearly articulated expectations of a self-determined life that transcends the traditional gender roles led us to suppose that there would be specific changes and potentials for conflict in how people lead their everyday lives. Because these processes are taking place to different degrees in urban and rural areas, some of the survey participants came from urban environments and others from rural environments. The sample was also systematically stratified according to the following groups of workers:

a. laborers and mid-level salaried workers in industrial posts with flexitime arrangements;
b. shop assistants working in department stores with part-time jobs;
c. industrial workers from factories with around-the-clock shift systems;
d. highly skilled computer staff from an international data processing center with an around-the-clock shift system;
e. geriatric nurses with different alternating shifts;
f. and finally freelance staff from a domain of the mass media with extensive freedom to structure their time but only limited job security.

(1993b, p. 15f.)

The methodological approach of the Munich research group (as reported in Jurczyk & Rerrich, 1993b, p. 16) is "*qualitatively oriented.*" They use theme-centered interviews with interview guidelines and a duration of 2 to 3 hours. The reason for this is that characteristic "modes of conduct of life cannot be captured using standardized surveys."

A procedure is required that goes deeply into the distinctive features of how the respective interviewee conducts his/her life, followed by a detailed analysis of a large number of single cases in order to arrive at a broader, differentiated picture.
(Ibid. p.17)

Thus the interviewees were not selected according to requirements for statistical representativeness. However, this does not mean that they were chosen arbitrarily. The study sample was collected by means of a theory-driven selection procedure in accordance with certain criteria. This theoretical basis for the procedure was Strauss's concept of "theoretical sampling" (ibid., p. 17). The particular way in which justice was done to the distinctiveness of each individual interviewee by using this kind of qualitative procedure is also demonstrated by the fact that in the research reports they were referred to as *individual persons*, i.e., not simply as "Mr. A." or "Mr. B.," but usually even using a full name: "Mr Modes" and "Mr Winkelmann" (Dunkel, 1993, pp. 203ff.), "Mrs. Hollweg" and "Mrs. Hillermeier" (Jurczyk & Rerrich, 1993c). This was perhaps intended as a special way of expressing the "subject orientation" as understood by the Munich project.

Against the background of the Munich group's sociological knowledge interest as thus described, the next step would now be – as mentioned above – to analyze the specific characteristics of our knowledge interest as a science from the standpoint of the subject, on the basis of which we can give grounds for the need to further elaborate the conduct of life concept developed by this group. In so doing we must make clear that the *science from the standpoint of the subject* as we understand it does in fact differ from the *subject orientation* of the Munich project. We can then proceed to address the question as to what the difference consists in. It is clear that we are in principle also addressing the question of the specific nature of the science from the standpoint of the subject as opposed to traditional *psychology*. However, this will not be the focus of our discussion, since we have already demonstrated the inability of the latter to address the problem of the "conduct of life" in a systematic way. To what extent such developments of thought as we have undertaken can be convincing or to what degree they may lead us astray strongly depends – as has repeatedly become apparent (for instance, Holzkamp, 1993, pp. 177ff.) – on whether one has found the right *starting point*. So where shall we begin? Or, to be more exact: what is the *core concept*, quasi the "germ cell" that can be taken as a basis for developing as seamlessly and stringently as possible all further characteristics of the knowledge interest of a science from the standpoint of the subject (in the conduct of life), and thus also for distinguishing it from other relevant approaches?

While, as we have shown, the Munich concept of the conduct of life – as "subject-oriented" as it is – *centers on society*, i.e., it takes the process of modernization of societal structures as the reference point for its analysis of the "conduct of life," the psychological version of the science from the standpoint of the subject to be elaborated in what follows is in some way *centered on the individual*. This focus on the individual has accrued to psychology as a science from the standpoint of the subject in the course of the distribution of labor between the social sciences and it therefore shares it with traditional psychology. But what does this mean specifically for psychology as a science from the standpoint of the subject (as opposed to traditional psychology)? We have previously given an account of our objectives elsewhere (XX).★ We proceed from the assumption that the common denominator of traditional psychology (including psychoanalysis) is, at least in the last analysis, the *external scientific standpoint*, which in this view cannot be abandoned without abandoning the standpoint of science – as a result of which the "individuals" are inevitably simultaneously relegated again to their position "on the other side," i.e., that of the subject matter of research. In the "hermeneutic" versions of psychoanalysis the opposing positions of the "interpreter" and the "interpreted" are also ultimately fixed and unalterable. In contrast, in the science from the standpoint of the subject the individuals concerned (experimental subjects, clients, etc.) are liberated from their fictive role as the subject matter of research and seen as standing at the side of the researchers. In order to pursue these objectives one can (as we have previously attempted) start with the concept of a "psychology from the generalized subject standpoint," by qualifying the role of the scientific "co-researcher" and by specifying psychology from the standpoint of the subject as "psychology in the 'reason discourse'," etc.

As I was thinking about the present chapter it occurred to me that these concepts might perhaps be easier to understand if I were to begin with a different concept that we have previously always included in our thinking, but rarely explicitly addressed, and that is the concept (originally coined by Marx) of *self-understanding* as the central intention of the knowledge interest of the science from the standpoint of the subject, which I am thus introducing tentatively as the sought-for "germ cell" for further development of our thought. Above all, "self-understanding" means "coming to an understanding with myself" about something that I think, in this case about the conduct of life, trying to make something I already "somehow know" comprehensible by reflection, to make the implicit explicit, what is unclear clear, that is (to use a nice expression coined by Hugh Mehan, 1979, p. 176) to transform my "tacit knowledge" into "known knowledge." And thus the *other* is potentially also included in the process of reaching self-understanding – insofar as something that has not previously been said (and is perhaps unsayable) is to be put into words. The other is challenged to – or it is suggested to him/her that s/he should – follow my attempt to express myself in words in order to find out whether *s/he* can achieve greater clarity, for instance, about his or her "conduct of life." In this sense, and only in this sense, the interest in achieving "self-understanding" is also an interest in "coming to an understanding" with others in order to find a *common language* about something that is always only available or "given" to each of us individually. This is what we mean when we speak of our "standpoint of the generalized subject" as incorporating each individual's particular perspective (see, for example, Holzkamp, 1991). Thus, in the context of the knowledge interest in (mutual) "self-understanding" nobody – and this is an important consequence – can treat the other as an object, because by doing so s/he would exclude her/him from the joint project of self-understanding. If the intention is to reach self-understanding, the intersubjective framework that I have posited must be adhered to. This also means that in research conducted within the frame of reference of the science from the standpoint of the subject the distinctive character of the *scientific* position or the position of the "scientist" can never be removed from the intersubjective framework of reaching an understanding by defining a standpoint that is external to those under investigation, but can only be seen as being *within* it – this is the *"co-researcher relationship,"* to which we will return later.

If I have an interest in "self-understanding," this implies that there is in fact anything at all to "understand" that is not simply self-evident, i.e., that in and behind things that appear to be unproblematic and "uni-dimensional," such as the conduct of everyday life (of which, after all, everybody has experience), problems and problem complexes are hidden that – if they are to become evident and "sayable" – need the effort of a (joint) self-understanding project. We can leave the attempt to give grounds for a knowledge interest in facts and circumstances that are truly unproblematic (if such facts and circumstances exist at all) to other research approaches.

They do not, at any rate, fall within the sphere of the knowledge interest of psychology as a science from the standpoint of the subject. In Critical Psychology the *difference* (which may even be a *discrepancy*) between what appears to be "*self-evident*" and more comprehensive or "deeper" structural relationships that can only be brought to light by processes of self-understanding has led to a *double set of basic concepts* that are always linked in some way to the two paired concepts of *remaining on the level of immediate appearances* and *transcending this level*. As a result of this duality, each aspect of individual experience can be conceptualized in two versions, both as a reproduction and duplication of what is "self-evident" and as a conceptual tool to penetrate the level of the obvious (on the cognitive level, for instance, in the form of "interpreting" versus "comprehending," and on the social level in the form of "instrumental relationships" versus "relationships between subjects," etc.; Holzkamp, 1983, chap. 7.5).

At the same time it became clear that these alternatives by no means exist only "in thought," but that to a greater or lesser extent they involve *real conflicts of power and interests*; that is, the conflict between my interest in penetrating what is immediately obvious in order to *gain more influence over my own conditions of life* and thus also in improving my *subjective quality of life* by going beyond the "self-evident," and the ruling interest in preventing this in order to *protect the existing power relations*. Thus, when I penetrate the self-evident not only may I be in a position to expand my influence on the conditions of my life, but I also run the risk that they could in fact deteriorate. It could then appear to be in my – though narrow and defensive – interest to content with the immediately accessible ("restrictive vs. generalized agency"; cf. Holzkamp, 1990). This might explain the persuasive power of such constructs of self-justifications and defences which make putting up with the obvious – by denying is self-curtailing implications – appear to be in one's own interest (it is in this context that critical psychologists have reinterpreted such psychoanalytic concepts as "repression," "defense" and "the unconscious"; Holzkamp, 1983). However, this means that having a (personal and academic) interest in gaining knowledge on "self-understanding" always at the same time implies an interest in finding out to what extent we can also construe, for example, our "detachment" as an avoidance of conflict, our "reasonable willingness to compromise" also as giving in, our "realistic attitude that we have finally arrived at as a result of set-backs" also as a denial of legitimate claims on life, and where and why we are "deceiving ourselves about something," "kidding ourselves," "giving in in our heads" or "shirking our responsibilities," etc. In short, it implies that we must, wherever necessary, see through our own ruses (doubtlessly several examples connected with the "conduct of everyday life" will immediately occur to all of us). Here it is important to emphasize that where we are concerned with reaching self-understanding, this can never mean seeing through each other's ruses or those of some *other person we have selected for this purpose*. Neither a therapist–patient relationship thus defined nor, especially for example, any political constellation where recriminations are being made and I see myself as entitled to suspect others and to expect their attempts to justify themselves, can be passed off as an offer of understanding/self-understanding to the other.

While we can support each other in our efforts to attain self-understanding, these efforts are, as explained above, inevitably tied to our own subjective standpoints, so that when other people try to understand and judge us without taking our views into account they do in fact exclude us from the project of reaching intersubjective understanding, i.e., refuse to accord us the status of a fellow human being by making us the "object" of their interests (however legitimized they may be).

Defining "self-understanding" as a project in which experiences that have not previously been articulated at all, or not clearly, are jointly "raised for discussion" poses the question as to what criteria a *scientific language* that would be fitting for the project of self-understanding must fulfill. Putting the question this way makes it clear that all scientific languages in which the external standpoint from which one wishes to make statements about others (even if they are about their "subjectivity") must be considered unsuitable from the start because the *reciprocity of perspectives* that is required for joint activities of self-understanding is excluded. This applies particularly to the scientific language of traditional psychology in which predictions of "expected" behaviors are made from predetermined conditions (since there is no language for them, "predictions" that experimental subjects or clients may make about behaviors of experimenters or therapists have no place in this system). The reciprocity implied in the project of reaching self-understanding can only be expressed in a language in which the *perspectives of those involved* can actually be shown *in their interrelatedness*; that is, in which the standpoint from which each person from his or her perspective can relate to the other with his or her perspective can be verbalized and communicated. Nonetheless, this is the "*discourse level of subjective reasons for actions*" that we have presented as an explication of the "language" of the standpoint of the subject (e.g., Holzkamp, 1993, p. 21). "Reasons" are, as such, always "first person," that is, they must logically be *my* reasons and when I speak of the "reasons" of other persons in this context, I recognize that these are *their* reasons that can only be accessed by *them* from *their* standpoints and *their* perspectives, which I cannot reduce to my own standpoint and my perspective. No one is the "object" of the other's point of view, no one has the privilege of being the speaker toward whom the other must remain silent – both are equally required to permit the other to express him- or herself and his or her reasons in the verbal communication process. The above-mentioned prerequisites for a scientific language as the medium of mutual self-understanding are thereby fulfilled.

The "reason discourse" thus defined, as the language of a psychological science from the standpoint of the subject (as we understand it), has been comprehensively and both theoretically and methodologically justified and conceptualized in opposition to the condition discourse of traditional psychology. However, since we believe that we have adequately described the special differences between the project of self-understanding as the core of the knowledge interest of psychology as a science from the standpoint of the subject and the sociological knowledge interest of the Munich group above, in what follows I shall now no longer present it in "abstract" and systematic terms, but (where necessary) address it within the context of our elaboration of our concept of the "conduct of life." In what follows our aim is to *reinterpret* the basic definitions of the "conduct of life" previously established by the Munich research group *in terms of "self-understanding"* and of the conceptions developed in that context. In the process it should become apparent to what extent or in what problem areas the knowledge interest of our science from the standpoint of the subject requires us to arrive at *conceptualizations and research questions that go beyond the Munich approach*. To the extent that we address the problem of the *empirical* realizability of our concept of the conduct of life from the standpoint of the subject we shall also review the above-mentioned *methodological procedure* used by the Munich project and reinterpret it from the viewpoint of previously developed methods of psychology as a science from the standpoint of the subject.

The "Relative Autonomy" of the Conduct of Life in the Discourse of Reasons

As is well known, the concept of the "conduct of everyday life" has not previously been addressed in the theory building of psychology as a science from the standpoint of the subject. In what follows we shall therefore introduce it as a new concept (which will likely also have consequences for our approach as a whole). In order to render this (for us) new issue accessible and developable we must first attempt to reformulate the *basic concepts* of the Munich group described above in the terms that we have already developed in the science from the standpoint of the subject, while at the same time also expressing them in a problem-centered form – insofar as that has not already been done. This is necessary because it is the only way that we can show to what extent it is possible to do so in a "seamless" manner and/or to what extent we must develop new ways of looking at the issues involved.

The Munich concept of the conduct of life is intended primarily – as shown above[2] – to present a new formulation of the "relationship between individual and society" that differs from traditional sociological notions, by introducing the conduct of life as a "*mediating category between subject and societal structures.*" These researchers see the "conduct of life" as an "*active effort*" of the individual who thus has certain "*degrees of freedom*," i.e., a "*relative autonomy*" from the prevailing circumstances and therefore not only "appropriates through work the conditions that s/he finds in society and organizes them" but "*change[s]* it, and in fact (together with others) *creates* it." How are we to reformulate this mediating relationship in the language of the science from the standpoint of the subject?

We do not limit the "societal conditions" to how they are defined by conventional sociology or the sociological theory of society, but understand them in their "subjectward" oriented aspects as meanings, constellations of meanings, configurations of meanings, etc. They are grasped in a very particular (not to say idiosyncratic) sense, as the epitome of societally produced, *generalized possibilities for and constraints on action* that subjects *can*, but by no means *must*, put into practice in the context of the interests of their own life practice. *Which* of the meaning aspects open to them as alternatives for action in such a "*relationship of possibilities*" the subjects actually *do* translate into action depends in our theory, as I said, on the *reasons* that they have – in accordance with their respective interests in life (that is, with their interest in increasing their influence on societal conditions and thus improving their quality of life). To put it more precisely: from the meaning constellations with which they are confronted subjects can *extract certain premises for action* that they *adopt as theirs* and from which, by implication or inference, certain intentions to act then arise that are, for them, sensible, in the sense that they are in their interest, on which they then, insofar as there are no resistances or impediments in the contingent reality that militate against it (i.e., all other things being equal), finally act (for more on the above section see, for instance, Holzkamp, 1983, chap. 7.4, 1993, p. 21f.).

From this résumé it is clear that in the context of the concepts of the science from the standpoint of the subject – i.e., in the medium of the scientific "reason discourse" – our conduct of everyday life must be regarded as "relatively autonomous" (in exactly the same sense as understood by the Munich group) since it is, like any other activity of human life, not "conditioned" by social structures, but rather simply grounded in them as possibilities for action. The degree or the "degrees of freedom" of the "relative autonomy" vis-à-vis the prevailing conditions need to be more precisely defined in two respects. First, what general aspects of an existing meaning constellation I can extract as my personal premises for action – that is, what alternatives I actually have at my disposal – depends on the historically evolved generalized possibilities for and/or restrictions on action themselves that are "objectified" in the respective concrete meaning constellation. I cannot make possibilities that do not (yet) generally exist the premises of my actions. Second, it also depends on my interests in life, in which the reason for my actions are rooted. This also implies that I do not have unlimited options, since such alternative actions that are not compatible with my interest in maintaining or increasing my influence on societal conditions and/or my quality of life are excluded from the start for "psychological" reasons. My actions can be at variance

> with my *objective* interests in life but not with … my interests in life *as I experience them as my situation*. The statement that human beings cannot consciously harm themselves contains so-to-speak the only material apriori of the "science from the standpoint of the subject".
> (Holzkamp, 1983, p. 350; emphasis altered)

Nevertheless, my subjective "autonomy" is by no means "determined" or restricted in some way as a result of being thus linked to my interests in life – even if the alternative actions that are in principle conceivable are not in fact all at my free disposal. It is, after all, *my* interests on which my respective options for action are based and if I consciously act against my interests in life this can never be seen as exercising my "freedom," but always only as having been imposed upon me (in whatever way that may have been) "from outside."

However, how can we reformulate in the terms of our theory the relationship between mere *appropriation* of the prevailing conditions in the course of the "conduct of everyday life" and their *creation/modification*, which the Munich group saw as qualifying the "relative autonomy" of the subject? We already have among our basic concepts what we might call a "slot" into which this could fit insofar as we have differentiated the above-mentioned "relationship of possibilities" into "two *possibilities*," that is, into an option for action "*under*" societal conditions and an option for action that "*broadens* our scope of influence" (Holzkamp, 1993, p. 368). If we assume that it is directly within my interests in life to change prevailing conditions through expanding my influence and improving my quality of life, the question immediately arises as to what reasons I could have for nonetheless contenting myself with the "first option" of acting in accordance with the prevailing conditions and thereby forgoing an increase in my quality of life. And this question links up again to our earlier thoughts about staying within the confines of what appears to be obvious (which we need to overcome through processes of self-understanding) or going beyond it. Thus seen, opting not to change the existing meaning structures and possibilities for action in my conduct of life can only be understood as having grounds or being sensible if it is assumed that I anticipate that any endeavor to go beyond the "self-evident" in an attempt to change the conditions would at the same time be to lay myself open to a *threat to the current stability of my conduct of life*. I would thus risk provoking conflicts that could result in my damaging the possibilities currently open to me to exert an influence on the prevailing conditions and of my everyday living. Here the *power relations* that we spoke about above come into play, although not in the form of a clear dividing line between the "powerful" and the "powerless," but as a *distribution* of power relations within everyday strategies of enforcement and defense, such as those to which Foucault repeatedly drew attention (and which will be of great relevance for our further considerations). The alternative of either changing the conditions under which I organize my life from day to day or accepting (limiting) conditions lies between the two poles of improving my quality of life on the one hand and defensively warding off threats on the other, as described above. Therefore, the self-justification and defense strategies, the risks of unconsciously doing oneself a disservice etc., and accordingly the necessity of recognizing our own self-delusions, have proved and will prove in future their relevance also for the above-mentioned "two possibilities" of which I can make use owing to the relative autonomy of my "conduct of life,". The above-mentioned relationship between the options for action that are theoretically always open to me in a meaning constellation and the premises for actions that I actually extract from them can thus now be seen in a different light. I will first (following this logic) only be able to become aware of the existing possibilities for action (to improve my quality of life) to the extent that I do not have to anticipate that the stability that I have achieved in the way I organize my life will be directly threatened if I act on these possibilities. And second, I will only be able to contemplate changing or expanding the meaning constellation in question to the extent that I have been able to transform the possibilities for action inherent in them into premises for my intended actions or the actions I actually carry out sufficiently to come up "against limits" that I can only overcome if I change the conditions in which I lead my life (including the power relations involved). The consequences of the dynamics of the conduct of everyday life implied in this will only later become completely understandable when we have expanded our concept of the "conduct of life" by reinterpreting it and made some important additions.

It follows from the above that the knowledge interest of our science from the standpoint of the subject by no means requires us to neglect the concepts that the Munich group developed in the context of their own sociological knowledge interest, nor, indeed, should we permit ourselves to do so. On the contrary, their analyses of the historical development of and increasing emphasis on the "conduct of life" in the course of processes of *"modernization," "rationalization"* and *"individualization,"* etc., that have taken place in society as a whole have a definite place among our basic concepts. Here they can be read as *those aspects of societal processes or conditions* that are "turned toward the subject" and can become *meaning configurations*, or in other words, generalized possibilities for action. However, we must then put the question as to what societal determinants can *enter into the mediation between the individual and society* at all in more precise terms, since none of the concepts used to characterize social structures and their history, such as "mode of production," "feudalism," "individualization," etc., which *cannot per se be reformulated as generalized possibilities of action for subjects*, are eligible here. It is (from the viewpoint of the science from the standpoint of the subject) so to speak a methodological "error" to ask, for example, without further ado, what influence "bourgeois class relations" or the growing "modernization or rationalization" of society have on the individual subjects without taking into consideration the fact that these are concepts that were *invented* by sociologists and social theorists and have not therefore necessarily become reality for individuals on whom they could potentially have an influence. Rather, in order to be able to formulate *hypotheses* about possibilities for and constraints on actions that result for the concrete subjects that are even halfway reasonable, we must first make a theoretical endeavor to elaborate the multifarious levels of mediation that exist between the structures in question and/or processes of society as a whole and the concrete everyday worlds of the individuals. If we leave out these levels of mediation we can, of course, still arrive at some kind of statistical regularities in the relationship between the global sociological categories and individual variables, for example the "conduct of life," but these will then (in the reference system of the science from the standpoint of the subject) remain totally uninterpretable. Retrospective ad hoc explanations cannot be considered a remedy, since they would hardly offset the theoretical deficit.

This all means, in principle, that it is not possible to sustain a clear distribution of labor between sociological research on the conduct of life and that based on the science from the standpoint of the subject, at least, not at this point. Neither can one (as I pointed out above) in the science of the subject simply factor out the social structural preconditions that have led to an increase in importance of and changes in the conduct of life as seen from the sociological perspective, but nor can one simply adopt these preconditions as they are, either. Instead, in the theory building of the *science from the standpoint of the subject* we need to use a problem-centered approach to analyze each of the levels of mediation between the socio-structural characteristics and the meaning constellations and possibilities for action given in the lifeworlds of the individuals sufficiently to arrive at a point where the question as to how they can be implemented in sequences from premises of action to projected actions to actions can be posed in a meaningful way. These are the "*meaning-reason analyses*" that we have called for as a central aim of our theory – and tried out (at least) in the analysis of the institutional preconditions of learning at school (Holzkamp, 1993, chap. 4) – and that are also indispensable for research on the conduct of life within a subject-science framework.

This concludes the first step of our attempt to reinterpret, that is, to formulate in terms of the science from the standpoint of the subject, the Munich concept of the "conduct of life" as a mediating link (Voß also occasionally speaks of a "missing link") between the individual and society based on the "*relative autonomy*" that a subject organizing or "conducting" his life has vis-à-vis society. We have learned two things from this endeavor. It has become clear, first, that such a reformulation is, by and large, relatively easy to achieve and, second, that we have – by introducing our conception of "reason analysis," which goes beyond a merely negative definition of the subject's "degrees of freedom" – also gained substantial information about the way in which opportunities for societal action are implemented in individual actions, about the necessary preconditions for actively changing existing societal conditions and about the contradictions and conflicts that must be taken into account in the process.

However, we must admit that what we have written here has had to remain comparatively non-specific, i.e., it is relatable to human activities in general to a greater or lesser extent and only applicable to certain examples of the "conduct of life." Before we can begin to utilize the above-mentioned positive definition of the subjective problems related to "relative autonomy" for our own concept of the conduct of life we must first include, in a second reinterpretive step, the *distinctive character* of the "conduct of life" as defined by the Munich group in our considerations. This is the "conduct of life" as an *everyday* activity of *organizing, integrating and constructing* everyday life in such a way that the various different and contradictory demands with which individuals are faced in their daily lives are rendered reconcilable with each other and can be "handled." How can such a conceptualization be reinterpreted in such a way as to be compatible with the science from the standpoint of the subject?

The Subjective Groundedness of the Elementary Cyclicality of the Conduct of Everyday Life

What is in a sense the most elementary specific feature of the "conduct of everyday life" lies in its above-mentioned character as a "self-reproductive system" organizing "everydayness"; that is, it has its own course that is independent of and follows a different trajectory from the course of a person's life as a whole. This course cannot be adequately represented by the conventional linear "stimulus–response" chains or, in the terms of action regulation theory, means–goal hierarchies. The *specific nature* of the conduct of life is also only inadequately described by the concept of the "automation" of sequences of action that would appear to be fitting here. In order to do justice to it we must rather take into account that linear forms of the organization of actions are sublated in cyclical forms. Although our going-to-bed routines (from washing to getting undressed – first taking off our shoes – up to the point where we slip under the bed covers) are in themselves linear action sequences (which can then be run through in a more or less "automated" fashion), they only become an element of our conduct of everyday life because we *repeat* them every night; that is, we integrate the linear action structure into a *cyclical* structure in which it attains its status within other routines that we also repeat – getting up (again) in the morning, having breakfast, going to work, etc. Such cycles are mediated by many different, externally imposed cycles (from the family rules about using the bathroom to the opening times of shops and institutional regulations on working hours). The different levels of the cyclicality here are linked to the cosmic day–night cycle to which the societal systems of repetition are adapted, if only loosely. Despite this, the cycle in which I organize my life does not run on its own, but (as I said above) *I* must get my own life activities "running": I must set the alarm clock (and I can also "*forget*" to do so – more or less consciously), I must go to school in the morning (and I can also refuse to do so, by feigning illness or by "playing truant"), etc. I can in fact (temporarily?) free myself completely from cyclical life organization, make the "night into day," "run away," "drop out," etc. However, then I will also (as we shall see more clearly later) have to bear the consequences, assume responsibility for doing so – and, moreover, I will inevitably soon have to get involved in another (be it old or new) cyclical mode of organizing my life.

When I ask myself *what function* the cyclical organization of my life has for me, what *reasons* I can have (in consideration of my interests in life) for constantly getting involved in such repetitive structures, what becomes evident (to me), even when I look at the issue from the global perspective, is the *substantial relief* from my coping efforts that I obtain from it. While I am relieved by biological or physiological regulation systems that take place outside of awareness from being potentially overstrained by the task of actively regulating my bodily functions (breathing, digestion, etc.), unlike subhuman beings, which are also relieved of the majority of these tasks by their biological endowment, at the level of actions I *am* responsible for how I reproduce my own everyday living. I myself also have to ensure that this does not *systematically overtax* me and prevent me from living my "actual life" (see below); and this is what makes my acceptance of the elementary cyclical organization of my conduct of everyday life functional. It is this that relieves me of the task of repeatedly re-extracting premises from the given meaning constellations to justify my actions and of establishing intentions to act on their basis. It is also unnecessary for me to clarify each time to what extent my intentions to act are in fact compatible with my interests in life. Rather, for me, since due to the cyclical nature of these routines I have "always" performed them and have been able to reproduce the bases of my life in this way, it is the most obvious thing to do to continue to rely on them. I consider them to be a matter of course, they are "self-evident" or are understandable in themselves, or to be more exact, they are justified by the mere fact that I have previously already executed the same action sequences; that is, they are "routines" in the sense that I include them in my conduct of my everyday life "*without reflecting anew on whether the premises for their justification are fulfilled*" (Holzkamp, 1993, p. 315). At the same time the linear action sequences also need no justification – if or insofar as they are elements of such action cycles. However, this does not mean that the cyclical routines of the conduct of everyday life are in any way excluded from the intersubjective reason discourse (i.e., that they can, for example, be considered to be "conditioned"). Instead, they are in a sense negatively justified, i.e., because one sees "*no reason expressly to re-examine the premises each time*" (Holzkamp, 1993, p. 315).

It becomes still clearer how the cyclical organization of my conduct of everyday life is grounded in my interests in life when we take into consideration a case in which my everyday cyclicality is (temporarily) *destroyed*, for instance, due to severe illness, the death of a relative, war, etc. In such extreme situations we literally do not know what to do (first). We lose control over our living conditions and find our existence fundamentally threatened. Accordingly, in order to overcome such crises (or at least to take the first step in that direction) we need to recover our "everyday life," that is, the cyclical routines of our conduct of everyday life. Only if we succeed in doing so do we once more know "how life should go on" or that "things will somehow go on." From this it also becomes understandable in what initially desperate and hopeless situations it helps to reconstruct my everyday routines. If I have come home from hospital after an operation with the prospect that I may soon die, things will seem "no longer as bad" to the extent that I have recovered my daily routines by performing familiar cyclical activities. This makes what is awful and inconceivable seem less real. If one has crawled unharmed out of the ruins after an air raid and has no idea whether friends and relatives are still alive or how life will go on, one begins, as far as possible, as a first or last resort, to reconstruct fragments of one's everyday cyclicality. Perhaps another survivor will soon say, "I'll try to find some hot water and some tea and make a cuppa" – and then one will see. If I am in detention, in prison, for instance, one of the things that is perhaps most stressful, apart from being deprived of my freedom, will be the fact that my own daily cycle is taken out of my hands by means of meticulous rules that are imposed from outside – signals for going to bed and for taking exercise in the yard, having my food passed to me through the hatch, wherever I have to go I am fetched and accompanied. I am thus almost completely at the mercy of the circumstances. This gets worse if I am prevented even from getting used to the imposed cycles and thus the illusion of a last vestige of autonomy is destroyed by mass accommodation with changing occupancies, refusals to inform me why I have been taken prisoner and when I will be released, frequent and arbitrary transfers, etc. I am thus deprived of the very foundations of existence (even if I am given enough to eat). Suicide is thus often de facto all that remains as the last means of escape – as is happening more and more often in the current practice of detention pending deportation instituted by the German government for non-German refugees (cf. XX).*

In what I have just written we can already detect the *time structuring* that is peculiar to the conduct of life on the level of cyclical everyday routines. Since here linear changes are subsumed in the cyclical movements that more or less return to themselves, the temporality is in a sense suspended and the cycles themselves seem to be beyond time: tomorrow I will get up again and the day after tomorrow too and also the day after that – and *so it goes on*. Perhaps it is this temporal quality of everydayness that is mainly responsible for the peculiar power of everyday banality to provide comfort. As long as or because things keep going on in the same way, actually not much can happen to me. Separations, losses and death are negated (I will, of course, die one day, but not yet and actually not at all). That is very likely one of the reasons why I so urgently need to reconstruct my everyday cyclicality when it has been destroyed. Without the illusionary bracketing of mortality, or to be more accurate, the impossibility of addressing mortality that it entails, I cannot actually go on living because my current existence is quasi relativized "in light of its end," disintegrated, destroyed. The fact that it is never completely possible to deny the vulnerability and fragility of my trust in the "eternity" of cyclical everyday life, that the repressed mortality in the background "rumbles" and occasionally shoots into awareness like lightning may in some cases be what is behind low spirits and states of hopelessness when their severity cannot be satisfactorily explained on the basis of the current situation.

Since everyday cyclicality is the vehicle of our fundamental security in life, it follows that my everyday life routines *cannot be the "whole of my life."* Although they are the basis of all else, they reduce my existential anxiety and guard my back, so to speak, however, "actual life" – productivity, excitement, happiness, fulfillment, joint struggles – nonetheless stands at right angles to the cyclicality of the conduct of life, although perhaps somehow in its folds. This is what makes the daily trials and tribulations of the repetitive unchanging routine bearable; indeed they may perhaps be pushed into the background by the consciousness-filling expanse of "actual life." This may entail a dynamic that really pushes the limits of everyday life, violating its rules and ignoring its daily demands – with the risk that we will perhaps never find our way back and thus lose the elemental basis from which alone "actual life" can develop. Conversely, the monotony of the "daily grind" itself may take on, even for me, an awareness-filling breadth – to the extent to which I am prevented from participating in "actual life" by reduced circumstances, illness, age and isolation – and, thus, resigned or even despairingly I may begin to ask myself why, or for what, I should actually get up every morning since (as we find in one well-known test item) "life is a strain for me."

At the same time we must take into consideration that the boundary between the "conduct of everyday life" and "actual life" can probably never be clearly drawn, that we cannot name any objective characteristics that belong to the one or the other, and that it depends rather on the respective context how

I experience or "interpret" the relationship between "everyday life" and "actual life." Thus, for example, when I go home after a long stay in hospital the modest autonomy of my everyday life that I have recovered may (for a while?) make me really happy, and when I grow old together with somebody close to me the everyday life that we share may itself increasingly take on qualities of an irrecoverable delight. Conversely, it is well known that ecstasies that are otherwise guaranteed, such as sexual fulfillment, are soon reduced to being an everyday routine if they are repeated cyclically (every Saturday evening) and thus lose their character of being "actual life" as opposed to daily routine. Nonetheless, it would seem to me to be indispensable to differentiate conceptually between the routine of everyday life and actual life, because otherwise one would not be able to grasp what is special about everyday cyclicality, its specific "emptiness" and the need to supplement it, and because one would otherwise not have a reference system that would make it possible to capture the essence of the characteristic cognitive limitations of the conduct of everyday life – how it remains caught up in the "obvious," etc. – precisely *as* limitations (I shall come back to this in more detail later).

In the above, so as to emphasize the specific characteristics of the cyclicality of everyday life, I initially presented the argument as if the "conduct of life" were simply a matter for the individual. In order to do so in some places I have had to use highly abstract expressions. For example, I had to ignore the fact that – where, for instance, "going-to-school" or "going-to-work" have been given as components of the daily cycle – the conduct of everyday life has always been subject to social demands. However, leaving out aspects in this way has meant that we have not yet been able to include in our reinterpretation efforts characteristics that the Munich research group considered central, i.e., the conduct of everyday life as an ongoing active "*integrative*" or "*constructive*" effort through which everyday life is organized in the face of multiple requirements. We will now focus on this in our further discussion – thereby reversing the above-mentioned abstraction (XX).*

What is it exactly that needs to be "integrated" by the conduct of everyday life?

Acknowledgment

The original German version of this chapter was published in 1995, Alltägliche Lebensführung als subjektwissenschaftliches Grundkonzept. *Das Argument*, 212, 817–846. We would like to thank Argument Press for granting permission for it to be translated and published in English.

Notes

* Editors' note: "XX" are place markers for additions in the manuscript. As mentioned in the introductory chapter, this text is an unfinished manuscript on which Klaus Holzkamp was working shortly before his death in November 1995.

1 As we find numerous collocations containing the word "subject" in the current discussion in the social sciences and psychology – for example, in addition to the "science from the standpoint of the subject" (*Subjektwissenschaft*), the "theory of the subjective" (*subjektive Theorie*), the "Critical Theory of the Subject" (*Kritische Theorie des Subjekts*), and "orientation toward the subject" (*Subjektorientierung*) – in the interests of clarity it is important to note that when in what follows I speak of the "science from the standpoint of the subject" etc. I am always referring to the approach of the science from the standpoint of the subject as it has developed since the early 1970s, together with Critical Psychology. Its development is associated not only with my own name, but also with such names as Ute Osterkamp, Volker Schurig, Ole Dreier, Wolfgang Maiers and Morus Markard.
2 To simplify matters, in what follows I quote from passages from the work of the Munich group that I have already cited without repeating the references. If necessary these can be relatively easily found in my earlier summary, which is (I would say) comparatively short. I have not expressly marked emphases added by myself in the present chapter.

References

Bolte, K. M. (1983). Subjektorientierte Soziologie: Plädoyer für eine Forschungsperspektive. In K. M. Bolte & E. Treutner (Eds.), *Subjektorientierte Arbeits- und Berufssoziologie* (pp. 12–36). Frankfurt/M.: Campus.

Cronbach, L.J. & Meehl, P.E. (1955). Construct validity in psychological tests. *Psychological Bulletin Vol. 52*. No 4 (pp. 281–302)

Dreier, O. (2008). *Psychotherapy in everyday life*. Cambridge: Cambridge University Press.

Dunkel, W. (1993). Kontrolle und Vertrauen: Die Herstellung von Stabilität in der alltäglichen Lebensführung. In K. Jurczyk & M. S. Rerrich (Eds.), *Die Arbeit des Alltags. Beiträge zu einer Soziologie der alltäglichen Lebensführung* (pp. 195–209). Freiburg: Lambertus.

Freud, S. (1955a/1973). Lines of advance in psycho-analytic therapy. In J. Strachey (Ed. & Trans.), *The standard edition of the complete psychological works of Sigmund Freud* (Vol. 17, pp. 159–168). London: Hogarth. (Original work published 1919)

Freud, S. (1955b/1973). Two encyclopedia articles: (A) Psychoanalysis and libido theory. In J. Strachey (Ed. & Trans.), *The standard edition of the complete psychological works of Sigmund Freud* (Vol. 18, pp. 235–254). London: Hogarth. (Original work published 1922)

Freud, S. (1958a/1973). On beginning the treatment. In J. Strachey (Ed. & Trans.), *The standard edition of the complete psychological works of Sigmund Freud* (Vol. 12, pp. 121–144). London: Hogarth Press. (Original work published 1913)

Freud, S. (1958b/1973). Remembering, repeating and working-through. (Further recommendations on the technique of psycho-analysis.) In J. Strachey (Ed. & Trans.), *The standard edition of complete psychological works of Sigmund Freud* (Vol. 12, pp. 145–156). London: Hogarth. (Original work published 1913)

Freud, S. (1963/1973). Introductory lectures on Psycho-Analysis: Resistance and repression (Lecture XIX). In *The standard edition of the complete psychological works of Sigmund Freud* (Vol. 16, pp. 286–302). London: Hogarth. (Original work published 1915–1916)

Holzkamp, K. (1983). *Grundlegung der Psychologie*. Frankfurt/M.: Campus.

Holzkamp, K. (1990). Worauf bezieht sich das Begriffspaar "restriktive/verallgemeinerte Handlungsfähigkeit"? *Forum Kritische Psychologie, 26*, 35–45.

Holzkamp, K. (1991). Was heißt Psychologie vom Subjektstandpunkt? *Forum Kritische Psychologie, 28*, 5–19.

Holzkamp, K. (1993). *Lernen: Subjektwissenschaftliche Grundlegung*. Frankfurt/M.: Campus.

Jurczyk, K. & Rerrich, M. S. (Eds.). (1993a). *Die Arbeit des Alltags: Beiträge zu einer Soziologie der alltäglichen Lebensführung.* Freiburg: Lambertus.

Jurczyk, K. & Rerrich, M. S. (1993b). Einführung: Alltägliche Lebensführung – der Ort, wo "alles zusammenkommt." In K. Jurczyk & M. S. Rerrich (Eds.), *Die Arbeit des Alltags: Beiträge zu einer Soziologie der alltäglichen Lebensführung* (pp. 11–45). Freiburg: Lambertus.

Jurczyk, K. & Rerrich, M. S. (1993c). Lebensführung, soziale Einbindung und die Strukturkategorie "Geschlecht." In K. Jurczyk & M. S. Rerrich (Eds.), *Die Arbeit des Alltags: Beiträge zu einer Soziologie der alltäglichen Lebensführung* (pp. 262–278). Freiburg: Lambertus.

Kudera, W. & Voß, G. G. (1990). Lebensführung zwischen Routinisierung und Aushandlung. Die Arbeitsteilung der Person unter Veränderungsdruck. In E.-H. Hoff (Ed.), *Die doppelte Sozialisation Erwachsener: Zum Verhältnis von beruflichem und privatem Lebensstrang* (pp. 155–176). Munich: Deutsches Jugendinstitut.

Lave, J., Smith, S. & Butler, M. (1989). Problem solving as everyday practice. In R. Charles & E. Silver (Eds.), *The teaching and assessing of mathematical problem solving* (pp. 61–81). Reston, VA: National Council of Teachers of Mathematics.

Lorenzer, A. (1974). *Die Wahrheit der psychoanalytischen Erkenntnis: Ein historisch-materialistischer Entwurf.* Frankfurt/M.: Suhrkamp.

Markard, M. (1984). *Einstellung: Kritik eines sozialpsychologischen Grundkonzeptes.* Frankfurt/M.: Campus.

Meehl, P.E. (1954). *Clinical vs. statistical prediction.* Minneapolis: University of Minnesota.

Mehan, H. (1979). *Learning lessons: Social organization in the classroom.* Cambridge, MA: Harvard University Press.

Mörth, I. & Fröhlich, G. (Eds.). (1994). *Das symbolische Kapital der Lebensstile: Zur Kultursoziologie der Moderne nach Pierre Bourdieu.* Frankfurt/M.: Campus.

Vetter, H.-R. (Ed.). (1991). *Muster moderner Lebensführung: Ansätze und Perspektiven.* Munich: Deutsches Jugendinstitut.

Voß, G. G. (1991). *Lebensführung als Arbeit: Über die Autonomie der Person im Alltag der Gesellschaft.* Stuttgart: Enke.

Weber, M. (2003). *The Protestant ethic and the spirit of capitalism* (D. Winter and U. Osterkamp, Trans.). New York: Routledge. (Original work published 1958)

4

THE MAZE AND THE LABYRINTH

Walking, Imagining and the Education of Attention

Tim Ingold

If you are educated to know too much about things, then there is a danger that you see your own knowledge and not the things themselves. Here I argue that walking offers an alternative model of education that, rather than instilling knowledge *in* to the minds of novices, leads them *out* into the world. I compare these alternatives to the difference between the maze and the labyrinth. The maze, which presents a series of choices but predetermines the moves predicated on each, puts all the emphasis on the traveler's intentions. In the labyrinth, by contrast, choice is not an issue, but holding to the trail calls for continual attention. Education along the lines of the labyrinth does not provide novices with standpoints or positions, but continually pulls them from any positions they might adopt. It is a practice of exposure. The attention required by such a practice is one that waits upon things, and that is present at their appearance. To "appear things" is tantamount to their imagination, on the plane of immanent life. Human life is temporally stretched between imagination and perception, and education, in the original sense of the Greek *scholè*, fills the gap between them. I conclude that the "poor pedagogy" provided by a mode of education that has no content to transmit, and no methods for doing so, nevertheless offers an understanding on the way to truth.

I

In his recent book, *At the Loch of the Green Corrie*, the poet Andrew Greig speaks thus of his friend and mentor, Norman MacCaig. His eye and heart were drawn to animals, says Greig, yet he was not particularly knowledgeable about them.

> He could name the commonest birds and that was about it. I think he didn't want to know more, believing that knowledge of their Latin names, habitat,

feeding and mating patterns, moulting season would obscure their reality. Sometimes the more you know the less you see. What you encounter is your knowledge, not the thing itself.

(Greig, 2010, p. 88)

In this, I think, Greig has touched on something quite profound, which goes to the heart of the meaning and purpose of what we call education. Does knowledge actually lead to wisdom? Does it open our eyes and ears to the truth of what is there? Or does it rather hold us captive within a compendium of our own making, like a hall of mirrors that blinds us to its beyond? Might we see more, experience more and understand more, by knowing less? And might it be because we know too much that we seem so incapable of attending to what is going on around us and of responding with care, judgment and sensitivity? Which of them is wiser, the ornithologist or the poet – the one who knows the name of every kind of bird but has them ready sorted in his head; the other who knows no names but looks with wonder, astonishment and perplexity on everything he sees?

I want to suggest that these alternatives correspond to two quite different senses of education (on this distinction, see Craft, 1984). The first is familiar enough to all of us who have sat in a school classroom, as pupils, or who have stood up before the class to teach. This is the sense of the Latin verb *educare*, meaning to rear or to bring up, to instill a pattern of approved conduct and the knowledge that supports it. A variant etymology, however, traces the word to *educere*, from *ex* (out) + *ducere* (to lead). In this sense, education is a matter of leading novices *out* into the world rather than – as it is conventionally taken to be today – instilling knowledge *in* to their minds. It is, quite literally, to invite the learner out for a walk. What kind of education is this, which one obtains by walking? And what is it about walking that makes it such an effective practice for education in this sense?

II

There are many ways of walking, and not all of them lead out. One way that does not, which you may recall from childhood, is the "crocodile." It is what teachers use for getting a class without mishap from one point to another. Children are expected to walk two abreast, in a neat line. If they pay attention to their surroundings at all, it is in the interests of safety, to avoid collision with traffic or passers-by. The path of the crocodile, however, is not a way of learning; this happens only at its destination, where once again the teacher stands before the class and addresses them. But when these same children – be they accompanied by a parent or guardian, with friends, or on their own – make their ways from home to school and back, they will walk quite differently. Now hurrying, now dawdling, alternately skipping and plodding, the child's attention is *caught* – or, in the view of an accompanying adult, *distracted* – by everything from the play of light and shadow to the flight of birds and the barking of dogs, to the scent of flowers, to puddles and fallen leaves, and to myriad trifles from snails to conkers, and from dropped coins to telltale litter. It is these trifles that make the street a place of such absorbing interest to the miniature detective whose eyes remain close to the ground (Ingold & Vergunst, 2008, p. 4).

For the child on his way to school, the street is a labyrinth. Like the scribe, copyist or draughtsman whose eyes are in his fingertips, the child follows its twists and turns, ever curious, but with no commanding view and no glimpse of an end. The challenge is not to lose the trail, and for that he needs to keep his wits about him. Walter Benjamin, fondly recalling his childhood days in Berlin around the turn of the 20th century, vividly describes the Ariadne's thread that he would follow in and around the Tiergarten, with its bridges, flowerbeds, pedestals of statues (which, being closer to the eye, held greater interest than the figures mounted on them) and kiosks hidden among the bushes. Here, says Benjamin, he first experienced what he only later found the word for. That word was "love" (Benjamin, 2006, p. 54).

But growing up, one learns to banish such childish follies. The crocodile devours the detective as discipline gobbles up curiosity. To recover what is lost, one has to go beyond the city, to take a walk in woods, fields or mountains governed by forces as yet untrained. For the adult, Benjamin remarks, it takes some effort to apprehend the city streets once again with the same acuity as a path in the countryside. To achieve this – to regain the labyrinth and lose oneself in it – "street names must speak to the urban wanderer like the snapping of dry twigs, and little streets in the heart of the city must reflect the times of day ... as clearly as a mountain valley." This art, Benjamin admits, is one that, having been lost in childhood, he acquired again only late in life (2006, pp. 53–54).

III

For most of us, disciplined by education and going about our business in the city, the streets are not a labyrinth. We walk them not for what they reveal along the way but because they afford transit from one point of call to another. We may still get lost in them, but that loss is experienced not as a discovery on the way to nowhere but as a setback in the achievement of a predetermined goal. We mean to get from here to there, and are frustrated by wrong turns and cul-de-sacs. For the urban shopper or commuter, then, the streets are not so much a labyrinth as a maze. Technically, the maze differs from the labyrinth in that it offers not one path but multiple choices, of which each may be freely made but most lead to dead ends (Kern, 1982, p. 13). It also differs, however, in that its avenues are demarcated by barriers that obstruct any view other than the way immediately ahead. The maze, then, does not open up to the world, as the labyrinth does. On the contrary, it encloses, trapping its inmates within the false antinomy of freedom and necessity.

Whether over- or underground, whether navigating the streets or the metro, urban pedestrians have to negotiate a maze of passages flanked by walls or high buildings. Once set on a particular thoroughfare they have no alternative but to continue along it, since it is walled in on either side.[1] These walls, however, are not usually bare. Rather, they are replete with advertisements, window displays and the like, which inform pedestrians of possible side-tracks they might choose to take, as and when the opportunity arises, to satisfy their desires. Every time there is a fork in the way, a decision has to be taken: to go to the left, to the right, or possibly straight ahead. A journey through the maze may thus be represented as a stochastic sequence of moves punctuated by decision points, such that every move is predicated upon the preceding decision. It is essentially a game-like, strategic enterprise. This is not to deny the tactical maneuvering that goes on as pedestrians and even drivers jostle with one another in making their ways through the throng of a busy street or subway. But negotiating a passage through the throng is one thing, finding a way through the maze quite another.[2]

In walking the labyrinth, by contrast, choice is not an issue. The path leads, and the walker is under an imperative to go where it takes him. But the path is not always easy to follow. Like the hunter tracking an animal or a hiker on the trail, it is important to keep an eye out for the subtle signs – footprints, piles of stones, nicks cut in the trunks of trees – that indicate the way ahead. Thus signs keep you on the path; they do not, like advertisements, tempt you away from it. The danger lies not in coming to a dead end, but in wandering off the track. Death is a deviation, not the end of the line. At no point in the labyrinth do you come to an abrupt stop. No buffers, or walls, block your onward movement. You are rather fated to carry on, nevertheless, along a path that, if you are not careful, may take you ever further from the living, to whose community you may never make it back. In the labyrinth you may indeed take a wrong turn, but not by choice. For at the time, you did not notice that the path divided. You were sleepwalking, or dreaming. Indigenous hunters often tell of those who, lured on by the prey they are following, drift into the prey's world, in which the animals appear to them as human. There they carry on their lives while lost, presumed dead, to their own people.

IV

The maze puts all the emphasis on the traveler's intentions. He has an aim in mind, a projected destination or horizon of expectations, a perspective to obtain, and is determined to reach it. This overarching aim may, of course, be broken down into a number of subsidiary objectives. And it may also be complicated by all the other, competing, aims that assail him from all sides. Choices are never clear-cut, and are rarely taken with sufficient information as not to leave a considerable margin of uncertainty. Nevertheless, in the maze, the outward cast of action follows the inward cast of thought. When we say that action is intentional, we mean that a mind is at work, operating from within the actor, and lending it a purpose and direction beyond what the physical laws of motion would alone dictate. Intentions distinguish the travelers in a maze from the balls in a game of bagatelle that – we suppose – have no idea of where they are heading and are quite incapable of deliberating whether to go in one way or another. In the maze, intention is cause and action effect.

Yet the intentional traveler, wrapped up in the space of his own deliberations, is, by the same token, absent from the world itself. He must perforce decide which way to go, but having resolved upon a course, has no further need to look where he is going. In the labyrinth, by contrast, the path follower has no objective save to carry on, to keep on going. But to do so, his action must be closely and continually coupled with his perception – that is, by an ever-vigilant monitoring of the path as it unfolds. Simply put, you have to watch your step, and to listen and feel as well. Path-following, in short, is not so much intentional as *attentional*. It draws the follower out into presence of the real. As intention is to attention, therefore, so absence is to presence. This is also the difference between wayfaring and navigation (Ingold, 2007, pp. 15–16). Of course there is a mind at work in the attentional wayfaring of the labyrinth, just as there is in the intentional navigation of the maze. But this is a mind immanent in the movement itself rather than an originating source to which such movement may be attributed as an effect.

V

Now between the navigation of the maze and the wayfaring of the labyrinth lies all the difference between the two senses of education with which I began: on the one hand the *in*-duction (drawing in) of the learner into the rules and representations, or the "intentional worlds," of a culture; on the other the *ex*-duction (drawing out) of the learner into the world itself, as it is given to experience. There is of course nothing new or radical in the suggestion that knowledge is relative to its cultural milieu. That every world is but a view of the world, and that these perspectives or interpretations are multiple and possibly conflicting, has become virtually the default position in the modern, or even postmodern, philosophy of education. Students are more than familiar with the idea that knowledge consists of representations, and they are savvy enough to realize that representations are not to be confused with the "real thing." This, as the philosopher of education Jan Masschelein observes, is not where the problem lies.

It lies rather in the way that a world that can be known only in its representations, in a plethora of images, slips from us in the very move by which we try to hold it in our sights. Our grasp of things is one that always leaves us empty-handed, clutching at reflections. We can no longer open to the world, nor it to us. "How," Masschelein asks,

> can we turn the world into something "real", how to make the world "present", to give again the real and discard the shields or mirrors that seem to have locked us up increasingly into self-reflections and interpretations, into endless returns upon "standpoints", "perspectives" and "opinions"?

How, in short, can we escape the maze? Masschelein's answer is, quite literally, "through exposure" (Masschelein, 2010a, p. 276). And this is precisely what is achieved by education in the sense of *ex*-duction – that is, by walking the labyrinth.

Education in this sense has nothing to do with such routine objectives as "gaining a critical distance" or "taking up a perspective" on things. It is not about arriving at a point of view. In the labyrinth there is no point of arrival, no final destination, for every place is already on the way to somewhere else. Far from taking up a standpoint or perspective from this position or that, walking continually pulls us away from *any* standpoint – from any position we might adopt. "Walking," as Masschelein explains, "is about putting this position at stake; it is about ex-position, about being out-of-position" (2010a, p. 278). This is what he means by exposure. It is not that exposure affords a different perspective or set of perspectives, for example from ground level, different from what might be gained from higher up, or from the air. Indeed, it does not disclose the world from any perspective at all. The walker's attention comes not from having arrived at a position but from being pulled away from it, from displacement.

VI

At first glance this conclusion seems remarkably close to that reached by the psychologist James Gibson (1979). Pioneering his ecological approach to visual perception, Gibson had proposed that we do not perceive our surroundings from a series of fixed points; nor, he argued, is it the task of the mind to assemble, in memory, the partial perspectives obtained from each point into a comprehensive picture of the whole. Rather, perception proceeds along what he called a *path of observation*. As the observer goes on his way, the pattern in the light reaching the eyes from reflecting surfaces in the environment (that is, the "optic array") undergoes continual modulation, and from the underlying invariants of this modulation, things disclose themselves for what they are. Or more precisely they disclose what they *afford*, insofar as they help or hinder the observer to keep going, or to carry on along a certain line of activity. The more practiced we become in walking these paths of observation, according to Gibson, the better able we are to notice and to respond fluently to salient aspects of our environment. That is to say, we undergo an "education of attention" (Gibson, 1979, p. 254; see also Ingold, 2001).

Despite the superficial similarity, however, the education to which the walker lays himself open through exposure, according to Masschelein, is quite the reverse of what Gibson had in mind. It is not a matter of picking up, and turning to one's advantage, the affordances of a world that is already laid out. Recall that the verb *attendre*, in French, means "to wait", and that even in English, to attend to things or persons carries connotations of looking after them, doing their bidding and following what they do. In this regard, attention abides with a world that is not ready-made but always incipient, on the cusp of continual emergence. In short, whereas for Gibson the world waits for the observer, for Masschelein the walker waits upon the world. As the path beckons the walker submits, and is at the mercy of what transpires. To walk, as Masschelein puts it, is to be commanded by what is not yet given but *on the way* to being given (Masschelein, 2010b, p. 46).

The philosopher Henri Bortoft, in his advocacy of the principles of Goethean science, makes much the same point through a clever reversal of the phrase "it appears." In the conventional and grammatically correct order of words, "it" comes before "appears": the thing exists prior to its disclosure, ready and waiting to be perceived by the moving observer, whose attention is attuned to what it affords. In walking the labyrinth, however, attention is moved upstream, to the "appearing of what appears." One is attending – waiting – for "it" to emerge. The appearing of a thing is tantamount to its emergence, and to witness the appearance is to be present at its birth. To say "appears it," Bortoft comments, "may be bad grammar but it is better philosophically," since it gets around the conundrum that otherwise leads us to suppose that things exist prior to the processes that give rise to them (Bortoft, 2012, pp. 95–96).

VII

Now to *appear things*, I suggest, is tantamount to imagining them. To imagine something is to appear it, to assist in its gestation and to attend its birth. Thus the power of the imagination lies not in mental representation, nor in a capacity to construct images in advance of their material enactment. Imagining is a movement of opening, not of foreclosure, and what it brings forth are not endings but beginnings. As we say colloquially, the propensity of the imagination is to roam, to cast about for a way ahead; it is not to follow a sequence of steps toward a predetermined goal. In this sense, imagination is the generative impulse of a life that is perpetually pulled along by the hope, promise and expectation of its continuation. In this life, as philosopher Gilles Deleuze asserts, there are no actuals, only virtuals – things that are *on their way* toward actualization, or to being given (Deleuze, 2001, p. 31). Such a life is not to be found in a record of achievements, nor can it be reconstructed like a curriculum vitae, by listing the milestones along a route already traveled. It rather passes between milestones, as a river between its banks, pulling away from them as it sweeps by. This is what Deleuze means by *a* life (rather than *the* life), carried on in what he calls the "plane of immanence" (ibid., p. 28). From everything I have said so far, it should be clear that this plane – of virtuality, of the appearing of what appears – is also the plane of the labyrinth. Immanent life, in short, is labyrinthine.

To explain what he means, Deleuze draws an example from an episode in Charles Dickens's novel, *Our Mutual Friend*. One Mr Riderhood, an unpleasant and disreputable man, has been rescued by onlookers following an accident on the Thames. His rowboat had been run down by a steamer. Close to drowning, he is carried to a nearby lodging, and the doctor is called. While his life hangs in the balance, the doctor's inconclusive investigations are greeted by his burly rescuers, and the mistress of the house, with a mixture of awe and hushed reverence. Eventually, however, the patient comes round, and as he regains consciousness the spell is lifted. Returning to his usual surly and bad-tempered self, Mr Riderhood scolds and berates the assembled company, which by then even includes his daughter, while his erstwhile saviors immediately recoil – their respect for life eclipsed by their contempt for this particular specimen of it. Neither Riderhood in this world nor Riderhood in the other, as Dickens wryly remarks, would draw any compassion from anyone, "but a striving human soul between the two can do it easily" (Dickens, 1963, p. 444).

As Dickens's tale reveals, the plane of immanence is suspended precariously between the biographical particularities of life and death, or of consciousness and coma: a suspension in which those particularities – decisions made, courses taken, goals achieved, crimes committed – are dissolved or placed in abeyance. It is just the same, as we have already seen, in the stories of indigenous hunters who also, in the pursuit of prey, find themselves in a zone of existential uncertainty where the balance of life and death, as between hunter and prey, can tip either way (Willerslev, 2007). Thus to walk the labyrinth is like balancing on cobwebs, where the ground itself is but a veil. Like the spider, we hang in there. Not that life, in this sense, is confined to critical situations. As Deleuze is keen to stress, "*A* life is everywhere, in all the moments that a given living subject goes through" (2001, p. 29). What, then, is the relation between the virtual moments of immanent life, lived along the ways of the labyrinth, and the actual moments marked by decision points in the maze? For do we not all, and at all times, have a foot in both concurrently?

VIII

It seems that the movement of a human life – perhaps in contrast to the lives of non-human animals – is temporally stretched. We are, so to speak, constitutionally ahead of ourselves. Upstream, coeval with the appearing of things, is the imagination; lagging behind downstream is our perceptual apprehension of a world that is already settled, and in which things are there to appear. That is why in every venture and at every moment, we are both fully prepared and utterly unprepared for things to come. What then leads, and what follows? The usual answer is to claim that as intentional beings – that is, as *agents* – humans deliberate before they act. This, of course, is to locate them, first and foremost, in the maze. Here the mind commands and the body submits more or less mechanically to its directions. Mastery, in this intentionalist account, is cognitive: if humans lead their lives, rather than merely living them, it is entirely thanks to their capacity to conceive of designs in advance of their execution, something of which animals – at least for a science of mind constructed on Cartesian principles – are deemed incapable.

To give priority to the labyrinth, however, is to invert this temporal relation between mastery and submission. Here, *submission leads and mastery follows*. Rather than a commanding mind that already knows its will trailing a subservient body in its wake, out in front is an imagination that feels its way forward, rooting for a passage through an as yet unformed world, while bringing up the rear is a perception already educated in the ways of the world and skilled in observing and responding to its affordances. A life that is led, then, is held in tension between submission and mastery, between imagination and perception, between the life we undergo and the things we do. And it is the former that sets the existential conditions for the latter, not the other way around. Life is not subservient to agency, but agency subservient to life. And the gap between the two, between the virtual and the actual — that temporal stretch by which imagination always outpaces perception — is no more, and no less, than *school*, in its original meaning (from the Greek *scholè*) of free time.

With this, we return to the theme of education, and to the philosophy of Masschelein. "Education," Masschelein argues, "is about making 'school' in the sense of *scholè*." And as the architect of *scholè*, the educator or teacher "is one who un-finishes, who undoes the appropriation and destination of time" (Masschelein, 2011, p. 530). He or she is not so much a custodian of ends as a catalyst of beginnings, whose task it is to unlock the imagination and to confer upon it the freedom to roam without aim or destination.

We should not, of course, confuse school in this sense with the institution familiar to Western societies that commonly goes by that name. For in its institutional history, the school has been largely devoted to corralling the imagination, to converting it into a capacity to represent ends in advance of their achievement. The object of the institution has overwhelmingly been to destine time, not to un-destine it; to complete the instillation of knowledge into the minds of students, not to unravel it (Masschelein, 2011, p. 531). It has been to assert the primacy of the maze over the labyrinth, and of mastery over submission. Thus the institution of the school and the free time of *scholè* are committed, respectively, to the contrary imperatives of *educare* and *educere*, of drawing in and leading out, inculcation and exposure, intention and attention. What the former appropriates, the latter holds in abeyance. It puts a delay on end-directed activity. On this plane of immanence, where nothing is any more what it was or yet what it will be, there is — as the saying goes — everything to play for. Unfinished, freed up from ends and objectives, common to all, the world is once more restored to presence. It touches us, so that we — together *exposed* to its touch (ibid., p. 533) — can live with it, in its company. Or in a word, we can *correspond* with it.[3]

IX

But if *scholè* is the time of being exposed together, it is also the time of tradition. Walkers in the labyrinth — like Australian Aboriginal youths as they follow the trails of their ancestors in the Dreamtime, when the world was incipient — retrace the footsteps of predecessors, becoming whom they once were. *All imagining, in this sense, is remembering.* For the monastic scholars of medieval Europe, it was much the same. To copy a liturgical text with pen and ink, or to read it by retracing the letter-line with the fingers while murmuring the corresponding sounds, was a following of tradition in the original sense of *traditio*. Derived from the Latin *tradere*, "to hand over," tradition meant something very different then from what it is commonly taken for today. It was not so much a corpus of knowledge to be passed from generation to generation as a performance by means of which, relay fashion, it was possible to *carry on*. Every story in the scriptures, like every trail in the landscape, would lay down a path along which this movement could proceed, and each trail – each story – would take the reader so far before handing over to the next (Ingold, 2013b, p. 741).

Whether in walking a trail or copying a text, the pedestrian or scribe submits to a line that forever pulls him out of position. Having no goal, no end in sight, always waiting, ever present, exposed yet astonished by the world through which he fares, he has nothing to learn and nothing to teach. His itinerary is a way of life, yet it is a way without content to transmit. There is no body of knowledge to be passed on. And because there is nothing to pass on, there are no methods for doing so. Thus between the conventional definition of education as instilling knowledge and the sense of education that we have explored here, as a leading out into the world, lies the difference between rich methodology and what Masschelein (2010b, p. 49) calls "poor pedagogy."

The notion of methodology belongs to the maze. In its deployment, it turns means into ends, divorcing knowledge-as-content from ways of coming to know, and thereby enforcing a kind of closure that is the very antithesis of the opening up to the present that a poor pedagogy offers. If a rich methodology offers us ready-made knowledge, poor pedagogy opens minds to the wisdom of experience: it pertains to the time of *scholè*, not to the institution of the school; to the labyrinth, not to the maze. The scribal art of copying is a case in point. The devotional life of the scribe unfolds in the labyrinthine twists and turns of the line he copies. Yet the logic of the maze has reduced copying, in our contemporary estimation, to plagiarism, the illegitimate usurpation of another's agency, as if there were no more to writing than the choice of words and their mechanical reproduction. And the same logic, applied to walking, converts the exploratory wandering of the child, on his or her way to school, into the disciplined march of the crocodile from a point of departure to a pre-selected destination. At the crocodile's end, the teacher turns to face her students and, looking back, articulates a perspective from its final vantage point. Perhaps, already prior to setting out, she will have already displayed a representation, in words and images, of what is to be expected. Hers is indeed a rich methodology.

It is a methodology, however, that sets a block on movement. Face-to-face, there's no way forward. Knowledge flies from head to head, but the heads themselves – and the bodies to which the heads belong – are fixed in place. To walk on is not to face and be addressed by those who stand in front but to follow those who have their backs to you. To copy is to do likewise: to join with the strokes of the pen, not to reflect or take a stand upon completed work. The farer in the labyrinth, abiding with the world and answering to its summons, following on where others went before, can keep on going, without beginning or end, pushing out into the flux of things. He is, as Masschelein would say, truly *present* in the present. The price of such presence is vulnerability, but its reward is an understanding, founded on immediate experience, that goes beyond knowledge. It is an understanding on the way to truth. For as Greig says of the poet: knowing little of the world, he sees the things themselves.

Acknowledgments

This chapter is revised from a paper originally presented at a conference to accompany the exhibition *Walk-On: From Richard Long to Janet Cardiff – 40 Years of Art Walking*, held at the University of Sunderland in June–August 2013. It was published in the same year in the eponymous volume, edited by Cynthia Morrison-Bell, Mike Collier and Alistair Robinson, by Arts Edition North, University of Sunderland, pp. 6–11. I went on to revise much of this material for my book *The Life of Lines*, published by Routledge in April 2015. For the ideas presented here I am especially indebted to Jan Masschelein and Ricardo Nemirovsky.

Notes

1 A recent visit to the gardens of the Palace of Versailles, outside Paris, afforded the same experience. In each square-shaped garden, dead-straight pedestrian avenues were lined on either side by high walls of trees, and led to enclosed groves with statues or fountains. I felt, in these gardens, an overwhelming sense of claustrophobia.
2 On the distinction between strategic navigation and tactical maneuvering, see de Certeau (1984, p. xviii).
3 I have discussed the notion of correspondence at greater length in Ingold (2013a, pp. 105–108).

References

Benjamin, W. (2006). *Berlin childhood around 1900* (H. Eiland, Trans.). Cambridge, MA: Belknap Press of Harvard University Press.
Bortoft, H. (2012). *Taking appearance seriously*. Edinburgh: Floris Books.
Craft, M. (1984). Education for diversity. In M. Craft (Ed.), *Education and cultural pluralism* (pp. 5–26). Philadelphia: Falmer Press.
de Certeau, M. (1984). *The practice of everyday life* (S. Rendall, Trans.). Berkeley, CA: University of California Press.
Deleuze, G. (2001). *Pure immanence: Essays on a life* (A. Boyman, Trans.). New York: Urzone.
Dickens, C. (1963). *Our mutual friend*. London: Oxford University Press. (Original work published 1865)
Gibson, J. J. (1979). *The ecological approach to visual perception*. Boston, MA: Houghton Mifflin.
Greig, A. (2010). *At the loch of the Green Corrie*. London: Quercus.
Ingold, T. (2001). From the transmission of representations to the education of attention. In H. Whitehouse (Ed.), *The debated mind: Evolutionary psychology versus ethnography* (pp. 113–153). Oxford: Berg.
Ingold, T. (2007). *Lines: A brief history*. Abingdon: Routledge.
Ingold, T. (2013a). *Making: Anthropology, archaeology, art and architecture*. Abingdon: Routledge.
Ingold, T. (2013b). Dreaming of dragons: On the imagination of real life. *Journal of the Royal Anthropological Institute*, *19*(4), 734–752.

Ingold, T. & Vergunst, J. L. (2008). Introduction. In T. Ingold & J. L. Vergunst (Eds.), *Ways of walking: Ethnography and practice on foot* (pp. 1–19). Aldershot: Ashgate.

Kern, H. (1982). *Labyrinthe*. Munich: Prestel.

Masschelein, J. (2010a). The idea of critical e-ducational research: e-ducating the gaze and inviting to go walking. In I. Gur-Ze'ev (Ed.), *The possibility/impossibility of a new critical language of education* (pp. 275–21). Rotterdam: Sense Publishers.

Masschelein, J. (2010b). E-ducating the gaze: The idea of a poor pedagogy. *Ethics and Education*, 5(1), 43–53.

Masschelein, J. (2011). Experimentum scholae: The world once more ... but not (yet) finished. *Studies in Philosophy and Education*, 30, 529–535.

Willerslev, R. (2007). *Soul hunters: Hunting, animism, and personhood among the Siberian Yukaghirs*. Berkeley, CA: University of California Press.

5

EMBODYING THE CONDUCT OF EVERYDAY LIFE

From Subjective Reasons to Privilege

Thomas Teo

Introduction

In this chapter I suggest that Holzkamp's (2013, 2015, chap. 3 in this volume) reflections on the *conduct of everyday life* and the conceptual network that surrounds this concept provide psychological solutions to basic core problems that critical psychologists and socially aware psychologists need to address: (a) the relationship between society and the individual and, deriving from this relationship, (b) a psychology that focuses on human subjectivity as it is lived, grounded but not determined by context. However, I suggest that Holzkamp provided only a first-order solution to the relationship between society and the individual, and, more importantly, that he provided only a partial solution to the problem of how critical psychology should consider the mediation between social structure and the conduct of everyday life.

By a *partial solution* I refer to a program that draws on local traditions that are embedded in philosophies of consciousness without an awareness of critical traditions focusing on the body. In suggesting *adding* body-based critical concepts, I imply that Holzkamp's (1983) critical psychology is a progressive research program that is able to assimilate and accommodate critical traditions from inside and outside the West, and that psychologists need to "move with Holzkamp beyond Holzkamp." In particular, I suggest that the notion of a conduct of life needs to add concepts of embodiment such as *habitus*, *performativity* and *privilege*, thus transcending the subject's reasons within a philosophy of consciousness. Whereas *habitus* is a concept that refers to the conduct of life within a society and *performativity* can be applied to an understanding of embodied social constructions the concept of *privilege* can be understood in relation to an *Other* within as well as outside a given society.

Society and the Subject

Critical psychologists understand that human mental life is culturally, historically and socially embedded. The notion of humans' societal nature can be traced in the Western world to Giambattista Vico (1668–1744), Georg Wilhelm Friedrich Hegel (1770–1831) and Karl Marx (1818–1883). In psychology, Holzkamp (1983) provided the clearest articulation of the relationship between society and individual life. The debates on this issue have shown that humans are individuals only to the degree that history and society enables them to be individuals because human consciousness is sublated in the history, culture and society they live in. Mental life is socially embedded and there is no unsocialized self. Thus, critical thinkers have suggested that society is not an external environment or an external variable, but rather a historically changing structure that constitutes the self and mental life, even as humans are not determined by societal structures (Holzkamp, 1983).

Holzkamp (1983) solved this first-order problem by reconstructing in an evolutionary dialectical mode the *societal nature* of human beings. He also demonstrated that in order to understand human subjectivities, psychologists require theories of society. But Holzkamp did not advance solutions to the second-order problems: Which theory of society should we privilege when society is changing? Why should we prefer a philosophy of consciousness over a philosophy of the body? Why should we privilege the subject's reasons? Indeed, since the 19th century the social sciences have accumulated a variety of theories on society, culture and history. The question arises as to whether it is sufficient to construct society as capitalist or bourgeois when one can add descriptions such as developed, industrialized, secular, democratic, liberal, neoliberal, multicultural, advanced, patriarchal, neocolonial, consumerist, leisure-oriented, communicative, information-based, technological, modern, postmodern, dialogical and so on, or combinations thereof.

The description of *capitalist* is insufficient to understand peculiarities of societies, histories and cultures that influence human subjectivity. For instance, technological developments and arrangements impact human subjectivity (see Chimirri, 2014; Schraube, 2013). Even within critical traditions, sophisticated theories of society have emerged that deviate from classical Marxist descriptions (e.g., Boltanski, 2012; Hardt & Negri, 2009; Harvey, 2005). Psychological experiences and understandings will differ based on theoretical choices, as might be the case for the understanding of mental life, consciousness, motivation, cognition and emotion in a particular society. In fact, a theory of society influences not only an understanding of mental life but offers suggestions for human resistance. Not only do psychological concepts provide looping effects (Hacking, 1994), but so do concepts of society.

More generally, and not without good reasons, grand theories, including grand theories of society (e.g., Marxist theories), have come under attack since the rise of post-structuralist thought. Within this stream of ideas it has been argued that instead of grand theories academics should endorse small local theories. For example, the analysis that a capitalist society produces alienated humans or neoliberal identities could be supplemented by the notion of a relational description of humans (Gergen, 2009). It should be epistemologically obvious to critical thinkers that a present-day concept of society needs to include some of the more recent critical debates in the social sciences from around the world. Critical psychologists need to follow up on these theories if they want to produce a current understanding of human subjectivity in specific worlds. I assume that Holzkamp would agree.

The Individual's Conduct of Life

Critical theory (the *Frankfurt School*) intended to solve the problem of the embeddedness of the person in society by including psychoanalysis in its research program. Critical psychology, especially in its later developments (Holzkamp, 1984, 2013), relied upon phenomenology and hermeneutic thinking for solving the *worldlessness* of traditional psychology. Indeed, to this day mainstream psychology remains a psychology without "being" because it has not been able to address adequately the reality that we "are" in the world. In my interpretation, Holzkamp made an important move when he acknowledged phenomenology: He realized that a Marxist framework is insufficient for a psychology of the person (or the subject, as he called it) and, thus, he included hermeneutic traditions that were part of his own intellectual history (see Teo, 2013).

Marxism, phenomenology and hermeneutics can be interpreted as having more in common than a surface reading might suggest. Marx taught that the human sciences must deal with real humans as they eat, produce, procreate and so on – in short, as they live their lives (Marx & Engels, 1932/1958). For Dilthey (1957), psychological *functions* need to be complemented by psychological *content*, which is formed through the meaning that humans give to their lives (see Teo, 2001). Such basic insights have only marginally found manifestation in mainstream psychology. But whereas Marxist ideas have moved into activity theory or cultural-historical psychology, Dilthey's ideas have influenced hermeneutic, phenomenological and existential thinkers. Admittedly, one should not overemphasize commonalities where differences exist: Marx might have had a hard time with Camus's (1955) idea that the only meaningful philosophical problem is answering the question of whether life is worth living or not and whether one should commit suicide. However, Dilthey could not envision what it means to live a life of poverty under the reality of extreme inequality. Yet, the tensions between these two traditions have enabled a dialectic for the possibility of theory development (Teo, 2001).

Holzkamp made a return to *Lebensphilosophie*, which in traditional Marxist thinking was considered bourgeois. Yet, I suggest that despite including concepts such as *Befindlichkeit* his concept of subjectivity remained part of a *Bewußtseinsphilosophie* that was not in contradiction to a Marxist approach, but part of it. The notion of the *conduct of life*, as Holzkamp pointed out, has a tradition in sociological discourses, but is equally embedded in a philosophy of life. The concept of a conduct of life is important to psychology because it connects psychologists to what should be central in the subject matter of psychology: subjectivity as it is lived and experienced in concrete circumstances.

Reflexivity and Human Kinds

Subjectivity and the concepts and actions that try to grasp it have a temporality, culture and society. Danziger (1997) demonstrated that psychological concepts have a history and that they are constructed for social purposes. Hacking (1994) identified *looping effects* between subjects and concepts, meaning that people begin to understand themselves through those psychological concepts, which in turn then reinforce the study of those categories through scientists. Martin and Sugarman (2009) summarized the literature in arguing that psychological concepts are socially constituted and value-laden, and point to the reactivity between concepts and subjects. As a critical psychologist one needs to add that this reactivity should be understood against the background of control, surveillance and power.

The reality of the history of concepts requires *reflexivity* on concepts that are used in psychological research, including in critical psychology (for the revival of reflexivity see, e.g., Finlay, 2002; Gao, 2012). Even if one argues that the concepts developed in natural-historical reconstructions may have a basis in representing a natural psychological world, it is also obvious that most of the concepts developed on a higher-order level do reflect particular traditions in psychology. Uniquely German, American or Danish psychological concepts, whether successful or not in a process of globalization, are sources *and* limits of understanding. Holzkamp (2013) talked about the *worldlessness* in traditional psychology and argued that it was a result of the designs used in mainstream research as well as in alternative approaches. But including the world in psychological research also means contextualizing one's own approach in a process of reflexivity as embedded in a particular world, as culturally and historically contingent.

This critique has been developed in postcolonial theory, indigenous psychology and social epistemology. Such approaches help us to understand in which ways the "conduct of everyday life" and the concepts that surround it require critical reflection as well. Indeed, as both Holzkamp and Danziger understood, psychological concepts not only describe forms of experiences, they also prescribe what we experience and, after a process of reflexivity, they allow us to conceive the limitations of our experiences when we engage with experiences from other critical programs, times or cultures. In a now widely used example, Danziger (1997) reported how teaching a course in Indonesia led him to challenge his European categories and to the realization of the incommensurability of Western and Indonesian psychology, which is based on Hindu and Javanese traditions.

In his book entitled *Provincializing Europe*, the Indian postcolonial historian Chakrabarty (2000) challenged the assumption that European history is world history, but also discussed the difficulty that a postcolonial scholar writing a non-European history was always required to refer to the center (Europe) but not vice versa. Although in psychology the situation is different, the reality is that European and especially American psychology are still dominant and require provincializing as well. Holzkamp understood that American psychology reflects American being, but at the same time, as I have argued regarding the character of German critical psychology (Teo, 2013), indigenousness applies to German critical psychology as well. Thus, reflexivity becomes an important aspect of critical work.

Holzkamp (2013) realized that the concept of the conduct of life is significant for a theory of subjectivity. He positioned *social structure* on one side, aware of the complexities of this concept, and the *conduct of everyday life* on the other, with "meaning structures" and "reason discourses" as mediating between the two. The concept of subjective reasons refers to the actions of persons and to the idea that actions, for which one does not have reasons, simply do not exist (or are not actions). I suggest that this argument, or laying out the problem in this way, is indebted too much to a philosophy of consciousness.

Holzkamp (2013) did not believe that sociological theories deal adequately with the concept of the conduct of everyday life because "subjective reasons" are not systematically investigated. This may be true but "subjective reasons" are not final in mediating between society and the person. The concept of "subjective reasons" is focused on the mind (as is, to a degree, the notion of concepts) and perhaps it is not *consciousness* or *subjective reasons* but the *body* that is central in mediating between society and the individual. The concepts of habitus, performativity and privilege make this point (see below).

Social epistemologies that demand reflexivity can be traced back to Marx but have been extended to many other social categories such as gender, ethnicity, "race," sexual preference, culture, disability and so on. Social epistemologies argue that social characteristics influence research in not only the questions but also the methods, interpretations and applications. Social characteristics influence how we do research and what terms we prefer. It is not surprising that a lesbian developed a theory of gender performance (Butler, 1989), critical disability studies were advanced by people with disabilities (Linton, 1998) and Holzkamp did not focus on the body or privilege. Social epistemologies are important because they do not apply to everyday but to academic life. Indeed, how is academic life conducted? How does the conduct of everyday academic life influence research? How does the conduct of marginal life influence theoretical orientations and research programs? The answers lead to the conclusion that subjectivity is historically, socially, culturally and indigenously embedded.

The mainstream is to a certain degree open to hearing about this issue. Arnett (2008) published in the *American Psychologist* an article with the title "Why American psychology needs to become less American," in which he pointed to the indigenous character of American psychology. Henrich, Heine and Norenzayan (2010) published an article on "The weirdest people in the world?" in the journal *Behavioral and Brain Sciences*. By "weird" the authors refer to people from Western, educated, industrialized, rich and democratic (WEIRD) societies, "more specifically American undergraduates who form the bulk of the database in the experimental branches of psychology, cognitive science, and economics, as well as allied fields" (p. 61). Such reflections show that mainstream American psychology is also a local psychology.

The point about social epistemologies is not only about sampling problems but about identifying how much an indigenous perspective guided Holzkamp's ideas as well as other studies on the conduct of everyday life. Globalization has enabled us to encounter traditions from other contexts, including China, India, the Philippines, Africa, Latin America and so on, where the majority of the world lives and where several indigenous psychologies have been developed. From the perspective of the *Other* from the periphery the conceptual network offered in the study of the conduct of everyday life does not include a study of White, or European, German or Danish *habitus*, *performativity* or *privilege*. From a critical perspective outside Europe or North America, privilege could be a much more important concept than *subjective reasons* (Martin-Baro, 1994).

Habitus and Performativity

I do not suggest the need to throw out consciousness or praxis philosophy but rather the need to complement it. Critical thought has provided psychology with concepts, which effectively mediate between social structure and the individual's conduct of everyday life, and which are indebted to a philosophy of embodiment. The concepts are significant because humans live their lives though their bodies as much as they do through their minds. Phenomenologists had an understanding of the significance of the body (e.g., Merleau-Ponty, 1945/1962), but most phenomenological treatments of the topic did not include a critical societal perspective (which is afforded by the concept of habitus, the feminist theory of performativity – in general, by feminist philosophers of the body – and by the concept of privilege). Society produces forms of subjectivity that are based on habitus, performativity and privilege that need to be accounted for.

Holzkamp (2013) envisioned a generalized universal human being when he argued that "the concept of 'subjective reasons for action' is … a universal characteristic of interaction between human beings" (p. 294), implying that actions for which one does not have reasons do not exist. I suggest that we perform actions of class, gender and privilege for which we may not have reasons. We are just in the habit of doing so and we may not be aware of our reasons. Reasons come into play once an *Other* engages us in a dialogue, or once we encounter radically different experiences that make us aware of our own habits.

For example, I may be using a certain amount of water per day without being aware that this is an act of privilege. This act may be part of my subjectivity but becomes a problem only when this privilege is pointed out to me or when I no longer have access to this privilege. Even labeling it as privilege may not occur to me unless I engage in a process of critical reflexivity. Nevertheless, the fact that I embody this privilege comes before any attempt to provide reasons, dialogues or reflexivity. This also means that the universal human being needs to be contextualized from the perspective of the marginalized *Other*. Moreover, it opens the study of the conduct of life to additional critical analyses of embodiment.

For the purpose of this argument, I would like to suggest embodied exemplars that mediate between social structure and the conduct of personal life without a recourse to reasons. Bourdieu (1979/1984) developed the concept of *habitus* to show that the conduct of everyday life may be based on constructing or appropriating embodied distinctions. The mediator between social structure and individuality is not a reason discourse but rather one's habitus. The French upper classes of the 1960s and 1970s did not solely rely on financial but also on cultural capital. For example, it was not accidental that "higher teachers" prided themselves for *not* watching television, which was perceived as a mode of entertainment for the masses. Going to operas, exhibitions, gala nights and galleries was also performed to demonstrate and experience membership in high society. In the conduct of everyday life embodied assumptions are made, for example, in that although visiting a museum is not the exclusive privilege of the educated classes, museums should be designed and organized for the educated or upper classes. A theory of power that focuses on cultural capital and habitus is intrinsically psychological.

Bourdieu originally related the concept of habitus to the conduct of life of the upper classes. Habitus is embodied class and not necessarily cognitive, or part of consciousness, or part of reason discourses. Habitus is not only a sociological but also a psychological category. Indeed, *habit* has a long tradition in psychology: William James (1890/1983) dedicated a whole chapter in his *Principles of Psychology* to the nature of habit. Habit for James was "the enormous fly-wheel of society, its most precious conservative agent. It alone keeps us within the bounds of ordinance, and saves the children of fortune from the envious uprisings of the poor" (p. 125). For James habit was something embodied (although he does not use this term), something physiological. He suggested that humans should make the nervous system their ally by making useful actions automatic and habitual as early as possible (ibid., p. 126). Of course, James did not ask what *useful* in a particular society meant and therefore James, in contrast to Bourdieu, lacked the critical dimension, meaning an analysis of power and the possibility of resistance. Although a critical concept of habit or habitus should not rely on James, such a concept can mediate between social structure and subjectivity and thus is a candidate for the analysis of the conduct of everyday life.

Bourdieu (1984/1988) later applied the concept of habitus to the *homo academicus* that he described as "objectively orchestrated dispositions" (p. 149), forms of professorial practices that can be explained by neither a subjective nor an objective teleology about the role of academia. Psychologists realized and emphasized that the concept of habitus not only allowed for the sociological study of the body and the socially structured body, but also for socialized subjectivity (Stam, 2009). Drawing on Bourdieu and Wacquant, Lizardo (2009) conceptualized socialization as practical and embodied, as motor-schematic mirroring (referring to the overstretched notion of mirror-neurons), as mimetic apprenticeship and as cross-modal mapping. The point here is not to show what one can do with the concept of habitus but rather to suggest that an embodied concept such as habitus can mediate between society and the subject, and thus overcome the division between the collective and the individual (Roth, 2014). "I" display a habitus in the conduct of "my" middle-class Western life and a psychological study should describe and analyze this habitus.

Butler's (1989, 1993) theory on the performance of gender is as much a psychological as it is a sociological, cultural, feminist, queer or ethical theory; it is transdisciplinary and based on situated knowledge. Butler's (1989) main argument regarding the performance of gender in everyday life is that neither nature nor nurture leads to gender but corporeal performances do. Drawing on Freud, Foucault and Lacan, she argues that the performance is not about the internalization or inscription of gender but rather about the active embodiment of gender. She suggests that gender is neither an illusion nor an ideology but rather something that is constantly produced and performed through bodies and language: "Such acts, gestures, enactments, generally construed, are performative in the sense that the essence of identity that they otherwise purport to express are fabrications manufactured and sustained through corporal signs and other discursive means" (p. 136). Performance means that the gendered body has no ontological status outside of the acts that constitute its reality. In the everyday conduct of life gender is performed, as are other identities, such as what it means to be Canadian, German or Danish. "I" perform my gender as I perform other identities in the conduct of my life, and a psychology of the subject needs to study that reality.

Rather than reducing subjectivity to the mind, Holzkamp's critical psychology needs more of the world, including critical theories that have emerged around the world. Butler allows us to think about the conduct of life as embodied practices, where subjective reasons for performances may be secondary. My request for reflexivity in concept construction is equally rooted in consciousness philosophy. Perhaps reflexivity is less important than *doing* and *embodying* things differently. Indeed, Butler understood that, and her theory of performance allows for acts of subversion and resistance. We can imagine how performative subversions regarding gender might look and we have seen them (e.g., challenging gender binaries). Butler's theory of gender performance is a critical theory of power and can easily be extended to other social categories.

For example, punctuality may play a role in the conduct of everyday life. But punctuality is not only a cultural value but partakes in the *subjectification* of individuals. The importance of punctuality reflects power that may not oppress insiders (from the perspective of the subject), but it may reflect power that constructs or constitutes identity, even a positive identity. The subject might either provide a variety of reasons for the importance of punctuality or just show embodied practices of punctuality without reasons. The point is that punctuality as part of everyday life may become a signifier, for instance, for modern Western performativity, as soon as the "*Other*" does not show the same appreciation for punctuality. The value-laden description "they are always late" makes sense only in a culture of punctuality. In the end, the performativity of *being late* in a culture of punctuality can be understood as a form of resistance.

Punctuality appears a trivial example, but there are many ways in which national or cultural performativity is established regarding the *Other* and in which dominance is maintained and reproduced in the conduct of everyday life. Insights into this may not be easily accessible to the insider and there might even be a denial in accepting notions of Western performativity. My own conduct of life can be a symbol for "civilized oppression" (see Fine, 2006), but "for me" it may be difficult to understand in which ways my own life has become a life of privilege and how my habits, presence and body contribute to oppression even if my words and my reasons may intend the opposite. I may not be privileged without reasons but privileged through my embodied practices.

Privilege

Performativity leads me to the study of privilege, which adds explicitly the concept of power to performativity. For instance, Whiteness studies have challenged established race relations in many countries. In the United States (and other countries) the law afforded holders of whiteness privileges and benefits. As Harris (1993) expressed it so aptly for the American legal system: "Whiteness as the embodiment of white privilege transcended mere belief or preference; it became usable property, the subject of the law's regard and protection. In this respect whiteness, as an active property, has been used and enjoyed" (p. 1734). The individual benefiting from whiteness does not need to engage in consciousness, reasons or discourses in order to enjoy privileges that are part of his or her embodied subjectivity.

Privilege often comes with a refusal to understand or to acknowledge how privileged people are involved in relations of privilege, domination and subordination (Cooks & Simpson, 2007). When studying the conduct of everyday life psychologists need to include the perspective of the *Other* as well as the privilege of the researcher, the habitus of privilege and the performativity of privilege. The observation, analysis and a possible critical dialogue between researcher and the *Other* would open studies on the conduct of everyday life to such new perspectives. The *Other* may help in provincializing psychology, including critical psychology, and may aid in provincializing the conduct of everyday life in rich countries. Moreover, the research situation itself is a context of privilege in which the researcher expresses his or her privilege.

Privilege applies not only to outside of society (Western privilege against the rest of the world) but also to within a society such as Germany or the United States. Indeed, debates on privilege emerged from discussions about male privilege in feminist discourses (McIntosh, 1988/2014). In many Western nations privilege is a significant dimension of interaction, social life and the conduct of everyday life. Male privilege and white privilege are "unconscious," as McIntosh (ibid.) argues, but *unconscious* is less precise than saying that we are often not aware of our privileges and that we even may be in denial (using psychoanalytic terminology). "Whites" think that their lives are neutral, normal and average (ibid., p. 17), but more importantly for the purpose of this argument, in the West and among the educated middle class we, whether White or not, conduct our lives as if they were neutral, normal and average. Privilege is not restricted to geographical, ethnic, gender or class advantages, but also divides people based on ability, nationality, religion, sexual orientation and so on. McIntosh asks whether dominance is not a better concept than privilege when referring to "unearned power conferred systematically" (ibid., p. 23). Yet, the subject might not be aware that he/she benefits because of the color of his/her skin and rather attributes it to achievements. In the conduct of my everyday life "I" live my privileges sometimes with and sometimes without reasons.

Privilege not only mediates between structure and the conduct of life but it also feeds back to theory development and the social sciences. Following Chakrabarty (2000) one can apply this argument to critical psychology, which is also based on Western privilege when it assumes that it need not address psychologies from India (Sinha, 1986), the Philippines (Enriquez, 1992), Latin America (Martin-Baro, 1994) or Africa (Hook, 2004). In contrast, I suggest that rather than viewing critical psychology as a closed system, it must be seen as an open program that may include ideas from the margins as well as from other centers. Critical psychology needs to be able to account for the subjectivity of the *Other*, a transgendered person, a person with disability and a marginalized person who experiences racism on a daily basis. It needs to include psychologies "from below" (see also Harding, 2008).

A theory of the conduct of everyday life needs to start with "ourselves" as academics with certain social characteristics that are often intersectionalized (see also Kendall, 2013). Such a theory begins not only with our theories and methods but with the concepts, traditions and the horizons that we use. It should begin with an analysis of our own habitus, performativity and privilege as we live our daily lives. But even if we need to begin with our own embodied practices and subjective reasons that we express linguistically, our theorizing cannot end with such considerations because our privileges can be ascertained only in living as the marginalized *Other* or in dialogue with the *Other* – who lacks the same privileges and can point to our privileges and advantages of which we may not be aware (see conscientization, Freire, 1997). Such an act is not a gesture of guilt but a sign of awareness and justice (see also Kendall, 2013, p. 67). Whereas reflexivity is linguistic and the dialogical is discursive, the conduct of life includes habits, performances and privileges that are not necessarily linguistic or discursive or practical in a traditional sense. Critical psychology needs to pay attention to such constituents of the conduct of everyday life.

Beyond the Subject

Holzkamp (2013) focused on the subject's reasons as the *via regia* to subjectivity. This theoretical move is indebted to a consciousness as well as to a subject philosophy that takes the reasoning subject as its final psychological entity. But if we move beyond reason and include embodiment, then the subject as the object of psychology relies neither on the mind nor on subject philosophy. It can include the notion of a relational constitution of the subject (Gergen, 2009; Levinas, 1961/1969). Although Holzkamp (2013) acknowledges the importance of relations, as do hermeneutic philosophers such as Gadamer (1960/1997), he does not consider a relational constitution of the subject matter of psychology.

A critical theory of the dialogue (Freire, 1997), invoked in relational practices of reflexivity, provides resistance because the *word* does not belong to the subject but to the interaction between a subject and the *Other*. For Freire, dialogue involves changing the world, but also love for the world, humility and hope. Dialogue sets the conditions for the possibility to transcend social structures and conducts of everyday life. At the same time dialogue has its own limitations, as does the philosophy of consciousness. This becomes evident in research on children (Chimirri, 2014) and on the marginalized who do not use *words*, but also with regard to self-righteous defenders of the status quo. Embodied forms of conducting one's life, including living one's privileges, can be challenged in critical dialogue but this does not mean that such privileges will be changed. Beyond dialogue alternative forms of embodiment (or an alternative habitus) may allow for critique and resistance in local contexts: for instance, when a man dresses as a woman during academic lectures while talking about assholism (Nunberg, 2012) as a personality trait.

In recent years there has been a debate about the consequences of inequality on the health and well-being of individuals (Prilleltensky, 2012; Wilkinson & Pickett, 2009). Epidemiological studies have shown that income inequality itself (and not just poverty) has an enormous negative effect on the psychosocial well-being of humans, ranging from mental illness to drug addictions, teenage pregnancies, higher rates of mortality and homicide (Sheivari, 2014). But the problem of understanding how a social structure such as income inequality produces such outcomes still remains. Authors have offered a psychosocial explanation that focuses on psychosocial mediators (e.g., trust, friendship), or a neo-material explanation that emphasizes a lack of infrastructure and other resources. The argument here is that to meaning structures and subjective reasons we need to add embodied practices of inequality that contribute to the negative outcomes in everyday life. Embodied practices of everyday life are class-based, gendered, racialized and inequality-based, and an awareness of such concepts and resisting their enactment may allow for a broader critical horizon on the topic of the conduct of everyday life.

References

Arnett, J. J. (2008). The neglected 95%: Why American psychology needs to become less American. *American Psychologist, 63*(7), 602–614.

Boltanski, L. (2012). *Love and justice as competences: Three essays on sociology of action.* Cambridge: Polity.

Bourdieu, P. (1984). *Distinction: A social critique of the judgement of taste.* London: Routledge & Kegan Paul. (Original work published 1979)

Bourdieu, P. (1988). *Homo academicus* (P. Collier, Trans.). Stanford, CA: Stanford University Press. (Original work published 1984)
Butler, J. (1989). *Gender trouble: Feminism and the subversion of identity*. New York: Routledge.
Butler, J. (1993). *Bodies that matter: On the discursive limits of "sex."* New York: Routledge.
Camus, A. (1955). *The myth of Sisyphus, and other essays*. New York: Vintage Books.
Chakrabarty, D. (2000). *Provincializing Europe: Postcolonial thought and historical difference*. Princeton, NJ: Princeton University Press.
Chimirri, N. A. (2014). *Investigating media artifacts with children: Conceptualizing a collaborative exploration of the sociomaterial conduct of everyday life*. Unpublished doctoral dissertation, Roskilde University, Denmark.
Cooks, L. M. & Simpson, J. S. (Eds.). (2007). *Whiteness, pedagogy, performance: Dis/placing race*. Lanham, MD: Lexington.
Danziger, K. (1997). *Naming the mind: How psychology found its language*. London: Sage.
Dilthey, W. (1957). *Die geistige Welt: Einleitung in die Philosophie des Lebens (Gesammelte Schriften V. Band)* [The mental world: Introduction to the philosophy of life (Collected writings, Vol. 5)]. Stuttgart: Teubner.
Enriquez, V. G. (1992). *From colonial to liberation psychology: The Philippine experience*. Diliman, Quezon City: University of the Philippines Press.
Fine, M. (2006). Bearing witness: Methods for researching oppression and resistance – A textbook for critical research. *Social Justice Research*, *19*(1), 83–108.
Finlay, L. (2002). "Outing" the researcher: The provenance, process, and practice of reflexivity. *Qualitative Health Research*, *12*(4), 531–545.
Freire, P. (1997). *Pedagogy of the oppressed* (20th anniversary rev. ed.) (M. Bergman Ramos, Trans.). New York: Continuum.
Gadamer, H.-G. (1997). *Truth and method* (J. Weinsheimer & D. G. Marshall, Trans.). New York: Continuum. (Original work published 1960)
Gao, Z. (2012). *Toward a psychological theory for practicing epistemological reflexivity*. Unpublished MA thesis, York University, Toronto.
Gergen, K. J. (2009). *Relational being: Beyond self and community*. New York: Oxford University Press.
Hacking, I. (1994). The looping effects of human kinds. In D. Sperber, D. Premack & A. J. Premack (Ed.), *Causal cognition: A multi-disciplinary approach* (pp. 351–382). Oxford: Clarendon Press.
Harding, S. G. (2008). *Sciences from below: Feminisms, postcolonialities, and modernities*. Durham, NC: Duke University Press.
Hardt, M. & Negri, A. (2009). *Commonwealth*. Cambridge, MA: Belknap Press of Harvard University Press.
Harris, C. I. (1993). Whiteness as property. *Harvard Law Review*, *106*(8), 1707–1791.
Harvey, D. (2005). *A brief history of neoliberalism*. Oxford: Oxford University Press.
Henrich, J., Heine, S. J. & Norenzayan, A. (2010). The weirdest people in the world? *Behavioral and Brain Sciences*, *33*(2–3), 61–83.
Holzkamp, K. (1983). *Grundlegung der Psychologie* [Laying the foundation for psychology]. Frankfurt/M.: Campus.
Holzkamp, K. (1984). Kritische Psychologie und phänomenologische Psychologie: Der Weg der Kritischen Psychologie zur Subjektwissenschaft [Critical psychology and phenomenological psychology: The path of critical psychology toward a science of the subject]. *Forum Kritische Psychologie*, *14*, 5–55.
Holzkamp, K. (2013). Psychology: Social self-understanding on the reasons for action in the conduct of everyday life. In E. Schraube & U. Osterkamp (Eds.), *Psychology from the standpoint*

of the subject: Selected writings of Klaus Holzkamp (pp. 233–351). New York: Palgrave Macmillan.

Hook, D. (Ed.). (2004). *Critical psychology.* Lansdowne: UCT Press.

James, W. (1983). *The principles of psychology.* Cambridge, MA: Harvard University Press. (Original work published 1890)

Kendall, F. E. (2013). *Understanding White privilege: Creating pathways to authentic relationships across race* (2nd ed.). New York: Routledge.

Levinas, E. (1969). *Totality and infinity: An essay on exteriority* (A. Lingis, Trans.). Pittsburgh, PA: Duquesne University Press. (Original work published 1961)

Linton, S. (1998). *Claiming disability: Knowledge and identity.* New York: New York University Press.

Lizardo, O. (2009). Is a "special psychology" of practice possible?: From values and attitudes to embodied dispositions. *Theory & Psychology, 19*(6), 713–727.

Martin, J. & Sugarman, J. (2009). Does interpretation in psychology differ from interpretation in natural science? *Journal for the Theory of Social Behaviour, 39*(1), 19–37.

Martin-Baro, I. (1994). *Writings for a liberation psychology.* Cambridge, MA: Harvard University Press.

Marx, K. & Engels, F. (1958). Die deutsche Ideologie [The German ideology]. In K. Marx & F. Engels (Eds.), *Werke Band 3* [Works: Volume 3] (pp. 9–530). Berlin: Dietz. (Original work published 1932; written 1845–1846)

McIntosh, P. (2014). White privilege and male privilege. In M. S. Kimmel & A. L. Ferber (Eds.), *Privilege: A reader* (3rd ed., pp. 15–27). Boulder, CO: Westview. (Original work published 1988)

Merleau-Ponty, M. (1962). *Phenomenology of perception* (C. Smith, Trans.). London: Routledge & Kegan Paul. (Original work published 1945)

Nunberg, G. (2012). *Ascent of the A-word: Assholism, the first sixty years.* New York: Public Affairs.

Prilleltensky, I. (2012). Wellness as fairness. *American Journal of Community Psychology, 49*(1–2), 1–21.

Roth, W.-M. (2014). Habitus. In T. Teo (Ed.), *Encyclopedia of critical psychology* (pp. 833–838). New York: Springer.

Schraube, E. (2013). First-person perspective and sociomaterial decentering: Studying technology from the standpoint of the subject. *Subjectivity, 6*(1), 12–32.

Sheivari, R. (2014). *The impact of income inequality on psychosocial well-being.* Unpublished MA thesis, York University, Toronto.

Sinha, D. (1986). *Psychology in a Third World country: The Indian experience.* New Delhi: Sage.

Stam, H. J. (2009). Habitus, psychology, and ethnography: Introduction to the special section. *Theory & Psychology, 19*(6), 707–711.

Teo, T. (2001). Karl Marx and Wilhelm Dilthey on the socio-historical conceptualization of the mind. In C. Green, M. Shore & T. Teo (Eds.), *The transformation of psychology: Influences of 19th-century philosophy, technology, and natural science* (pp. 195–218). Washington, DC: American Psychological Association.

Teo, T. (2013). Backlash against American psychology: An indigenous reconstruction of the history of German critical psychology. *History of Psychology, 16*(1), 1–18.

Wilkinson, R. G. & Pickett, K. (2009). *The spirit level: Why more equal societies almost always do better.* London: Allen Lane.

6

THE ORDINARY IN THE EXTRA ORDINARY

Everyday Living Textured by Homelessness

Darrin Hodgetts, Mohi Rua, Pita King and Tiniwai Te Whetu

Much ink has been spilt regarding the meaning of everyday life. The term is often used as a general catchphrase for the ordinary, typical, repetitive, mundane and shared fabric of social life (Hodgetts & Stolte, 2013; Silverstone, 2007). Everyday life encompasses personal actions, shared rituals and the reproduction of sociocultural structures. The everyday constitutes the relational glue that bonds a cluster of evolving and shared domains of life within routines that are often taken-for-granted. It is often conceptualized in terms of routine, flow and the mundane or "ordinary," which is disrupted from time-to-time by extraordinary events (Highmore, 2002; Lefebvre, 1991a). Such disruptions include illnesses, job losses, housing evictions or the death of loved ones. This orientation entrenches stability and certainty as central to our understanding of the everyday. For many people of more modest means this orientation is problematic because their lives are often characterized by disruption and extraordinary events, such as evictions, unemployment, food insecurity and exclusion. Disruption often provides a more accurate normative basis for daily lives that are punctuated from time to time by instances of flow and the ordinary where respite is gained.

Engaging with these extraordinary lives allows us to broaden our engagements with diversity within the quotidian. This chapter considers the significance of a group of homeless Māori men's efforts at gardening, cooking and engaging in traditional Māori material practices that, on Tuesdays and Thursdays, bring moments of flow and routine to their disrupted lives.[1] Our analysis is emplaced within a particularly significant site for everyday life within Māori culture, the *marae*. More broadly, this chapter constitutes an attempt to think through issues central to an engaged and culturally responsive psychology of everyday life. We do this by exploring how engagements in ordinary activities aid a group of older Māori homeless men in responding to extraordinary circumstances.

By way of further conceptual background, everyday life remains a polysemic concept that has been investigated through explorations of boredom, walking, eating and shopping; the use of objects such as food, money and plastic; and the relevance of places such as the shopping mall and home (de Certeau, 1984; Highmore, 2002; Sheringham, 2006). Scholars have considered the wider significance of mundane acts, things and places in reproducing sociocultural patterns of life, including ethnic, class-based and gendered inequalities (Hodgetts & Stolte, 2013). In grappling with the complexities and contractions of the everyday, scholars commonly invoke binarisms, such as the mundane and extraordinary, local (particular) and global (general), flow and disruption, constraint and freedom, structure and agency, personal experience and public discourse, domination (alienation) and resistance (Hodgetts & Stolte, 2013). Polarisation of the ordinary and the extraordinary is problematic because the everyday can be fluid and unpredictable as well as certain and routine. Everyday lives can remain constant, featuring continuity, as well as change and disruption (ibid.).

Following key theorists of the everyday (de Certeau, 1984; Lefebvre, 1991b; Simmel, 1903/1997), it is possible to draw upon these tensions to emphasize a dialectical understanding, which sees the everyday as a social process forged through the general (societal) being reproduced through the particular (local) activities of daily life. As a site of contestation, the everyday is woven out of both structure and agency, and conformity and creativity. Taking a similar orientation, Simmel (1903/1997) focused on incidental events or accumulated moments that make up everyday life in order to understand the broader patterning of social life. According to this approach, the specific resembles the general, but is not reducible to it (de Certeau, 1984). Simmel extracted general arguments out of detailed considerations of specific events such as dinner with friends, and studied these as situations indicative of city life. His work typifies attempts to bridge the gap between philosophical abstractions and detailed empirical engagements with actual everyday lives that are typically written out of history (Highmore, 2002; Sheringham, 2006). The everyday is approached as both a medium in which people are immersed and an abstract theoretical category.

For Māori homeless men participating in this research, distinctions between the ordinary and extraordinary, flow and disruption are particularly complex. They live disrupted lives punctuated by moments of the mundane. These men are reduced to seeking engagements in ordinary aspects of life, such as resting, socializing, cooking and eating in the extraordinary circumstances of lives characterized by having no place to call one's own. Their engagements in such ordinary activities are subject to constant threat of disruption by officials seeking to "clean up the streets" (Mitchell & Heynen, 2009). Their street lives are typically an extension of growing up poor, and thereby developing the skills necessary to survive adversity early in life (Hodgetts, Stolte, Nikora & Groot, 2012). Becoming homeless is not an abrupt disruption to normal domiciled life, but the continuation of multi-generational trauma associated with colonization (Groot, Hodgetts, Nikora & Leggat-Cook, 2011; Hodgetts et al., 2011). Structural disruptions to Māori society are played out in these men's contemporary lives. For these men, homelessness is an ordinary extension of growing up indigenous and poor in a colonial society. As indigenous people, Māori are much more likely to be homeless than members of the settler society due to such colonial practices of dislocation, land confiscations and structural violence (Groot et al., 2011). Our participants face challenges in retaining a strong sense of self and place whilst being at threat of losing themselves to the streets (Snow & Anderson, 1987). We document how affirmation of their cultural identities as Māori, claims to belonging and engagements in ordinary cultural practices, comprise common responses to histories of oppression that allow these men to hold on to their humanity and survive street life (Groot et al., 2011).

Scholarship on extraordinary circumstances in the everyday (Baumel, 1995; Davidson, 1984; Des Pres, 1977; Fitzpatrick, 1999; Kelly, 2008; Martin-Baro, 1994; Shokeid, 1992) provides one starting point for our exploration of how Māori homeless men, leading extraordinary lives, periodically engage in culturally patterned normality at a marae on Tuesdays and Thursdays. Following Kelly (2008) we propose that to understand how people survive adversity we need to study the ordinary as well as the extraordinary in their lives. However, maintaining more of a dichotomy between ordinary and extraordinary, Fitzpatrick (1999) introduces the idea of *extraordinary everydayness* to inform an analysis of the implications of broader structural shifts in society for the conduct of daily life in the 1930s Soviet Union. Such scholarship reveals that, when faced with extraordinary circumstances (e.g., life under Stalinism or in a death camp) people seek the ordinary and in doing so embrace their group heritage by engaging in culturally patterned practices. As we will show, personal connections and the preservation of reciprocity, loyalty, solidarity and sharing buffer such people against adversity (Davidson, 1984; Luchterhand, 1967).

Conduct of the Present Study

This research was initiated through an ongoing research collaboration with the Auckland City Mission and was conducted at the Ngāti Whātua (Māori tribal group indigenous to central Auckland) Orakei Marae. Fieldwork involved weekly visits to the Marae garden between October 2012 and April 2013, which allowed us to get to know the participants and contribute to gardening and related activities at the marae. After each site visit, we completed field diary entries on our observations and conversations with participants and discussed these with each other. Photography provided a means of documenting spaces, practices, relationships and events at the garden. We engaged in a range of conversations with participants and conducted audio-recorded interviews with eight people from three distinct groups: (1) two representatives from Ngāti Whātua who had established the garden and who garden with the men on a daily basis; (2) one representative of the Auckland City Mission who was involved in the garden since its inception; (3) five homeless men ranging in age from 54 to 69 years. All were Māori from outside the Auckland region and were kaumatua.[2] Recorded interviews were conducted using a mix of Māori and English language, were conversational in style and were conducted after we had

FIGURE 6.1 Research in action depicting Tiniwai (researcher) and Tuku (participant).

been participating at the garden for 4 months and had built up meaningful relationships with the participants. Our intent was to allow participants to contribute to the topics of discussion and lead us into important areas of interest to them.

We conducted this research in a manner that respected and contributed positively to the mauri[3] of the research site by observing traditional practices of engagement between men. We embraced the ethnographic turn in social research and developments in indigenous psychologies that advocate for the use of case-based methods characterized by closer, more engaged and reciprocal relationships between researchers and participants (Hodgetts, Chamberlain, Tankel & Groot, 2013; Hodgetts & Stolte, 2013). Figure 6.1 depicts our research in action and Māori men of a similar age caring for each other and their respective whakapapa.[4] In such engagements, Māori men speak in sensitive tones with one another and observe patient turn-taking. Figure 6.1 also exemplifies how our culturally patterned approach to this research was focused on spending time with and building relationships with these men, and treating the research as a secondary activity (Hodgetts et al., 2013).

Research in psychology often pays scant regard to relationships between researchers and participants. Psychologists tend to be more concerned with getting the right number of interviews conducted, scales filled out and observation sheets completed. Psychologists often conduct research in socially incompetent ways when working in real-world settings. Our disciplinary training in research often leads to "drive-by" research whereby we swoop into people's lives, "grab" information and escape it.

In the process, psychologists often disrupt the flow of participant's daily lives and offer them little in return. Central to our approach in this research was an effort to minimize such disruptions to participants' everyday lives. We drew scantily on our training as researchers in psychology and relied more on our personal and cultural skills as Māori men. We had all learned how to engage respectfully with older Māori men from childhood and knew not to pressure these men for recorded interviews. We spent every Thursday for 7 months with these men in the garden working until they were ready, in the 4th month, to be recorded. We (Darrin, Mohi and Pita) were also aware of our status as middle-aged to younger men and that we needed to engage with these older men as kaumatua (eldery Māori man) from our subordinate cultural positioning. The interviews were also made possible by Tiniwai's status as a kaumatua of some note in his own iwi (tribe). To accompany such a kaumatua in a marae setting is to be seen to be acting under his stewardship, which made this research project possible.

Conceptually, our analysis involved extracting general arguments out of detailed considerations of specific events, such as lunchtime at the garden (de Certeau, 1984; Simmel, 1903/1997). Following Lefebvre (1991a, 1991b), we treat daily emplaced practices in the garden as the starting point for social analysis. Our engagements with particular practices, material things and the Marae garden space provided a basis for developing a theoretically informed interpretation from the bottom up. This involved documenting how our participants respond to adversity through small acts of participation and human connection associated with being Māori, growing food, cooking, conversing and reminiscing. Reflecting the centrality of Māori culture to the garden and participants' ways of being, our analysis also exemplifies the importance of psychologists drawing upon cultural concepts germane to participant groups in order to extend understandings of the everyday lives of these groups (cf. Schraube & Osterkamp, 2013). Using Māori cultural concepts as central conceptual elements in our research contributes to an interpretation more relevant to our participants and their sense of self, place in the world and everyday lives.

The Marae as Space for Care within a Landscape of Despair

Different locales of everyday life can both hurt and heal people (Stolte & Hodgetts, 2015). The concept of *landscapes of despair* can be used to refer to homeless people's use of extraordinary spaces such as streets, doorways and motorway over-bridges to create an urban landscape of everyday life that is associated with disruption, stress, despair and illness. In contrast, the marae offers a more ordinary *space for care*,[5] which is characterized by inclusion, respite, hope and health. Our research documents how these Māori homeless men, Ngāti Whātua and the Auckland City Mission work together to create a *space of care* by embracing Māori traditions and practices that are central to these men's ways of being. These efforts need to be understood against a historical background of disruptive colonial occupation of the area, and

Māori resistance and efforts to reinstate normality by keeping the culture and links between Māori people and this place alive.

The Orakei marae garden in Central Auckland is a nationally significant site for Māori resistance to colonialism and reconciliation. It has been a site of contestation from the initial European occupation of Auckland in the 1800s. In 1873 the Crown government began a systematic process of alienating Ngāti Whātua from their lands using the Native Lands Act. By the 1950s, Ngāti Whātua was eventually evicted from their remaining lands. The efforts of Ngāti Whātua to regain this land culminated in the formation of the Orakei Māori Action Committee made up of hapū (tribal) members. This group and their supporters peacefully occupied the site for 507 days, until they were forcefully removed in 1978 by hundreds of police officers and soldiers. Some 222 people were arrested for trespassing on "Crown land." As a result of the Waitangi Tribunal commission of enquiry, in 1991 considerable tracts of land (including the Marae site) were returned to Ngāti Whātua after over 150 years of illegal occupation by the settler society. Subsequently, Ngāti Whātua have worked to reconstruct a marae on this site.

Marae have always functioned for Māori as key sites for everyday activities and as repositories within which people can meet, greet, eat, conduct community business, realize their cultural heritage and express collective rights (Rangihau, 1992; Walker, 1992): For Māori, the marae is also "a place that pulsates with the mauri, the essential spirit or metaphysical sense of being part of the community and of the land" (Te Awekōtuku, 1996, p. 35). In recounting the establishment of the garden for homeless people as part of Orakei marae, a Ngāti Whātua representative invokes aspects of his tribal history and associated colonial disruptions. A key issue raised in this account is how Ngāti Whātua feel an affinity with homeless Māori, given their own history of disruption and displacement:

> One of our leaders went to one of those sleep-over nights teaching people about homelessness with the Auckland City Mission. And he could identify with the homeless people and sort of started a conversation about how we could help ... I was asked if I could help run a garden to aid the city mission. And they came every Tuesday and Thursday and they just wanted to come back and do it every week ... They are Māori and this is a marae and they have the reo ... [the Māori language]. They came and they just felt at home. And they had a place to come to for their wairua [spirit or human essence] and to just be themselves ... You know, as a people we could identify with them because we were homeless in our own land. You know, we had nothing left ... You know, we almost got wiped out. So that was our aroha [love and compassion] to them. We couldn't have it that we owned all of this and we left them over there. They have their own home places that they've moved away from, but we were trying to give them a place where they felt comfortable ... And that was generated from our tipuna [ancestors] ... We are giving respect to our ancestors by helping other people. The manaakitanga [care] that we got

from our ancestors we have to carry that on … They're in town [landscape of despair], but up here they've got the peacefulness [space for care]. They're Māori so they know this. They're part of our reconciliation of our land.

This extract exemplifies how displacement, disruption and crises can spark humane reactions on the part of the oppressed (cf. Martin-Baro, 1994), which constitute a key element of the efforts of local people to retain their own culturally patterned ordinariness. Ngāti Whātua learned what it is like to be homeless during their turbulent colonial history and the continued occupation by the settler society in the greater Auckland region. Regardless, they are determined to maintain marae life and manaaki or host and care for visitors in this place.

It is important to see the marae in the context of the broader chaotic landscape of these men's extraordinary lives in Auckland. We know from work on daily disruption and transgression that homeless people's rights to the city and daily activities are regularly ruptured and denied (Mitchell & Heynen, 2009). The marae gives these men somewhere to come and go from, to belong and to realise traditional Māori protocols and ways of being. In contrasting the broader landscape of despair (city) and space for care (marae), Rātā (a homeless participant) reveals a key tension across these sites: "At the marae we have our [Māori] rules. Outside of here in Auckland are other people's [settler society] rules." Māori protocols implicit for the marae are deeply felt by our participants. These men leave the extraordinary world of homelessness and the settler society that textures the broader cityscape for them as a landscape of despair, and re-enter the ordinary Māori world of the marae that they are more in sync with every Tuesday and Thursday. The extraordinary and ordinary materialize for these men as they traverse across these contrasting settings. In the city, like other Māori homeless people they feel deeply out of place and are treated as such through processes of displacement and exclusion (Groot et al., 2011). At the marae, they experience an emplaced and deeply felt reconnection to the Māori world. We observed a transition in self during our travels with participants in a van from the city center to the marae during which their use of English and Māori languages changed:

> The transition of reo across spaces. English used in the city, but as they get in the van to go to the garden and the language slowly changes to te reo [Māori language], and is rumaki [fully immersed] by the time they are working in the garden.
>
> (Fieldnotes, Pita, February 21, 2012)

As the Auckland City Mission explains:

> The guys are fluent te reo [Māori language] speakers. You can come onto the gardens sometimes … and you won't hear much English … That's being washed with the aroha [love, nurturing] and the comfortableness of a marae setting, which is healing, it's soothing, it's strengthening … That whole way of

being is a remembering from childhood … People come back, there's a calmness of self of spirit … It's replaced the feelings and emotions that you might have coming out, because last night was a crappy night, I was hungry and the cops moved me on or even if nothing like that happened and it was just like, you know, "here I am again under a bloody bridge" or whatever, you can't say that when you come out here, "here I am again in the garden" it's like "great!"

This transition also reflects how everyday life is often played out across a range of settings that are culturally patterned and which carry particular expectations for human action and engagement. These sites come to form a lifescape of linked, interwoven and contrasted settings across which people go about their everyday existence. As we will show, the marae exists for these men within a patchwork of a distant home, the streets, the mission and other agencies, fringe spaces and the marae. Different locales materialize the ordinary and extraordinary for these men in different moments of their everyday lives. Having the marae to belong to provides our homeless participants with a more stable base for the expression of themselves as Māori people.

By observing cultural protocols for conducting oneself at the marae, and relating to others through a shared indigenous language, these men's heritage is brought to life. They do not just re-enter the Māori world at the marae, but also recreate it through their culturally patterned actions in this space for care. They realize a space for Māori ways of being, which provides respite and certainty in their exhausting and uncertain lives. Although none of our homeless participants are from or have ancestral links to Orakei Marae, these men can still gain a deeply felt sense of belonging and participation in this space. The space is culturally familiar to them:

> On the marae you pick up on the protocol straight away. Like the locals told me about a bit of the history here and "I recognize your protocol". When I got to know and understand the kuia [older female leader] here, we got on with each other which was really good. I knew things that she didn't know and she knew things I didn't know. Was a good combination. Sharing like my iwi [tribal group] and your iwi sharing things, which is a good thing … I think the greatest thing about it is that being Māori, no matter what iwi you're from or hapu [sub-tribal group] at least there's a connection as tangata whenua [people of the land], Māori to Māori.
>
> (Miro)

Enacting heritage and one's knowledge and skills feeds these men's sense of being and allows them to resist losing themselves to the streets (Snow & Anderson, 1987), which is a profound and pervasive danger of homelessness. They feel able to share their knowledge with local Ngāti Whātua people, and are also open to benefiting from the knowledge and hospitality of the local people. These men are more relaxed, familiar and open in this place than they are on the streets. Time at the marae provides a space for building one's strength, contemplating one's situation and considering possibilities for the future:

> The gift of the marae. It's like being at home on the marae, any marae will comfort you and that's like being at home. It's normal. There's no tension. It is being open with each other. It is being like that on the marae. It's the people themselves ... Good for understanding and being yourself ... I get strength in knowing my te reo [Māori language] and in being here ... To me it's very important in keeping and building my inner confidence. Being able to be Māori here is important to my confidence. Know the differences between who I really am or who I am supposed to be in this world of ours. Half the time I am lost [on the streets]. Now, what is my purpose? I can find it here. Just taking the time here to work on it on a day-to-day basis [Figure 6.2] ... I miss the old days where everything was always set out, especially as a child: Māori way of growing up. Always take the lessons from our koroua's [male elders] and kuia's [female elders]. Just the structure in life that's hard to keep going. That's what I notice here is rebuilding that confidence in what you were taught back at home ... And at least we know that we contribute to the whenua [the land] here. And I have faith in this marae and what they are trying to bring back that structure and we contribute to that, you know.
>
> (Miro, 53, Tuhoe)

Participating in ordinary activities, whilst in the marae garden, results in reflection, a traditional sense of being and emotional connections for Miro. His account invokes how the tentacles of this place and time reach back to other places and times, as well as processes of colonial disruption to Māori ways of being and efforts many Māori make to regain traditional life structures. The marae garden manifests as a site where Māori culture is appreciated, preserved and enacted. Being in the marae garden involves reconsidering one's place in the Māori world and what it means to belong somewhere.

Relevant here is the cultivation of self-respect and recognition in that if Māori people care for the marae and garden – as Miro is depicted doing in Figure 6.2 and in his account – they have an opportunity to care for and respect themselves (cf. Moon, 2005). This is significant because in the Māori world everyone and everything, including plants and spaces, are imbued with a mauri (life force or essence). When people engage with a marae garden with good intent they help create a positive mauri for the garden. The importance of reciprocity in these processes emerges in that the men are not simply recipients of charity, but also contribute to broader agendas of care in growing food to feed people who must access a foodbank (cf. Moon, 2005). The mauri of the garden is enhanced in that the men know they are working to the dialectical reproduction of the marae as a space for care for themselves and others.

Briefly, it is crucial to note that a marae is more than simply a static site for everyday events. This place materializes history and culturally patterned relations and ways

FIGURE 6.2   Miro in the marae garden.

of being. Such spaces are anchored in tradition, but are also alive and evolving through interaction and use. In turn, the marae becomes generative of culturally patterned practices, relations and selves. For these men, the marae locates aspects of their "truth of being"; where through spending time, participating and *dwelling* they can realize themselves (Heidegger, 1971). Despite living disrupted lives, these men can achieve some unity between self and the marae space through ordinary everyday activities such as gardening, cooking and culturally patterned interactions. The marae is a place for these men to recognize themselves and to be recognized by others as Māori men with worth. Below, we focus further on gardening and cooking as key practices that texture the marae as a place for Māori homeless men in Auckland to gain respite, engage in the ordinary, re-member who they are, and simply be and belong.

Gardening, Cooking and Having Lunch at the Marae

Our homeless participants went to Orakei Marae to garden, cook, have lunch and engage in spiritual practices, such as karakia.[6] This section focuses on these ordinary practices that texture the marae as a place for Māori homeless men in Auckland to belong. We consider how this particular garden, like other gardens, constitutes a culturally loaded space that is textured by emplaced human actions, cultural practices, identities and relationships (cf. Li, Hodgetts & Ho, 2010). Such gardens weave together nature, thought, memory and daily practice in culturally patterned ways that integrate people, things and places. As an ordinary practice, gardening can provide new growth at the same time as rooting people in the past. We will document how culture and history are literally sown into the ground of the marae garden. Lefebvre's (1991b) work on the dialectics of place informs our exploration of how small emplaced acts or local practices such as gardening, cooking using a purpose-built barbecue and a "boil-up pot" reproduce the marae garden as a space for taha Māori (traditional Māori practices). We also draw on Latour's (2005) account of actor network theory to consider the interwoven nature of the men, their practices, specific objects and the marae space.

Gardening is an everyday activity recognized across cultures for providing a focal point for developing social ties, self-reflection and respite (Li et al., 2010). Gardens provide somewhere to go, to be one's self, to just think (Gross & Lane, 2007). Gardens are not mute backdrops for human action. In everyday life people occupy such spaces as embodied beings whose material practices inflect interests, desires and needs into the physical environment (Li et al., 2010). Gardens say something about the people who create and use them and can become central to re-membering ways of being.[7] Gardening involves reshaping a physical space, turning it into a place that reflects the efforts and culture of gardeners. In addition to the activity and time spent in the garden, the presence of the cultural objects such as deities invokes the spiritual texturing of the marae space (Figure 6.3). Reflecting on the presence of the deity, Rātā notes: "That post shows this is a Māori garden and he is part of us cos we're also helping the plants grow here."

Gardening is an ordinary, unremarkable and generally domiciled activity that in this case is being conducted by men living extraordinary lives. It is an activity with profound implications because heritage is expressed and these men re-embed themselves through things Māori. According to Miro: "It's about tatou, te wairua o te tangata" (spiritual connection of us with other people and this place). For many Māori, a garden is part of a person and the person is part of the garden because gardening reconnects people with those who have passed and been returned to Papatuanuku (earth mother) (Moon, 2005). This link is emphasized by our participants:

> I like gardening. It reminds me of my early days working in the same manner when I was growing up with my koro/tipuna [grandfather/ancestor] ... My contribution is "ki te nakinaki haere" [tilling the soil around the plants] and seeing the growth of all the "hua kai" [food crops], such as riwai [potatoes], kamokamo [type of squash], paukena [pumpkin], kaapeti [cabbage], hopere, rikii [onions], reweti [kale], toomato [tomato], kumara [sweet potato], kai rapeti [lettuce], me nga otaota [weeds].
>
> (Rātā)

Processes of re-membering are manifest in physical efforts to enact one's traditions and shared cultural practices learned as a child. We see "the intervention of tradition as central to processes of remembering and belonging to a place" (Fortier, 1999, p. 42). Creating a garden on Māori land as an adult reproduces aspects of an earlier,

FIGURE 6.3 Deity texturing the garden as a Māori space.

fondly re-membered time and place. The past is brought into the present. This is particularly evident in accounts of having learned about how to behave on the marae from previous generations as children (Rangihau, 1992).

Producing certain food by gardening has been described as traditionally the primary work of Māori (Moon, 2005). Specific types of food are also associated with Māori gardens. For example, watercress and puha (sow thistle) are significant plants that one of our participants went to the trouble of transplanting onto the marae site to transform it into a "truly Māori garden" (Tuku):

> Tuku had dug up some puha from the side of the road and was adding it to his puha patch on sight [sic]. Such food is familiar to Tuku and his re-membering of growing up Māori. He is adding traditional gardening practices on sight and also has a watercress patch that we photographed [Figure 6.4]. Totara picked the watercress plants from Western Springs and transplanted them to a creek on sight. He dug out two areas about two meters square and planted it. The plants have spread down the stream.
>
> (Fieldnotes, Darrin, October 25, 2012)

Engaging in mundane activities such as developing one's watercress patch lends understanding, legacy, custom, acceptance and belonging to participants' work on the marae. Growing traditional plants provides a sense of continuity for our

FIGURE 6.4 Mohi and Tuku working on watercress patch.

participants, which contributes to the cultivation of the marae garden as a space for shared heritage and culturally patterned belonging.

Part of the homeless person's task is to rebuild a sense of place, home and comfort somewhere new. Deaux (2000) termed this process of identity re-situation as "*remooring*" – that is, the ways in which "people connect identity to a system of supports in the new environment" (p. 429). One potent resource in the construction of continuity is to connect the present to the past. To engage in the present in ordinary activities from the past is central to surviving disruption and extraordinary circumstance. For our participants, gardening provides continuity across periods in life. In the process, time and space collapses in that they are doing what they had done in the past with grandparents as part of a hapū (sub-tribal group). As the second Ngāti Whātua representative states:

> The key thing is connection. By being with us it reminds them of whanangatanga [relationships]. You know, working as an iwi [tribe], working as a hapū reminds them of where they're from and what was going on when they were boys. And I hear lots of stories about life down where they are from.

Through engagements in traditional cultural practices and ways of interacting at the marae that are alluded to here, these men work to rejoin a community and their cultural heritage.

The Ordinary in the Extra Ordinary

Retelling the significance of the marae garden invokes a nexus of relationships and meanings that weave people into place and exceeds the physical restraints of time and space. We know from the accounts of death-camp survivors that personal connections can buffer people against adversity and stop a person from giving up on life (Davidson, 1984). Support and cooperation is linked to a sense of common predicament and enhances the chances of not only survival, but also the preservation of humanity through participation in cultural traditions. Central to such efforts is the preservation of culturally patterned relationships through acts of reciprocity, loyalty and sharing (Davidson, 1984; Luchterhand, 1967):

> Most of all it is a communal garden and an opportunity to practice whakawhanaungatanga [the process of establishing relationships] and manaakitanga [hospitality and kindness] ... The most fun thing is being with the others ... that go there the same time on Tuesdays and Thursdays. I like all there is to do with gardening and am comfortable with mates.
>
> (Rātā, 56)

Such extracts reflect the interconnection of these men with each other and this garden space. It speaks to the texturing of the setting through the enactment of friendship and mutual support in a way that affords care and wellness.

For indigenous people dislocated by time and space such familiar practices and associated everyday objects act as conduits for reconnection. Recent research explores issues of authenticity and reconnection for indigenous people through relationships with material objects that contribute to culturally anchored identities (Krmpotich, 2010). As Jones (2010, p. 181) notes: "when we look at how people experience and negotiate authenticity through objects, it is the networks of relationships between people, place and things that appear to be central, not the things themselves." Culturally inflected objects take on mnemonic functions and are used to re-enact and reconsider past and present relationships and shared practices, and facilitate ties with both local people here now and loved ones from the past back home. Processes of connection and belonging anchored through the use of culturally imbued objects and spaces are intensified for these men who have been dislocated (Jones, 2010). We are less interested here in the treasures and rare artifacts explored in previous indigenous research, and are more concerned with the everyday objects, including a barbecue, boil-up pot and particular types of food.

Figure 6.5 depicts the barbecue area that was developed by Ngāti Whātua for the homeless gardeners to engage in ordinary cultural routines surrounding food preparation and consumption. Also depicted is a typical lunch break involving the use of the barbecue and boil-up pot[8] to cook meat and traditional vegetables from the garden (Figure 6.6). It is through the use of the boil-up pot that we witness the timelessness of Māori culture and the men's participation in tradition and the past in the present (cf. Fortier, 1999). The lunch space was created in the garden so that these men could engage in communal eating practices that they are often prevented from engaging in when on the streets. Lunchtime is a particularly significant event for these men who have few other spaces in the broader *landscape of despair* to take the time to cook a meal without threat of disruption in the form of being moved on by security guards. As the second Ngāti Whātua representative comments:

> The BBQ is for them to have a proper feed, you know ... The best part of being up here is their kai [food]. Cooking their feed and sharing their kai ... With them not having hot kai on the streets they look forward to cooking here, meat and veges. They're not disrupted. Sit down and enjoy their kai without getting pushed out.

Māori value communal eating, and the cooking area constitutes the materialization of manaakitanga (practices of hosting and caring for others). Having a space and facilities to take the time to cook and share food in lives characterized by disruption creates a stabilizing event.

Evident here is the dialectical production of a culturally textured space and inhabitants through the mundane everyday practices of preparing and sharing lunch. The barbecue area materializes manaakitanga (care) as central to the living marae and speaks of the men's inclusion in this place. In turn, our participants' use of the barbecue to cook lunch contributes dialectically to the production of the living marae. Figure 6.5 and 6.6 reflects cultural processes that connect people, objects and spaces. Via deceptively simple and often taken-for-granted activities of cooking and observing associated rituals, such as karakia (incantations), the men can further salvage their heritage and selves. We marked lunch as a key event in our fieldnotes on several occasions:

> We broke for lunch. The kai came from the garden and included kumara [sweet potato], and kamokamo [type of squash] and was cooked on the BBQ Rimu had built ... Miro was head chef and had brought a few sausages along ... He was saying that the people from the marae would come along and use the BBQ. He didn't say this in a way that came across as "this is our BBQ", but in more of a way to complement [sic] the facility that had become a socially-shared space for anyone who wanted to come and cook a feed.
> (Fieldnotes, Pita, February 21, 2012)

It is through ritual practices such as cooking traditional dishes, karakia (incantations) and communal eating that Māori men, bodies, pots and places are combined into a cultural milieu. Having grown most of the ingredients for the meal adds depth to these men's bonding through food and the cultivation of a sense of connection with people and place, tradition and culture at lunchtime. This is particularly significant when we realize the broader functions of food. Food is much more than a commodity and is such a human thing. Food is about tradition. Food is a focal point for care and relationships. It is a basis for extending hospitality. Food epitomizes care and connection. Food functions to remind these men of who they are, where they are from and where they belong.

FIGURE 6.5 The barbecue and pot.

FIGURE 6.6 Lunchtime.

The people, objects and space depicted in Figure 6.6 do not simply reflect everyday practices, but, in concert, also create opportunities for these practices (Latour, 2005). At lunchtimes we witnessed how human relations implicate non-human objects and spaces. In this context, mundane cultural objects do not simply reflect social practices, but also create opportunities for cultural practices and identities to be re-enacted. The pot and barbecue call for cultural re-engagement in the form of cooking a communal meal and hosting others. In considering such processes we can transcend the Cartesian dualism that separates mind and body, person and place, people and things. Processes of re-membering and retention of group identities for indigenous people are often associated with the possession of significant artworks and cultural objects such as carvings and cloaks (Krmpotich, 2010). We would argue that such processes also encompass more mundane everyday objects, including the boil-up pot (cf. Latour, 2005). It is through daily activities such as lunch breaks and the use of such mundane objects that these men can realize themselves as interconnected within the Māori world (Heidegger, 1971), which is also part of them, and which they come to know through practical experience and participation (Merleau-Ponty, 1962).

Discussion

For many people, everyday life is characterized by freedom, creativity, inclusion and flow. For others, it is characterized by disruption, prejudice, exploitation and repression. Our research shows that it is fruitful to think in pluralistic terms in order to avoid glossing diversity and inequalities in the everyday (Hodgetts et al., 2010). Literature on experiences of the ordinary during horrific historical events (Baumel, 1995; Davidson, 1984; Des Pres, 1977; Fitzpatrick, 1999; Kelly, 2008) allows us to shed light on the extraordinary as the terrain of everyday life for people facing adversity. In the process, we can see how the extraordinary character of our homeless participants' lives on the streets does not imply the absence of the ordinary. Like other groups facing the extraordinary, our participants' engagements in the ordinary allow them to reconnect to their heritage and culture, and in the process retain their humanity. Ordinary small acts of decency, self-sacrifice, solidarity, teamwork, sharing and mutual care that represent rudimentary humanness are not out of place within their extraordinary situations. Even in extreme and dehumanizing circumstances there is routine, predictability and opportunities for care and self-discovery (Baumel, 1995; Davidson, 1984).

The routine that comes with going to the marae on Tuesdays and Thursdays needs to be seen against the backdrop of a more chaotic existence within which our homeless participants experience constant ruptures and displacement. Seeking routine and normality in cultural connection at the marae garden is central to how these men live through and survive street life. Mundane acts of gardening and cooking anchor these men. But more than this, the garden provides ontological proof of their existence, efforts and value as cultural experts. In many respects, the marae garden takes the men beyond homelessness and street life and back into the Māori world. Our participants present themselves as more than vagrants through participation in Māori cultural practices. The marae garden is both a physical location and an imagined everyday space where these men can put down roots, reflect and make a place for themselves.

Broader lessons for a social psychology of everyday life can be taken from this project. Human beings are culturally situated beings who reproduce their sense of self and place through material practices and ongoing emplaced interactions. A social psychology of everyday life needs to delve into these processes and issues of difference in order to produce knowledge that is relevant to the groups of interest. Embracing difference also enables us to avoid the common practice in psychology of homogenizing human experience to fit with the globally dominant USian approach that seeks universal, rather than situated, knowledge (Hodgetts et al., 2010). Our analysis exemplifies the importance of local cultural concepts for understanding the everyday for indigenous homeless people. Using Māori cultural concepts as conceptual elements in our research contributes to an interpretation more germane to our participants' lived realities and ways of being in the world.

A vibrant and useful social psychology of everyday life of the sort we are seeking works to rehumanize people who are dehumanized on a daily basis. Our approach to this research was informed by ongoing discussions regarding the need for psychology to rediscover human beings and to stop losing sight of them through an over-reliance on quantification or overly technocratic conversation analyses (Hodgetts et al., 2013; Hodgetts & Stolte, 2012). We drew from the ethnographic turn in psychological research and embraced a case-based orientation to the marae garden. This approach is characterized by closer and more engaged relations between researchers and participants than is typically evident in psychological research.[9] Case-based research strategies provide a means of contextualizing social issues in a manner that is recognizable to people affected by these issues (Flyvbjerg, 2001; Hodgetts & Stolte, 2012). Our approach allowed us to learn more about the everyday lives of our participants organically by involving ourselves in mundane activities, such as gardening, sharing lunch and being in a particular place. By sharing these activities and enacting our common interests in Māori culture, we behaved in a respectful manner that met with cultural expectations for reciprocity in research that are particularly prominent for indigenous groups (Hodgetts et al., 2013). This requires a careful balance to avoid appropriation of the indigenous into the Western canon. It also requires us to engage in processes and relationships that lie beyond our formal training in psychology. Hegemonic training in research methods modeled on the physical sciences within psychology often leads us to disrupt the everyday lives of our participants through our research practices. The style of research in which we engaged in our project operates in a more flexible manner where we try harder to fit into everyday events (Hodgetts & Stolte, 2012). Our research approach forces us to operate in more flexible ways methodologically. We do not want methods that rupture flows of events. We want to fit in as much as possible. This means not being hung up on getting the perfect interview or set of quotations. Not everything we need to understand this place and associated practices resides in direct quotations from participants. We learned much more by prioritizing our relationships and by gardening with these men, sharing lunch and being Māori on the marae with them. Approaching the garden project as a culturally patterned case also supported our efforts to promote inclusion and equity in knowledge production, and to embrace an ethics of reciprocity in research.

Notes

1. Māori are the indigenous people of New Zealand.
2. Elderly Māori men who possess a range of Māori cultural knowledge, language and life experience that contributes to whanau (relationships), hapu (sub-tribe) and iwi (tribe) decision-making.
3. Life force created through human interactions.
4. Everyone from their families who came before and will come after them.
5. This concept was developed in recognition of the health-enhancing aspects of particular places that have healing effects.
6. Thanking deities for the food and acknowledging the plants.
7. The concept of re-membering is used to take recollection beyond cognition and to engage with how through material and emplaced actions people recall who they are and can reconnect with their heritage and cultural groups.
8. Such pots are much sought after and are a source of pride and a common conversation piece that invokes humorous exchanges around the intricacies of stews. Typical marae boil-up pots could be five times the size shown in Figure 6.5.
9. Notable exceptions here would include some variants of community, humanistic, critical, liberation and indigenous psychologies that emphasize the importance of meaningful engagements with people. However, such psychologies are often marginalized in the discipline globally and considered "unscientific," as if engaging in meaningful exchanges with research participants is somehow a bad thing.

References

Baumel, J. (1995). Social interaction among Jewish women in crisis during the Holocaust: A case study. *Gender & History*, 7, 64–84.

Davidson, S. (1984). Human reciprocity among the Jewish prisoners in the Nazi concentration camps. In Y. Gutman & A. Saf (Eds.), *The Nazi concentration camps* (pp. 555–572). Jerusalem: International School for Holocaust Studies.

Deaux, K. (2000). Surveying the landscape of immigration. *Journal of Community and Applied Social Psychology*, 10, 421–431.

de Certeau, M. (1984). *The practice of everyday life* (S. Rendall, Trans.). Berkeley, CA: University of California Press.

Des Pres, T. (1977). *The survivor: An anatomy of life in the death camps*. New York: Oxford University Press.

Fitzpatrick, S. (1999). *Everyday Stalinism: Ordinary life in extraordinary times – Soviet Russia in the 1930s*. Oxford: Oxford University Press.

Flyvbjerg, B. (2001). *Making social science matter: Why social inquiry fails and how it can succeed again.* Cambridge: Cambridge University Press.
Fortier, A. (1999). Re-membering places and the performance of belonging(s). *Theory, Culture & Society, 16,* 41–64.
Groot, S., Hodgetts, D., Nikora, L. & Leggat-Cook, C. (2011). A Māori homeless woman. *Ethnography, 12,* 375–397.
Gross, H. & Lane, N. (2007). Landscapes of the lifespan: Exploring accounts of own gardens and gardening. *Journal of Environmental Psychology, 27,* 225.
Heidegger, M. (1971). *Poetry, language, thought.* New York: Harper & Row.
Highmore, B. (2002). *The everyday life reader.* Routledge: London.
Hodgetts, D., Chamberlain, K., Tankel, Y. & Groot, S. (2013). Researching poverty to make a difference: The need for reciprocity and advocacy in community research. *The Australian Community Psychologist, 5,* 46–59.
Hodgetts, D., Drew, N., Sonn, C., Stolte, O., Nikora, L. & Curtis, C. (2010). *Social psychology and everyday life.* Basingstoke: Palgrave Macmillan.
Hodgetts, D. & Stolte, O. (2012). Case-based research in community and social psychology: Introduction to the special issue. *Journal of Community & Applied Social Psychology, 22,* 379–389.
Hodgetts, D. & Stolte, O. (2013). Everyday life. In Teo, T. (Ed.) *Encyclopedia of critical psychology.* New York: Springer.
Hodgetts, D., Stolte, O., Nikora, L. & Groot, S. (2012). Drifting along and dropping into homelessness: A class analysis of responses to homelessness, *Antipode, 44,* 1209–1226.
Hodgetts, D., Stolte, O., Radley, A., Groot, S. Chamberlain, K. & Leggatt-Cook, C. (2011). "Near and far": Social distancing in domiciled characterizations of homeless people. *Urban Studies, 48*(8), 1739–1753.
Jones, S. (2010). Negotiating authentic objects and authentic selves: Beyond the deconstruction of authenticity. *Journal of Material Culture, 15,* 181–203.
Kelly, T. (2008). The attractions of accountancy: Living an ordinary life during the second Palestinian *intifada. Ethnography, 9,* 351–376.
Krmpotich, C. (2010). Remembering and repatriation: The production of kinship, memory and respect. *Journal of Material Culture, 15,* 157–179.
Latour, B. (2005). *Reassembling the social: An introduction to actor-network theory.* New York: Oxford University Press.
Lefebvre, H. (1991a). *Critique of everyday life.* London: Verso.
Lefebvre, H. (1991b). *The production of space.* Oxford: Basil Blackwell.
Li, W., Hodgetts, D. & Ho, E. (2010). Gardens, transitions, and identity reconstruction among older Chinese immigrants to New Zealand. *Journal of Health Psychology, 15,* 786–796.
Luchterhand, E. (1967). Prisoner behaviour and social system in the Nazi camp. *International Journal of Psychiatry, 13,* 245–264.
Martin-Baro, I. (1994). War and mental health (A. Wallace, Trans.). In A. Aron & S. Corne (Eds.), *Writings for a liberation psychology.* Cambridge, MA: Harvard University Press.
Merleau-Ponty, M. (1962). *The phenomenology of perception.* London: Routledge.
Mitchell, D. & Heynen, N. (2009). The geography of survival and the right to the city: Speculations on surveillance, legal innovation, and the criminalization of intervention. *Urban Geographies, 30*(6), 611–632.
Moon, P. (2005). *A Tohunga's natural world: Plants, gardening and food.* Auckland: David Ling.
Rangihau, J. (1992). Being Māori. In M. King (Ed.), *Te Ao Hurihuri: Aspects of Maoritanga* (pp. 183–190). Auckland: Reed.

Schraube, E. & Osterkamp, U. (2013). *Psychology from the standpoint of the subject: Selected writings of Klaus Holzkamp*. Basingstoke: Palgrave Macmillan.
Sheringham, M. (2006). *Everyday life: Theories and practices from surrealism to the present*. Oxford: Oxford University Press.
Shokeid, M. (1992). Exceptional experiences in everyday life. *Cultural Anthropology*, 7, 232–243.
Silverstone, R. (2007). *Media and morality: On the rise of the mediapolis*. London: Wiley.
Simmel, G. (1997). *Simmel on culture* (D. Frisby & M. Featherstone, Eds.). London: Sage. (Original work published 1903)
Snow, D. A. & Anderson, L. (1987). Identity work among the homelessness: The verbal construction and avowal of personal identities. *The American Journal of Sociology*, 92, 1336–1371.
Stolte, O. & Hodgetts, D. (2015). Being healthy in unhealthy places: Health tactics in a homeless lifeworld. *Journal of Health Psychology*, 20(2), 144–153.
Te Awekōtuku, N. (1996). Māori people and culture. In R. Neich, M. Pendergrast, J. Davidson, A. Hakiwai & D. C. Starzecka (Eds.), *Māori art and culture* (pp. 26–49). London: British Museum Press.
Walker, R. (1992). Marae: A place to stand. In M. King (Ed.), *Te Ao Hurihuri: Aspects of Māoritanga* (pp. 15–27). Auckland: Reed.

7
SITUATED INEQUALITY AND THE CONFLICTUALITY OF CHILDREN'S CONDUCT OF LIFE

Charlotte Højholt

Conduct of Everyday Life: Participation in Social Conflicts

This chapter contributes to the discussions about conduct of life with a focus on *conflicts* of everyday living and their relatedness to broader social conflicts. In this way, the chapter touches on discussions about critical and political dimensions of the study of the conduct of everyday life. This provides a focus on the unequal conditions persons live with in relation to dealing with these conflicts.

In this way, the chapter discusses how analyses of people's (in this case children's) conduct of everyday life may point to structural inequalities in a concrete way by addressing the social conflicts with which personal problems are entwined. Dilemmas, contradictions and conflicts of everyday life are interwoven with political conflicts: for example, concerning how the education system should prioritize with regard to working with social problems or working in a more isolated approach for the purpose of obtaining good marks in relation to national tests and global competition. Such conflicts are continually negotiated in the social practice of the school, but participants are positioned differently in relation to these processes.

Even in critical analyses, conditions of everyday life are often conceptualized in *abstract* ways, for instance related to different kinds of deviancies in social background or to unambiguous categorizations and reproduction of social order. This may lead to serious problems for our analytical work. One problem is that the critique may become about abstract factors and we have to make guesses about the meanings they have for those involved, and thus to estimate the meanings from "outside." Another related problem is a kind of displacement of problems – *from* social dilemmas and into different kinds of individual deficiencies.

I will discuss these general dilemmas through concrete examples from children's conduct of everyday life across social contexts, where different parties have different kinds of responsibility and conflicting perspectives on the children. A key point is that the social and political conflicts *about* children lead to personal problems *for* children. In this understanding, the concrete dilemmas of children may teach us something about the social conflicts in and about the institutional arrangements where children live their daily life.

Abstract understandings of human conditions easily point to some kinds of individual deficiency and, as an answer to that, some kind of compensation. In the Danish context, we confront social policy characterized by increasing preventative and compensatory interventions earlier and earlier in children's and their families' lives. These political solutions to structural problems have been followed by research identifying the interventions as *part of the problems* and as contributing to marginalization (Højholt, 2011; Juhl, 2014; Kousholt, 2012a, 2012b; Morin, 2007; Røn Larsen, 2011).

Due to this paradox, I will initiate the discussions with a short investigation of the theoretical challenges in relation to conceptualizing the social conditions of everyday life as a question of "social background" or "social heritage," which is the dominating discourse in Denmark (across different kinds of political ideologies). We may approach the dilemmas in relation to conceptualizing meanings of social conditions through an investigation of widespread ways of conceptualizing the implications of social circumstances for the individual. The critical analysis is not meant to question whether social conditions such as family resources have meanings, but to explore how we can understand meanings – perhaps in quite different ways than we are used to.

In continuation of these challenges, I will discuss the concept of conduct of everyday life (Holzkamp, 2013) in relation to children's life across a plurality of contexts and together with peers. Subsequently, an example from fieldwork in and around the school is presented.

In this way, the analyses emphasize that persons' lives and engagements are distributed between several contexts and that the conduct of everyday life is a fundamental collective process, i.e., subjects conduct their life in collaboration with other subjects (Dreier, 2008; Kousholt, 2011). Here we will see this emphasis pointing to *social coordination and conflicts* as central problems of the personal conduct of life and how it has consequences for understandings of "agency" as well as "self-understanding."

"Social conflicts" are often understood as either societal conflicts between societal groups or relational conflicts between persons. The aim in this chapter is to point to both, or rather to the inner connections between them. This way of working with the concept of social conflict is rooted in an understanding of social practice as – as a starting point – conflictual (Axel, 2002; Lave, 2008). It is to approach conflicts as connected to different ways of dealing with common societal dilemmas and contradictions – conflicts become related to "structured human traditions for interaction around specific tasks and goals" (Hedegaard, Chaiklin & Juul Jensen, 1999, p. 19).

There is a broad and long-standing tradition in psychology to analyze social inequalities, structures of power and marginalization of human beings and, in relation to this, to discuss the inner connections between human life conditions and subjective agency (e.g., Burman, 2015; Lave, 2011; McDermott, 1993; Mehan, 1993; Nissen, 2012). One of the theoretical challenges in relation to this is how to conceptualize social conditions *in a concrete way*, to pave the way for situated analysis of unequal conditions for taking part in institutional arrangements (Dreier, 2008), instead of displacing problems into abstract conceptualizations about social background. At the same time, we confront the dilemma that the critique may become rather implicit, which seems to be a dilemma in the situated analysis I argue for in the following. It is a pressing challenge to make the political aspect of social practice more explicit and related to what people try to organize in their life and how they are hindered in relation to that.

In relation to direct critical analyses more explicitly to social conditions of people's everyday life, and in order to explore these conditions as they are experienced and handled by persons, we need concepts to analyze how concrete dilemmas of everyday life are entwined with structural inequalities and political conflictualities. In the chapter, political conflictuality is discussed as social conflicts about how societal problems should be understood and handled, and it is argued that we find these conflicts in our situated analysis of people's interplay in everyday life. Personal conduct of life is entangled in social coordination and conflicts, and in the situations of everyday life persons make up the conditions for each other through interplay, where social possibilities are structurally and unequally arranged. With the concept of *situated inequality*, I want to draw attention to the social distribution of possibilities for taking part in and influencing different social contexts.

Social Inequalities Conceptualized as a Question of Intergenerational Transmission

Concerning children's "problematic" conditions, it is prevalent to focus on children's family background and to conceptualize specific, deviant and isolated variables or backgrounds. This way of isolating some aspects in abstract variables are quite well criticized in psychology (Burman, 1994; McDermott, 1993; Mehan, 1993; Røn Larsen, 2012a), but are still dominating in practice.

Especially the professional practices aimed at supporting children in difficulties have a tradition of interpreting problems with relation to the social backgrounds of the children, focusing on how professionals must compensate for a lack of family resources. This turns interventions toward special support for individual children identified as "special" due to different kinds of tests and categorizations (Kousholt, 2010; Røn Larsen, 2011). In the formulations of aims for such interventions, as well as in the argumentation for social as well as educational policy in Denmark, the main purpose is to "break with social heritage."

Searching for the scientific formulations of this widespread understanding of a kind of automatic process of transfer between children's family backgrounds and their performance in school led me to comprehensive investigations of "intergenerational transmission." In the following I will present and quote some of the concepts and formulations from such investigations to illustrate insights as well as problematics in relation to creating knowledge about these processes and conceptualizing their meanings to those involved.

Characteristic of these often large-scale longitudinal studies is that quite a lot of different issues are compiled in a scientific model of factors and variables. It could, for instance, be "parenting quality received" and "social competence" (Shaffer et al., 2009) or "the intergenerational processes that place families and children at risk for a broad variety of social, behavioural, and health problems" (Serbin & Karp, 2003, p. 138). A third study focuses on the impact of parental worklessness on "children's cognitive ability, education attainment, behaviours, attitude to school, academic aspirations" (Barnes et al., 2012). The last-mentioned study finds associations between parental worklessness and early cognitive academic and behavioral development of young children (at age 7); "however we needed to allow for other factors that influence these outcomes and that are also correlated with parental worklessness – so-called 'interlinked risk factors'" (i.e., households affected by worklessness are, for example, also more likely to have characteristics such as a single parent, living in income poverty, family instability, a parent with a long-term limiting illness etc.) (ibid., p. 6).

This is mentioned to illustrate how connections between different "factors" in people's everyday lives are set up, as well as the built-in notions about the complexity of interrelations between factors. How can we gain knowledge about interrelated meanings? It is, for instance, also stated that:

> Children in workless families were more likely to be bullied, to bully others and to be unhappy at school but this was *not* due to the worklessness itself but rather attributable to other characteristics of the households, such as lone parenthood or parental health (i.e. the interlinked risk factors).
>
> (Barnes et al., 2012, p. 7)

Furthermore, it is written in several places that so-called "protective factors" may change the picture. It is stated that it is difficult to identify specific factors that protected young people from the "negative outcome" the entire study points to. However, there was evidence that positive school experiences (child likes school, has friends at school), school characteristics and parents' engagement in their children's education reduce or remove the association between parental worklessness and poor academic outcomes (Barnes et al., 2012, pp. 9, 10). In continuation of this, some of the studies advocate for more research involving, among other things: experiences of being parented, beliefs and current parental practice (Shaffer et al., 2009, p. 1238), as well as "a broader ecological model of risk" (Saltaris et al., 2004) and "a presumption of cultural and ethnic 'environment' distinctly interacting with genetics and physiology to produce self-reinforcing behaviours that may be passed from one generation to another" (Markward, Dozier, Hooks & Markward, 2000, p. 237).

Thus, the reading illustrated an acknowledgment of complexity, interplay and interrelated meanings, but still the very concepts of "transmission," "prediction" and "mechanism" seem unchallenged and turn the interventions toward "these individuals" living in "a stressful environment with a lack of emotional and financial support" (Saltaris et al., 2004, p. 105). Such concepts are used, for instance, as in the following formulations: "parental stimulation predicts the intellectual functioning of preschool-aged offspring" (ibid.); "In light of these indications of intergenerational transfer of risk by the time the second generation reached school age, we became interested in uncovering the potential mechanisms contributing to the continuity of maladjustment" (ibid., p. 107). So, "these individuals" become the center of focus, at the expense of the meanings of the problematic conditions.

Another characteristic of these studies is the close connection to policy and intervention. Some of the papers end in paragraphs like "Applications and implications for social policy," in which it is stated that "Issues of intergenerational transfer of risk are central to the field of human development. However, their importance extends further because identifying risk factors provides crucial information that can be used in developing social, educational, and health policy" (Serbin & Karp, 2003, p. 141). Moreover, Shaffer et al. conclude: "Developmental studies such as these are crucial to highlighting possible opportunities for intervention" (2009, p. 1238).

Therefore, it does not seem strange that social policy and professionals working with interventions regarding children in difficulties are strongly connected to exactly the figure of thought about intergenerational transmission.[1] In the many-sided conflicts about the problems, it appears legitimate, scientific and professional to focus on intergenerational transmission. Nevertheless, this is turning the interventions toward "these individuals" and toward concepts connected *to the intergenerational transmission* and not to the concrete conditions of everyday life.

It cannot be said that this kind of research overlooks everyday life, since we gain an insight into problematic conditions for conducting daily life as a family, but it does not provide an insight into how daily life is conducted, how problems are experienced by the persons living with them or about their perspectives on the care for the children – even though some of the investigations themselves underline how such issues may change the picture of transfer.

Qualitative studies working with such questions point to the ways problems are experienced very differently by the parents than by the professionals (Juhl, 2014; Kousholt, 2012a). In such studies, the parents emphasize the social conditions that were the point of departure of the research (for instance, economic problems, housing problems, a lack of network and support – and also difficulties and conflicts in relation to the way the children are met, received and involved in the educative contexts). However, the professionals emphasize psychological concepts of attachment, parents being attentive, having good eye contact, etc. – concepts associated with the black box of "transmission."

This field of research seems to illustrate that we lack insight into the social practice of these cross-contextual processes. In an overview of "The intergenerational transmission of poverty," it is acknowledged that "Contrasting evidence is presented, and it is recognised that unmeasured sociological or psychological factors may be important" (Bird, 2007, p. ix).

Even more striking in the concept of transmission is the missing involvement of other contexts in the life of the children, contexts such as the school and child institutions. When these contexts are included in the research, they seem to be comprehended as "arenas" where the negative consequences of the family background are displayed, and not as social practices connected in the daily life of the children, with situated meanings going across the contexts and where social conflicts form contradictory conditions for the involved participants. In that way, the social practice of, for example, the school and the way this social practice makes up different conditions for the children is overlooked (Kousholt, 2010; Ljungstrøm, 1984). There seems to be a bracket around the situated interplay in these practices and around the meanings of the general dilemmas, contradictions and conflicts involved in the differentiations of children and their possibilities here. Such dilemmas are central to the following analysis, where I will try to unfold an approach to social practice in which situated meanings and conflicts are included.

Some studies focus directly on the intergenerational transmission of poverty and, even though one could expect such studies to concentrate on social conditions, the question turns into a focus on quality of parenting, nurturing and socialization. A nuanced overview of the literature takes as a point of departure that "Poverty is not transferred as a 'package', but as a complex set of positive and negative factors that affect an individual's chances of experiencing poverty, either in the present or at a future point in their life-course" (Bird, 2007, p. v). Furthermore, it is pointed out that "This is a controversial area, which can seemingly blame the poor for their poverty. As a result, liberal researchers have tended to avoid such issues, leaving the terrain open to the right wing" (ibid., p. ix). With the concept of "cultures of poverty," it is suggested that "the poor have a different culture to the rest of society which is characterised by deviant attitudes, values and behaviours" (ibid., p. ix). But the concept of culture of poverty is challenged in this paper as well:

> Some research has suggested that social class has a powerful influence on behavioural, social and psychological variables (Singh-Manoux and Marmot, 2005), but contradictory findings suggest that it is "very difficult to make any comprehensive cross-cultural generalisations about the poor other than that they lack money and are often socially and politically marginalised" (Rigdon, 1998:17, in Moore, 2001).
>
> (Ibid., p. 29)

The "contrasting evidence," as well as the political positions in the scientific debates, seem to illustrate *the conceptual dilemmas* as well as their connections to political ideologies. As a final theme, I want to comment on the point Bird formulates about "combining" human agency with structural factors and involving agency in the research – but in this economic model these become independent factors:

Being a poor child increases the chances of being a poor adult but this is not always the case, and other factors can operate independently to affect well-being over the life-course. Although highly context specific, household characteristics and initial endowments have been found to be important – an individual's asset bundle, their capabilities and characteristics, and their power to exercise agency.

(Ibid., p. v)

In such formulations, assets, characteristics and agency are set up as isolated. I find the overview of these investigations, their contradictions and internal debates illustrative for the theoretical dilemma of analyzing agency, social interplay and concrete meanings of social conditions, as well as different ways of dealing with different kinds of challenge in everyday life. The great paradox is that attention to unequal conditions of everyday life in the concept of transmission – and in the interventions – is turned away from just the social conditions.

Could we in a psychological framework unfold situated analyses of everyday life pointing to the personal meanings of unequal conditions? And could we in this way encourage possibilities for understanding how agency, in contrast to an independent variable, is entangled in the conflictuality of social practice?

Personal Conduct of Life and Social Conflicts

The concept of "conduct of life" is developed as a way to unite social structures and personal meanings in our understanding and to be used in concrete empirical analysis of persons' efforts at integrating, planning and prioritizing everyday life. Klaus Holzkamp has argued that in order to overcome a psychology, where subjects are enclosed in psychological special functions, we need concepts that can capture the richness and complexity of people's everyday life. He presents the concept of conduct of life as a way to conceptualize the active creative processes involved in leading a complex everyday life (2013, 2015, chap. 3 in this volume; Dreier, 2015, chap. 1 in this volume; Kousholt, 2015, chap. 13 in this volume; and for a conceptual background, see also Jurczyk et al., 2015, chap. 2 in this volume).

In relation to the discussions in this chapter, I will emphasize how such formulations highlight ordinary processes often overlooked in theorizing: everyday life and its practices cannot "live itself" – every day a subject must choose, for example, to get out of the bed (or not); how to organize the morning in relation to the tasks to be carried out in other places; often to coordinate with others about who will accompany the children to school, who will buy the food, who can stay at the meeting so that I can catch the train, etc. Even routines must every day become prioritized and planned and persons make quite a lot of choices during an "ordinary day," which must be adjusted with other persons and affairs. In their complex everyday lives, persons pursue many concerns across several social contexts (Dreier, 2011).

The persons we cooperate with in our research are in a process of conducting their life in relation to such specific conditions, demands and preferences, and at the same time, they are developing *their ways* of taking part in different places, organizing daily life and influencing significant contexts in their life. The question of conducting one's life cannot be limited to a question of repeating what others have done before or adjusting to some kinds of given conditions. To live implies to *arrange* conditions, together with others, to look for possibilities, to revise plans and pursue ideas. Therefore, the possibilities for developing conduct of life are connected to possibilities for participation *and influence* in different places (elaborated in Højholt & Kousholt, 2015).

The recent developments in our research communities emphasize that persons live across various contexts and their lives and engagements are distributed between several contexts (Dreier, 2008) and that the conduct of everyday life is a fundamental collective process – subjects conduct their life in collaboration with other subjects and in relation to different matters in their lives (Chimirri, 2013; Kousholt, 2011). This movement points to *social coordination and conflicts* as central problems of the personal conduct of life (Axel, 2002, 2011). Furthermore, social practice is experienced in different locations and positions and from different perspectives in relation to this specific practice and its main concerns. Through a common interest in just this, the participants develop different standpoints about, for example, how to organize and change this practice and how to pursue its concerns.

"Reasons for actions" are in this understanding related to what other persons do and how a person estimates what they will do – individual actions enter into collective actions and the "outcome" of personal choices, plans and objectives must be understood on the basis of the social practice they are part of and are intertwined with (Dreier, 2008, p. 34). Self-understanding appears as an intersubjective matter and in continuous change related to historical scopes of possibilities for taking part in different kinds of practice, related to how other persons take part, related to access to communities, etc. When conduct of everyday life is interwoven in social coordination, negotiations and possibilities for creating something together with someone, personal conduct implies investigating social possibilities. Such possibilities are structurally and unequally arranged and are grasped by persons with different positions, experiences and perspectives.

So, developing conduct of life is a conflictual process entwined with different social conditions and in continuation of this we may study the concrete meanings of structural inequalities and social problems in the concrete *interplay* between participants in daily situations and *from* the perspectives of concrete persons, or, we could say, from the perspective of everyday living.

Conflicts about, with, between and *for* Children

In relation to children, their developmental challenges are entangled in social coordination, communities and conflicts, and the responsibility in relation to children is politically distributed among adults in a privatized, individualized and conflictual way. Parents, teachers, pedagogues and psychologists are *connected* through the content of their tasks and, at the same time, they have different kinds of responsibilities and perspectives (Andenæs & Haavind, 2015; Højholt, 2006; Pedersen & Nielsen, 2009).

In continuation of this social structure, children are at one and the same time gathered in institutional communities (such as, for instance, a school class) and continuously differentiated into various kinds of categories (such as, for instance, the good pupils, the ones who receive special help, the ones who do not know how to behave, etc.). These differentiations are conflictual: different parties such as mothers and fathers, teachers, pedagogues, psychologists and politicians have different perspectives on the differentiations and on the children. For instance, they disagree about whether a child can stay in regular school or should be sent to a special institution, or about how the school should prioritize in relation to inclusion and working with school communities, which are often set up as a contradiction to working in a more focused way to obtain competences.

Furthermore, the differentiations become "at stake" in the interplay between the children themselves and the children relate to them in their communities, and vice versa. The interplay between the children constitutes conditions for educational strategies that often acquire other significations for the children than they were originally intended to have. Typically, the adults do not know how, for example, sending a child to compensative special education may have significations for the child's conditions for taking part in the communities of the class; neither do they know how, for example, a conflictual boy's community constitutes participatory conditions for the child they are trying to help (Højholt & Kousholt, 2014, 2015; Morin, 2008; Røn Larsen, 2012a).

Following different kinds of cases over the years, our research has shown that "behind" the practice of identifying individual children, we find a complex landscape of conflicts between different groups of professionals and parents, as well as among the children (Højholt, 1993, 2001, 2006). The point is that processes around children in difficulties can be seen as particular "intensifications" of *general conflicts* about children, and about the concept of learning and education policy. In particular, when problems are pointed out, the dispute is: Who has the responsibility?

The collaboration regarding the problems is loaded with conflicts linked to broader debates about what is relevant in relation to learning, how difficulties ought to be understood (and handled) and how tasks should be distributed. For the moment, these very general conflicts are frequently formulated in concepts to do with the task of the school in the global competition that have a focus on increasing competences (Pedersen, 2011) or a (not as dominating) focus on common goods in a welfare state and the task of including and providing equal educational opportunities to different children (Højrup & Juul Jensen, 2010).

Theoretically, these conflicts may be formulated as concerning the question of how to influence the development of common practice. In more general terms, one could analyze the conflicts as being about directions and influence in relation to the change of social practice and as related to its many-sided concerns (I will return to this in relation to the example p.154ff). For example, the different persons involved in the school develop different perspectives on what is important to prioritize in relation to their shared problems. Subsequently, the different perspectives can be seen as connected as well as conflictual. They are not coincidentally different, but structurally different and structurally connected.

In such a theoretical approach, the disagreeing parties are not seen as "randomly disagreeing." Their different perspectives can be analytically linked to their different positions, and their different types of responsibilities and contributions are differentiated in a complex practice structure (Dreier, 2008; Højholt, 2006). Their perspectives on the problems are formed by the tasks they have in relation to the children and how they are part of the conflicts, for example, as a child, a parent, a teacher or a pedagogue (Axel, 2002, 2009; Dreier, 2003).

To conduct their everyday life, children have to orient in this social complexity and negotiate their participation and influence on what is occurring (Højholt & Kousholt, 2015; Stanek, 2013). These processes are not easy, but involve common efforts, coordination and flexibility. Still, these seem to be challenges in children's lives that we as adults often overlook, as long as it takes place in a quite unnoticed way, then it is "just children playing," and when the movements among the children become stuck, we notice it as *specific problems* often related to a specific child and a specific background (cf. the section on intergenerational transmission) or diagnostic category. When we overlook the social complexity of children's daily lives and the *ordinary difficulties* in relation to conducting a child's life, we overlook the general basis for the conflicts and how the children are positioned differently in relation to managing the general challenges.

An Example: The Boy Who Couldn't Get the Ball – and didn't Have any Roller Skates

In school, children are in a situation of competition as regards academic tasks, as well as with regard to positioning and influence among themselves. In this way, school life is characterized by a plurality of agendas related to learning, as well as to social life in general. As McDermott (1993) illustrates, the children must at one and the same time learn new things and show that they already know how to do them. The children relate to the competition and the differentiations of competences, and they must also navigate in social communities, dealing with positions, relations, fun, friendships and conflicts among their peers (Højholt & Kousholt, 2014, 2015; Røn Larsen, 2011; Stanek, 2013).

Due to the previously mentioned differentiations, the children participate from different positions and with different conditions in relation to managing the double agendas of school life. The classroom does not set the same conditions for different children. Sometimes it is stated that when children perform differently in the same classroom, it must be due to circumstances other than what is taking place there – compare the discussion about intergenerational transmission above. In a social practice approach, the social life of the classroom must be analyzed as situated ways of relating collectively to the historical agendas of the school. The school not only measures differences, but constitutes differences.

So, in school, children are learning to take part in a specific practice and they are engaged in relating to the possibilities, as well as the contradictions, that exist here – they are engaging in the meanings that this has for them in a concrete way. Thus, the classroom has quite different meanings to the children, and what the adults do and say, as well as their rules (often meant to situate the children equally, but with different meanings for the children as well as for their parents), become involved in the strategies of the children and may have unforeseen meanings for them.

This is illustrated when I observe school life from Peter's perspective. He seems to be working hard to achieve a position in the group of boys, but he also has to handle the conflicts between his parents and the teachers: conflicts about him, about whether he is able to behave in school or not, whether he is lying or not, who is responsible for the noise and trouble in the classroom, etc. The teachers think he is badly brought up at home and the parents think the teachers are inflexible and traditional in their teaching style.

These quarrels relate to the aforementioned political conflicts about what ought to happen in school and about the distribution of responsibility between the adults. The teachers think the pedagogues in the preschool class should have taught the pupils more discipline, since the noise in the classroom makes it very difficult to carry out the teaching and they think that Peter should have waited one more year before joining the class. Such conflicts can be seen as conflicts about the distribution of responsibility in relation to learning, as well as about the very concept of learning. In the conflicts, learning becomes isolated from social life in a scholastic way and is comprehended as if the social life stands in the way of learning (Axel, 2009; Dreier, 2003; Juul Jensen, 2001, 2007; Lave, 2011). Under the pressure, the teachers find that the pedagogue has prioritized "the social" at the expense of learning. This is also related to the underlying conflict about discipline – in these conflicts, discipline becomes detached from the common organization of social practice as an obstacle to play, community and democracy. The involved parties have different conditions in relation to promoting learning and different perspectives on the priorities of the school and how the difficulties should be understood and addressed.

At the end of some lessons in the class, I observe a repeated conflict, a struggle to get the football first, which seems to be of great importance for positioning in the football game during the break. This moment accentuates the structural divisions in school between children's self-organized play and adult-regulated teaching. To be allowed to leave their chairs, the children must complete their school tasks, pack their school bags and remain quiet.

One boy, William, is acting outstandingly in combining the double agendas – organizing his close friends in a way that will satisfy the teacher. Peter also tries to use this strategy, but he is placed at a table alone and he is in increasing strife with the other boys, as well as with the teacher. Peter gets to the ball too quickly and William and some other boys argue that Peter must not touch the ball: "it is not allowed," "you are not allowed to do so are you?" The teacher becomes involved and yes, they are right, this is not allowed and Peter must put the ball back. As usual, William is the one who gets the football first and organizes the football match during the break, while Peter must try to take part from a peripheral position.

The situation repeats itself at the end of the next lesson, but now Peter is so keen to get the ball that it becomes a problem in relation to putting the sheet of paper correctly in the folder, as he has been told to do. William is immediately on guard: "Peter, you must not take the ball." It seems that in such a situation, Peter is in trouble with regard to asserting himself during lessons, as well as during the breaks. His attention is split in a kind of *personal conflict of priorities*. The abstract divisions and structural conflicts around him – among the adults as well as among the boys – become personal conflicts for him. In this way, the conflict can be analyzed from Peter's perspective as a problem for his conduct of life in relation to connecting friendships, school life, academic performance, football and math.

All children deal with conflictual agendas related to taking part in the lessons as good pupils, having fun with each other, developing friendships and communities, influencing their activities, competing for resources and positions, dealing with conflicts and solidarity, etc. The problem for Peter seems to be the way the conflicts are *displaced into his person* – and to his social background – and how this displacement moves back and forth between the adults as an abstract question of guilt. This could be seen as a psychological construction of the discussed concept of transmission, and in this way social problems become privatized and their rootedness in societal dilemmas becomes obscured (Motzkau & Schraube, 2015).

The background is, among other things, implicit conflicts not being addressed. Often we individualize children's conflicts, but these conflicts can be seen as subjective ways of dealing with general conflicts about the concerns of the school. The participants in the school are focused on achieving future competences and on immediate cooperation at the same time. To carry out the teaching, the teacher needs the children to behave in certain ways and prepare themselves for this practice. In one situation, a boy does not know the answer to a question or where in the book the teacher is working (he is engaged in something else together with another boy) but the teacher concludes that this must be an exception, because she knows he is a good pupil. In another situation, things are interrupted because Peter does not have a pencil. The teacher empties Peter's school bag and ascertains that the contents have not been updated for a long while. A girl sitting in front of Peter solves the situation by lending him a pencil to continue the lesson, but to the teacher the situation seems connected to the conflicts with Peter's parents: they should take care of this, and teaching pupils (and parents) to prepare the school bag is part of her task as a teacher. The teachers explain the feeling of powerlessness and isolation in relation to these problems, and in this situation of pressure and lack of possibilities to act the quite ordinary situation[2] turns into an illustration of the specific problems related to Peter's background. One could say that the matter is contradictory here, and due to the way these contradictions are handled, those involved reach an impasse.

In the process, Peter becomes more and more exposed to the premises of the conflicts and he loses influence on the common conditions. Still, he tries to change his situation, for example, in relation to a period in the spring when the children want to go roller-skating. The pedagogues at the institution who are responsible for the children's leisure time explain that Peter has taken a pair of the institution's roller skates and then lied about them being his own. Some confusion arises, partly because of the problematic communication with Peter's parents and partly because Peter explains (during a long interrogation) that a pedagogue who is not at work that day had given him the roller skates.

The Constitution of School Problems, Subjective Reasons and Personal Agency

The episode of the roller skates illustrates several points. I will try to systematize some of the points into three problem issues: (1) the abstract interpretations of the difficulties versus a search for insight into Peter's personal reasons for taking part in school life as he does; (2) situated inequality; (3) the discussions about "agency."

Peter's strategies for taking part in the life of the school – in the academic agenda of the teachers, as well as the social life of the lessons, breaks and leisure time – are categorized as "deviant behavior." As the processes evolve, Peter's actions become more and more unambiguously comprehended as an expression of his individual disadvantages. The very comprehensions become part of the conflicts and become threatening to the involved parties (are the teachers the problem? The mother? The pedagogues who did not teach Peter "how to behave"?). The possibilities for *presenting problems* in the school seem to be a very significant part of the way they become problems. Still, analyzing the categorizations and the way the divergence between perspectives often becomes obscured by an apparent agreement about "blaming the social background" does not seem enough to understand the actions of those involved and their unequal possibilities for taking part (Røn Larsen, 2012b).

Focusing on the "result" of the conflictual processes – the construction of "pupil identities" – (cf. Mehan, 1993, p. 260) seems to remain in the social labeling of Peter's strategies, and for a psychology of the subject it is important to explore personal "reasons" and "social meanings" as different aspects of the same problem. Where "personal reasons" point to Peter's engagement *in relation* to his conditions, "social meanings" point to how other persons act in relation to his actions.

Analyzing the everyday life of the school as situated social practice and by thus (re)placing Peter's actions in their social connections, they do not look so special. Following Peter's conduct of life in and across different contexts (in our observations as well as in our analyses) might offer insight into his perspectives and reasons. In the group interviews Peter and the other children talk about friends and the meanings of having friends, and Peter tells me that he is best friends with some of the boys I see him trying to connect with, but is increasingly being rejected by. We need more knowledge in order to learn about the content of these social conflicts, as well as the content of the political conflicts about the school, and the argument is that we need concepts to analyze reasons for actions in connection with situated (and unequal differentiated) conditions for taking part in the practice of the school. To understand the many-sided matter, we need to be curious about personal reasons.

The meanings of the children's strategies are social, and therefore they are also interpreted differently, and this is part of what I have tried to discuss as "situated inequality." Among the professionals, the episode of the roller skates thus appears to be a matter of Peter's lies, and precisely "lying" is a theme of the conflicts between the adults in relation to Peter. Peter mediates between his teachers and his parents, and they do not agree about when to believe him. Discussions on this issue appear to take up attention at the expense of the dilemmas in the everyday life of Peter. So, what Peter does becomes interpreted in the conflicts and in relation to the adults' categorizations of him. Lots of conflicts among the children (involving many children) are represented by the teachers as being to do with the problems with Peter. In this way, the process of displacement becomes a kind of "generalization of the special": It is everywhere that he is "special," the special appears everywhere and therefore has little to do with what is going on in these contexts. In such a generalization, the problem has nothing to do with the general conditions.

This very detached way of understanding problems is part of the problem. It is hiding the conflicts and presenting the situations as quite mysterious and a question of strange individual behavior – and such an alienation calls for understanding through abstract concepts about social background.

With this I want to illustrate how *personal "agency" is interwoven with the ways social conflicts develop*. In discussions of intergenerational transmission, personal agency was involved as an independent variable – and also beyond statistical accounts, personal agency is often involved as something some persons "have" and a way of nuancing the automatic transmission. When agency is not closely connected to concrete conditions of social practice, the relations between social possibilities and personal performance seem to stay mysterious and beyond analysis. With this I want to emphasize how subjective ways of taking part – and developing the same – are related to dealing with concrete dilemmas in everyday life and its *coordination with others*. This interplay is not static, but must be seen as processes where the way in which conflicts and problems unfold influences further conditions for cooperation. To elaborate this, I will illustrate how different processes of conflicts may unfold.

Following different cases in school life, situated analyses illustrate how different perspectives are sometimes connected and the conflicts are "generalized" and understood through different perspectives in relation to the "same concern" – the concerns are many-sided, contradictory and compounded (Axel, 2011). Like this, the involved parties might see themselves and each other as contributing to "the same project" from different positions and with different possibilities and contributions. In such processes, the conflicts may lead to development of understanding, which opens up possibilities to act and a kind of extension of cooperation (Højholt, 2011). As stated before, the parties are connected through the same ambition, but still experience the requirements of this ambition differently. The disagreements of the participants provide an opportunity to expand our understanding of the practice in question. An exploration of the conflicts can contribute to knowledge on the subject matter and to the development of the practice.

At other times, several parties give up on the substance of conflicts, and giving up seems to constitute difficult conditions for interaction and various parties seem to lose influence and their personal grasp of the issues. In these processes, the children sometimes give up strategies for taking part in lessons as well (Højholt, 2012; Højholt & Kousholt, 2015). Thus, the development of self-understanding and agency should not be seen as determined by but related to social possibilities for taking part in social practice.

Situated Inequality and Political Aspects of Social Practice

In this chapter I have tried to illustrate how problems in the personal conduct of life may be understood as intertwined with compound and political conflicts. I have tried to do this through analyses of personal meanings of structural conditions in the situated interplay between participants in daily situations, such as school, and from the perspectives of concrete persons.

The example is intended to point to the *situated inequality in the classroom*, instead of displacing the conflicts in and about the school to abstract concepts about social background, poorly functioning families, psychological deficiencies, lack of cultural capital, etc. Critical analyses sometimes also seem to analyze social differences in a way that refers to different kinds of lack of personal resources in other places – in the understanding often related to a quite ambiguous power of the school. In contrast, the chapter's discussions argue for analyzing the contradictions of the school. In such an approach, the question of power and influence in school is at stake in political conflicts about priority and distribution of resources and responsibility in relation to the general education of children (Busch-Jensen, 2013). In a social practice approach, political questions may be seen as part of the social life related to connecting different aspects of multifaceted concerns.

The boy in the example is in this perspective not just acting to "live up to a category" or "to reproduce a culture," he is also struggling to conduct a contradictory life. His personal agency is interwoven with the ways social conflicts develop in his life. In this way, analyses of people's conduct of everyday life may be productive in order to criticize structural inequalities and highlight the political conflicts with which personal problems are entwined.

In research, we may explore the *content* of these conflicts and analyze the contradictory conditions in relation to these conflicts, as well as the possibilities for cooperation that these conflicts reveal. In relation to doing so, we need, among other things, theoretical developments to conceptualize the inner connection between societal and political conflicts and contradictions in everyday life, to analyze how social conflicts also become conflictual *for* persons when they conduct their everyday life.

Political discussions about the school point to broader societal conflicts (McDermott, 1993; Varenne & McDermott, 1998) as well as conceptual abstractions (Holzkamp, 2013; Burman, 2015). To be able to analyze connections between conceptual, political and personal problems, the concept of personal reasons appears central: reasons point to subjective experiences of conditions related to conducting one's life. This is a theoretical endeavor to analyze situated interplay between participants – children organizing their breaks; adults organizing their shared care for children – as intersubjective ways of relating to structural conditions and contradictions in a continual and conflictual coordination.

In continuation of this, individual and compensative interventions cannot work in isolation. The above analyses suggest working with a democratization of the social practice of the school and the collaboration about the school as well as a democratization of the social practice of research (Kousholt, 2015, chap. 13 in this volume). Furthermore, the analyses point to methodological development in relation to conceptualizing the inner connection between problems in the personal conduct of everyday life and the social conflicts of which this conduct is a part. I find it especially relevant to elaborate on the connections between political conflicts about, for example, societal need for competent individuals, care for children and social control, and *personal conflicts of priorities* in the conduct of everyday life.

Moreover, situated analyses of the conflictual coordination between and around children may inspire the professionals to be curious about this interplay, instead of closing down investigations with abstract categorizations or displacement of problems to a question of intergenerational transmission. Such efforts could be directed toward possibilities of participation in learning communities, involvement of different perspectives, distribution of influence and promotion of relevant conditions at the disposal of the persons in difficulties.

Notes

1 And the other way around – research and political strategies interrelate and have consequences for the tasks of professional practice.
2 Looking into school bags in general may illustrate this and (at least in Denmark) the very notion evokes bad conscience among parents.

References

Andenæs, A. & Haavind, H. (2015). Sharing early care: Learning from practitioners. In M. Fleer & B. van Oers (Eds.), *International handbook on early childhood education*. Dordrecht: Springer.

Axel, E. (2002). *Regulation as productive tool use: Participatory observation in the control room of a district heating system*. Roskilde: Roskilde University Press.

Axel, E. (2009). What makes us talk about wing nuts? Critical psychology and subjects at work. *Theory & Psychology, 19*(2), 275–295.

Axel, E. (2011). Conflictual cooperation. *Nordic Psychology, 20*(4), 56–78.

Barnes, M., Brown, V., Parsons, S., Ross, A., Schoon, I. & Vignoles, A. (2012). *Intergenerational transmission of worklessness: Evidence from the Millennium Cohort and the Longitudinal Study of Young People in England*. London: Department for Education (DFE), Centre for Analysis of Youth Transitions, Institute of Education, National Centre for Social Research, corp creators. Retrieved from http://dera.ioe.ac.uk/15563.

Bird, K. (2007). *The intergenerational transmission of poverty: An overview* (ODI Working Paper 286, CPRC Working Paper 99). London: Overseas Development Institute and Chronic Poverty Research Center.

Burman, E. (1994). *Deconstructing developmental psychology*. London: Routledge.

Burman, E. (2015). Towards a posthuman developmental psychology of child, families and communities. In M. Fleer & B. van Oers (Eds.), *International handbook on early childhood education*. Dordrecht: Springer.

Busch-Jensen, P. (2013). Grappling with the structural from a situated perspective. *Psychology in Society*, *44*, 1–21.

Chimirri, N. (2013). Expanding the conduct of everyday life concept for psychological media research with children. In A. Marvakis, J. Motzkau, D. Painter, R. Ruto-Korir, G. Sullivan, S. Triliva et al. (Eds.), *Doing psychology under new conditions* (pp. 355–364). Toronto: Captus Press.

Dreier, O. (2003). Learning in personal trajectories of participation. In N. Stephenson, L. Radke, R. Jorna & H. J. Stam (Eds.), *Theoretical psychology: Critical contributions* (pp. 20–29). Toronto: Captus Press.

Dreier, O. (2008). *Psychotherapy in everyday life*. Cambridge: Cambridge University Press.

Dreier, O. (2011). Personality and the conduct of everyday life. *Nordic Psychology*, *63*(2), 4–23.

Hedegaard, M., Chaiklin, S. & Juul Jensen, U. (1999). Activity theory and social practice: An introduction. In M. Hedegaard, S. Chaiklin & U. Juul Jensen (Eds.), *Activity theory and social practice* (pp. 12–30). Aarhus: Aarhus University Press.

Højholt, C. (1993). *Brugerperspektiver: Forældres, læreres og psykologers erfaringer med psykosocialt arbejde* [User's perspectives: Parents', teachers' and psychologists' experiences with psycho-social work]. Copenhagen: Dansk Psykologisk Forlag.

Højholt, C. (2001). *Samarbejde om børns udvikling* [Collaboration on children's development]. Doctoral dissertation, University of Copenhagen, Gyldendal.

Højholt, C. (2006). Knowledge and professionalism: From the perspectives of children? *Journal of Critical Psychology*, *19*, 81–160.

Højholt, C. (2011). Cooperation between professionals in educational psychology: Children's specific problems are connected to general problems in relation to taking part. In H. Daniels & M. Hedegaard (Eds.), *Vygotsky and special needs education: Rethinking support for children and schools* (pp. 67–86). London: Continuum Press.

Højholt, C. (2012). Communities of children and learning in school: Children's perspectives. In M. Hedegaard, K. Aronsson, C. Højholt & O. Ulvik (Eds.), *Children, childhood and everyday life* (pp. 199–215). Charlotte, NC: Information Age Publishing Inc.

Højholt, C. & Kousholt, D. (2014). Participant observation of children's communities: Exploring subjective aspects of social practice. *Qualitative Research in Psychology*, *11*, 316–334.

Højholt, C. & Kousholt, D. (2015). Children participating and developing agency in and across various social practices. In M. Fleer & B. van Oers (Eds.), *International handbook on early childhood education*. Dordrecht: Springer.

Højrup, T. & Juul Jensen, U. (2010). Moderne fællesgoder eller postmoderne kynisme? Mellem velfærdsstat og konkurrencestat i teori og praksis. In K. Thorgård, M. Nissen & U. Juul Jensen (Eds.), *Viden, virkning og virke* (pp. 17–59). Frederiksberg: Roskilde Universitetsforlag.

Holzkamp, K. (2013). Psychology: Social self-understanding on the reasons for action in the conduct of everyday life. In E. Schraube & U. Osterkamp (Eds.), *Psychology from the standpoint of the subject: Selected writings of Klaus Holzkamp* (pp. 233–341). Basingstoke: Palgrave Macmillan.

Juhl, P. (2014). *På sporet af det gode børneliv: om vanskelige betingelser for småbørns hverdagsliv – analyseret fra et børneperspektiv* [On the good life for children: Difficult conditions for young children's everyday lives – analyzed from the children's perspectives]. Doctoral dissertation, Roskilde University, Denmark.

Juhl, P. (2015). Toddlers collaboratively explore possibilities for actions across contexts: Developing the concept conduct of everyday life in relation to young children. In *Dialogue and debate in the making of theoretical psychology*. Toronto: Captus Press.

Juul Jensen, U. (2001). Mellem social praksis og skolastisk fornuft [Between social practice and scholastic rationality]. In J. Myrup (Eds.), *Temaer i nyere fransk filosofi* (pp. 195–218). Aarhus: Philosophia.

Juul Jensen, U. (2007). The struggle for clinical authority: Shifting ontologies and the politics of evidence. *BioSocieties, 2*(1), 101–114.

Kousholt, D. (2011). Researching family through the everyday lives of children across home and day care in Denmark. *Ethos, 39*(1), 98–114.

Kousholt, D. (2012a). Family problems: Exploring dilemmas and complexities of organizing everyday family life. In M. Hedegaard, K. Aronsson, C. Højholt & O. S. Ulvik (Eds.), *Children, childhood, and everyday life: Children's perspectives* (pp. 125–139). Charlotte, NC: Information Age Publishing.

Kousholt, D. (2012b). Børnefællesskaber og udsatte positioner i SFO: Inklusion og fritidspædagogik [Children's communities and exposed positions in leisure time institutions: Inclusion and leisure time pedagogy]. In P. Hviid & C. Højholt (Eds.), *Fritidspædagogik og børneliv*. Copenhagen: Hans Reitzel.

Kousholt, K. (2010). *Evalueret: Deltagelse i folkeskolens evalueringspraksis*. Doctoral dissertation, Aarhus University.

Lave, J. (2008). Situated learning and changing practice. In A. Amin & J. Roberts (Eds.), *Community, economic creativity and organization* (pp. 283–296). Oxford: Oxford University Press.

Lave, J. (2011). *Apprenticeship in critical ethnographic practice*. Chicago, IL: Chicago University Press.

Ljungstrøm, C. (1984). Differentiering og kvalificering. *Udkast, 2*.

Markward, M., Dozier, C., Hooks, K. & Markward, N. (2000). Culture and the intergenerational transmission of substance abuse, woman abuse, and child abuse: A diathesis-stress perspective. *Children and Youth Services Review, 22*, 237–250.

McDermott, R. P. (1993). The acquisition of a child by a learning disability. In S. Chaiklin & J. Lave (Eds.), *Understanding practice: Perspectives on activity and context* (pp. 269–305). Cambridge: Cambridge University Press.

Mehan, H. (1993). Beneath the skin and between the ears: A case study in the politics of representation. In S. Chaiklin & J. Lave (Eds.), *Understanding practice: Perspectives on activity and context* (pp. 241–268). Cambridge: Cambridge University Press.

Morin, A. (2007). *Børns deltagelse og læring: På tværs af almen- og specialpædagogiske lærearrangementer* [Children's participation and learning: Across general and special education learning settings]. Doctoral dissertation, Danish School of Education, Aarhus University.

Morin, A. (2008). Learning together: A child perspective on educational arrangements of special education. *ARECE – Australian Research in Early Childhood Education, 15*, 27–38.

Motzkau, J. & Schraube, E. (2015). Kritische Psychologie: Psychology from the standpoint of the subject. In I. Parker (Ed.), *Handbook of critical psychology*. London: Routledge.

Nissen, M. (2012). *The subjectivity of participation: Articulating social work with youth in Copenhagen*. London: Palgrave Macmillan.

Pedersen, M. & Nielsen, K. (2009). Læring, konflikter og arbejdsdeling – en udvidelse af den socialt situerede læringsforståelse. *Psyke & Logos, 2*, 652–671.

Pedersen, O. K. (2011). *Konkurrencestaten*. Copenhagen: Hans Reitzel.

Røn Larsen, M. (2011). *Samarbejde og strid om børn i vanskeligheder: Organiseringer af specialindsatser i skolen* [Cooperation and conflict about children in difficulties: Organisation of special support in school]. Doctoral dissertation, Department of Psychology and Educational Studies, Roskilde University, Denmark.

Røn Larsen, M. (2012a). A paradox of inclusion: Administrative procedures and children's perspectives on difficulties in school. In M. Hedegaard, K. Aronsson, C. Højholt & O. S. Ulvik (Eds.), *Children, childhood, and everyday life: Children's perspectives* (pp. 143–160). New York: Information Age Publishing.

Røn Larsen, M. (2012b). Konflikt og konsensus i tværfagligt samarbejde omkring børn i vanskeligheder. *Nordiske Udkast, 40*(1), 52–72.

Saltaris, C., Serbin, L. A., Stack, D. M., Karp, J. A., Schwartzman, A. E. & Ledingham, J. E. (2004). Nurturing cognitive competence in preschoolers: A longitudinal study of intergenerational continuity and risk. *International Journal of Behavioral Development, 28*(2), 105–115.

Schraube, E. & Osterkamp, U. (2013). *Psychology from the standpoint of the subject: Selected writings of Klaus Holzkamp.* Basingstoke: Palgrave Macmillan.

Serbin, L. & Karp, J. (2003). Intergenerational studies of parenting and the transfer of risk from parent to child. *Current Directions in Psychological Science, 12*(4), 138–142.

Shaffer, A., Burt, K. B., Obradovic, J., Herbers, J. E. & Masten, A. S. (2009). Intergenerational continuity in parenting quality: The mediating role of social competence. *Developmental Psychology, 45*(5), 1227–1240.

Stanek, A. H. (2013). Understanding children's learning as connected to social life. In A. Marvakis, J. Motzkau, D. Painter, R. Ruto-Korir, G. Sullivan, S. Triliva & M. Wieser (Eds.), *Doing psychology under new conditions* (pp. 365–374). Toronto: Captus Press.

Varenne, H. & McDermott, R. (1998). *Successful failure: The school America builds.* Oxford: Westview Press.

8

"THERE IS NO RIGHT LIFE IN THE WRONG ONE"

Recognizing this Dilemma is the
First Step Out of it

Ute Osterkamp

There is no right life in a wrong one. This quotation from Adorno usually provokes ambivalent reactions. In view of the experience that we presumably all share, namely that much of what happens and what one does doesn't work or "goes wrong," i.e., fails to ensure what one is striving for, the quotation often meets with agreement. However, at the same time it calls into question a tendency that is central for coping with life under conditions of alienation, that is, under conditions on which we are dependent but over which we have no control. The usual way of coping with this situation is to attempt to keep some leeway by trying to fulfill respective demands and expectations as well as necessary, or at least better than other people do. Thus, Adorno's dictum that there is no right life in the wrong one questions an essential means of coping with life under the prevailing conditions. Accordingly even those who agree with this view in principle only accept it with the proviso that it is only valid in general and not in every case and, above all, not for those who are critical of the prevailing power relations.

Nevertheless, it is precisely this idea that criticism of the prevailing conditions raises us above them that Adorno calls into question. Instead he stresses that the

> detached observer is as much entangled as the active participant; the only advantage of the former is insight into his entanglement, and the infinitesimal freedom that lies in knowledge as such. His own distance from business at large is a luxury which only that business confers. This is why the very movement of withdrawal bears features of what it negates.
>
> (2005, p. 26)

The idea that we are, for whatever reasons, personally strong enough to resist the impact of restrictive conditions on our own ways of thinking and acting implies, as he points out, the idea of being better than others, which is an underhand way of justifying existing power relations: "It is as old a component of bourgeois ideology that each individual, in his particular interest, considers himself better than all others, as that he values these others, as the community of all customers, more highly than himself" (ibid., p. 27).

The notion that we are personally immune to the demoralizing effects of the prevailing conditions that we perceive in others is, as Adorno explains, tantamount to "severing the moral principle from the social and displacing it into the realm of private conscience ... It dispenses with the realization of a condition worthy of men that is implicit in the principle of morality" (2005, p. 94). However, a morality that abstracts from the basic premises that enable us to live it, is, as Adorno puts it, "itself a deformation of good ... it aims at alleviation, not cure, and consciousness of incurability finally sides with the latter" (ibid., p. 94). It is based, as he explains, on lies and forces us to lie, while with every lie we undermine the resistance to the conditions that compel us to lie: "A man who lies is ashamed, for each lie teaches him the degradation of a world which, forcing him to lie in order to live, promptly sings the praises of loyalty and truthfulness" (ibid., p. 30). Under these premises interpersonal relations will be guided essentially by mutual mistrust and efforts to find out what the other persons are about in order not to be outwitted by them. "Nobody believes anybody, everyone is in the know" (ibid., p. 30). At the same time Adorno views lying as a technique "enabling each individual to spread around him the glacial atmosphere in whose shelter he can thrive" (ibid., p. 30).

A first step toward overcoming restrictive conditions will thus be, says Adorno, to be totally clear about the demoralizing effects that this has on our own ways of thinking and acting, rather than simply seeing them in other people or consoling ourselves with the thought that our actions are at least less problematical than theirs. To call into question restrictive conditions in a manner that is not subjectively grounded, i.e., based on our own experiences of constantly being prevented from doing what we consider necessary under the prevailing conditions, is, as Adorno stresses, to misuse "critique of society as an ideology for ... private interest" (2005, p. 26). It is an "ideology for those wishing with a bad conscience to keep what they have" (ibid., p. 39). Such criticism remains focused on maintaining one's own position of relative superiority over others; it is a kind of "critical" coming to terms with the prevailing conditions. Effective critique of social reality presupposes, to quote Adorno, "sufficient involvement in it to feel it itching in one's fingertips, so to speak, but at the same time, the strength to dismiss it" (ibid., p. 29). Nonetheless, Adorno does not further explain why and how the awareness of our active involvement in the social reality we want to overcome will enable us to free ourselves from it. Yet by bracketing out this question he indirectly supports a view that he simultaneously calls into question elsewhere in his writings, namely that it is a question of simple enlightenment and/or personal strength of character as to whether we are able to act in accordance with our own insights and interests or not.

At the root of Adorno's deliberations is the experience of German fascism and the question as to how it was possible "that something like Auschwitz could have occurred in the midst of more or less civilized and innocent people" (2003, p. 30).

To find an answer to this question, he stresses, a turn to the subject is be required. By this, in contrast to the view of traditional psychology, Adorno does not mean that we should investigate individual ways of thinking and acting from the external standpoint with its focus on developing and improving the strategies and techniques to shape and control other people's behavior or performance. He is far more interested in analyzing the psychological conditions that have led "normal" people to support the fascist system more or less uncritically, if not enthusiastically. However, since Adorno does not see any way of changing the current societal conditions, in the final analysis his argument remains oriented toward changing the individuals. Thus, he states in his article "Education after Auschwitz":

> Since the possibility of changing the objective – namely, societal and political – conditions is extremely limited today, attempts to work against the repetition of Auschwitz are necessarily restricted to the subjective dimension. By this I also mean essentially the psychology of people who do such things ... What is necessary is what I once in this respect called the turn to the subject. One must come to know the mechanisms that render people capable of such deeds, must reveal these mechanisms to them, and strive, by awakening a general awareness of those mechanisms, to prevent people from becoming so again.
>
> (2003, p. 20f.)

Even if the awareness of these mechanisms "does not straightaway eliminate the unconscious mechanism, then it reinforces, at least in the preconscious, certain counterimpulses and helps prepare a climate that does not favor the uttermost extreme" (ibid., p. 31f.). The greater the awareness of these mechanisms, the greater is the likelihood that "people would better control those tendencies" (ibid., p. 32).

Since Adorno more or less neglects the possibility that societal conditions can be changed he also fails to consider the question as to how subjects perceive this possibility. Nevertheless, in avoiding this question he indirectly reproduces the conventional opposition of the individual and society, according to which the only option open to the individual is obviously to submit to the current conditions without question and to try to get the most they can out of them or to avoid being affected by them as far as possible. This mode of coping with the situation always requires us to work on ourselves, which includes keeping a check on all insights and impulses for action that could impair our good relations with those who have the say in a given situation. The main method required for such a "turn to the subject" is, as Adorno concludes, to exercise critical self-reflection and to encourage others to do so. "One must labor against this lack of reflection, must dissuade people from striking outward without reflecting upon themselves. The only education that has any sense at all is an education toward critical self-reflection" (2003, p. 21). Yet he does not further discuss the question as to under what conditions such critical self-reflection subjectively appears necessary and possible. What is clear for him, however, is the direction that such self-reflection must take. Since psychoanalysis has shown, as he explains, that "all personalities, even those who commit atrocities in later life, are formed in early childhood, education seeking to prevent the repetition must concentrate on early childhood" (ibid., p. 21). Adorno considers the "inability to identify with others" as one of the main factors contributing to Auschwitz and indifference to the fate of others as an essential prerequisite for the submissiveness with which the majority of German people complied with fascist measures and helped to implement them against those who were excluded as different. "The coldness of the societal monad, the isolated competitor, was the precondition, as indifference to the fate of others, for the fact that only few people reacted" (ibid., p. 30). Social relations were, as he emphasizes, determined merely by a "business interest": "One pursues one's own advantage before all else and, simply not to endanger oneself, one does not talk too much. That is a general law of the status quo. The silence under terror was only its consequence" (ibid., p. 30). Since Adorno sees this reciprocal coldness "as the condition for disaster" (ibid., p. 31), he also sees this as the starting point for effecting change. However, he points out, simply calling for people to show more love and kindness to each other is to no avail since such appeals would be part of a system that produces this coldness, so "The first thing is therefore to bring coldness to the consciousness of itself, of the reasons why it arose" (ibid., p. 31). He sees these reasons as residing "in the domain of the individual" meaning, following the explanatory model of psychoanalysis, that they are due to an impaired early childhood. In his view the main cause of problematic development is "the lack of love" that the individuals have experienced in their past. Individuals who have not experienced love cannot give love and are themselves not lovable – developments we must become aware of in order to be able to counteract them (ibid., p. 30f.).

Yet Adorno goes on to point out that neither mutual indifference toward each other nor mutual isolation from each other precludes the wish to bond but that they even imply it to a certain degree – as a compensation for the inner void. Adorno speaks here of the "herd drive," the "banding together of people completely cold who cannot endure their own coldness and yet cannot change it" (2003, p. 30). Such a merging is guided by "the very willingness to connive with power and to submit outwardly to what is stronger, under the guise of a norm" (ibid., p. 23). It "either become[s] a ready badge of shared convictions – one enters into them to prove oneself a good citizen – or produce[s] spiteful resentment, psychologically the opposite of the purpose for which they were drummed up" (ibid., p. 23). Nonetheless, submitting to rules and norms "that cannot be justified by the individual's own reason" (ibid., p. 23) entails not only disregarding one's own subjectivity but also disregarding the others as subjects. "People who blindly slot themselves into the collective already make themselves into something like inert material, extinguish themselves as self-determined beings. With this comes the willingness to treat others as an amorphous mass" (ibid., p. 26f.).

Lack of interest in the situations of others and the reasons they might have for their ways of acting is, as Adorno points out, characteristic not only of everyday thinking, but also of scientific thinking. This is manifested in the "primacy of the general over the particular" according to which the particular is seen as a "through-station" to the general without any significance of its own. Thus subordinating the particular to the general would, as Adorno points out, "all too quickly [come] to terms with suffering and death for the sake of a reconciliation occurring merely in reflection – in the last analysis, the bourgeois coldness that is only too willing to underwrite the inevitable" (2005, p. 74). To counteract the neglect of the particular in favor of the (alleged) general, Adorno calls for a concept of science in which the particular is not simply a "through-station" but both the starting point and the endpoint of scientific research.

> Knowledge can only widen horizons by abiding so insistently with the particular that its isolation is dispelled. This admittedly presupposes a relation to the general, though not one of subsumption, but rather almost the reverse. Dialectical mediation is not a recourse to the more abstract, but a process of resolution of the concrete in itself.
>
> (Ibid., p. 74)

However, what Adorno has to say about what such a dialectical mediation would look like remains relatively vague. He discusses dialectical mediation not as one and the same process comprising both individual and societal development, but, similarly to the conventional severance of individual and society, as separate processes on the individual and societal levels. Thus on the one hand he states:

> Nothing less is asked of the thinker today than that he should be at every moment both within things and outside them – Münchhausen pulling himself out of the bog by his pig-tail becomes the pattern of knowledge which wishes to be more than either verification or speculation.
>
> (Ibid., p. 74)

On the other hand, he speaks of an "emancipated society" that "would not be a unitary state, but the realization of universality in the reconciliation of differences" (ibid., p. 103). Instead of propounding the goal of abstract equality, which is "all too compatible with the most insidious tendencies of society" (ibid., p. 102), emancipatory politics "should point to the bad equality today … and conceive the better state as one in which people could be different without fear" (ibid., p. 103). Such statements are consistent with the perspective of social relations in which "the free development of each is the condition of free development for all," as Marx and Engels had formulated it in the *Communist Manifesto*. Nevertheless, if this vision is not to remain at the level of a mere utopia the task of a critical social science/psychology must be to clarify what it can contribute to the practical realization of such a humanization of social/societal relations.

It is here that Critical Psychology comes into play. It agrees with many of Adorno's statements, and in particular with his view that a critical social science must start with the subject. However, there are differences of opinion as to what this means in concrete terms. Critical Psychology goes further than Adorno in that, starting from the insight that we always perceive reality through the medium of the concepts available to us, it has chosen to make the prevailing understanding of human subjectivity itself the focus of its analyses and examines how it functions to justify existing power relations. In extensive analyses we attempted to trace the phylogenetic development to the societal existence as the species-specific mode of human life (for an overview see, for example, Charles Tolman, 1994). In contrast to a life at the pre-human level, here the individuals are, in principle, able to join together to pursue the shared aim of creating the conditions of their lives in accordance with their own experiences and hopes instead of having only to make the best possible use of the circumstances in which they happen to find themselves. In this context, we coined the term "generalized agency." It refers to the fact that the specifically human ability consciously to determine the conditions under which we live rather than simply having to accept them as they are can only be realized on a supra-individual level, i.e., together with others and through coming to a shared understanding about the subjective necessity and possibility of exerting such a substantial influence on the development of society. In this sense Critical Psychology does not see human subjectivity as limited to the individual, but rather as being manifested in the specifically human capacity to determine the conditions of our life instead of merely adjusting to them. Thus seen, the self-determination of the individual can only be achieved by determining the conditions that determine our views and actions. In this context, to act with awareness means to act in accordance with our own insights and interests. However, it is only necessary to become clear about our own interests to the extent that this has consequences, i.e., that we see a possibility of exerting an influence that will result in change. In turn, our interests themselves develop, are modified and become more precise as we realize them in practice. Therefore, in a psychology from the standpoint of the subject as understood in Critical Psychology, "subjectivity" is not seen as something residing within individuals that can be captured, evaluated, shaped or controlled in one way or another from an external standpoint. Rather, human subjectivity manifests itself in our capacity to determine the conditions of our life instead of being determined by them.

Seen in this way, our actions as human beings are determined neither by our (innate or acquired) personal dispositions nor by the conditions under which we live, but are rather rooted in our capacity to expand our influence on the life conditions that we share together, in accordance with our interests and needs as we perceive them. Following Leontiev, it can thus be said that this capacity is not "given" to us but that we must realize it – both cognitively and practically. In this sense, in order to exercise our generalizing agency we need to transcend the level of the immediately obvious, by including an intermediate phase in which we attempt to establish the preconditions that will allow us to tackle the pressures jointly, instead of having to submit to them. In this sense, the standpoint of the subject does not refer to single individuals, but is rather, as Holzkamp calls it, the standpoint of a "generalized" subject. This involves the task of developing a meta-standpoint from which the self-limiting function of the common self-defenses become visible – as well as the ways in which the defenses interact to reproduce conditions that enforce such a defensive-restrictive behavior on us. This meta-standpoint results, as Holzkamp points out, from a process "in which the individual learns, in a kind of 'social de-centering' to abstract from her/his own standpoint and conceive her/himself as 'the other for the other'" (1983, p. 292; see also 2013b, p. 326). It requires us to recognize that each person has a particular view on the problem in question "which is absolutely on a par with my own, and in comparison to which my own view is in no way privileged or advantaged" (ibid., p. 325). In this approach, it is not the "irrationality" of individual actions that is the problem. Instead, it is the tendency to dismiss thoughts and actions that do not match our own ideas of a "right" life as irrational, irresponsible, etc. that is the subject of analysis. In other words, we will recognize and overcome the narrowness of our conduct of everyday life only if we can avoid falling into the trap of assuming that our particular perspective on the problem is the only valid one and a measure for judging the "rightness" or "wrongness" of what other people are thinking and doing. Rather, the main task of a psychology from the standpoint of the subject will be to help to transcend this narrowness by conveying the insight that our own view of the world is merely one particular segment of the whole whose complexity can only be comprehended if the perspectives of the others are also taken into account.

Only if we have a concept of generalized agency can we become aware of the inhumanness of reducing human subjectivity and agency to the individual. We have conceptualized the alternative of either being reduced to the individual "struggle for survival" or fighting against conditions that enforce this struggle on us by distinguishing these two options for action as restrictive or generalized agency. They draw attention to the fact that even under restrictive conditions two different kinds of action are possible. We can either "voluntarily" confirm our subjection to established power systems by trying to outdo others in order to avoid being outdone by them, or we can engage in the struggle against circumstances that enforce such a mutual disempowerment on us together with the "petty antipathies, uneasy conscience and brutal mediocrity" (to cite Marx, 1975, p.178) that are the corollary of such a "licensed existence." Which of these options individuals choose is less a question of their personal disposition than it is dependent on the concrete circumstances and available opportunities for action. In this sense, the expanded notion of human agency also implies a more comprehensive understanding of individual responsibility. It comprises not only our own actions, but also the societal conditions and, with them, the possibilities open to others to overcome the restrictions in their lives. Thus, a psychology that starts from the standpoint of the subject does not aim to advise people how to lead a "right" life, however it may be defined. Instead it highlights the many ways and situations in which we ourselves hinder the development of our potential agency by defending our actual stance as the only right one and dismissing any suggestion that it may be wrong. We can only continue the claim that we are right or at least better than others if we succeed in silencing those who have good reason to see things differently. Hence, what is important is to understand that the concepts of generalized and restrictive agency are not intended as directions for action but to be used only to clarify the societal preconditions and implications of our own actions they address the question of how far they are in line with our own realization that we are responsible for what we are doing and how far they are primarily defensive, i.e., directed at fending off all insights that could require actions that we feel would overtax us. Whenever we use these concepts to analyze the limitedness of views and actions merely as a problem of others, we inevitably reproduce the prevailing practice of seeing the problems as lying primarily in the individuals' lack of knowledge about the true causes of their difficulties and how they should be dealt with. We will then see our main task as being to impart to these others the "right" way to view and deal with the problems, and judge them according to their capacity or willingness to follow the instructions given to them.

Therefore, in contrast to the conventional practice of seeing ourselves only as victims of oppression or engaged in the fight against it, from the standpoint of the subject the struggle to overcome constricting conditions will only be successful if we do not ignore our involvement in them but explicitly address it. However, in order to be able to admit our active entanglement in suppressive structures that we seek to overcome we should not see this entanglement as our "personal" failure, but reflect upon it as a universal problem that is only negotiable at a supra-individual or societal level, that is, a problem that is shared. In other words, whereas in the light of the prevailing practice of polarizing the individual and society social conditions appear to us to be an external framework that we should utilize as effectively as possible for our own personal development, but for which we are not responsible, the concept of "generalized agency" comprises a broader concept of responsibility. It is not limited to the individuals' compliance with prevailing values and standards, but is concerned with the values and standards themselves in that it includes the task of clarifying the function they may have in justifying social imbalances. Since generalized responsibility is part of generalized agency, this does not, as it may appear in an individualistic view, place excessive demand on the individual. Rather, it is a precondition for recognizing how the common practice to reduce human agency and the responsibility to the individual is due to its restrictive and manipulative nature.

The external standpoint, from which such a focus on the individuals as the source of the problems appears to be natural, is based on the separation of theory and practice, and this, in turn, serves primarily to protect us from recognizing our co-responsibility for the practical realization of what we have recognized as necessary. Thus, dissociating theory and practice proves to be a most reliable means of combining opposition to established systems of power with coming to terms with them. It renders even the most trenchant criticism of restrictive conditions harmless – both for the status quo and for those who criticize it. Hence, our questioning of existing power relations will only be serious and potentially powerful and lasting if it addresses the many ways in which we find that our concrete efforts to act in line with what we have recognized as necessary are frustrated. By questioning the conventional separation of individual and society the concept of generalized agency in fact turns the relationship between the individual and society upside down, insofar as the interests of individuals do not have to be subordinated to the interests of society in general, but are subsumed in them. Yet this is only ensured under the premise that the individuals themselves have a notion of the fundamental unity of the societal and individual development and, thus, by implication, also of the societal dimension of anything that they do and think. In this perspective the dualism of the universal and the particular is misleading insofar as the universal can only emerge from the particular. If it is defined in contrast to the particular, it is merely a particular interest in the guise of universality, i.e., an interest of those who have the power to define how the "universal" must be read. In contrast, in a human science "universality" is not something fixed, but a never-ending process that does not take place over the individuals' heads but evolves out of their everyday activities and experiences and their endeavors to gain a more comprehensive perspective on them and to find out how far what they are doing meets their own claims and expectations on life (cf. Osterkamp, 2014).

To stay with Adorno's Münchhausen metaphor, we do in fact in a sense have to pull ourselves by our own hair out of the "bog" in which we are stuck. This is, however, only possible if we see the compulsion to lie "in order to live," and the violation of our personal integrity it implies as a shared problem that can only be overcome if we do not claim to have already reached a position above the bog from where we can help those out of it who still are mired in it. Thus, Critical Psychology also shares Adorno's emphasis on the importance of self-reflection as pivotal for a science whose aim is not to optimize the means of shaping and controlling individuals, but to develop a scientific language that enables individuals to recognize the societal dimension of what they are doing and striving for. However, here again Critical Psychology goes beyond Adorno insofar as it focuses above all on the question as to how the general limitations of our own thinking and action affect others and, hence, also our relationships with them and consequently also whether we will be able jointly to overcome the conditions that are disempowering all of us. Such a self-reflection that relates to the effects of our actions on social and societal relations requires us to communicate with those who are more or less directly affected by them. Correspondingly, with reference to Marx, Holzkamp uses the term "social self-clarification," meaning an orientation toward reaching a meta-standpoint that renders it possible to consider individuals' differing views on the problems at hand relative to the different positions they have within given power relations and the constraints and obstacles associated with them (see also Holzkamp, 2015, chap. 3 in this volume).

The specific scientific language for such a psychology that aims at "social self-understanding" is, as Holzkamp emphasizes, the "reason discourse" (chap. 3 in this volume, p. 85; see also Holzkamp, 2013b, p. 281ff). It is based on the recognition that all actions, no matter how strange they might appear to us, have their grounds, i.e., that individuals always have reasons for what they are doing. Looked at in this way, the problem is not the lack of reason or irrationality of the actions of others, but our own tendency to dismiss all thoughts and actions as being irrational or lacking in reason as soon as they contradict our own notions of what is "right" and should be done. By denying that other people have reasons for their actions, as Holzkamp points out, we deny them their subjectivity; that is, we see them primarily in terms of how we can use them for our own ends, which, in turn, we consider to be beyond any need for critical scrutiny. Thus when we deny that others have reasons for their actions we are at the same time also defending against the conflicts that we would experience if we accepted our co-responsibility for overcoming the restrictions on other people's scope of action. In this context Holzkamp speaks of "pre-reflective features of inter-subjective relations" that are characterized by "*centered views, irreversibility of standpoints and thus the impossibility of integrating the other's standpoint as an (however contradictory) aspect of one's own*" (2013b, p. 332). Such "*centered* relationships" are, as he goes on to explain, "the formal side of meaning/reason complexes which, in one way or other, factually contain the exclusion, suppression, negation, disregard of the – individual or collective – other's interests in their life and dispositive power over it" (ibid., p. 333).

Since from the perspective of a psychology from the standpoint of the subject others are a potential part of my own subjectivity, negating their subjectivity, i.e., the grounds they have for viewing the problems in the way they do, always also curtails my own subjectivity, i.e., my possibilities of a self-determined life. Nonetheless, as nobody will consciously choose or accept the self-disempowering implications associated with such restricted and self-centered views and actions, it can be assumed, as Holzkamp points out, that we are dealing here with

> unconscious or only partially conscious experiences as, for instance, social views whose "one-sidedness" and restrictedness – often in adopting established readings – appear so "self-evident" that alternative ways of thinking remain invisible or repressed, thus constituting the tacit knowledge to be developed into voiceable (and reflectable) knowledge in the process of social self-understanding.
>
> (2013b, p. 332)

In other words, recognizing the fact that all views and actions, whether we understand them or not, have reasons makes it necessary to clarify what conditions are preventing us from incorporating the reasons that others have for what they are doing. Seen in this light, dismissing other people's views and actions as groundless is tantamount to negating also our co-responsibility for creating the prerequisites for realizing a generalized agency and responsibility. Nonetheless, I will have to dismiss the actions of others as irrational if I do not feel able to assume my co-responsibility for overcoming the preconditions that make them act in the way they do.

Put in another way, whenever I judge other people's actions I am arguing from an external standpoint that is characterized by the separation of theory and practice, and this, in turn, serves primarily to protect us from recognizing our co-responsibility for the practical realization of what we have recognized as necessary and hence also from experiencing the obstacles and intimidations that are liable to occur when established ways of thinking and acting are challenged. However, since judging others has become, as it were, second nature to us, it will hardly resolve the dilemma or lead us out of the bog if we simply try to refrain from "incorrect" ways of thinking. The task is rather to reach an understanding about the concrete conditions in which we "spontaneously" tend to reproduce ways of thinking and actions despite being aware of their restrictive and disempowering implications. Consequently, in a psychology from the standpoint of the subject, the main focus will be on the possibility of unwittingly reproducing the conditions we want to overcome.

Thus, being aware of the problematic nature of the external standpoint and its inherent orientation toward governing and controlling the actions of other people by no means protects us from falling back into the habit of denying their subjectivity by negating the reasons for their actions if we do not feel able to respond to them. It simply enables us to recognize the self-disempowering quality of such behavior and to call into question the concrete circumstances that make the "regression" to it appear reasonable. Hence, in order to overcome the opposition of theory and practice, we need, first of all, to have a conceptualization of their dialectical relationship. We can only be open to new insights to the extent that we can see ways of putting them into practice. A critical psychology that is satisfied with drawing attention to the need to change the prevailing conditions but fails to analyze the obstacles that stand in the way of such a change implicitly supports the ideology of the individuals as being themselves responsible for what they make of their lives. We cannot therefore overcome our entanglement in the opposition between theory and practice simply by being aware of the problems to which it leads. It is also not sufficient to draw attention to alternative perspectives such as those offered, for example, by Critical Psychology. We can only extricate ourselves from our implication in the prevailing thought patterns if we accept that we share the responsibility for the practical realization of the options we have shown to be possible by means of our critical concepts and comprehensive analyses. Only under these circumstances will we experience the objective and subjective obstacles that stand in the way of this realization and thus establish the empirical basis necessary to clarify the true function of prevailing blinkered views and their persuasive power. In other words, we can merely perceive these obstacles if we remain conscious of the fact that elaborating critical concepts that render visible the reality that in the prevailing view is systematically blotted out of awareness is only an important preliminary to the actual task, which is to raise for discussion the many obstacles that we will face if we attempt to act in line with our expanded understanding of the problems. To the extent that this does not happen, Critical Psychology also sees the objective obstacles essentially as subjective limitations, for example, as an expression of practitioners' personal inadequacies or their failings as practitioners. In this way, however, we contribute to the pressures we want to overcome, that is, we reinforce, for instance, the practitioners' perception that they must maintain the semblance of being able to manage their work and that their colleagues and clients who do not behave in the way they think they should are the only obstacle to their doing so (see, for instance Holzkamp, 2013a, pp. 87–111). Under such circumstances it is hardly possible to come to an understanding about the specific form of oppression that is prevalent under capitalist conditions, i.e., the fact that we are forced to act "voluntarily" against our better judgment and conscience while, at the same time, being prevented in many ways from voicing these contradictions. Conceiving of theory and practice as opposites thus means, as Holzkamp concludes,

> nothing other than neutralizing theory's critical potential for practice and making practice as smoothly integrable and feasible as possible. Or, to put it the other way round, we will only make progress when we no longer divide ourselves (or allow ourselves be divided) into theoreticians and practitioners.
> (2013a, p. 111)

References

Adorno, T. W. (2003). Education after Auschwitz. In R. Tiedemann (Ed.), *Can one live after Auschwitz? A philosophical reader* (pp. 19–33). Stanford, CA: Stanford University Press.

Adorno, T. W. (2005). *Minima Moralia: Reflections on a damaged life*. London: Verso.

Holzkamp, K. (1983). *Grundlegung der Psychologie*. Frankfurt/M.: Campus.

Holzkamp, K. (2013a). Practice: A functional analysis of the concept. In E. Schraube & U. Osterkamp (Eds.), *Psychology from the standpoint of the subject. Selected writings of Klaus Holzkamp* (pp. 87–111). London: Palgrave Macmillan.

Holzkamp, K. (2013b). Psychology: Social self-understanding on the reasons for action in the conduct of everyday life. In E. Schraube & U. Osterkamp (Eds.), *Psychology from the standpoint of the subject: Selected writings of Klaus Holzkamp* (pp. 233–341). London: Palgrave Macmillan.

Marx, K. (1944/1975). A contribution to the critique of Hegel's philosophy of right. In K. Marx & F. Engels, *Collected works, Vol. 3*, (pp. 175–187). Moscow: Progress.

Marx, K. & Engels, F. (1848/1976). The manifesto of the Communist Party. In K. Marx & F. Engels, *Collected work*, Vol. VI. (pp. 477–519). Moscow: Progress.

Osterkamp, U. (2014). Subject matter of psychology. In T. Teo (Ed.), *Encyclopedia of critical psychology* (pp. 1870–1876). New York: Springer.

Tolman, C. W. (1994). *Psychology, society and subjectivity: An introduction to German critical psychology*. London: Routledge.

9

EVERYDAY LIFE IN THE SHADOW OF THE DEBT ECONOMY

C. George Caffentzis

Debt: The Counter-Revolution of Everyday Life

In this chapter I will examine some dimensions of everyday life that have been affected by the development of a debt economy (with special emphasis on the United States, the place I know best and where I have been involved directly in anti-debt organizations for the last few years). I will contrast the consequences for everyday life when the working class's primary monetary relationship with capital is through debt rather than the wage. I conclude with an examination of the anti-debt movement that is appearing in the United States and is aiming to constitute a "revolution of everyday life" in the shadow of the debt economy.

Everyday Life, the Theory of Needs and Debt

The development of a science or theory of everyday life and the question of the conduct of everyday life is directly connected with an attempt to understand the dynamics of action outside of the immediately defined labor and valorization processes that largely were coincident with waged labor deployed in the confines of an officially recognized workplace like a factory, office, mine or farm. This science would be especially important for Marxists and other anti-capitalists who must deal with questions like: If the Marxist analysis of capitalism is correct, why have the workers not united, broken their chains and won the world long ago? Why is anti-capitalist revolution so difficult to achieve, if, as a contemporary adage puts it, the mathematical ratio is 99 to 1 in favor of those oppressed and exploited in capitalism?

Theorists like Henri Lefebvre and the Situationists attempted to locate and chart the course of what is the counter-revolutionary "hidden variable" of capitalist life that was immediately before our eyes and that would explain this paradox of revolution. Their answer was: *everyday life itself* (Debord, 1970; Lefebvre, 1991, 2002, 2005; Vaneigem, 2012). Within everyday life we find, on the one side, the forces binding the mass of the working class to capital and, on the other side, the hidden liberating revolutionary forces waiting to explode. The Situationists – partly disciples of Lefebvre and partly his nemeses – made the "revolution of everyday life" the central formulation of the solution of the Marxian paradox both theoretically and practically.

A major problem, however, with Lefebvre and his associates' analysis was its disconnection of the two spheres of life in capitalism: the productive and the reproductive, work and the everyday life. The banishment of the study of everyday life outside the official workplace seemed to grant it an autonomy from the "economic." Although Lefebvre is never given to drawing precise definitional lines around the territory of everyday life, he seems to have located it in the sphere of use-values (i.e., the usefulness of things that are discovered in the "work of history," as Marx (1976, p. 125) would have put it).

> Taken together, products and works make up the "human world." But where and in what sphere is the relation between living men and objects of consumption actualized? Where do they become goods in the concrete sense of the term? How are they appropriated? In everyday life, that sphere where needs and goods meet … Alongside the scientific study of the relations of production which is the province of political economy, there is thus a place for the concrete study of appropriation: for a theory of needs. Such a study enfolds philosophical concepts and makes them concrete; in a sense it renews philosophy by bringing it back into the sphere of real life and the everyday without allowing it to disappear within it.
>
> (Lefebvre, 1991, p. 91)

I reject the bifurcation of the conceptual field between the theory of needs and political economy or between production and reproduction; in the process I too revive philosophy in a way that can lead to a "philosophy of debt" that would be useful to those participating in the emergence of a debtors' movement in the United States and beyond.

Everyday Life and Debt

Given that a standard assumption of theorists of everyday life is, as Lefebvre claims in the passage above, that the value-creating sphere of life (the labor and valorization process of political economy) must be kept distinct from the process of inventing and satisfying needs, *working-class* debt was rarely included in the analysis of either everyday life or political economy. Why?

From the side of political economy this lacuna is understandable. Marx and his contemporaries were writing at the beginning of a transitional phase of the "indebtedness of the working class" in the 1860s (around the time of the formation of the first credit unions in Germany and the end of imprisonment for debt).[1] Working-class debt at that time was a relation between worker and worker, worker and boss or worker and shopkeeper, but by the beginning of the 20th century there was the beginning of indebtedness to banks and large merchant capital firms (with installment plans) (Cross, 1993, p. 148). If one examines the working class's confrontations with the courts in the 19th century, most of the plaintiffs were either employers or small shop-owners doing business with workers. Marx had no idea that eventually the majority of the working class in the United States would be customers of capital's financial sector. Only when the wage became steady enough and ample enough to act as collateral for a bank loan could workers qualify as debtors to financial institutions. This occurred after World War II on a mass scale first in the United States and later on in Europe, long after Marx wrote *Capital*.

In fact, the extension of credit to the working class is still uneven to this day. The World Bank estimates that about 2.5 billion people have no connection with a banking system. I am told that in Mexico at least until the 21st century most waged workers still did not have access to credit cards and other financial vehicles. The main exceptions were government workers whose jobs were (once) relatively secure and whose wage had the character of collateral. Therefore, these workers were especially hurt in the financial crisis of 1994–1995.[2]

The category of alienation is especially crucial here in ways that Marx did not develop (compared to the elaborate analysis of alienated [or estranged] waged labor and the production of commodities in both his early and late writings; Marx, 1961, pp. 67–83, 1976, chap. 8: "The buying and selling of labor power"). Part of the reason for this lack of balance between the attention paid to working-class wages and working-class debt was that the workers were only beginning to expect to be paid monetary wages in the period Marx is writing, whereas the proletariat had not yet entered into the status of debtor with respect to financial institutions and capital as a whole (Linebaugh, 1991, pp. 436–438).

Whenever Marx writes of creditors and debtors he speaks of capitalists, never of the working class, and when he speaks of debt, he speaks of profit debt (i.e., debt incurred in order to make a profit), never of use-value debt (i.e., debt incurred in order to purchase and consume a use-value).[3] In fact, Marx's definition of the value of the commodity labor power "is the value of the means of subsistence necessary for the maintenance of its owner" (Marx, 1976, p. 274). In other words, if the wage were equal to the value of labor power, it should satisfy the worker's subsistence needs and not require the worker to be in debt. As a consequence, working-class debt to banks and other financial agencies was inconsequential in Marx's analysis of capital and the notion of debt was unnecessary for the understanding of class relations in the industrial capitalism of his day. It would take more than half a century before workers would proceed from the ambivalent conquest of monetary wages to the entrance to the realm of credit and debt.

Marx summed his view of debt as a purely capitalist concern in the following passage: "The use-value of money lent out is its capacity to function as capital and as such to produce the average profit under average conditions" (Marx, 1981, p. 474). So much then for the long-term blindness to working-class debt in political economy, let us now look at the absence of working-class debt from the side of the theory of needs in the conduct of everyday life.

Those like Lefebvre who were writing in the post-World War II era and bemoaning the consumer society (while developing the theory of false needs) were not attending to the consequences for workers of the increasing indebtedness that was binding them to capital (Lefebvre, 2002, pp. 10–11). For Lefebvre and his collaborators seem to have neglected the fact that in order to "shop 'til you drop" most workers must "charge it." Indeed, working-class debt immediately becomes the dark mirror image of consumerism (i.e., the increased future work required to pay the debt).

The moralistic critique of consumerism and of the attention workers pay to commodities permeates the Leftist literature on everyday life in the 1960s to the present, including at times the writings of Lefebvre and the Situationists. The real problem, however, is not the pleasure that workers derive from commodities' use-value – as if the working class has been turned into a pack of pigs through a flick of the Circes of capitalism's commodity wand – but rather the price workers pay for this pleasure (whether it be "real" or "fancied"): the debt to capital, which is an appropriation of future waged labor.

It is only when the working class becomes indebted to capital that we can speak of the "colonization" of everyday life, in Debord's sense (cited in Lefebvre, 2002, p. 11). But when debt enters into the basic metabolism of the working class, it constitutes the *counter-revolution of everyday life*, i.e., debt makes the satisfaction of needs an essential part of the alienation of the worker and consequently helps explain his/her incapacity for revolutionary action.

Otherwise, debt is literally business as usual among capitalists. Certainly, the notion that there is one everyday life with a unified phenomenological structure is impossible to hold in a class society. Thus, can one assume that the everyday lives of successful capitalists and that of workers with precarious wages have much of interest in common? Hardly.

Infact, one outstanding class difference (both historically and experientially) is in the way that debt enters into the everyday lives of workers versus the capitalists. Debt does not enter into the capitalists' enjoyment of the use-value of their commodities. Debt for them is largely profit debt (money borrowed to make more money). Debt enters into working-class life in the form of use-value debt which has consequences that can be elucidated by extending an insight of Lefebvre's, who notes that there was a structural series characteristic, from the Marxist perspective at least, in the working class's everyday life until recently: need–labor–pleasure (Lefebvre, 2005, p. 11). This is the abstract structure of the puritan work ethic: *you must work before you enjoy the satisfaction of your needs or desires*. In his comments on this triadic series, Lefebvre notes that radical movements of the 1960s and 1970s tore the triad apart, valorizing pleasure and devalorizing labor while calling for "zerowork" and "refusal of work."

Working-class debt has had an even greater disintegrative effect, however, than these movements. It is important to note, for our purposes, what happens to the triad when debt is introduced into the everyday life of the proletariat. The triad becomes a quadrinomial series: need–debt–pleasure–labor. In a way, the introduction of "use-value debt" (i.e., debt incurred to buy commodities in order to enjoy their use-values) allows for the immediate pleasurable satisfaction of a need (or desire), hence valorizing pleasure (where the so-called "consumer society" becomes capital's response to the "revolt against work"), but the price of this "debt deal" is the deferral of labor into the future. This reversal of the temporal relation between pleasure and labor has a profound impact on workers' everyday life, especially given the rise of a debt economy and the increasing number of needs (and desires) satisfied by debt. It makes the pleasure of the satisfaction of needs and desires contingent, and instead of leading to the liberation from work, the pleasure derived from using the use-value of the commodities purchased creates a future of repression in an environment when the final step, waged labor, is neither guaranteed nor remunerated at an increasing level.

On the contrary, as capital's political economy shifted from Keynesianism to neoliberalism and the debt economy became hegemonic, the precarity of future waged labor turned into an inbuilt feature of life. Increasingly the proletariat's place in the debt economy becomes paradoxical: the more needs are satisfied through debt incurred on the basis of future waged labor, the more perilous this assumption of future waged labor becomes. Instead of liberation from work, this period has seen waged labor's increasing "necessity" to pay off past debt before a new day can begin, but in order to deal with this necessity, new debt is incurred, a bad infinity is created indeed, with revolution receding until it becomes a vanishing point on the horizon.

Four Kinds of Creditor–Debtor Class Relations and their Differential Place in Everyday Life

The relation of capitalists' everyday life to debt is one of the mainstays of literature from *Merchant of Venice* to *Buddenbrooks* to *Wall Street*, but the entrance of the debt economy into the proletariat's everyday life is a relatively recent development, as I have noted above. Though there have been thousands of studies of the wage relation and its impact on workers' everyday life, there are very few that have taken the restructuring of everyday life by debt as their theme (prominent among the exceptions are Graeber, 2011; Ross, 2014).

In order to take on this task (i.e., to construct a philosophy of debt), some prolegomena need to be dealt with. For example, it is important to distinguish four kinds of class-differentiated creditor–debtor relations in order to make clear what kind of debt we are dealing with.

It is important to recognize that debt is not one relation between creditor and debtor, although many analysts leave it at that. Debt has class dimensions that are important to distinguish since they have very different consequences for everyday life. Let me specify the logical possibilities of the indebtedness relation ("x→y" meaning "x lends to y") between capitalists (C) and workers (W) as creditors or debtors:

(a) C→C
(b) C→W
(c) W→C
(d) W→W

The first category is the standard form of debt in a capitalist society from its beginning. Capitalists borrow money from other capitalists (individually and/or collectively in the form of banks and other financial institutions) largely in order to "make money." This kind of debt is "profit-debt" (as defined above). In most capitalist societies this type of debt is the largest in monetary volume and it is crucial for the functioning of capitalist economy. That is why financial capital and banking appear at the beginning of capitalism along with primitive accumulation (of labor power), since it is a direct way to create the capitalist class in an operational manner. For with C→C debt capitalists look beyond their immediate interests (their own factory, farm, mine or office) into the whole realm of capitalist production. This debt creates a collection of capitalists (bankers) who are materially interested in other capitalists' business. Historically speaking, this kind of debt was a first step in capitalist class formation (we might call it the "primitive accumulation of the capitalist class") that took place the moment when the "blood and fire" of the enclosures in Europe and the conquest of the Americas became the crucible for making the world working class in the 16th century.

C→C debt is suffused with suppressed inter-class struggle, for a capitalist gets into debt in order to appropriate workers' labor that is always done in the midst of struggle (whether open or covert) while a financial capitalist loans money to a fellow capitalist in order to appropriate interest from the profits the latter appropriates. However, as Marx points out:

> [Interest] represents this character of capital as something that falls to it outside the production process and is in no way the result of the specifically capitalist character of this production process itself. It presents it not in direct antithesis to labour, but, on the contrary, with no relationship to labour at all, merely as a relation between one capitalist and another.
>
> (1981, p. 506)

In this kind of debt, workers are kept out of the ideological action. If they feel the impact of inter-capitalist debt (e.g., their employer is forced to declare bankruptcy because s/he/it defaults on her/his/its loan obligations to a bank), they appear as innocent bystanders in the fallout.

To see how the class struggle affects C→C debt, one simply needs to ask, what determines the interest rate of this debt? As Marx puts it, there is little of nature but much of convention determined by power to it:

> The prevailing average rate of interest in a country, as distinct from the fluctuating market rate, cannot be determined by any law. There is no natural rate of interest, therefore, in the sense that economists speak of a natural rate of profit and a natural rate of wages.
>
> (1981, p. 484)

Clearly, the average rate of profit and zero are its limits, since capitalists would not borrow money and go through a cycle of production only to give all his/her/its profits to the bankers, and the bankers do not lend their money for nothing. But within these limits, the rate of interest is determined by intra-capitalist conflict (called "competition"), custom and legal tradition, which do not include workers. What is revealed in C→C debt, however, is the capitalist common, or, as Marx puts it: "Here capital really does emerge, in the pressure of its demand and supply, as *the common capital of the class*, whereas industrial capital appears like this only in the movement and competition between particular spheres" (1981, pp. 490–491).

The second category, C→W debt, is the form of credit that developed in the early 20th century after a long period when workers had no collateral. With the qualifications noted in the previous section, this debt is "use-value debt." It was only after World War II that the wage, for many white, male workers, became stable enough for them to be able to qualify for loans (home mortgages, medical debt, student loans, auto loans, etc.) from banks, mortgage companies and the like. This kind of debt has grown inordinately in the last half-century and has become a central aspect of everyday life in the United States (and increasingly in Europe as well).

In this debt relationship the temporal order is reversed compared to the wage relation. The worker debtor receives the money before s/he performs the work needed to earn a wage large enough to pay back the debt's principal and interest to the capitalist creditor. The creditor is temporally vulnerable to the debtor and so the creditor class has developed a whole battery of painful, terrorizing instruments throughout history – tortures, enslavement, servitude, eviction, repossession, foreclosure and psychic torments – in order to guard against the worker debtor using the social surplus implicit in debt without repaying it to the creditor. For the existence of loanable wealth implies that there is more wealth available than is needed to simply reproduce the society. The instruments of torture were often seen as ways to "remind" the debtor of the obligation to repay the debt. But there is another function to these instruments: to repress the deep (almost innate) conviction that in an equitable communal society, those in trouble have the right to tap the social surplus (Caffentzis, 2007).

The third category, W→C debt, might appear trivial, for, after all, how do workers put capitalists in their debt, given the power hierarchy implicit to capitalist society? In actual fact, some of the largest forms of debt in the United States are exactly of this kind, although they are not categorized in this way. The two kinds of debt that capitalists incur to workers are "wage debt" and "pension debt." Wages and pensions are some of the largest monetary categories in contemporary capitalism, yet the wage-relation involves first that workers work before they are paid their wages (from one week to one month) and second that pension funds are loaned to capitalist firms (in the form of bonds). Indeed, the latter category in dollar terms is quite large, comprising even in the late 1990s 10% of corporate debt that in 2010 was approximately $25 trillion. If those ratios still hold, then there would be a good part of $2.5 trillion in corporate bonds that workers, through their pension funds, loaned to the capitalist class! Certainly, given the fuzziness of the distinction between stocks and bonds, this should be considered a conservative figure.

In 2010 the total wages paid in the United States was $6 trillion (Johnston, 2011). All or almost all of this $6 trillion was "lent" to the capitalists during a pay cycle, being the exchange value of the labor power on the labor market in 2010 for different periods of time and without interest. So if a worker receives $100 at the end of the week, the capitalist had the use of the labor power before paying for it, i.e., s/he had the use of a commodity worth $100 for a week before paying for it. Thus the worker lent the capitalist, interest free, the equivalent of the weekly wage. True, the capitalist received this loan in the form of a commodity (labor power) and not money, but s/he/it is still in a more profitable condition than if s/he/it had to pay the worker before working! For example, the capitalist could invest the $100 that s/he/it did not have to pay at the beginning of the work-week and earn interest for a week on the money. If the capitalist repeated this for 52 weeks, at an interest rate of 5% a year, the capitalist would yield an extra $5 over the year. Generalizing this scenario, we see that would yield $300 billion (= 5% of $6 trillion) per year for the capitalist class as a whole. In effect, that is the working class's structurally imposed loan to the capitalist class. Of course, there have been many times when the capitalist not only gained interest, but s/he/it reneged on the wage payment and absconded with the workers' product, i.e., the capitalists used the temporal asymmetry between work and the wage to steal from the worker.

The fourth category, W→W debt, is the least examined, but it is essential to mention it if we are to understand the conduct of everyday life of the working class and its historic possibilities. The biggest creditor to the working class, I suspect, is the working class itself. I can't prove this assertion because there is no statistical category that specifies this type of loan, since it is most often contracted "off the books" and as part of a wider set of exchanges, gifts and plain cooperative behavior of a "don't mention it" character. Workers were "lending" to their family members (especially their children and siblings), workmates, drinking buddies, fellow gang members and select co-religionists long before capitalist institutions like banks were. Though payday loans are a multi-billion dollar business today, they are a sign of the breakdown of working-class communities, because the practice of friends and relatives lending money to friends and relatives "until the end of the month" is a sign of the strength of solidarity within the workers' community (Strike Debt, 2014, pp. 125–129).

Credit unions that began as mutual aid organizations also complemented these individual-to-individual loans within the working class. The credit union can be seen as the modern version of the tontine ("invented" in 1652 by an Italian financier), and even older forms of rotating savings and credit associations were documented in China in the 700s CE and in Japan in 1275 CE. The modern credit union formally began in Germany in the 1850s and 1860s (at the time of the drafting of Marx's *Capital*); by the end of the 19th century they had spread throughout Europe and in the first decades of the 20th century became the basis of workers' credit organizations in the United States. The resulting institutions are not trivial, economically speaking. In fact, according to Wikipedia's article on Credit Unions: "Credit unions in the United States serve 96 million members, comprising 43.7% of the economically active population … Total credit union assets in the U.S. reached $1 trillion as of March 2012" (Credit Unions, 2014). To get a sense of the size of credit unions with respect to the overall banking system, we should remember that the total assets of US commercial banks (that largely do C→C lending) is about $14.42 trillion.

So W→W debt is far from a negligible aspect of the everyday life of debt in the United States, but we will leave it to one side in examining the different forms of alienation and estrangement that C→W debt engenders.

It is important to distinguish between these different forms of debt because the ethical consequences of defaulting on C→W debt are quite different from defaulting on W→W debt. Indeed, by deliberately confusing the distinction between the two kinds of debt, the positive ethical attributes of the latter (solidarity and sharing of social surplus in emergencies) are appropriated by the former, so that not paying back a student loan debt from a multi-billion-dollar bank is made to be comparable to not paying back your old Uncle Joe when he needs the money for funeral expenses for his wife, your aunt!

The Dilemma of Debt Alienation in the Conduct of Everyday Life

When Marx turned his formidable powers of analysis to the everyday life of the working class, the worker was not yet a debtor to a financial capitalist. Some 150 years later, however, it is time for a fundamental economic-philosophical analysis of debt that emerges from Marxist studies of capitalism. In fact, in this part of the chapter I will follow the young Marx's analysis of "Estranged Labor" in a new debt key. I will discuss how: (1) debt estranges one from the objects purchased by it; (2) debt estranges one from one's self; (3) debt alienates one from others in the shame and guilt associated with it; (4) debt alienates one from the sense of class oppression.

Debt Estranges Debtors from the Objects Purchased by it

Marx points out that a key aspect of capitalist society is that the worker does not possess the object s/he labored to produce. As a recompense, one owns what one buys in most cases. But the objects that one purchases through debt have a different presence than commodities that are purchased outright. For these "debt-objects" appear to be at a hostile distance from the debtor. When the debtor is enjoying their use-values as if they were possessed, they at the same time open an ontological gap between the subject and the object. There is a built-in insecurity and precarity with the use-values of debt-objects, since if one does not pay the debt, the object's use-value is threatened, not because it loses its useful qualities, but rather because it can be repossessed by the creditor and a commodity has no use-value to one if one cannot use it! Just as in "Estranged Labor," where Marx observes that "the object which labor produces – labor's product – confronts it as *something alien*, as a *power independent* of the producer" (Marx, 1961, p. 69), so too in the realm of debt there is a similar loss of realization and indeed the desired object (or, the objectified desire) becomes an alien power that is independent of the debtor.

So as we follow the debtor from his/her waged workplace to his/her home, the physical center of everyday life, s/he enters the front door of a treasury of objects that are continually crying out that they are not his/hers, but at the same time the debt used to purchase them is definitely the debtor's. To be surrounded by the objectification of desire and at the same time to recognize that the objects are not really your property is a central experience in the everyday life of the debtor. This is most explicit in the so-called "home" that is mortgaged, i.e., the prime symbol of security and of the privacy of life is turned on its head when the home's value is "underwater," i.e., its value sinks below what the house can fetch on the real estate market. Just as King Midas's touch froze and killed all objects valuable for the purposes of life, so too debt puts objects purchased by its means under a precarious spell.

Alienation of the Debtors from Themselves

Debt also puts oneself at a distance from oneself, for the act of entering into an indebted state is to give over one's life, work and creativity to the creditor for a certain period of time (which can stretch to infinity, i.e., death). However, just as debt-objects have a duplicitous estranging character, appearing as the debtor's and simultaneously open for dispossession by the creditor once the debt is in default, the *act* that made their purchase possible is duplicitous and estranging as well. The estrangement arises from the exchange of *present* satisfaction of use-value needs and desires for *future* work and wages. This makes the comfortable certainty of the immediate satisfaction of needs and desires illusory, because the satisfaction is poisoned by the recognition that it is attached to the uncertainty of the future. How often has it happened that the increase in one's credit card maximum is taken as a signal to purchase more on credit, as if the debt-creating act of "charging it" was a typical example of commodity–money exchange. Such typical exchanges instantaneously shut down the mutual obligations of buyer and seller (under normal conditions); this is not the case with the purchasing of debt-objects. The seller might be free of future obligations, but the buyer is certainly not. S/he is entangled with the consequences of indebtedness for an indeterminate future, during which time s/he is estranged from his/her own self.

Alienation of Debtors from Other Debtors

One of the most impressive and at first baffling features of working-class indebtedness is the frequent combination of debtors feeling *shame* at being in debt to the capitalist and their *hatred* toward other debtors. This disturbing combination makes for tremendous difficulties in organizing to fight various forms of injustice operated under the cover of debt that one does not find in struggles around wages and working conditions.

First, the shame prevents debtors from openly revealing their plight to other debtors. For the fear of being identified as a debtor per se arises from the anxiety and vulnerability that the condition of indebtedness creates. This fear is intensified when the debtor is in default of his/her debt payments. Why this is the case has been the study of a number of thinkers, from Nietzsche to Graeber and Lazzarato, but whatever the cause, the result is the creation of a self-inhibiting resistance to challenge the condition and a sense of being in the wrong the minute one begins to refuse the debt.

Second, this infernal situation is compounded by another development that is only uncovered by organizing against debt: the deep hatred many debtors have to other debtors (and such debtor-hating debtors always appear, sometimes quite dramatically, in public forums). This state is a version of Sartre's famous false double consciousness or "bad faith," appearing in the realm of debt, for the debtor continually rejects his/her identity as a debtor, "I am not like them (the other debtors)," but then again, by the shame they express in the violence of this displacement, they must conclude that they have good reason to hate themselves but cannot admit it (Sartre, 1956, pp. 112–116).

Debt Alienates the Debtor from the Class Struggle

One of the distinctive effects of debt is the understanding of the class struggle it creates or, more accurately, annihilates. The wage-relation makes it plain that there is a direct relationship of exploitation between the collective worker and the boss. The workers create surplus value for the capitalist. But with debt the debtor is individualized, and the exploitation seems to vanish in the air. For there is no way to tell whether the person next to you is indebted to the same bank or financial institution. The workers' immediate awareness of their collectivity is therefore lost in the creditor–debtor relationship. For example, determining who exactly is your creditor is increasingly difficult to understand, as the loan is sliced up in "securitized" bundles and farmed out to many different investors or it is sold on the secondary market to collection agencies trained in the tortures of the Spanish Inquisition.

There is a different logical structure to debt and wages that leads to different organizational challenges. Wages are in their nature collective. As a waged worker one is inevitably thrown into the same work condition with other workers and, for all the divisions – race, gender, skill, etc. – there are commonalities: (1) the capital–labor conflict that leads to collective action and organization (or, at least, it must be continually repressed); (2) the cooperation on the job that inevitably is required for any real work to be accomplished. Together, these commonalities are the foundation of collective wage struggle.

Debt tends to be individualizing and alienating. Debtors do not necessarily know each other unless they reveal their condition to others, and they are often too ashamed or guilty to do so. It is therefore necessary in any organizing around debt to bring the identity of the debtor to the surface and create the collectivity that is continually being repressed and decomposed by the creditor class.

Moreover, debt also has its ideological character. It is supposed to be a "fair exchange" between creditor and debtor. But in actual fact the creditor gains an interest payment (often many times the principal given the miserable "miracle" of compound interest) and in so doing receives a return for the risk incurred. But refusal to pay back the loan plus interest is considered to be immoral and unfair. The debtor is made to be ashamed, even to feel that s/he has committed a secular sin. Thus, instead of experiencing her/his own exploitation, the debtor is put into the position of justifying it. Hence, all the subjective elements necessary for the launching of the class struggle in any historical circumstance modeled on wage struggles are undermined in the everyday life of the debtor.

The Politics of Debt: Making Visible

Given these different kinds of estrangement, a movement against debt must confront from the start the everyday creation of much "incapacity building," i.e., estrangement and loss of power. In this the debtors' movement to come is similar to feminism and the gay movement of the past, for in order to begin to organize debtors one must overcome to some extent their inhibitions, their guilt and shame that brings about the accumulation of an "invisible army of debtors" that must come to visibility in order to have the power to undo the debt economy (i.e., an economy where in order to satisfy one's basic needs one must incur large debts) on a mass level.

That is why one of the first steps in forming debtors' groups is to offer one's own debt to collective scrutiny. It is only when this "inner sanctum" is opened to the light of public scrutiny that one can begin to join in the struggle. This revelation is a very powerful moment in the formation of a debtors' movement group, and the anxiety surrounding it can be intense. But there is a widely reported sense of liberation that follows this moment of revelation similar to the voluntary "coming out" rites in the gay movement. It offers the hope that the multiple forms of alienation typical of the debt relation reviewed above could be overcome.

From Occupy to Strike Debt

The power of the debt revelation was discovered in the Occupy movement sites. At least as far as I know, it was in these sites that the first-observed handwritten signs and cardboard placards openly declaring how much debt the bearer had accrued were produced. These debt revelations attest to the fact that it is only in the "commoning," i.e., the cooperation in creating the institutions of social reproduction, practiced in the Occupy site that the collective confidence of the Occupiers in each other had reached a pitch that could allow these revelations to come forth and overcome the trained incapacity instilled by the multiple alienations of debt. It was not enough to have a debt that was unjustly entered into, was managed corruptly and was having eviscerating consequences on your life in order to prompt revolt or, even, open protest. The power to make such protest or, even, revolt needed that self-liberation that could only come with the "revolution against the everyday life of a debt society" that the Occupy movement provided in the United States (for even that 2- to 3-month period between September 17 and Christmas of 2011).

It is no accident therefore that the student loan debt movement and other anti-debt organizations were formed as "offshoots" of the Occupy movement. For example, although I had been writing about debt in its various forms in a class context since 2007, it is only with the Occupy eruption that I could join with others to form actual anti-debt organizations.

In November 21, 2011 (a few days after the enclosure of Occupy Wall Street's occupation of Zuccotti Park), all these revelations were transformed into an organization, Occupy Student Debt Campaign (OSDC). The group started with the basic activist operating procedures of the Occupy movement, i.e., not making demands on the state, but going ahead to accomplish your ends directly. Since it was clear, however, that an immediate debt strike would be unfeasible, OSDC's organizational "hook" was the conditional pledge: "As members of the most indebted generations in history, we pledge to stop making student loan payments after one million of us have signed this pledge." Within the space of about a month nearly 3,000 student loan debtors came forward to take the pledge, there were also hundreds of faculty members who took the pledge of support:

> We support the Debtors' Pledge of Refusal and the principles on which it is based:
> ★ We believe that any student loan should be interest-free.
> ★ We believe the federal government should cover the cost of tuition at public colleges and universities.
> ★ We believe that private non-profit and for-profit colleges and universities, which are largely financed through student debt, should open their books.
> ★ We believe that the current student debt load should be written off.
> We also pledge to urge our unions and professional organizations to recognize this campaign of moral support for the debt refusers.

This response showed that there was enough anger and energy to motivate debtors to take some risky steps. There was also faith enough in OSDC to support its radical approach. The hope of the campaign was that both the pace of pledging and the creation of a nationwide network would create enough political power to begin to change the behavior of the private student loan sharks and the governmental vultures. However, neither hope was realized in the coming months. After the first month's euphoria in December, the following 3 months showed that the pace of pledging had come down to a trickle and, though there was a lot of interest expressed, there were few affiliates created in the country. As these facts began to be clear, we thought that we should see what else would be needed to stimulate the pledge activity and the formation of affiliates. This led to OSDC planning a set of events in April and on May Day that would re-enter our pledge and our direct action strategy into the center of the student loan debt discussion. The key event was on April 27, 2012 – Trillion Dollar Day ($1TD) – when we organized demonstrations in New York City spotlighting the fact that total student debt had just passed the one-trillion-dollar mark, making student loan debt larger than credit card debt by a couple of hundred billion. The event was a success, it was widely seen through live feed and awareness of our strategy (compared to the legislative approaches of the other student loan debt organizations) increased. In the following month 1,000 additional pledges came in. Nevertheless, the ratio of creative energy to actual pledges and affiliates was quite sobering.

Ironically enough, though visible anti-student loan debt pledgers were in the thousands, in the same period there were more than six million in the invisible army of student loan defaulters (Lewin, 2012). This gives a sense of the ratio of the visible and invisible "armies" and of the political problem it poses. For as long as it is considered almost 1,000 times more acceptable to default on a loan individually than to collectively pledge to confront the system, there will be no movement with the power to change the balance of forces between capitalist creditors and proletarian debtors (however creative the tactics used to "stay under the radar" and live "off the grid").

After May Day and continuing into the summer a core group in OSDC and others involved with Occupy Wall Street (OWS) began having public assemblies around debt. They felt that it was not enough to address student loan debt, but a more comprehensive approach to debt, dealing with credit card debt, housing debt, medical debt, fringe finance (like pay-day loans), is necessary. Slowly these discussions led to the formation of a new organization, Strike Debt (SD). What exactly were the relations between SD and OWS and SD and OSDC was not clear in the summer of 2012, even though (or because) many people were involved in all three organizations. Certainly, these relations are still being discussed and debated, but increasingly SD is moving away from seeing itself as a part of OWS while the OSDC has largely merged with SD.

Whatever the organizational connections, and however slow it has been in agreeing on principles and program, SD began its work with two projects that proved to be quite successful. One is the Rolling Jubilee (RJ) and the other is *The Debt Resisters' Operation Manual* (DROM) (Strike Debt, 2012, 2014). The RJ is an ingenious *political* use of the secondary market for loans that blends the style of a charitable organization with the tactic of turning some capitalists' shady game of bait and switch against such capitalists themselves. When a loan is in default, the bank that offered the loan is often willing to sell it on a secondary market for just pennies on the dollar. Most often a "bottom-feeder" collection agency is willing to buy the loan at a greatly reduced price and use all the tricks at its disposal to squeeze as much out of the defaulter as possible. But is it necessary for a predatory agency to buy these loans? No. Why couldn't a not-for-profit, politically motivated anti-debt organization buy these loans on the secondary market as well? It could. Were only sharks allowed in the secondary market pool? No, it wasn't true. And so after consultation with tax lawyers, collection agency "traitors" and other knowledgeable folk, the RJ started to roll and first bought $5,000 worth of medical debt and, after a telethon that fired the imagination of many, received more than $500,000 (from many who were undoubtedly debtors themselves) to buy back and liberate thousands of randomly chosen debtors from their debt worth more than $12 million as of today.

Here indeed is the realization of Brecht's wisdom in his poem, "All or Nothing": only the hungry can feed the hungry, and in parallel, only the debtors can free the debtors from their debts. Though in embryo and long after the crisis of 2008, we are witnessing the formation of a debtors' movement in response to the debt economy and its counter-revolution of everyday life.

Notes

1. Imprisonment for debt ended in England with the Debtors Act of 1869. The following is a list of countries and dates marking the end of imprisonment for debt: France, 1867; Belgium, 1871; Ireland, 1872; Switzerland and Norway, 1874; Italy, 1877; Scotland, 1880. There is no comparable date for the United States because this legislation went state by state.
2. Interview with Alfonso Ramierez, October 29, 2013.
3. See Marx, "On James Mill," where he gives an early account of the credit system that treats the capitalist and the poor worker quite differently: "The antithesis between capitalist and worker between large and small capitalists becomes even greater in that credit is given only to him who already has and is a new opportunity for the rich man to accumulate; or in that the poor man either confirms or denies his whole existence according to the arbitrary will and judgement that the rich man passes on him and sees his whole existence depend upon this arbitrariness" (cited in McLellan, 2000, p. 124).

References

Caffentzis, G. (2007). Workers against debt slavery and torture: An ancient tale with a modern moral. Retrieved from http://tinyurl.com/DROMCaffentzis4.
Credit Unions (2014, August 15). In *Wikipedia, the free encyclopedia*. Retrieved August 15, 2014 from http//en.wikipedia.org/wiki/Credit_Unions
Cross, G. (1993). *Time and money: The making of consumer culture*. London: Routledge.
Debord, G. (1970). *Society of the spectacle*. Detroit, Mi: Black and Red.
Graeber, D. (2011). *Debt: The first five thousand years*. New York: Melville House.

Johnston, D. C. (2011, October 19). First look at US pay data, it's awful. *Reuters*. Retrieved from http://blogs.reuters.com/david-cay-johnston/2011/10/19/first-look-at-us-pay-data-its-awful.

Lefebvre, H. (1991). *The critique of everyday life* (Vol. 1). London: Verso.

Lefebvre, H. (2002). *The critique of everyday life: Vol. 2. Foundations for a sociology of the everyday*. London: Verso.

Lefebvre, H. (2005). *The critique of everyday life: Vol. 3. From modernity to modernism*. London: Verso.

Lewin, T. (2012, September 28). Education department report shows more borrowers defaulting on student loans. *New York Times*, p. A16.

Linebaugh, P. (1991). *The London hanged: Crime and civil society in the eighteenth century*. London: Allen Lane.

Marx, K. (1961). *Economic and philosophical manuscripts of 1844*. Moscow: Foreign Languages Publishing House.

Marx, K. (1976). *Capital* (Vol. 1). London: Penguin.

Marx, K. (1981). *Capital* (Vol. 3). London: Penguin.

McLellan, D. (Ed.). (2000). *Karl Marx: Selected writings*. Oxford: Oxford University Press.

Ross, A. (2014). *Creditocracy and the case for debt refusal*. New York: OR Books.

Sartre, J.-P. (1956). *Being and nothingness*. New York: Washington Square Press.

Strike Debt. (2012). *The debt resisters' operation manual* (1st ed.). Retrieved from www.strikedebt.org.

Strike Debt. (2014). *The debt resisters' operation manual* (2nd ed.). Oakland, CA: PM Press.

Vaneigem, R. (2012). *The revolution of everyday life*. Oakland, CA: PM Press.

10

FROM CRISIS TO COMMONS

Reproductive Work, Affective Labor and Technology in the Transformation of Everyday Life

Silvia Federici

Introduction

The recognition that *everyday life* is the primary terrain of social change and within it we find a critique of institutional and political orthodoxy has a long history. Already Marx and Engels, in *The German Ideology* (1968), contrasted the study of the material conditions of our existence to the speculations of the Neo-Hegelians. A century later, the French sociologist Henry Lefebvre and the Situationists appealed to "everyday life" as an antidote to the bureaucratic French Marxism of the time. Challenging the Left's concentration on factory struggles as the engine of social change, Lefebvre argued that social theory must address the life of the "whole worker" (Lefevbre, 1947/1991, pp. 87–88) and set out to investigate how "everydayness" is constituted and why the philosophers have constantly devalued it. In this process he inspired and anticipated a new generation of radicals, starting with the Situationists, as his discussion of "consumerism," technological alienation and his critique of work in capitalist society set the stage for much of the literature of the New Left.

It was only with the rise of the feminist movement, however, that the critique of "everyday life" became a key to that comprehensive understanding of society that Lefevbre was seeking in his work. By rebelling against women's confinement to reproductive work and the hierarchies constructed through the sexual division of labor, the women's movement gave a material basis to the critique of everyday life and uncovered the "deep structure," the "arche," underlining and binding the multiplicity of daily acts and events that Lefebvre had sought for but never truly grasped.[1] From a feminist viewpoint it became possible, in fact, to recognize that the foundation of everyday life is the process of "reproduction," intended not only as procreation, but as the complex of activities – mostly performed by women – that on a day-to-day and generational basis reproduce our life and, at the same time, re/produce people's capacity to work (Federici, 2012c, especially part 1). In other words, feminists have shown that "everyday life" is not a generic complex of events, attitudes and experiences searching for an order. It is a structured reality, organized around a specific process of production, the production of human beings – which, as Marx and Engels pointed out, is "the first historical act" and "a fundamental condition of all history" (Marx & Engels, 1968, p. 48) – and its epicenter are domestic labor and gender relations. A theoretical and practical revolution has followed from this discovery that has transformed our concept of work, politics, "femininity" and the methodology of the social sciences, enabling us to transcend the limits of the traditional psychological viewpoint, which individualizes our experiences and separates the mental from the social.

At the core of the feminist "revolution" there has been the recognition that we cannot look at social life from the viewpoint of an abstract, universal, sexless social subject, because the racial and sexual hierarchies that characterized the social division of labor in capitalism, and especially the divide between the waged and the unwaged, produce not only unequal power relations but qualitatively different experiences and perspectives on the world. Second, while all experiences are subject to societal construction, it is of special significance that in capitalist society the reproduction of daily life has been subsumed to the reproduction of the labor force and it has been constructed as unpaid labor and "women's work."[2] For in the absence of a wage, domestic work has been so naturalized that it has been difficult for women to struggle against it without experiencing an enormous sense of guilt and without becoming vulnerable to abuse. For if it is natural for women to be good housewives and mothers, then those who refuse that work are not to be treated as workers on strike, but as "bad women." Third, if domestic work has been subsumed to the needs of the labor market, and if the family and the home are centers for the reproduction of the workforce, then familial, sexual, gender relations are "relations of production" and we should not be surprised by the contradictions that permeate them and by our inability to make them fulfill our desires. This realization has certainly been for women a liberating experience, and we can say that it has given the "everyday access to history and political life" (Lefebvre, 1961/2002, p. 41), revealing that *the personal is political*,[3] and the private/public divide is a political ruse, hiding the exploitation of women and mystifying their unpaid work as a "labor of love."[4]

It is important to stress that the feminist critique of everyday life has been not only theoretical but practical and political as well, triggering a democratization process that has left no aspect of our life, even our most intimate relations, unchanged (Federici, 2012d). Thanks to it, for the first time battering and rape in the family, traditionally condoned as conditions of housework, have been seen as crimes against women. The right of husbands to control their wives' bodies and to demand their sexual services against their will has been denied. In several countries, the feminist movement has led to the legalization of divorce and the right to abortion. More broadly, women have transformed their everyday interaction with the world, asserting a new power with regard to language, knowledge, relations with others, especially with men, and the expression of desire. Even the sexual act has been placed on a more egalitarian basis, as many women have begun to refuse the "fast sex" typical of marital life, advocating their right to sexual experimentation and to a sexual intercourse more conforming to the configuration of the pleasure-points in their bodies. Most important, the feminist movement established that women would no longer accept a subordinate social position and a relation to the state and capital mediated by men. This in itself has produced a social revolution, forcing significant institutional changes, such as the censoring of many practices and policies discriminating on a gender basis. Thus, from the viewpoint of Lefebvre's problematic, we could say that the feminist movement "has rehabilitated" (Lefebvre, 1947/1991, p. 87) and revalorized everyday life, making a searing critique of some of the most important institutions by which it has been structured. However, to the extent the movement could not turn its critique of the family and what I call "the patriarchy of the wage" into a critique of other forms of exploitation, and it equated "liberation" with "parity," "equal rights" and access to wage labor, it could not escape its cooptation by governments and the United Nations, which, by the mid-1970s, were ready to embrace edited forms of feminism as key elements in the restructuring of the world economy. As I have written elsewhere (Federici, 2014), two considerations plausibly motivated the decision of the United Nations to intervene in the field of feminist politics and appoint itself as the agency in charge of de-patriarchalizing the international power structure. First, the realization that the relationship between women, capital and the state could no longer be organized through the mediation of the male/waged workers, as the Women's Liberation Movement expressed a massive refusal of it and a demand for autonomy from men that could no longer be repressed. Second, there was the necessity to domesticate a movement that had a great subversive potential, being fiercely autonomous (until that point), committed to a radical transformation of everyday life, and suspicious of political representation and participation. Taming the movement was especially urgent at a time when, in response to the intractable "labor crisis" of the mid-1970s, a global capitalist counter-offensive was under way, aiming to re-establish the command of the capitalist class over work discipline, and dismantle the organizational forms responsible for factory workers' resistance to exploitation. It is in this context that we must place the launching of the Decades on Women and the first International Conference in Mexico City in 1975 that marked the beginning of the institutionalization of the feminist movement, and the integration of women in the globalizing world economy. As we know, in the space of a decade, as many obstacles to female wage employment were removed, women entered the waged workforce in large numbers, but, with that, the feminist revolution of everyday life came to an end. Reproduction, as a terrain of feminist struggle, was abandoned, and soon the feminist movement itself was demobilized and could not muster a serious opposition to the increasing dismantling of the welfare programs that, since World War II, had been an essential part of the social contract between capital and labor. Even more problematic, perhaps, is that in fighting for equal opportunity and waged work the feminist movement contributed to relegitimize the flagging work ethic and counter the refusal of work that had been so prominent in the workplaces of the 1960s and 1970s across the industrial world. Certainly, the lesson that we have learned in this process is that we cannot change our everyday life without changing not only its immediate institutions but also the political and economic capitalist system that governs their permutations. Otherwise, our struggles to transform our "everydayness" can be easily digested and become a launching pad for a rationalized system of relations more difficult to challenge. This is the situation that we are presently experiencing, which confronts us with an immense "crisis of reproduction" and, in response to it, a variety of initiatives that propose more cooperative forms of reproduction but, in the absence of a broad political project, may provide a safety valve to the social frustrations produced by the neoliberal regime.

In what follows I discuss this emerging "politics of the commons," asking how it may transform our reproductive relations and under what conditions it may become the path to a society not ruled by the logic of the state and the market. I first look, however, at the current reproduction crisis, with particular reference to the situation in the United States, which is the one I am most familiar with and the one that best exhibits the developments I have mentioned.

Everyday Life as Permanent Crisis

While some feminists have read the changes that have taken place in the lives of American women since the 1970s as an instance of progress, I argue that in many respects both women and men are today in a more difficult economic and social position than they were at the time when the feminist movement took off. Even the evidence of more egalitarian relations is very spotty. Undoubtedly, the expansion of the female wage labor force has increased women's autonomy from men. Also, as Nancy MacLean has pointed out, the fight for entrance in male-dominated jobs has contributed to "our own era's heightened consciousness concerning the social construction and instability of the categories of gender, race and class" (MacLean, 1999, p. 68).

Women, however, have entered the waged workforce at the very moment when waged work was being stripped of the benefits and guarantees that it had previously provided, making it impossible for them to negotiate the sort of changes in the organization of the work and the work-week that could enable them to reconcile work outside the home with the care of families and communities. Few jobs provide childcare or a schedule compatible with homemaking, even when it is shared. As for the commercialization of domestic work, that is, its organization as a purchasable service, this much-hailed development has proven to have serious limitations, like the high cost and low quality of the services provided. We now know, for instance, that the fast food that many workers rely upon is one of the leading causes of obesity that now affects many children. An option for those who have a steady income is hired domestic labor, but the present conditions of paid domestic work, and the fact that those employed are mostly immigrant women who seek this employment because of the harsh economic conditions in their countries of origin, rule this out as a solution.[5] Added to this is the fact that the cuts in social services – such as education, healthcare and in particular hospital care – have brought back to the home a significant quantity of housework, particularly with regard to the care of children, the elderly and those with illnesses or disabilities. Thus, the independence that entrance in waged work had promised has proven to be an illusion, at least for the majority, so much so that even among career-bound women there has recently been a return to the home and revalorization of domesticity (Matchar, 2013). Tired of struggling in a workplace that no longer tries to care for the workers' reproduction, still assuming they have wives at home, many women, in middle-class families at least, have presumably "thrown in the towel" and dedicated themselves to providing their families with a "high-quality" reproduction: baking bread, growing vegetables, shopping for nutritious food, schooling children at home and so forth. As Emily Matchar points out in *Homeward Bound* (2013), the newly reclaimed domesticity is also shaped by ecological concerns and the desire to know where food comes from, leading to the refusal of convenience food and generally industrially produced goods. Many women opting for it are also affected by the DIY (Do It Yourself) movements and are not as secluded as their mothers, becoming bloggers to spread and acquire information. But these are individual solutions that do not address the problems that the majority of women are facing and only deepen the social distances among them. They are a manifestation of the rise of a new individualism pursuing the "good life," but not through a social struggle for the "common good" (ibid.).

Because of the double load to which many are condemned, the long hours of work and low wages that are now prevailing, and the cuts of essential reproductive services, for most women everyday life has become a permanent crisis. In the United States, proletarian women on average work about 50 hours a week, 35 or more outside the home and about 3 hours a day in the home. If we add the (expanding) transport time and the time spent preparing to go to work we see that little time is left for relaxation or other activities. Furthermore, much of the work that women do is emotional/affective labor – pleasing, exciting, comforting, reassuring others – a task that, especially when performed for the market, is very draining and over time leads to a profound sense of depersonalization and incapacity to know what one really desires (Hochschild, 1983). This too, compounded by the economic downturn and the precarization of life, explains why women are twice as likely to suffer from clinical depression and anxiety than men. The figures are staggering. Women form the majority of the 15 million adults in the United States affected by depression. Some 40 million women suffer daily from anxiety; one in five will suffer from depression at some point in her life (Mayo Clinic Staff, 2014). Similar statistics come from other countries and the numbers are on the rise. In the United States, indicators also show a decline in happiness for women over the last decade and, most significantly, a decline in life expectancy that is especially pronounced for working-class women, who between 1990 and 2008 have lost 5 years of their lives compared with their mothers' generation.[6]

But the crisis of everyday life is not limited to women. Overwork and, at the same time, insecurity with respect to employment and the possibility to plan for the future are now pervasive problems, affecting all social groups and ages. There is also a breakdown in social solidarity and family relations. For in the absence of a steady wage, families are falling apart, at the very time when the forms of organization that, as late as the 1960s, characterized working-class communities are also disintegrating, unable to resist the impact of economic restructuring, gentrification and enforced mobility. Clearly the neoliberal restructuring of the world economy is mostly responsible for this situation. But as Leopolda Fortunati points out in her introduction to *Telecomunicando in Europe* (Fortunati, 1998) – a study of the impact of communicative technology on the reproduction of everyday life in Europe – we are also witnessing the consequence of the inability of the various social subjects who structure everyday life to mediate their interests and find forms of organizations enabling them to resist the devastating consequences of "globalization." Men's refusal to accept women's autonomy, for instance, as reflected in the increasing male violence against women, has contributed to weakening social bonds. Under these circumstances, everyday life, which is the primary terrain of mediation and confrontation among people, has been allowed to shipwreck; it has become a terrain from which many are fleeing, unable to sustain interpersonal relations that appear too laborious and difficult to handle (ibid., p. 27). This means that care-work, either by family members or friends, is not attended to, with consequences that are especially severe in the case of children and the elderly (Federici, 2012b). To what degree this is true can be judged by the new trend that is developing in Germany, which is to send elderly relatives, especially when affected by Alzheimer's disease, to be cared for abroad (Haarhoff, 2013).[7] Interpersonal, face-to-face communication, a key component of our reproduction, is also declining, both among adults and between adults and children, diminished in quantity and content and reduced to a purely instrumental use, as the Internet, Facebook and Twitter gradually replace it.

In brief, one of the most prominent facts concerning everyday life at present is a "crisis of reproduction" in the twofold sense of a drastic decline in the work of caring for other people, beginning with family members, and an increasing devaluation of everyday life to which the new communication technologies contribute, although they are not its primary cause. In this case as well statistics are telling. As we have seen, life expectancy is diminishing, and so is the quality of life, as daily experience is characterized by a profound sense of alienation, anxiety and fear. Mental disorders are rampant, for many fear that dispossession and homelessness may be just around the corner and experience a destabilizing lack of projectuality. What is most worrisome is that now these pathologies seem to affect even children, plausibly caused by the collapse of the care-work that family and school once provided. To what extent these mental disorders are "real" or are constructed – by doctors and pharmaceutical companies with the tacit assent of parents and teachers – in order to medicalize the unhappiness of a generation of children who, both at home and at school, are denied time, space and creative activities is difficult to tell. What is certain is that never have so many children and such young children been diagnosed with so many mental illnesses. By 2007 the number of mentally ill children had risen to 35 times the number in 1990 (Angell, 2011). One in five, including toddlers, according to the Center for Disease Control, may suffer a mental disorder (Williams, 2013). These include depression, hyperactivity, attention-deficit disorders. And, for all, the "cure" is a variety of psychoactive drugs that the schools and families liberally administer, so that by the time they are 10 years old some children take up to seven pills a day, even though their negative effects on their mental development are well known.

The reality is that in today's society children are the great losers. In a world where monetary accumulation is all, and all our time must be "productively" engaged, satisfying children's needs is a low priority and must be reduced to a minimum. This, at least, is the message that comes from the capitalist class, for whom children today are essentially a consumer market. There is almost a desire to erase childhood itself as a non-productive state, for instance by teaching toddlers – as some economists recommend – how to manage money and how to become wise consumers, and submitting them to an "attitude test" as early as age four, to presumably give them a good start in the race for economic competition. But the erasure of childhood proceeds also in working-class families, as parents are more and more absent from home and face severe economic crises that are a constant source of despair and rage. Adults, whether parents or teachers, have no time, no energies and resources to dedicate to children. They may teach them to speak, but not to communicate (Fortunati, 1998). And, judging from the spread of child abuse, they clearly see them as a disturbance. It is a worrisome sign of the intense crisis of parent–child relations we are now experiencing in the United States that between 2001 and 2011 more than 20,000 children – 75% of them under the age of four – were killed by their families, this being four times the number of troops killed in Iraq and in Afghanistan in the same years (Jilani, 2011; BBC, 2011).[8]

"Riprendiamoci la vita" – "Let's Retake our Own Life"[9]

How to stem this flight from the terrain of daily relations and reproduction? How to reconstitute the social fabrics of our lives and transform the home and the neighborhood into places of resistance and political reconstruction? These, today, are some of the most important questions on humanity's agenda. They are certainly the motivating force behind the growing interest – practical and philosophical – for the production of "commons"; that is, the creation of social relations and spaces built on solidarity, the communal sharing of wealth and cooperative work and decision-making (Caffentzis & Federici, 2013).

This project – often inspired by the struggles of indigenous peoples and now shared by a variety of movements (feminist, anarchist, green, Marxist) – responds to a variety of needs. First, there is the need to survive in a context in which less and less of the state and market provide the means of our reproduction. In Latin America, as Raúl Zibechi has well documented in his *Territories in Resistance* (2012), women in particular, in the 1980 and 1990s, pooled their resources to support their families, in the face of harsh austerity measures that left their communities demonetized or dependent on the remittances of those who have migrated. In Lima, women have created thousands of committees – shopping and cooking committees, urban garden committees, glass of milk (for children) committees, etc. – that provided different forms of assistance, and for many made a difference between life and death (Zibechi, 2012, pp. 236–237). Similar forms of organization have developed in Chile, where, after the Pinochet coup of 1973, in the face of devastating impoverishment and political repression, the popular kitchen "never stopped" (Fisher, 1993, pp. 177ff.). In Argentina as well, elements of a "collectivization" or socialization of reproduction appeared in the crisis of 2002, when women brought their cooking pots to the *piquetes* (Rauber, 2002, pp. 115–116). In Colombia, proletarian women, in the early 1990s, constituted themselves as *madres comunitarias* to care for children living in the streets. Begun as a voluntary initiative, after a prolonged struggle the *Madres Comunitarias* project is currently undergoing a formalization process whereby about 70,000 *madres* by 2014 will receive a small salary from the country's welfare department (UNC, 2014). But their work is still performed on the basis of communal solidarity, with the salary gained barely enabling them to survive and provide for the care of the children.

Neither in the United States nor in Europe have we seen the kind of collectivization of reproductive work mentioned above. However, more communal and self-managed forms of reproductive work are beginning to appear also across the "developed" world. Both in the United States and Europe urban gardens and Community Supported Agriculture are now well-established practices in many towns, providing not only vegetables for the pot but various forms of instruction especially for children, who may attend classes there on how to plant, how to preserve food and how to make things grow (Federici, 2012a, pp. 141–142).[10] Time banks, once a radical project, are currently spreading in mainstream America, as a means of acquiring services without monetary exchanges and above all acquiring new support networks and friendships.[11]

All such initiatives may appear small things in the face of the enormous disasters – social and ecological – that we are facing. But in a context of growing impoverishment and the militarization of everyday life, leading to paralysis, withdrawal and distrust of neighbors, these signs of a will to cooperate are encouraging. They are signs of a growing realization that to face the crisis alone is a path to defeat, for in a social system committed to the devaluation of our lives the only possibility of economic and psychological survival resides in our capacity to transform everyday practices into a terrain of collective struggle.

There is a further reason why it is crucial that we create new forms of social bonding and cooperation in the reproduction of our everyday life. Domestic work, including care-work and affective work, is extremely isolating, being performed in a way that separates us from each other, individualizes our problems and hides our needs and suffering. It is also extremely laborious, requiring many, often simultaneous, activities that cannot be mechanized, performed mostly by women as unpaid labor, often in addition to a full-time waged job. Technology – communication technology in particular – undoubtedly plays a role in the organization of domestic work, and is now an essential part of our daily life. But, as Fortunati argues, it has primarily served to replace, rather than to enhance, interpersonal communication, allowing each family member to escape the communication crisis by taking refuge in the machine (Fortunati, 1998, pp. 27–28).[12] Similarly, the attempts by companies in Japan and the United States to robotize our reproduction – with the introduction of nurse-bots (Folbre, 2006) and love-bots customized to satisfy our desires – are more signs of a growing solitude and loss of supportive relations than alternatives to it, and it is doubtful that in the future they will enter many homes. This is why the efforts that women above all are making to deprivatize our everyday lives and create cooperative forms of reproduction are so important. Not only do they pave the way to a world where care for others can become a creative task rather than a burden, they also break down the isolation that characterizes the process of our reproduction, creating those solidarity bonds without which our life is an affective desert and we have no social power.

Here, too, however, the danger of cooptation or "institutionalization" must be a pressing concern. For as long as more cooperative forms of re/production are surrounded by a sea of capitalist relations, the production of commons remains a contested terrain. Beside the risk of constructing gated communities and fetishizing localist solutions, we must consider the trend to view "the common" as "a third" (type of property) beside private and public, market and state, rather than an alternative to them (Bollier & Helfrich, 2012). But in this case "commoning" can only provide a safety valve to the excesses of neoliberalism (Caffentzis, 2014). It is crucial, then, that the commoning of our everyday life be constantly tested for its capacity to increase our autonomy and "delink" our reproduction from dependence on capitalist relations. Elsewhere, in an article written with George Caffentzis, we have outlined some of the criteria that help us test the capacity of "commoning" projects to go beyond the status quo. As we wrote in "Commons Against and Beyond Capitalism" (Caffentzis & Federici, 2013):

> i. Commons are not things, but social relations. Nevertheless, they must guarantee the reproduction of our life, according to the principle that all the wealth produced should be shared, and used for common enjoyment and not for commercial purposes and profit making.

ii. Commons also require a community as they entail obligations as much as entitlements; and they require collectively chosen regulations stipulating how the wealth we share will be utilized and cared for.

iii. To become a principle of social change, the production of commons must transcend the "politics of survival" and create not only *communities of care* but *communities of resistance*. To do so, however, we must oppose all social hierarchies so that a *common interest* can be created.

Commons, in this context, are both *objectives* and *conditions* of our everyday life and struggles. In an embryonic form, they represent the social relations we aim to achieve, as well as the means for its construction. They are not a separate struggle but a *perspective* we bring to every struggle and every social movement in which we participate. It only remains to be added that this is not a utopia but a reality already in the making. As a member of a Zapatista community put it: "Resistance is not merely refusing to support a bad government, or not paying taxes or electric bills. Resistance is constructing everything that we need to maintain the life of our people" (Zapatistas, 2014, p. 70).

Notes

1 As he wrote, "daily life, like language, contains manifest forms and deep structures that are implicit in its operations, yet concealed in and through them" (Lefebvre, 1981/2005, p. 2).
2 The first feminist document to analyze domestic work as work producing labor power was Dalla Costa (1972/1973).
3 On the origin of this slogan, see Carol Hanisch (1969).
4 See on this subject "Wages against Housework" (1975) in Federici (2012c, pp. 15–22).
5 On the "globalization of care," see Ehrenreich and Hochschild (2002).
6 See Olshansky (2012) and Potts (2014). Also, the March 2013 issue of *Health Affairs* reported that life expectancy in the United States has lost ground in the past decade compared to other countries so that the United States now ranks at the bottom of 21 industrialized nations for life expectancy. But the drop was especially notable for non-educated white women, who on average could expect to live 5 years less than their mothers (Kindig & Cheng, 2013). Suicide, too, for women, especially middle-aged ones, has sharply increased in recent years. However, men are still leading in the number of suicides. See Parker-Pope (2013), quoting figures issued by the Center for Disease Control.
7 Haarhoff reports that about 7,000 elderly Germans have been "delocalized" and now live in nursing homes in the Czech Republic, Greece, Hungary, Spain and Thailand (2013, p. 15).
8 See also the discussion of the Presidential panel titled "Every Child Matters" on National Public Radio (NPR, 2014). The United States leads the developed world in child abuse deaths, according to this organization. More than 20,000 American children have died over the past decade in their own homes because of the actions of family members, with about 75% being under 4 years of age and nearly half being under one. The US child maltreatment death rate is 3 times higher than Canada's and 11 times that of Italy.
9 "Riprendiamoci la Vita" was the slogan chanted by feminists in Italy in the 1970s in many demonstrations, to qualify a struggle that exceeded any specific demand, aspiring instead to free their bodies and daily lives from the hold of the state.

10 Community Supported Agriculture (CSA) is the name of a number of initiatives that have grown in recent years in the Unites States whereby, in various regions, "consumers" establish a direct connection with the producers, in this case the farmers, paying in advance for the coming crops and sharing the risks, to then receive periodically boxes of fruit and vegetables, with the possibility of visiting the farm where they are produced and sharing the work.
11 ABC News report entitled "Diane Sawyer's Hometown in Kentucky Saves Money By Helping Each Other Out," broadcast on January 15, 2014 (http://abcnews.go.com/blogs/headlines/2014/01/saving-money-helping-others-with-timebanking), commented on the growing practice of time-banking in the United States. The reporter stated that there were time-bank efforts going on in 42 states.
12 Fortunati, however, warns against assuming that communicative technologies are by themselves responsible for the communication crisis we are witnessing. Rejecting this type of "technological determinism" that ignores that the "consumers" are active political subjects, she argues that communicative technologies intervene in a social reality already "structurally organized in an alienated way" (Fortunati, 1998, p. 38). That is, the crisis of family relations is the ground enabling technologies to break into and dominate our daily life (ibid., pp. 34–48).

References

Angell, M. (2011, June 23). The epidemics of mental illness: Why? *The New Yorker*.

BBC. (2011, October 18). Michael Petit: America can fix problem of child abuse fatalities. Retrieved from www.bbc.news/15361466.

Bollier, D. & Helfrich, S. (Eds.). (2012). *The wealth of the commons: A world beyond market and state*. Amherst, MA: The Levellers Press.

Caffentzis, G. (2014). Divisions in the commons? Ecuador's FLOK Society versus the Zapatistas' Escuelita. Paper presented at the Creative Alternatives to Capitalism Conference, held at the CUNY Graduate Center, New York, May 24, 2014.

Caffentzis, G. & Federici, S. (2013). Commons against and beyond capitalism. *Upping the Anti: A Journal of Theory and Action*, 15, 83–99.

Cochrane, K. (2010, April 29). Why do so many women have depression? *Guardian*. Retrieved from www.theguardian.com/society/2010/apr/29/women-depression-allison-pearson.

Dalla Costa, M. (1973). Women and the subversion of the community. In M. Dalla Costa & S. James (Eds.), *The power of women and the subversion of the community*. Bristol: Falling Wall Press. (Originally published in Italian as *Potere femminile e sovversione social*, with S. James's "Il posto della donna." Padova-Venice: Marsilio, 1972)

Ehrenreich, B. & Hochschild, A. R. (2002). *Global woman: Nannies, maids and sex workers in the new economy*. New York: Henry Holt and Company.

Federici, S. (2012a). Feminism and the politics of the commons in an era of primitive accumulation. In S. Federici, *Revolution at point zero: Housework, reproduction and feminist struggle* (pp. 138–149). Oakland, CA: PM Press.

Federici, S. (2012b). On elder care work and the limits of Marxism. In S. Federici, *Revolution at point zero: Housework, reproduction and feminist struggle* (pp. 115–125). Oakland, CA: PM Press.

Federici, S. (2012c). *Revolution at point zero: Housework, reproduction and feminist struggle*. Oakland, CA: PM Press.

Federici, S. (2012d). Women's liberation and the struggle for democratization. Paper presented at the 2nd Congress on Critical Political Analysis, on the theme of "Democracy," University of Basque Country, November 19–20.

Federici, S. (2014). Andare a Pechino: Come le Nazioni Unite Hanno Colonizzato il Movimento Femminista. In S. Federici, *Il Punto Zero della Rivoluzione: Lavoro Domestico, riproduzione e lotta femminista*. Verona: Ombre Corte.

Fisher, J. (1993). Chile: Democracy in the country and democracy in the home. In *Out of the shadows: Women, resistance and politics in South America* (pp. 177–201). London: Latin American Bureau.

Folbre, N. (2006). Nursebots to the rescue? Immigration, automation and care. *Globalizations*, 3(3), 349–360.

Fortunati, L. (Ed.). (1998). *Telecomunicando in Europa*. Milan: FrancoAngeli.

Haarhoff, H. (2013, June). Les Allemands exportent aussi leurs grands-parents. *Le Monde Diplomatique*, 14–15.

Hanisch, C. (1969). *The personal is political*. With a new explanatory introduction (2006). Retrieved June 15, 2014, from http://carolhanisch.org/CHwritings/PIP.html.

Hochschild, A. R. (1983). *The managed heart: Commercialization of human feeling*. Berkeley, CA: University of California Press.

Jilani, S. (2011, October 24). America's child abuse epidemic: Four times more children have been killed this decade than US soldiers in Iraq and Afghanistan. Their assailants? Their families. *Guardian*. Retrieved from www.theguardian.com/commentisfree/cifamerica/2011/oct/24/america-child-abuse-epidemic.

Kindig, D. A. & Cheng, E. R. (2013). Even as mortality fell in most US counties, female mortality nonetheless rose in 42.8 percent of counties from 1992 to 2006. *Health Affairs*, 32(3), 451–458.

Lefebvre, H. (1991). *The critique of everyday life* (J. Moore, Trans.). London: Verso. (Originally published in French in 1947 as *Critique de la vie quotidienne*. Paris: L'Arche Editeur)

Lefebvre, H. (2002). *The critique of everyday life: Vol. 2. Foundations for a sociology of the everyday* (J. Moore, Trans.). London: Verso. (Originally published in French in 1961 as *Critique de la vie quotidienne II: Fondements d'une sociologie de la quotidienneté*. Paris: L'Arche Editeur)

Lefebvre, H. (2005) *The critique of everyday life: Vol. 3. From modernity to modernism (Towards a metaphilosophy of daily life)* (G. Elliott, Trans.). London: Verso. (Originally published in French in 1981 as *Critique de la vie quotidienne: III. De la modernité au modernisme (pour une mé- taphilosophie du quotidienne*. Paris: L'Arche Editeur)

MacLean, N. (1999). The hidden history of affirmative action: Working women's struggles in the 1970s and the gender of class. *Feminist Studies*, 25(1), 43–78.

Marx, K. & Engels, F. (1968). *The German ideology*. Moscow: Progress Publishers.

Matchar, E. (2013). *Homeward bound: Why women are embracing the new domesticity*. New York: Simon & Schuster.

Mayo Clinic Staff. (2014). Depression in women: Understanding the gender gap. Retrieved March 10, 2014, from www.mayoclinic.org/diseases/in-depth/depression/art-20047725.

National Public Radio (NPR). (2014, February 25). Panel charged with eliminating child abuse. Retrieved from www.npr.org/2014/02/25/282359501/panel-charged-with-eliminating-child-abuse-deaths.

Olshansky, J. (2012). Differences in life expectancy due to race and educational differences are widening, and many may not catch up. *Health Affairs*, 31(8), 1803–1813.

Parker-Pope, T. (2013, May 13). Suicide rates rise sharply in U.S. *New York Times*, p. A1.

Potts, M. (2014, September 3). What's killing poor white women? *The American Prospect*. Retrieved from http://prospect.org/article/whats-killing-poor-white-women.

Rauber, I. (2002). Mujeres piqueteras: El caso de Argentina. In F. Reysoo (Ed.), *Economie mondialisée et identités de genre* (pp. 107–123). Geneve: IUED.

Universidad National de Colombia (UNC): Agencia de Noticiasun. (2014, March 9). *Madres comunitarias: del voluntariado a la formalidad*. Retrieved from www.agenciadenoticias.unal.edu.co.

Veneigem, R. (2013). *The revolution of everyday life* (D. Nicholson-Smith, Trans.). Oakland, CA: PM Press. (Originally published in French in 1967 as *Traité de savoir-vivre à l'usage de jeunes generations*. Paris: Gallimard)

Williams, M. (2013, May 16). Mental disorders rising in children. *The Atlanta Journal-Constitution*. Retrieved from www.ajc.com/news/news/2013/05/16.

Zapatistas. (2014). *Autonomous resistance* (1st-grade textbook for the course "Freedom according to the Zapatistas") (El Kilombo, Trans.). Retrieved from www.schoolsforchiapas.org/library/autonomous-resistance-grade-textbook.

Zibechi, R. (2012). *Territories in resistance: A cartography of Latin American social movements*. Oakland, CA: AK Press.

11
FROZEN FLUIDITY

Digital Technologies and the Transformation of Students' Learning and Conduct of Everyday Life

Ernst Schraube and Athanasios Marvakis

Digital technologies seem to have the potential to radically transform the learning and teaching relations at universities. A range of fundamental learning activities, such as reading, writing and communication, are being integrated into digitization processes. Moreover, in terms of the learning situation itself (courses, lectures, etc.), a series of transformations from face-to-face to virtual learning worlds are under way, supplementing or replacing traditional learning arrangements via digital platforms and structures. Today, many universities automatically establish a digital platform for every course (using, for example, the *Moodle* learning management system) offered to students who attend campus to study, while courses and programs are increasingly offered exclusively online (as, for example, in the form of *MOOCs*, the *Massive Open Online Courses*). This movement toward the digital reorganization – or reconstitution – of learning relations is fundamentally changing the process and content of learning, as well as the students' conduct of everyday life. Since digital technologies facilitate certain learning activities and relationships while hindering or even preventing others, this movement to digitalization is not free from inconsistencies and contradictions. Digitalized learning has justifiably fueled the hope of, for example, broader learner participation and more symmetrical learner–teacher relations. However, it also comes with the dangers of distraction, a new quality of freezing and one-sidedly fixing learning relations, as well as a temptation to relapse into instrumental transfer and internalization models and an inscription of defensive learning. Such a situation calls for an analysis of the digitalization of higher education that helps to identify and explain its possibilities and limits; an analysis that raises fundamental questions about the ready embrace of digital technologies in higher education to date (Winner, 2009) and identifies processes of learning where digital technologies can clearly contribute as well as processes where they cannot.

The debates on the digitalization of teaching and learning in higher education have long focused primarily on issues related to the development and design of technical systems, and their utilization by teachers, students and administrations. More recently there has been a marked shift in the discussion toward students as learning subjects, their experiences, activities and participations (a shift also more generally visible in the social study of technology; Schraube, 2013; Schraube & Sørensen, 2013). "The history ... of initiatives bringing technologies into education," explains the philosopher of education Jan Derry, "shows a change in focus of attention from an early emphasis on the technology itself towards a greater concern with the details of learning and the learner" (2008, p. 506). In this chapter, we start from this development and focus on the relevance of digital technology for learners and their learning activities. We ask, how and why do digital technologies actually expand or undermine students' learning processes? By introducing and developing a variety of analytical concepts highlighting the decisive elements of the learning activity we aim to contribute to a more nuanced understanding of the contradictory significance of digital technologies for students' learning. Although there is a plethora of learning theories, conceptualizations of learning systematically developed from the perspective of the learners are still in their infancy. Therefore our focus is on the question of learning. What is learning? How to integrate learners into learning theory and reflections on digital technology? Why, how and to what end does learning take place, and what are the best possible conditions for learning? We not only discuss these questions in detail to get a view of the digitalization of higher education from the perspective of the students and their learning processes, but also because the profound changes in the material learning structures under way are calling for a similarly profound investigation into the nature of learning. Our concern here is to rethink these issues as a basis of thinking ahead – to invite imagining and re-imagining of the kinds of learning worlds we are in the process of creating, and what meaning these can have for the activity of learning and people's conduct of everyday life.

We start by conceptualizing learning as a basic human activity for appropriating and changing the world, rooted in our conduct of everyday life (as opposed to taking the instrumental internalization or transfer models of learning as our starting point). Such a view regards learning as an essential part of the human access to the world, as an activity taking place in and through participation in social practices. Drawing on situated and participatory learning theory, and especially on the work of Klaus Holzkamp, we develop this approach to learning as arising from the standpoint of learning subjects by identifying the crucial role of the fluid, mutual entanglement of learning and teaching. Thus our analysis is especially concerned with the fluidity of learning and teaching and the ways in which digital technologies can facilitate its unfolding. Taking the example of Roskilde University, we indicate the possibilities of how such a concept of learning can be implemented in higher education, and describe learning and teaching practices that systematically seek to integrate the students' perspective. Based on such a concept of learning we show how the digitalization of the students' learning environment can catalyze but also freeze the fluidity of learning and teaching.

Understanding Learning as Participation in Social Practice from the Standpoint of the Learning Subjects

The Transfer Model of Learning and its Limits

In educational research, the concept of learning appears to have shifted in the wake of the profound social changes over the past decades (in catchwords – from Fordism to neoliberalism). In the *internalization* or *transfer model* prevalent in the twentieth century, learning is regarded as a transfer of knowledge from a teacher to a learner; in the learning process, the learners internalize the transferred knowledge and absorb it drop by drop as it trickles into them as if through a funnel (critical discussions of the model e.g. in Dupont, 2013; Freire, 1970/2012; Ingold, 2015, chap. 4 in this volume; Packer, 2001). In contrast, the idea of active, relational and contextual learning is now gaining ground, where learning is viewed as a process happening in a social world (e.g., Engeström, 1987; Hedegaard & Chaiklin, 2005, Illeris, 2007; Kontopodis, Wulf & Fichtner, 2011; Lave & Wenger, 1991; Marvakis, 2014b; Sørensen, 2008). Such an approach integrates not only, on the one hand, the social, cultural and material dimension of learning, but also, on the other hand, the *subjective dimension*, the perspective and agency of the learning subject, and thus seeks to take this into account in understanding learning relations. Higher education policies have also acknowledged the need for learning concepts to include the contextual dimension including the learning subjects, and have expressly promoted "student-centered learning" – such as, for example, in a recent report presented to the European Commission on modernizing higher education (European Commission, 2013, p. 40).

However, even though hardly anyone in the *study of learning* today would vigorously defend a traditional internalization model, the notion of internalization is still very much alive in current *educational theory and practice* as well as in the *everyday understanding* of learning. From both the learning and teaching perspective, the internalization model is readily cited as soon as the discussion turns to how people learn. Students typically respond to the question "What do you understand by learning?" with such statements as "A relatively boring process by which I absorb what the teacher says, and reproduce it in the exam." Or, to take an example from everyday family life: "How does my child learn to swim?" – "First, by watching me demonstrate the movements, and then more or less internalizing them."

The internalization model (with its different variations) can be traced back to behaviorism's classical and instrumental conditioning with learning interpreted as an outer-directed process producing reactions and behavioral change (i.e., learning) in individuals (e.g., Skinner, 1954, 1968). In such a conceptualization, the learning process as well as the educational practices intended to initiate and regulate learning appear as instrumental and determined – as a set of *fixed procedures* defined without recourse to the learning subject. In such an approach, one finds an affinity, neither coincidental nor unimportant, to a mechanistic and even technocratic view of learning (Kvale, 1976).

The transfer and internalization model has been subjected to a broad critique, and here we highlight some of the core problem areas. One major limitation of this model lies in how it entirely excludes the learner's activity, subjective reality and conduct of life. Since the learning conception lacks the analytical tools to portray the learner's subjectivity, the learning experience, intentions, problems, actions, etc. as well as the social world and societal contexts in which learning activities are inevitably grounded, these all remain entirely excluded from the research perspective. Nevertheless, the learning subject cannot be separated from the activity of learning. Learning is not just an isolated activity induced in a classroom but an activity rooted in a person's conduct of life. It is an activity integrating a person's activities based on everyday problems and interests as well as the ideas and senses of how a person wants to live her/his life. It is an activity that involves other persons and which happens in and across the different contexts of everyday life (Dreier, 2015; Holzkamp, 2015, chap. 3 in this volume p.65). With the conceptual structure of the transfer and internalization model unable to address or explicate the subjective dimension of learning and the learner's conduct of life, one can talk here of a *discursive void and privatization* of the learning subjects in the dominant learning theories of the 20th century.

This also indicates a further problematic aspect of the transfer model, since *learning* is viewed as *a direct result of teaching*. In this way, learning is reduced to teaching: what is taught corresponds to what is learned. As a result, if one wants to understand *learning*, it would appear to be enough to analyze *teaching*. When examined in more detail, this limiting parallelization proves to seriously distort – if not invert – the learning process. As already mentioned, a learning process, by definition, cannot exist without a learning subject. This does not mean, of course, that one cannot learn something from a teacher; rather the misunderstanding consists in the idea of a linear transfer from what is taught to what is learned. Holzkamp termed this equating of teaching with learning as the *teaching–learning short circuit* (2013, p. 121) and analyzed in detail how the conceptual reduction of learning to teaching can not only be found in everyday thought and classical learning models, but actually also in relational, sociocultural theories of learning (1993).

There is, though, a grain of truth in this supposed equating of teaching and learning that is worth extracting and examining. Learning and teaching form a reciprocal relationship, are closely connected and intimately linked – and that proximity is evident in some languages having only one word to express both meanings. The Danish verb *at lære*, for example, not only describes the act of "learning" but also "teaching." In modern Greek, the verb μαθαίνω potentially includes both "learning" and "teaching," and requires additional information to clarify unequivocally which activity is meant. However, the issue here is not to assume a close interrelation between learning and teaching. Rather, it is precisely that the transfer model is not based on the mutual entanglement of learning and teaching, but reduces learning to teaching, or substitutes learning for teaching; what the teacher teaches is regarded as what the learner learns. The essential fiction of this view lies in conceptualizing learning as a *mere result* of teaching.

Developments in learning theory have attempted to systematically address this problem by, for instance, introducing the concept of *situated* and *distributed learning*.

In this case, learning is conceptualized as the learning subject's increasing participation in society and social practices, as a problem-oriented expansive process in which, through the learning process and the help of teachers, learners expand their own agency and conduct of life, increasing their involvement in and disposition over those aspects of the world relevant for them. As Jean Lave and Etienne Wenger explain, the theory of situated learning is based on an idea

> about the relational character of knowing and learning, about the negotiated character of meaning, and about the concerned (engaged, dilemma-driven) nature of learning activity for the people involved … [It implies] emphasis on comprehensive understanding involving the whole person rather than "receiving" a body of factual knowledge about the world; on activity in and with the world; and on the view that agent, activity, and the world mutually constitute each other.
>
> (1991, p. 33)

The Learning Matter: Not Neutral Technicalities but Conflictual Societal Meanings

Situated learning theory anchors the activity of learning in the world. Learning is understood as a process of exploring the world and participating in social practices. These social practices are always complex and contested entities. The concrete outcome of and prerequisites for *my* learning are realized by appropriating societal meanings as they are situated and distributed in a variety of societally produced tools: mental tools (e.g., concepts), social tools (e.g., relations, subjectivities), objective tools (e.g., external objects, things, artifacts) guiding – not determining – *our* activity. In such a perspective, learning articulates participation in the action possibilities that are situated and distributed in these produced tools. These tools – and thus my actions as well – refer to the ambiguous, conflictual and contradictory character of societal reality represented in societal meanings.

However, the conflictuality of reality and the respective societal meanings is not taken seriously in the dominant conceptualizations of learning and organized educational practices. Instead, conflicts and contradictions are replaced by some neutral, technical unambiguity in the semantics of social meanings. Rather than societal meanings conceived of as conflictual social fields, they are modeled on the analogy of operating guidelines for technical equipment. Such a reading of societal meanings leaves no space for conflictual "deviations," and only allows for faithful appropriation based on the semantic differentiations of technical operating guidelines. Yet making societal meanings appear unambiguous delegitimizes any problems with or resistance to a straightforward subordination to authoritative social meanings, and posits a conceptual simplicity that is either a chimera of social scientists or a politically motivated camouflage of powerful practices. But can social meanings really be just as unequivocal, as seemingly banal as the instructions on an espresso machine?

We need to be careful not to reduce social meanings to a knowledge equivalent to that required for passing a school test, which reduces the world we need to get to know into a very narrow social practice. The tools we use for learning, together with the social meanings situated in them and distributed by them, are products of societal labor. As such, they are informed by the ambiguities, conflicts and contradictions in society (to name but a few examples: knife, gender, alienation, equality, friendship or cellphones). The terms "situated" and "distributed" do not refer just to a semantic space, but to social battlefields (with their differentiations), and thus also refer to particular standpoints articulated in specific perspectives on interpreting the social meanings. Therefore, methodologically speaking, social meanings are not just terms that name different things; they also articulate particular social, political and epistemological standpoints, including the subject's awareness of his/her particular position in society. As an example, we could take the "knife"; we can cut bread with it but also our veins. Whereas in Christian culture the thereby committal suicide is seen as a sin to be avoided, it appears in Japanese samurai culture as the peak of virtue. Thus, what is learned if one learns or should learn about the handling of a knife? Which societally produced meanings are for the learners in the offing with a "knife"? Even a knife – as an aspect of societal reality and as an entity conceiving/reflecting on this societal reality – refers to a social phenomenon and, in Lave and Wenger's words in the quotation above, "to the negotiated character of meaning."

It is exactly this ambiguous, contradictory character of societal meanings that opens up a plurality of conflicting possibilities for subjects' learning. If social meanings really could be expressed as unambiguous technicalities merely needing to be memorized, empirical research into how real subjects act in their social reality would be superfluous. Learning would be far easier, since the information could be deduced from an extensive description of social reality, and students would merely need to be "instructed" (or the information "transferred" or "taught"). Here, learning would solely be a *technical process* of inducing and performing. However, this is far removed from our societal reality, necessities and human potentials. Learning is always learning *of* and *through* contradictions – learning amid socially contested meanings. The contradictions in social reality are also visible in the way we learn, our learning practices, and appear to us as subjects not as supposed semantic gaps waiting to be filled, like a glass of water or a bank account. In the words of Frigga Haug:

> The contradiction permeates the individuals' experiences and memories as empty spaces, silences, senselessness, denial, as something wanting to be freed from suppression … Such contradictions in learning are experienced as crises, as breaks with the familiar, as unrest and disorder. As a result, the pressure to learn is created by situations of distress and difficulty.
> (2003b, p. 212; translation by the authors)

Hence, learning – as participation in the action possibilities situated and distributed in societal meanings – cannot be reduced to an active or passive *interiorization* of specific semantic aspects of these meanings; it requires subjects to encounter and respond to the conflicts, contradictions, politics, battles, standpoints inherent in them. As a result, the unfolding of learners' *subjective sense* is a productive and transformative process, and cannot be reduced to interiorizing external – supposedly neutral and technical – information. The emergence of subjective sense relies on a particular practice we could call *subjective semiosis* (Brockmeier, 1988). Encountering contradictions in my learning activities necessarily includes compromises; potentially it also requires the removal or erosion of learning sediments, fundamental relearning, but equally requires creative and ingenious integrations and transformations (Mergner, 1999).

Theorizing Learning from the Standpoint of the Learning Subjects

Since the learning activity is located on the side of the learning subjects and not on the side of those teaching (which does not exclude the possibility of teachers also becoming learners), elaborating a precise concept of learning requires a fundamental shift in perspective in learning theory and the development of a concept of participatory learning systematically structured from the standpoint of the learning subjects. In the words of Lave: "Questions about learning are almost always met by educational researchers with investigations of teaching. This disastrous shortcut equates learning with teaching" (1996, p. 158). Consequently, she calls for "a reversal in perspective so that the vital focus of research on learning shifts from transmitters, teachers or care givers, to learners" (ibid., p. 155) and "an analysis of learners as subjects" (ibid., p. 158). In the next step, we take a more detailed look at this task and outline basic concepts of a learning theory systematically developed from the standpoint of the learning subjects. In elaborating such an approach, we draw on Holzkamp's work on learning and expand his perspective by considering the relationship of learning and teaching.

Seen from the standpoint of the learners, Holzkamp explains, learning is an inherent part of the ongoing activities of everyday living. In more or less every aspect of our conduct of life, we see, experience, do and recognize things in new ways, and in this process we inevitably learn new things about ourselves, others and the world. Building on the tradition of action theory, Holzkamp described this as co-learning or *incidental learning* (Bourdieu & Passeron used the term *osmotic learning*, 1979), distinguishing it from *intentional learning*. Intentional learning refers to an activity standing out from the flow of everyday activities in which learning itself turns into a topic. This learning activity is initiated by an interruption, a problem in the conduct of life; in the ongoing everyday activities, subjects find themselves confronting a dilemma where they are no longer able to act as desired, and they cannot advance as wished within their previous horizon. In other words, the dilemma can only be resolved by a new impetus: by learning. For this reason, Holzkamp talks of a *learning loop*, a detour that constitutes intentional learning; learning takes us on a roundabout route that ultimately – whether successful or not – flows back into our everyday activities and conduct of life.

Consequently, in intentional learning, an action problem is transformed into a *learning problem*, and since the learning activity has an intention (which by no means has to be entirely clear in one's mind) and wants to move something (the initial problem), Holzkamp talks of the *act of learning*. The learning problem is of crucial importance for the question of learning or, as we can now say more precisely, for the act of learning. Without learning problem, no genuine learning. The learning problem can also be taken on from others (e.g., from teachers), or developed together with others – however, it is essential that the learner conceives the learning problem as his/her own. "Learning does not start by itself," Holzkamp emphasizes,

> simply because I am subjected to some demands from a third party; my learning cannot be planned over my head by some instances responsible for that learning (such as teachers or school authorities). Subjecting me to learning *demands* does not in itself lead to *acts* of learning, since demands only become acts if I consciously can adopt them as a learning problem – and that in turn requires at the very least that I realize where I really do have here something to learn.
>
> (1993, p. 184f.; translation by the authors)

Since learning is not limited to incidental learning in the ongoing activities of everyday living but can also represent a particular act in itself, and since every act is based on reasons, Holzkamp goes on to ask what reasons learners could have for their learning activities. This question points to the contextual basis of the act of learning. Holzkamp noticed that we can differentiate two typical kinds of subjective reasons for learning. How these are realized depends on the degree to which subjects merely view learning as a means to avert restrictions or threats, or as offering the potential to expand their influence over the conditions of their life and enhance the quality of their lives. Hence, he concludes, one can distinguish between defensive and expansive reasons for learning – in short, *defensive* and *expansive learning* – with the latter as learning to expand my influence over the conditions of my life and the former as seeking to avert expected curtailments of my opportunities should I refuse to learn, or protect opportunities already existing.

Thus, in defensive learning, I learn because otherwise I am threatened by possible sanctions: for example, I take part in a course merely because it is mandatory for completing my degree. In defensive learning, then, the primary objective is not an interest in the learning content or matter, but demonstrating learning results and so warding off or evading possible threats and constraints associated with a failure to meet the particular learning demand. In this sense, defensive learning is primarily other-controlled and directed, and largely indifferent to the content of what is learned; the constellation of reasons for defensive learning could even lead to the dissolution of the learning problem as such and a reinterpretation of the learning demand purely as a question of the action appropriate to achieve the end (without learning), such as, for example, by posing the question: "How can I pass an exam whether I learn something in the process or not?"

In contrast, the learning problem lies at the heart of expansive learning. In this case, the learning subject takes on the anticipated efforts and risks of learning, assuming that the enhanced access to the world through learning will result in an increased influence over the conditions of his or her life, and greater subjective life-quality. Hence, in expansive learning, the learning process is not principally directed to meeting external demands, but oriented to the factual necessities emerging in the process of adopting the learning problem and engaging with a learning matter that is still partially inaccessible. "All learning (to overcome a learning problem)," Holzkamp explains, is "directed to enriching my access to the world and increasing my ability to influence the conditions of my life and is thus, in terms of intention, 'expansive learning'" (1996, p. 125; translation by the authors).

Defensive and expansive learning represent analytical concepts, i.e., are not terms developed to externally categorize or rate the learning process of others. Instead, these are terms offering an understanding of learning processes from the perspective of the learning subject. Here, one should also note that a learning activity may involve elements of both defensive and expansive learning.

Expansive learning, Holzkamp adds, comprises two key phases – *affinitive* and *definitive learning phases*. The starting point of the *affinitive learning phase* is the learning problem and the point where we seem to be making no further progress. In affinitive learning phases, we expose ourselves to the learning matter and contemplate it in another way, seeking to find a different mode of access to move us forward. Given the partial inaccessibility of the learning matter, the process of exposing and engaging with it leads to a series of unseen difficulties. As a result, learning cannot simply succeed by establishing a straight-lined learning plan and a linear following of an anticipated learning goal. Rather, absolutizing goal-directedness itself frequently leads to just that one-sidedness, fixation, etc., that expansive learning is seeking to overcome. Therefore, in genuinely productive expansive learning the goal-directed learning process is always complemented by a virtually reverse affinitive movement in the learning process; an exploratory movement of de-centering, gaining distance and overview, withdrawal and contemplation etc. With the words of the anthropologist Tim Ingold (2015, chap. 4 in this volume, p.103), this is more an *attentional* than an *intentional* process (see also Højholt & Røn Larsen, 2014, p. 65f.). Phases of affinitive learning, Holzkamp emphasizes, essentially require "the absence of threat, stress, and pressures, i.e., the possibility of trust, and above all (including all of these): peace and tranquility" (1993, p. 485; translation by the authors).

The *definitive learning phase* is complementary to the affinitive learning phase. In the definitive learning phase, we center the openness and synthesize and extract the essential from the wealth, carrying the learning problem on a new level – until, on the basis of this new level, new difficulties arise that again require a new affinitive learning phase. Hence, affinitive learning, including its alternation and interplay with definitive learning, represents a decisive phase in the learning process. As Holzkamp underlines, the "alternation between affinitive and definitive learning phases is … the constitutive element of an expansive mode of learning" (1993,

p. 481; translation by the authors), and without it, no real learning, creativity and new thinking can take place.

The strength of Holzkamp's learning theory consists in being systematically grounded in a theory of experience and action where learning is conceptualized from the standpoint of the learners. The concepts he introduces, such as incidental and intentional learning, learning problem, defensive and expansive learning, or affinitive and definitive learning phases, relate to the learning activity of the individual subject. Yet with these terms so radically related to individual learning, are they too narrow or even individualistic? Although Holzkamp attempts to carefully include the social preconditions of learning in his analysis, his focus is on the institutional learning relations (especially school) and their implications for pupils' learning processes (e.g., 1993, chap. 4). He does not systematically deal with the intersubjective dimension of learning and the relationship between learning and teaching. For this reason, Holzkamp's learning theory may appear individualistic, and at this point needs to be further developed. Haug, for example, has recognized this problem and, working on the basis of a situated and participatory theory of learning, has examined the connection between learning and teaching, and the role of teachers in learning processes (2003a, 2009; see also Langemeyer, 2005). We can now build on this point in the next stage of our argument: For developing a precise concept of learning, we also require a notion of how learning and teaching are linked. Naturally, this is a huge topic. Here, we are focusing solely on learning and teaching's original connection and reciprocity – an aspect we view as crucial for our initial question on the relevance of digital technologies for students' learning.

Fluidity of Learning and Teaching as a Basic Element of Expansive Learning

The task of separating out just one discrete act – the learning act – from our ongoing everyday activities and the continuous *flow of action* (Giddens, 1984) is necessarily based on a separation already existing societally, if not initially facilitated by such a separation. Because incidental learning is increasingly insufficient in the socio-historical process as a basis for participating in social practices – for example, work – the requisite learning needs and possibilities were separated in society. Should individual subjects want or have to participate and partake in the societal process, they are confronted with these antecedent societal "offers," yet also have to position and relate themselves to them, since these "offers" are – as conditions and meanings – the mediators of their own actions. Logically, only after relating myself to these societal "offers" can I take on the task of specifying for myself particular learning actions. This form of activity, referred to by Rubinstein as *learning labor* (1958/1977), does not emerge as an individual initiative or necessity for action, but initially arises *from* and *for* the subjects' participation in multiple (pre-existent and more or less societally organized) *communities of practice* (Lave & Wenger, 1991) or *action contexts* (Dreier, 2008; Højholt, 2008).

Hence, the learning act including the development of a learning problem is not left to isolated individual activities or coincidences (Marvakis & Petritsi, 2014). Learning *labor* – as a moment of participation, partaking and sharing – is always societally interwoven and mediated in multiple ways; moreover, it is supported by a whole societal organization of education. This societally organized integrative process of education exists and is realized only as a combination of learning and teaching.

Participating in the educational process assumes (and simultaneously facilitates) a dialectical relationship between learning and teaching that is concretely articulated in each historical period, i.e., organized socially as discrete learning relations and educational practices. Since each type of institutionalized education (e.g., kindergarten, school, university) channels and organizes the relation of learning and teaching in a particular way, the question arises of the kind of channeling and how appropriate it may be for the specific learning matters.

At colleges and universities the educational practices represent a particular form and structuring of the learning–teaching relationship. On the one hand, we have the activities of learning, on the other hand, the activities of teaching; accordingly, the relationship between learning and teaching is fixed as *functional*, with the learning and teaching activities assigned to specific working positions: the learner becomes a "student" and the teacher a "lecturer/professor." This functional positioning of the persons is a reality in the learning–teaching practices of today's universities.

However, the history of learning shows that not all the learning relations are structured in such a fixed manner. In the original basic form of learning, localized in the – still pre-institutionalized – activities of everyday living, the learning–teaching relationship is constituted not as functional but as *logical positions*. Learning as a social process situated in relation to others unfolds as a continuous open back-and-forth between logical positions of learning and teaching in and between people. This *fluidity of learning and teaching* (Marvakis, 2014a, 2014b) forms a basic element in expansive learning, and is the nucleus of productive and vibrant learning relations.

As an example, here, one can imagine a 4-year-old realizing that he cannot swim, and that both he and his parents want him to learn. The parents show their son the swimming strokes, and ask their son to imitate their movements, practice them in water and essentially internalize them. But the boy has no intention of imitating the strokes. Instead, he jumps into the water, ducks under the surface, and then asks his father to buy him diving goggles. "But how can you learn to swim if you won't learn the proper strokes?," his father asked, and insists that his son imitates him, though without any evident success. The son continues to duck under the surface. His father is first puzzled, then annoyed. Suddenly, he thinks that getting used to going underwater is actually quite important for the process of learning to swim; could jumping in and learning how to move easily underwater even be a basic step in learning how to swim safely? So he buys his son diving goggles. The boy learns to move underwater and then starts to appropriate – together with many other movements – the classic swimming strokes. Soon, he happily swims both underwater and on the surface.

This example illustrates how, starting from an action problem (not being able to swim), learning does not simply occur as the internalization of knowledge and skills (for instance, swimming strokes), but as a shared process of exploring the world (in particular, the meaning complex of body, movement, water and air) and developing agency that first gains its explorative and productive power through the mutual entanglement of learning and teaching. Even if Holzkamp did not systematically analyze the learning–teaching relationship, his concept of *cooperative learning* already includes central moments of the transition from more fixed functional positions to a fluid back-and-forth between the logical positions of learning and teaching in expansive learning. As Holzkamp notes:

> We [use the term] *cooperative learning* ... for interpersonal learning relations in which – in the interest of unhindered expansive learning – asymmetries concerning knowledge or skills of the participants are not removed, but always accessible and liable for justification through knowledge-seeking questions. Within this process, the better arguments seem no longer to be bound to the more superior person, but can shift from person to person, but also within the person.
>
> (1993, p. 509; translation by the authors)

As formal learning relations and institutionalized educational practices developed, it was definitely productive to expand the logically fluid positions of learning and teaching by functional positions. Bringing together those with sophisticated knowledge as well as the capability and opportunity to do research, such as teachers in higher education, with those eager to learn offers a new quality and potential in expansive learning processes. This new form, though, already harbors a danger of reinterpreting learning in a way that tends toward the transfer model, a tendency further intensified by the nature of the work of those teaching. What is the task of a well-paid teacher? Telling the students "how to do something" – and with that, we are already moving toward the trap of equating learning and teaching, and advocating a notion of learning as the transfer of knowledge and skills from the knowing and skillful to the unknowing and unskillful.

However, a closer look at the conditions of teaching and learning in higher education reveals that to this day the fluidity of learning and teaching represents one key form of learning, even if it is not *the* key form. Asked about situations in which they really learn something, students often emphasize the importance of mutual questions and explanations in discussions with one another and their teachers as a means of enabling them to immerse themselves in a particular problem area and start to understand phenomena in their context. Many of those involved in teaching also similarly emphasize how they value their work precisely because they are engaged in a constant process of learning with and from their students. In fact, one can find specific learning arrangements at universities that are especially designed to facilitate the fluidity of learning and teaching (such as, for example, seminars, workshops, conferences, etc.). In short: even though it is not expressly named as such, the fluidity of learning and teaching forms a very real dimension of today's academic learning practices.

You have a point – as one objection might start – I can see the problem with the transfer model and the fiction of directly planning learning processes, and also a need for systematically integrating the subjective dimension of learning and the perspective of the learners into learning and teaching theory. If we do not, then we produce one-sided and paralyzing learning relations that fail to take into account the experience and concrete learning activities of those principally involved and, in this way, generate more learning difficulties than productive learning processes. Moreover, a shift toward participatory learning also requires participatory educational structures and a learning environment supporting such an approach. Yet isn't the development of such learning relations pure pie in the sky, and has little to do with the reality of life at university today? Actually, until now our analysis has focused on the *activity of learning* and the search for analytical concepts allowing this to be understood from the standpoint of the learning subjects, and we have not yet explicitly addressed the educational structures. However, the educational structures are of central importance. They form the social and technological framework for the learning activities; rather than (causally) determining learning, they facilitate particular learning activities and relationships and prevent others, they define the horizon of possibilities for the *how, what and why* of learning. Together with the learning and teaching activities, they constitute a *learning regime*. Therefore, as a further brick for understanding digital technology and learning, we turn now in our analysis to the educational structures of universities. We conceive these structures – in line with our approach to understanding learning from the standpoint of the learners – as the *students' learning environment*. In fact, over the last decades a series of reform universities in Europe and the United States have been establishing learning environments and educational practices supporting participatory learning (e.g., Aalborg University, Emory College, Maastricht University, Roskilde University and many others; see Andersen, 2015). Taking Roskilde University as an example, we present in the following some basic organizational principles of a learning environment that facilitate expansive learning and outline how these can be implemented in practice.

Participatory Learning Practices in Higher Education, Structured from the Standpoint of the Learning Subjects

When we talk of participatory learning and of the influence of learners on the practice of their learning activities, then we are also addressing the possibility of the learners' influence on their learning environment and institutionalized educational practices. Indeed, in the context of their democratization, universities have recognized the need for the participation of their students in developing teaching and learning practices and established a variety of forms of student influence on university life. These included, on the one hand, introducing *formal organs of representative*

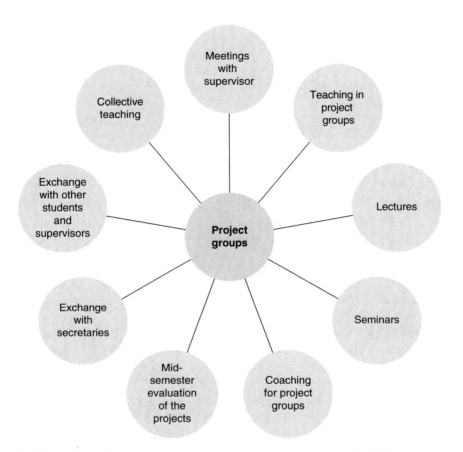

FIGURE 11.1 Basic structure of the learning environment at Roskilde University (Dupont, 2013, p. 33; translation by the authors). Reproduced with permission.

participation in university bodies (such as department councils, faculty council, etc.) where decisions are taken on structural aspects of the degree programs and the university; on the other hand, more *informal types of participation* were also created that are specifically related to the *content* of learning and studying. Some universities took a further radical step in the question of student participation, establishing *formal models of co-determining content*. This started from the premise that there must be more to genuinely studying than just listening to a professor giving a lecture; in fact, it must be more the other way round, with students themselves able to influence the content of what they learn, and decide on the topics and issues they will investigate in depth during their studies.

Since Roskilde University (RU) was founded 40 years ago, this idea of *students participating in decisions on the content of what they learn* forms the fundamental educational principle in the practices of teaching and learning. From their first semester, students study the issues and problems they have chosen in a particular field, with their *problem-oriented project work* continually supervised by a member of the faculty staff (Andersen & Heilesen, 2015; Salling Olesen & Højgård Jensen, 1999). In addition, lectures, seminars and other events are offered in connection with the projects. However, the main focus of learning is on the students' problem-oriented project work, and all other forms of learning and teaching are structured around this. Figure 11.1, by Søren Dupont, head of the Center for University Education at RU, provides an overview of the university's learning environment.

Basic Principles in Problem-Oriented Project Work

Rather than students starting their degree programs by learning about the theory and practice of one single discipline (such as, for example, psychology), learning in problem-oriented project work starts from problems in contemporary society (Andersen, 2015; Berthelsen, Illeris & Poulsen, 1985). In a group-formation process usually held in the first week of each semester and lasting 3 days, students take their own experience as a basis for deciding on a particular problem or set of problems they would like to address in their project (with the topics in the first semesters adopting an interdisciplinary approach while increasingly focusing on one discipline in later semesters). Since the project groups usually comprise 4–7 students, one of the initial difficulties they face is precisely developing and jointly agreeing on the problem addressed in the project. In the process of group formation, the academic staff can make suggestions on formulating the problem to be investigated (e.g., relating it to their own research). Students can then take up these suggestions or develop their own ideas, discussing and honing them with other students and teachers, ultimately deciding independently on the particular problem dealt with by their project and the approach adopted. Where possible, the project is mentored by the teaching staff most familiar with the particular topic investigated (Andersen & Dupont, 2015). In the group meetings with supervisors, all the many issues and difficulties of learning through research are discussed. In this process, the supervisor acts as a critical participant in the discussions, helping to give the project work the requisite scholarly substance. Students work for an entire semester on their project. In formal terms, the project work accounts for half of their study hours for any given semester. The remainder of the required study time is taken up with lectures and seminars providing an introduction into different subject areas, schools of thought and disciplines designed to expand and deepen the scholarly horizons of the students and their projects. The lectures are usually supplemented by seminars in which students work in small groups together with a member of the teaching staff on readings and issues relevant to the lectures.

The crucial factor in this approach to learning is that the students themselves define the content of the learning problem and work independently at their projects. In this way, the learning subjects are genuinely included in the learning and studying activities, since they can thus make their experiences and the action problems that they perceive in today's society into their learning object. Project work enables an immediate integration of learning and students' conduct of life; the students can directly implement their questions and interests in the learning and studying process, which facilitates the possibility of expansive learning. In addition, since they determine the object of their learning and studying themselves, they develop a new relationship to the faculty. Students want to know things from their project supervisor in their own immediate interest; on the basis of their project work, they ask questions to help them understand their problem better and improve their research. Moreover, the other way round, the teaching staff learn from their students, from the problems they pose, the theoretical and methodological approaches adopted, empirical insights, and all the questions and difficulties that they experience in the course of their project work.

In this way, the meetings for project supervision together with all the other lectures, seminars, etc., related to the project work can represent a learning environment facilitating expansive learning and the fluidity of learning and teaching. Of course, expansive learning spaces can only represent just a *possibility* for expansive learning. It does not automatically lead to expansive learning. Even in an expansive learning environment, students can have good reasons for simply wanting to pass a project, irrespective of whether they really learn something in the process or not. However, without such an environment, the possibilities of expansive learning are seriously hampered.

Learning relations seeking to promote expansive learning are not independent of societal developments or free from contradictions. The RU model, for instance, also has to deal regularly with a variety of contradictions evident, for example, in project work exams. In the exam situation, teaching staff are removed from the potentially fluid logical positions of learning and teaching, and forcibly placed in the functional position of an examiner who awards grades that play a part in determining the students' future chances (for this reason, in the first years after the RU was founded, there were neither exams nor grades; instead, the projects were critically reviewed and evaluated together by students and the teaching staff. In 1974, though, the Danish Ministry of Science, whose remit also included higher education, ordered exams to be introduced; today, these examinations are conducted as group exams). Interestingly, despite all the contradictions and the growing pressure to standardize higher education (for instance, through implementing the Bologna Process), the principle of self-determined problem-oriented project work has managed to develop intact for over 40 years, and today appears more vibrant than ever. The RU model shows that developing expansive learning relations at universities is not a flight of fancy, but is – at least at some universities – a firmly established reality whose basic elements – above all, problem-oriented project work – have also been adopted by schools and other universities.

Digital Technologies, Expansive Learning and the Fluidity of Learning and Teaching

In today's university learning environment, digital technologies play a dual role. On the one hand, computers, iPads, cell phones, email, Internet, etc., form an essential component in the material foundation of learning relations that can be used in individual learning activities; on the other hand, digital things are not only a component, but a constitutive moment of the learning relations themselves. This is not only because the digital things, linked to and with each other, form an inter-objective network and hence should not merely be seen as a means used for a particular end, but more accurately as contradictory *forms of life* (Winner, 1989) or *materialized action* (Schraube, 2009); it is also because, on the basis of the new technologies, digital learning spaces and platforms are created that constitute a new virtual learning environment and learning practice. This movement toward a digital reconstituting of learning relations is fundamentally transforming students' learning. It is a movement not free from contradictions and inconsistencies, which facilitates particular learning activities and relationships but also prevents others. For this reason, there is a need for a critical look at the dialectic of digitalizing learning relations at university, and a detailed analysis of the implications this process has for the various aspects of student learning. In conclusion here, we now offer some thoughts on how far digital technologies can contribute to the development of expansive learning and the fluidity of learning and teaching.

Digital technologies and expansive learning are not antithetical. On the contrary, digital technologies can indeed productively expand students' learning processes and explorative project work. The central question, however, is at which points exactly they are really relevant for the learning activities, and can actually support and enhance the various activities and phases of expansive learning. Digital technologies can only play a secondary role in decisive learning phases – above all, in developing the learning problem and in the affinitive and definitive learning phases. In these learning phases, the subjects themselves have to focus on, consider and reflect on the learning matter in a manner where digital devices and systems can, at most, provide only very limited support. Expansive learning, though, builds on access to objectified knowledge in its various literary, visual or acoustic forms where digital technologies can play a significant role in the learning process. They greatly facilitate the search and utilization of pertinent sources of knowledge, and in addition provide new possibilities of access to and working with empirical material. Digital technologies can also function as a catalyst in the development of the fluidity of learning and teaching as a central moment in expansive learning simply because they can provide access to texts, materials and other sources of knowledge in a new way, and these can be considered and discussed in shared – and interactive – processes.

Here, we can take an example from a methods course dealing with the practice of interviewing. As an exercise on the course, students interviewed each other about an issue in their current project. The interviews were digitally recorded in audio and video, and uploaded onto the course's digital platform directly afterwards. From there, they could then be projected onto the seminar room's Smart Board, and analyzed by a small group of students and teaching staff. Since the discussion was on the development and better understanding of conversation practices in interviews, the contributions were considered in the light of how far they contributed to this aim. In this process, the functional positions of teachers and students could shift in favor of the logical positions in the fluid back-and-forth of learning and teaching among all participants, and a collective immersion in the learning matter – the practice of interviewing. Certainly, such shifting positions would also be possible without digital technologies, but they enabled the materials to be presented to a group in different forms (film, audio, text) in a new and simple way. Moreover, since the digital technologies allowed the material to be dealt with interactively, they opened up new possibilities for those involved in the learning process to develop the fluidity of learning and teaching.

However, one can also identify a reverse movement. Expansive learning requires learning relations that support the students' influence on both the *environment* and *content* of learning. Since digital learning platforms and online courses establish a reconfiguration of the involved learning subjects in time and space as well as new possibilities of one-sidedly reorganizing and hierarchizing the learning relations, the potential influence is shifting drastically to the side of the teachers as well as the administration/management. While the classic non-digital course is held in a definite time period in a defined seminar room on campus, the virtual classroom is open 24/7 and can be accessed online from anywhere. This not only offers the potential to massively expand the use of teaching time as well as the space defined by teaching, but equally massively expands access to the students and their conduct of life in that space and time, as well as opens up the possibility of logging their activities in detail. This drastic expansion of the "classroom" into a "control room," with the potential of greater monitoring and regulation by teachers, embodies the danger of reverting to the transfer model of learning and paralyzing the fluidity of learning and teaching. The activities of learning and teaching are getting locked into functional positions, while the teachers define stipulated courses and content by themselves, and the students have to "learn" what is prescribed for them in digital space. Such a displacement in participation and relapsing into equating teaching and learning is not an inevitable result of digitalizing learning relations. Nevertheless, in the present digital systems and e-learning practices it is structurally inscribed as a possibility for teachers and administrations – an inscription already evident in the description of digital learning platforms (such as Moodle) as *learning management systems*. Learning is regarded as a process that teachers can administratively plan and manage. This reversal, though, is most apparent in the theory and practice of e-learning. "What is e-learning?," Ruth Colvin Clark and Richard Mayer ask in their volume on the topic, and explicate: "we define e-learning as instruction delivered on a computer by way of CD-ROM, Internet, or intranet" (2011, p. 10). In fact, the discussions on *e-learning* usually deal exclusively with *e-teaching* and a notion of teaching that systematically excludes the subjective dimension of learning, the students' real learning processes and their conduct of everyday life, as well as the conflictual, contradictory character of learning matters and societal meanings. Here, societal meanings only seem to be read as unquestioned givens, but not as challenges and issues to be explored in the act of learning.

Furthermore, the development of learning management systems, e-teaching and online courses has to be viewed historically in the present social context of the economic utilization of teaching. In his analysis of the political economy of digitalizing educational practices in North American universities, historian of science and technology David Noble notes:

> We are now witnessing the commodification of the educational function of the university, transforming courses into courseware, the activity of instruction itself into commercially viable proprietary products that can be owned and bought and sold in the market.... The universities ... are becoming the site of production of – as well as the chief market for – copyrighted videos, courseware, CD-ROM's, and websites.
>
> (2004, p. 27)

Noble's analysis shows how, in the context of digitalization, marketing and the utilization interests in the computer and publishing sector and university management, digital courses become commoditized products that, frozen up in a new way, are increasingly withdrawn from the influence of students – and also of teachers. Such a one-sided fixation, however, structurally excludes the fundamental preconditions required for expansive learning (such as the students' interests in learning, the self-determined development of learning problems, the possibilities of affinitive and definitive learning phases, and a learning approach to contradictions) and profoundly inscribes into the digital learning environments a dichotomized positioning of teachers and learners as well as a transfer of merely authoritative knowledge.

The social impetus to automatizing and digitalizing the learning relations at universities should not be underestimated. Even if the idea of an "automatic professor machine" (Winner, 2014) may be an exaggeration, it exaggerates in the direction of a truth already overtaken by real events (with, for example, schools in Korea using robots as teachers; Sang-Hun, 2010). With the growing homogenization of teaching and learning and the further de-personalization of subjective learning activities, the productive, dialogical dynamisms in teaching and learning processes are becoming ossified. Developing expansive learning relations thus requires comprehensive theoretical and practical reasoning that, from the standpoint of the learning subjects, continually analyzes the potentials and limits of digital technologies for learning activities. The boundaries have to be precisely drawn; if not, this brings with it the danger of a severe impoverishment and freezing in the practice of learning and its most productive moment – the fluid back-and-forth of learning and teaching.

References

Andersen, A. S. (2015). History of Roskilde University. In A. S. Andersen & S. Heilesen (Eds.), *The Roskilde model: Problem-orientated project learning and project work* (pp. 63–78). New York: Springer.

Andersen, A. S. & Dupont, S. (2015). Supervising project. In A. S. Andersen & S. Heilesen (Eds.), *The Roskilde model: Problem-orientated project learning and project work* (pp. 121–140). New York: Springer.

Andersen, A. S. & Heilesen, S. (Eds.). (2015). *The Roskilde model: Problem-orientated project learning and project work*. New York: Springer.

Berthelsen, J., Illeris, K. & Poulsen, S. C. (1985). *Grundbog i projektarbejde: Teori og praktisk vejledning*. Copenhagen: Unge Pædagoger.

Bourdieu, P. & Passeron, J.-C. (1979). *The inheritors: French students and their relations to culture*. Chicago: University of Chicago Press.

Brockmeier, J. (1988). Was bedeutet dem Subjekt die Welt: Fragen einer psychologischen Semantik. In N. Kruse & M. Ramme (Eds.), *Hamburger Ringvorlesung Kritische Psychologie*, (pp. 141–184). Hamburg: Ergebnisse Verlag.

Colvin Clark, R. & Mayer, R.-E. (2011). *E-learning and the science of instruction: Proven guidelines for consumers and designers of multimedia learning*. San Francisco: Pfeiffer.

Derry, J. (2008). Technology-enhanced learning: A question of knowledge. *Journal of Philosophy of Education*, 42(3/4), 505–519.

Dreier, O. (2008). Learning in structures of social practice. In K. Nielsen, S. Brinkmann, C. Elmholdt, L. Tanggaard, P. Musaeus & G. Kraft (Eds.), *Qualitative stance: Essays in honor of Steinar Kvale, 1938–2008* (pp. 85–96). Aarhus: Aarhus University Press.

Dreier, O. (2015). Learning and conduct of everyday life. In A. Larraín, A. Haye, J. Cresswell, G. Sullivan & M. Morgan (Eds.), *Dialogue and debate in the making of theoretical psychology*. Toronto: Captus Press.

Dupont, S. (2013). Vejledning, læring, kompetence og dannelse. *Spor: Tidskrift for Universitetspædagogik*, 2, 1–45.

Engeström, Y. (1987). *Learning by expanding: An activity-theoretical approach to developmental research*. Helsinki: Orienta-Konsultit.

European Commission. (2013). *Report to the European Commission on improving the quality of teaching and learning in Europe's higher education institutions*. Luxembourg: Publications Office of the European Union.

Freire, P. (2012). *Pedagogy of the oppressed*. New York: Bloomsbury. (Original work published 1970)

Giddens, A. (1984). *The constitution of society: Outline of the theory of structuration*. Cambridge: Polity Press.

Haug, F. (2003a). *Lernverhältnisse: Selbstbewegungen und Selbstblockierungen*. Hamburg: Argument.

Haug, F. (2003b). Erinnerung an Lernen. *Journal für Psychologie*, 11(2), 194–213.

Haug, F. (2009). Teaching how to learn and learning how to teach. *Theory & Psychology*, 19(2), 245–274.

Hedegaard, M. & Chaiklin, S. (2005). *Radical-local teaching and learning: A cultural-historical approach*. Aarhus: Aarhus University Press.

Højholt, C. (2008). Participation in communities: Living and learning across different contexts. *Australian Research in Early Childhood Education*, 15(1), 1–12.

Højholt, C. & Røn Larsen, M. (2014). Læring som et aspekt ved børns engagementer i hverdagslivet. In C. Aabro (Ed.), *Læring i daginstitutioner: Et erobringsforsøg* (pp. 64–83). Frederikshavn: Dafolo.

Holzkamp, K. (1993). *Lernen: Subjektwissenschaftliche Grundlegung*. Frankfurt/M.: Campus.

Holzkamp, K. (1996). Lernen. Subjektwissenschaftliche Grundlegung: Einführung in die Hauptanliegen des Buches. *Forum Kritische Psychologie*, 36, 113–131.

Holzkamp, K. (2013). The fiction of learning as administratively plannable. In E. Schraube & U. Osterkamp (Eds.), *Psychology from the standpoint of the subject: Selected writings of Klaus Holzkamp* (pp. 115–132) (A. Boreham and U. Osterkamp, Trans.). Basingstoke: Palgrave Macmillan.

Illeris, K. (2007). *How we learn*. London: Routledge.

Kontopodis, M., Wulf, C. & Fichtner, B. (Eds.). (2011). *Children, development and education: Cultural, historical, anthropological perspectives*. New York: Springer.

Kvale, S. (1976). The psychology of learning as ideology and technology. *Behaviorism, 4*(1), 97–116.

Langemeyer, I. (2005). Contradictions in expansive learning: Towards a critical analysis of self-dependent forms of learning in relation to contemporary socio-technological change. *Forum: Qualitative Social Research, 7*(1), Article 12. Retrieved from www.qualitative-research.net/index.php/fqs/article/view/76/155.

Lave, J. (1996). Teaching, as learning, in practice. *Mind, Culture, and Activity, 3*(3), 149–164.

Lave, J. & Wenger, E. (1991). *Situated learning: Legitimate peripheral participation.* Cambridge: Cambridge University Press.

Marvakis, A. (2014a). Learning. In T. Teo (Ed.), *Encyclopedia of critical psychology* (pp. 1069–1075). New York: Springer.

Marvakis, A. (2014b). *Στρατηγικές και πρακτικές μάθησης* [Learning strategies and practices]. Thessalonika: Epikentro.

Marvakis, A. & Petritsi, I. (2014). Solidarity, not adjustment: Activism learning as (self)education. In T. Corcoran (Ed.), *Psychology in education: Critical theory~practice* (pp. 129–143). Rotterdam: Sense.

Mergner, G. (1999). *Lernfähigkeit der Subjekte und gesellschaftliche Anpassungsgewalt: Kritischer Dialog über Erziehung und Subjektivität.* Hamburg: Argument.

Noble, D. F. (2004). *Digital diploma mills: The automation of higher education.* New York: Monthly Review Press.

Packer, M. (2001). The problem of transfer, and the sociocultural critique of schooling. *Journal of the Learning Sciences, 10*(4), S493–514.

Rubinstein, S. L. (1977). *Grundlagen der Allgemeinen Psychologie.* Berlin: Volk und Wissen. (Original work published 1958)

Salling Olesen, H. & Højgård Jensen, J. (Eds.). (1999). *Project studies: A late modern university reform?* Frederiksberg: Roskilde University Press.

Sang-Hun, C. (2010, July 10). Teaching machine sticks to script in South Korea. *New York Times*, p. A19.

Schraube, E. (2009). Technology as materialized action and its ambivalences. *Theory & Psychology, 19*(2), 296–312.

Schraube, E. (2013). First-person perspective and sociomaterial decentering: Studying technology from the standpoint of the subject. *Subjectivity, 6*(1), 12–32.

Schraube, E. & Sørensen, E. (2013). Exploring sociomaterial mediations of human subjectivity. *Subjectivity, 6*(1), 1–11.

Skinner, B. F. (1954). The science of learning and the art of teaching. *Harvard Educational Review, 24,* 86–97.

Skinner, B. F. (1968). *The technology of teaching.* Englewood Cliffs, NJ: Prentice Hall.

Sørensen, E. (2008). *The materiality of learning.* Cambridge: Cambridge University Press.

Winner, L. (1989). *The whale and the reactor: A search for limits in an age of high technology.* Chicago, IL: University of Chicago Press.

Winner, L. (2009). Information technology and educational amnesia. *Policy Futures in Education, 7*(6), 587–591.

Winner, L. (2014, June 9). The automatic professor machine [Video file]. Retrieved from www.youtube.com/watch?v=vYOZVdpdmws.

12
THE POLITICS OF HOPE

Memory-Work as a Method to Study the Conduct of Everyday Life

Frigga Haug

Drawing on Gramsci's thoughts on how theoretical concepts relate to common sense, I delineate the relation between theory and everyday understanding as a basic challenge in the study of the conduct of life and introduce memory-work as a possible approach to deal with it. A brief outline of memory-work's development is supplemented by basic assumptions underlying and supporting this approach. In a short excursus, I address a current discussion in critical psychology about implicit suppositions about the human subject. My reference to Gramsci is linked to a short presentation of the *Female Sexualization* project (Haug et al., 1999), which provides an initial answer to the urgent need for research in the area of *body and feeling*. Then I introduce memory-work, its individual steps and theoretical foundations. The memory-work project is related to conduct of life in two ways: first, through the general question of how individuals could be genuinely empowered to take control of their own conduct of life. Second, this question is then related to the ideas underlying the *Four-in-One-Perspective* political project, a proposal to understand individual life as taking place in four main areas (work-life, reproduction, self-development and politics) and always being challenged to bring these four areas together in one conduct of life instead of spending one's whole life only in one or two areas unhappily and subordinated (Haug, 2011); this in turn, is broken down into anticipatory memory-work – in other words, work with hope.

Starting from Antonio Gramsci

In *Selections from the Prison Notebooks*, Antonio Gramsci discusses the connection between common sense and science, critiquing an earlier author neglecting the relevance of theory:

He really does capitulate before common sense and vulgar thought, since he has not put the problem in exact theoretical terms and is therefore in practice disarmed and impotent. The uneducated and crude environment has dominated the educator and vulgar common sense has imposed itself on science rather than the other way round. If the environment is the educator, it too must in turn be educated.

(Gramsci, 1971, p. 435)

Gramsci's statement maintains the importance of understanding the everyday in theoretical terms in order to recognize how the everyday is actually lived in practice. In other words, we have a lot of work ahead of us – work rather reminiscent of Baron Münchhausen reputedly pulling himself out of a swamp by his own hair since we ourselves, involved and entangled as we are in everyday life, have to mobilize our experience of everyday and yet, at the same time, gain a distance from it so that it does not engulf us.

In this context, memory-work does indeed offer an approach that we might fruitfully adopt. To begin with, negatively – not by setting priorities and principles, nor by constructing a categorial superstructure and then seeing whether our everyday life fits into it. Instead, positively, we can start directly with our conduct of everyday life, looking at precisely those points where we experience crises and conflicts, where the old order no longer functions and there is a search for new rules, habits and approaches: in brief, where there is suffering, and hence where the subject seeks to change the way s/he lives her/his everyday life.

But even then, one would still have just as many individual narratives, neither sorted nor orderly, and have only just started the work of grasping this in theoretical terms. One needs to identify how the general – that is, the theoretically resilient – can be mined from the individual or, in other words, how the general appears in the individual. Since everyday life in its entirety is constantly shifting and changing, we have to attempt to grasp it through those changes.

The Origins of Memory-Work

In political and historical terms, memory-work began with the crisis of the avant-garde model that forced the members of a socialist women's group to realize that they themselves were the children of just those same conditions they wanted to enlighten others about. Writing our own memories of the political process, we learned that we had to combat such blocking feelings as envy and jealousy, feelings we thought we had long overcome, and fight with incompetences. But we also learned that, in turn, we possessed some unusual skills – for example, thanks to our education, we had the ability to think abstractly and distance ourselves. To understand just what this means, it may be appropriate to recall the origins of memory-work.

In the wake of the severe shock at finding ourselves the children of these social relations, we deduced five lessons from the experience. These, elucidated below, became rather like fundamental theorems, and mark the beginning of memory-work.

a. We were mistaken in thinking of ourselves as a kind of avant-garde of the women's movement; even though we never put this so bluntly in these terms, we implicitly believed it. As the children of the same social relations, though, we realized that we bore similar marks, encountered similar obstacles and had the same flaws and possibilities as any other woman. This insight changed our long-term politics and, in my case, also changed my ideas on how to conduct research. To find out what happens in the process of women's socialization, we could actually take ourselves and each other as "empirical material" and as "objects of research" – an approach simultaneously making our research easier and more difficult.
b. We needed to assume that we are also reproducing the dominant culture and ideology. As a result, we also needed to study those contexts and examine our lives as female producers of culture and ideology.
c. We painfully acquired knowledge of the politics of language. From a very early stage, we concretely experienced how language conducts politics through us, and is not simply a mere tool to be used more or less skillfully.
d. We were aware of our inability to speak about women while retracing theories of knowledge and other social, cultural, etc. theories, and felt this was our own ineffectiveness. Now, though, we realized it was due to the complete absence of women within these theories.
e. We recognized that a vast unknown territory lay before us – the knowledge of how women work themselves into society. As women, we were the experts who "knew" how this was done, since we lived it day and night.

These insights were both painful and fascinating. In general, we had learned to critique structures somehow external to and independent from us, yet thinking about ourselves as part of those social relations confronted us with a need to see ourselves as reproducing just this very society, and as entangled in it both in our bodies and minds, as well as through our emotions and thoughts. Changing our politics was difficult, but it was fascinating to discover ourselves as an area of research, and convince other women throughout Germany and abroad to do the same. It was even more difficult to change ourselves: how should we work with our feelings and the ways we spontaneously conceived everyday practice? How should we explain the links we sensed between feelings, attitudes and everyday practices? This was the birth of memory-work. And it began with what became known as the actor-victim debate: The proposition that women's oppression can only be understood if we take into account how we ourselves are participators, actively reproducing this oppression ourselves.

Brief Excursus on the Concept of the Subject

This debate refers to a discussion (still unresolved) within the critical psychology in which we had to clarify how to conceptualize the human subject when conducting subject research. As I understand Ute Osterkamp (e.g., 2015, chap. 8 in this volume), she presently regards the subject as corrupted by prevailing power relations and prepared to suppress others in order to exercise its own agency (even if only a restrictive agency). She attempts to identify ways to alter this situation through a joint leap into changing the world. She and I both share a critical intention directed at liberation. However, in my case, I consider the subject as fragile, a battleground in itself, where it wrestles with prevailing power structures to exercise agency of its own volition. In this process, the subject embodies the state, seeks to arrange itself more or less with it, and also offers resistance. There are differences, which are gender specific, not only in the way subalternities are maintained, but also established. I regard gender relations as relations of production; in other words, the reciprocal positioning of men and women is intertwined with power relations. For my research, then, I need to pose the complicated question of *how* a subject consents to being dominated – in contrast, Osterkamp asks *why* a subject consents to exercise domination – which is actually a question directed to men. With the *how*-question, then, I need to undertake comprehensive explorations examining the conduct of everyday life in a variety of ways, and cannot know what I will find.

Further Support for Working with Individual Memories

One constant and major source of inspiration and support for my memory-work project came from Marxist philosophy as well as belles-lettres, in particular, works by Christa Wolf, Herbert Marcuse, Walter Benjamin and, as a concrete example, Antonio Gramsci (for more detail, see Haug, 1999, pp. 23–42).

Gramsci's concept of common sense embraces two dimensions simultaneously: common thoughts and ideas, full of prejudices and superstitions, and yet at the same time a kind of basis that refuses to be fooled, and for this reason provides a foundation to build on. Gramsci rejects the view that, at different times and in different states of consciousness, common-sense experiences are amassed uncritically and then, as needed, one or the other can be selected, put forward to justify and explain one's own actions and decisions. Instead, common sense is not just the basis on which individuals engage with the world and seek to act to fulfill their needs, but also obstructs the capacity to act to achieve emancipation. Common sense is contradictory; at the very least, it is incoherent. An individual's rational grounds are culturally anchored, and so depend on collective individual practices and how their engagement with the world is embedded. As a result, one can have a scientific approach to knowledge and still be guided by superstitions in many everyday decisions, arrange things for the well-being of all and, in another dimension of one's thoughts, believe it quite proper to give all power and agency to a leader. Therefore, Gramsci concluded that each person has to give an account of herself or himself depending on the stratum of the maturity of her/his judgments, and whether s/he could argue for such judgments as commensurate with the most advanced thought of the age. Gramsci thus pointed to the importance of drawing up an inventory of the traces of common sense within ourselves; through the process of seeing and reordering this list, we become enabled to develop a greater capacity to act in the sense that we ourselves affirm (Gramsci, 1971, Q. 11, § 12).

Female Sexualization

Memory-work started from the assumption that its inquiry initiates in a personal crisis, that it politically rejects the avant-garde model and at first emerged from the simple desire to stay together – to be a new kind of political family. This came together with a theoretical crisis. I gave a seminar on sexuality and power together with Wolfgang Fritz Haug. I arrived with my socialist women's group, and we easily understood the theories on sexuality and the body yet, at the same time, did not understand them or, rather, could not identify with them. We could only memorize them, but not really recognize them. In the wake of this experience, we began our study on *Female Sexualization*, working on it for 2 years. We published our findings in a book that became a classical text of memory-work (Haug et al., 1999; for a discussion, see, for example, the collection of articles in Hyle, Ewing, Montgomery & Kaufman, 2008).

At that time, our *Female Sexualization* project began very much as an experiment, with hesitation and doubts over our relationship to our own bodies – an issue where no final answer was found. We soon discovered that something as concrete as one's own body proved to be a conceptual abstraction. One does not encounter one's body as such, but only parts of it. Everyone has a different problem with a different part – stomach, legs, breasts, hair, nose, mouth, chin and so on, and everywhere there are flaws and stigma needing to be corrected, or if that proves impossible, they have to be hidden by cheating. How that happens in detail is an empirical question. A considerable amount of material on this subject can be found in Erving Goffman's *Stigma* (1963), a book always fruitful to read and re-read. In this area, in a comprehensive incompetence, one acquires competences and a bad conscience, since you are not the way you present yourself, and so always run the risk of being caught out (we adopted the terms *competence/incompetence* for these practices from the *Ideological Theory* project; see also the entry in Haug, Haug & Jehle, 2010).

In brief, the body quickly turned out to be a rich depository of rules and resistance, and, above all, guilt, morals, ideology and the state, which uses its laws to direct our behavior – for example, through the law on abortion, but also laws on how we deal with our bodies, its size, prescriptions on nutrition, exercise and so on.

The first propositions we developed included the hypothesis that dividing up the body into individual parts opens it up to power and submission under external rules demanding obedience, and anchored in an ideology of morals. We formed working groups on parts of the body – and to suggest who would be expected to cope with the topics of breasts or stomachs in our first projects, we ourselves divided the women in the project into "stable" and "labile." We then recommended the latter group to research into their own relationship to such topics as hair, since we thought these were rather more neutral, and less emotionally laden. However, the idea that hair could be "neutral" proved to be a serious error since, of course, hair does not only grow on the head. The details of this study can be found in the book on the project (Haug et al., 1999; see also Haug, 1992, 1999). The book also contains the first discussion of the subsequent methodological guidelines.

Memory-Work: A Theoretical and Methodological Outline

A number of basic assumptions need to be examined to clarify whether the memory-work method might prove a suitable approach to enrich studies on the conduct of life. These assumptions are not new discoveries of the project first applied in memory-work. Instead, they combine a variety of positions, partly from the cultural-historical school, partly from critical psychology, Marxism and linguistic theory. In the following, I outline some of the basic theoretical guidelines from memory-work that ought to be familiar to any group using this method, and should be discussed by them.

Working on the general assumption that personalities are constructed just as in the meaning of the scene written down, that there is a tendency to eliminate contradictions and that, on the whole, language is used politically, the written-down memories are, in the context of this assumption, systematically analyzed and examined. It is advisable to follow the individual steps in sequence: noting down the characteristics, actions and emotions the author herself includes in the scene. The purpose is to find how meaning is suggested, and, in general, how language is informed by politics. When the written scene has been dissected into its individual components in this way, conclusions can be drawn in one single step on how the construction of self and others appears to be. In retrospect you see how the initially apparent issue has ultimately shifted into a different problem readable under the surface of the account, virtually as a kind of author's second message that wants to be heard (more on this later).

The analytical steps in working with personal memories range from establishing the construction of self to the construction of others, and finally to problem displacement.

Given that individuals make their own history, but do not make it as they please (Marx), we also assume that this applies equally to the construction of each individual's personality. To encourage distance and a more relaxed approach, necessary to facilitate self-change as a component of changing the conditions, the first step is to consider the joints in this construction – in other words, for change to be conceivable, what seem to be self-evident ways of behaving, thinking and feeling have to be transposed into the status of the "non-self-evident." In a memory-work group project (and it is always a group, since a group is needed for the work, as a mirror, as dissent, confirmation or fantasy) this process occurs through questions being asked about an everyday scene that has been written down. These questions relate to some shared assumptions about writing, the choice of language and construction. These are, as one might say, questions about the grammar of the written scene. At the same time, through the experience gained in discussing many such written scenes, I would suggest not allowing the text to become too abstract and removed from the real world. I am also including here an initial practical guide, which can be skipped if the reader does not intend to work directly with memory-work.

How are the Others in the Scene Constructed? First Answer and Insight: they are Nearly Always Missing

Abstractly, each participant knows that nobody can live her everyday life without others. Since such a memory-work group in particular involves a collective attempt to live part of feminist culture, all of the group members regard an individual woman's self-perception as resembling Robinson Crusoe on a desert island having to tackle everything by herself as scandalous, which necessitates individual efforts to achieve a resolution.

At the same time, the group should discuss the issue of tracing back events to personality, the inability to perceive others, and social circumstances as factors contributing to a self-perception that is culturally supported in our individualistic society. In this context, developing our own culture becomes an urgent task, and one that relates to individual development and freedom.

How Does the Construction of One's Own Personality Occur?

Our personalities are not innate, given to us or predetermined. Instead, they are constructed by the self. This self-construction within pre-existing structures implies that a personality has a story, a past. We take this insight from the cultural-historical school of the early Soviet Union, namely from Vygotsky and Leontiev. We attach meaning to our personas and use this meaning, or understanding of our personality, to determine the steps we take in the near present and distant future.

Eliminating Contradictions is an Important Strategy in Memory

We tend to disregard anything that conflicts with the unified image we present to ourselves and others. For example, if one wants to create the impression of a capable, feisty and fun-loving person, one naturally hides and covers up all signs of imbalance, of fear and insecurity. It is important, as Gramsci put it, to work coherently oneself, but this entails the need for self-reflection to remain capable of acting despite contradictory reasons for action. At the start of any movement there are contradictions, and these provide the motivation to move forward. In contrast, in our idea of our own self presented to others, it is easy to cover up uncertainties and we can very quickly manage merely to display what is a coherent image. In a narrated version of the self, contradictions often appear in the thread of the narrative as gaps or empty spaces that then need to be covered up – for example, when someone characterizes herself as a lone fighter against her parents, and only mentions in passing at another point that she has seven siblings; or when a harmony is reported requiring seemingly incomprehensible rituals, such as always meeting at a set time even though the people have nothing to say to each other. The individual materials are full of inconsistencies that one can already identify when one merely applies what Gramsci calls a *sensu commune*, the "healthy" part of common sense during the collective discussion of a narrative. This act of eliminating contradictions, which is mostly semi-conscious, may become transparent in the written experiences as we document the details that do not fit. Deconstruction work is aimed primarily at drawing out these contradictions and breaking points in our experiences. It presents them in a new light and connects them to other developments, choices or ways of life. Hence, in order to facilitate change, we need to disturb the graveyard-like silence of sameness, creating a sense of mental unrest. When we achieve this sense of mental unrest, we can realize that certain emotions are disquieting and destabilizing, and the memory-work is set in motion.

Construction of Meaning

In our everyday life, we strive to endow ourselves with coherent meaning, creating the image of ourselves in which we believe. In every communicative situation, we attempt to convey this image, or present different images to different audiences. Meaning construction is a continuous process. We talk about ourselves and expect others to receive the messages we sent out in the form we intended. Thus, the construction of meaning is also a process that requires the others' agreement. Meaning is transmitted primarily by language, but also by gestures, appearance and expression.

The Politics of Language

In methodological terms, memory-work is language analysis, examining the language we use as a medium of consent, participation and submission. For this reason, the research object is the text, not the person.

In discussing an experience documented in written form, working with language use is of key importance. How does the writer use language to convey the intended meaning without triggering doubts? In this critical analysis, one prerequisite is to realize that language is not merely a tool that we can use as we choose. Instead, in our use of the language, politics speaks through us and regulates our construction of meaning. Thus, as it were, we have recourse culturally to a number of ready-made meanings that we can access. When we write, they strongly suggest themselves to us, dictating a meaning we may not even have intended – and this is especially the case when we use language less reflectively and more naively. Of course, the more we try not to stand out as personalities and seek to attribute normality to our experiences, the more we use these ready-made meanings.

Text Dissection

When we want to discover how the author's language expresses the intended meaning about the experience, we need to deconstruct the meaning in the text. The first step in this process is to gain a distance to the realm of conveyed meaning. In itself, this is not an easy task since most reports of individual experiences rely on empathy and sympathetic understanding, and successfully elicit these in everyday communication. As a result, there is a tendency to cultivate therapeutic discourses of sympathy, and apply a "psychologizing" approach to relate connecting stories. However, this approach and practice is not merely theoretically unproductive, but also obstructs insights by inviting group members to form alliances with those less inclined to actively apply analytical tools, thus merely heightening a perception of suffering ("you poor thing, was your father really that bad?" etc.).

For this reason, it is absolutely essential to establish distance to work with a text. One method of creating that distance is to question the text. Since every question also has a kind of theory about the subject underlying it, we try to keep the questions as simple as possible. In this way, we can control the implicit theory better, and avoid falling prey to common prejudices. The questions about the text only relate to the use of language – following basic grammatical rules. The sentences contain a subject, a verb, an object, perhaps adjectives or adverbs. They provide information about the person writing the text, her emotions and actions, and about other individuals. Starting from this basis, we then split the text into its elements, placing them in vertical columns. The aim here is to identify how the writer constructs herself – that is, her personality – and how she thus creates meaning and coherence. In addition, we also consider how she has constructed other people in the text in relation to her.

Linguistic Particularities

The division of language also includes another column that we have called "linguistic particularities." In this column, we list, for example, how far the narrative is written with impersonal subjects. This often reveals how the writer herself disappears almost completely, at least as an active agent, and instead is other-directed. It becomes evident that in the situations she describes, she is unable to do anything actively; her experiences are presented solely as if impersonal subjects decide on the narrative development – for instance, using such phrases as "hunger grabbed me," "fog enveloped me," "the dark surprised me," "the sky exploded," where movement and activity appear compressed. Since none of the subjects in these phrases are people, the narrative subject herself does not act as an active agent. The use of negated verbs ("did not run") is another particularity, as is the frequent weakening of actions by modal verbs such as can, or would like, both of which make the narrator less important in the narration. In some cases, the narrative subject manages with just one to two active verbs, or in other cases may always use the same verb, such as "said." These particularities are discussed below to consider whether using the same verb repeatedly is due to limited expressive language or also demonstrates the hopelessness of the situation – given the way the situation unfolded, there was nothing else to say.

Empty Spaces – Gaps – Contradictions

Some elements do not reference the written text as such, but need an inquiry into what is not mentioned. For example, here one column lists "empty spaces" – the elements not expressed in the written account but necessary for the narrative's plausibility – while another column is headed contradictions. The implication of these columns becoming part of the project is that individuals, in order to remain agents, have to lend a sense of cohesiveness to their narratives and self-perception. They then need to eliminate the contradictions that may appear in this process, or just ignore certain individual elements.

Problem Shifting

In the final stage, the different constructions are readable in the context and give the narrative a new meaning – a process we have termed "problem shifting." At the start of our work we could unanimously decipher a message that was the motive of the narrative expressed in contemporary common-sense terms. However, after analyzing the language use, we can now read an entirely new message. The reading gained through reconstruction is different from the author's intended meaning. Nevertheless, since she has written the narrative down, it illustrates her semi-conscious awareness of the context in which she is living. Quite often, such a context may be summarized in such sentences as "one cannot do anything alone" or "if you do not listen to advice, you are lost," which sound like pebbles smoothed by truth. They are the thoughts not expressed yet wanting to be said.

This does not mean that the first narrative was not true; in fact, both narratives are true. The second shows how the author can wriggle out of the usual traps where she talks up her self-confidence, since she now has gained an insight into her construction of self. Hence, this step is the most important in the memory-work process, since it offers a possible way out of the habitual and a chance to grasp other possibilities.

Finally, the last suggested reading of the text can then be compared with the initial one – a reconstruction based on a deconstruction of the initial statement deduced in agreement. Frequently, in contrast to the new meaning elicited after the deconstruction process, it is surprising to realize how meager and ideologically informed the earlier intended message was. However, this does not mean that one is true and the other invalid – after all, both messages are from the author. The circumstances producing one at the cost of the other show just how odd our dealings are with ourselves, and how we struggle with ambiguity and knowledge in everyday life.

A Summary of Kinds

Every author writing an account of an everyday situation first writes in the dominant language. For us to understand her account, she has to write with the appropriate feelings and use a rational and logical structure to create what seems, at first glance, a non-contradictory narrative with a beginning, middle and end. The dominant language then reveals the dominant cultural pattern, while the language use conveys experience. For that reason, imagining experience is also a political process that occurs almost automatically. By complying with the expectations that correspond to feelings, mental processes and reactions, one can ensure that one has really experienced what is related, and it is not merely a fictional account. If the account was told as a story, the expression would naturally underline the story.

Yet only the describing subject is able to view this process as a development, and not as the experience of a class goal. We assume that we can find evidence of semi-conscious things, departures and contradictions in the experience, and that these are often revealed in narratives through inappropriate words, senseless pieces, a reasonless silence or contradictory statements. These are also experiences, yet conflict with the dominant meaning of the experience gained. We compare the single experience with the potential of a single person in the world. It seems possible to assume that every single person has a need to escape from the conditions in which she is acting and to attain competence, autonomy and co-determination on every important issue. The conditions in which she is acting have a political and methodological dimension, as well as a dimension critical of domination. Each woman in the research group can analyze her own texts, how she makes compromises and how she falls in line or submits, and in this way discover how to retain her agency within contradictory structures. Her way of life, attitudes and patterns of processing conflict become legible as a solution once functional, but today seemingly nothing more than suitable for 4-year-olds. At the same time, you wish for the complete ability to act, comprehensive solutions, and the ability to create a living culture of contradiction instead of a culture of inequality. From this position, you can work for the possibility of a freer life, and so it may therefore become a vision, a possibility to make something happen that you wanted or divined. This search takes a collective form. The language needed is discovered in the process, and the material is the undiscovered knowledge contained in the described experiences. This is a process that is never finished.

Finally Back to Emotions: a Term as Abstract as Body

It is advisable to study special feelings like love or hatred. To deal with emotions you have to deal with language. But looking at our pieces of memory, they quite commonly do not discuss emotions. The column we have reserved for the emotions remains empty. Since we know the account of everyday experience included a wide spectrum of emotions, we at least can say that we have no language for our emotions. In most scenarios, it seems as if an absence of feelings is required to make our observations appear reasonable.

To introduce movement into this situation, one could make provocative and contradictory statements to trigger further research on the subject, stating, for example, that "evidently, women – supposedly such an emotional gender – are unable to express feelings," or "something happens to the emotions and feelings of women in our society; they wilt, are prohibited or unnamed." What does it mean when activities are narrated without mentioning feelings even though we know these actions are accompanied, steered, blocked or perpetuated by feelings, and yet we still consider our written account as describing a carefully structured and valid experience? Perhaps this could be the start of a new research project. From my experience, the following always holds true: In the experiences documented by women, feelings are highly peripheral even when the accounts deal with an experience of antagonistic feelings. In addition, measured on the scale of possible human passions, the feelings have to be regarded by the group as mainly superficial.

We find a similar pattern in dealing with motivation, the reasons for action, which are such a key subject for analysis in critical psychology (where conditions and patterns of meaning and reason are analyzed to reveal the socially mediated dimension of human agency). Our extra "motivation" column is also usually empty, as if women lived and acted without motivation. Just as in the case of the question about feelings, this too provides a suggestion for further research. When related to the narrator's self-construction, it then seems as if "She constructs herself as devoid of interests." If we examine impersonal subjects or consider the construction of others, it might then become evident that a woman has constructed herself as powerless, weak or other-directed. Alternatively, after some more research, we might then formulate the hypothesis that women have not achieved the status of subjects.

Sometimes, feelings are mentioned: for instance, when love appears as self-abandonment, enraptured, ensnared or enchained. The particular position of women in relation to feelings requires its own study, in the interest of women, where an appropriate language would also be acquired.

Alexandra Kollontai, who took part in the Russian Revolution, wrote about women's love as a prison that women need to liberate themselves from to become, in her words, "free as the wind and lonely as the grass in the steppe (1977, S. 277; translation by the author)." Simone de Beauvoir offered a similar diagnosis, recommending the less dramatic solution of earning one's own living to escape economic subalternity. It remains questionable whether this brings the freedom needed to love. What remains complicated is female abandon of the self, living with herself against herself until she gains her self.

In short, the experience of feelings shows these to be something quite amorphous and without knowledge, something that overcomes you, which does not make you stronger, but weakens you; the point being to find a way to use emotions to strengthen oneself, to escape from prison, and yet give to others.

Remembering the Future

To return to the main theme of the conduct of everyday life: how does the above exposition relate to the conduct of life project discussed here? Throughout my life, my work has been dedicated to analyzing and elucidating the involvement of one's own actions in suppression. My first publication on the question of whether women were actually only victims – of the conditions and of men – unleashed a kind of furore, not least because of the political pretension that if we do not liberate ourselves on our own, it will be without consequences for us (as Peter Weiss says in his novel *The Aesthetics of Resistance* (1975/2005)). It is not easy to take the step out of subalternity, where one experiences other-determined states as if they were volitional, and to embrace the self-conscious determination of deciding how one's own life should unfold. In this process, we face the prevailing culture even in our habits, and are blocked by the inflexibility of the everyday. If we leave the individualizing isolation and join others to organize ourselves and jointly challenge prevailing culture, we find ourselves confronting the totality of the social structures of the division of labor and power.

For just this approach, I have developed a project that has been discussed for some years among very different groups in society. Entitled the *Four-in-One-Perspective* (Haug, 2011), this project seeks to overcome customary divisions and reintegrate differences in a balanced totality. The project addresses the employment sector – where we spend a lot of time earning our living and at the same time do socially necessary labor – and includes as reproductive work care, love and friendliness in the world; it addresses each person's own development where we are an end and not a means; and finally, it addresses the appropriation of the political, instead of leaving it to representatives and only suffering the consequences, as we all know only too well from the crisis in the global economy. The idea is to live and experience these four areas of human activity in more or less equal parts of our time – say about 4 hours each. Put politically, this means fighting for the radical reduction of wage labor time for everybody connected with the right and duty to have a working place. Culturally, it means participation in the social of caring for each other as a source of enjoyment and a duty for everybody, for men and women; as a human project it also means to take the development of your own possibilities and capacities into your own hands, in culture and art, in knowledge, etc; politically it also means to be responsible for society and really participate in radical democracy.

Usually, society happens to us. It is something we have not created, and so we have to arrange ourselves in a given. But in reality, people make their own history and have to participate in producing the conditions of life, the prerequisites of their way of life; in other words, they need to act politically, and view themselves as politically responsible. In periods of crisis, persevering in subalternity clearly shows how delegating responsibility conjures up ideas of fate and destiny, instead of identifying points where one can and has to intervene. On the whole, this is also a call to live differently, to take responsibility for one's life or to understand Marx's statement in his "Theses on Feuerbach" (1976) on the coincidence of changing circumstances and self-change as a categorical imperative to connect these different spheres of life, learn the art to live them and thus change your own life by abandoning the historically grown division of labor that renders the many subaltern and poor, while allowing development for very few (1976).

Anticipatory Memory-Work

To allow this political proposal to move from the level of a sheer concept into our everyday lives, we have used the method of memory-work in an anticipatory way. Ultimately, this is about a different conduct of life and, in this process, our potential to actually intervene and posit ourselves as subjects of change. The idea that there is nothing you can do, the sweeping paralysis that grips the individual, does indeed derive from the widespread prevailing view that there is, in essence, only a now. We do not regard ourselves as moments in a historical process from whose movement and constant change we could and have to draw our strength. As soon as one grasps the workings of society as constant change and movement in particular power relations, one finds out which dimensions are changeable and intervenes at that point. To do so, one needs a compass to co-determine the direction of change, that is, to create an image of the desired future as in, for instance, imagining a dismantling of power, the empowerment of all, a good life without fear, and so on.

Hence, the conduct of life project would not only be something descriptively formulated in retrospect, but a hope, a utopia, which we want to become reality from the outset. We have written scenes of everyday life in which our lives took place as equally as possible in the four areas mentioned above. In concrete terms, this not only meant making ourselves aware of our conduct of everyday life and keeping a record of it, but also gradually at the same time, and in a draft form, accelerating change in it into the desired direction. In this way, we brought our political beliefs down to the level of our everyday actions, and could experience them in a schematic form with the resistances opposing their realization.

This was a very difficult process, yet not without its humorous moments. To summarize it as succinctly as possible, one can say: The movement toward the political sought to make the previous personal life impossible. It is not primarily in the area of the work–family balance, as it is commonly called, that there is a difficult compatibility problem, but politics is only possible when I give up love and friendship. And it is only then that one can think of one's own realization, and have the strength and time for artistic development. In that sense, late though it is, we can awaken Alexandra Kollontai's phrase to new life: women have to emerge from the prison of love to develop their own personalities.

But happiness as a goal is something different. Here, to clearly see what one has become entwined in, one needs to investigate one's own entanglement and the affirmation one has performed. Then, simultaneously, it will become apparent that a different model of society can only be initiated at all in a collective culture; the changes that are necessary challenge the conditions; and only when one acts does one profit from self-change. In other words, when one takes into consideration the coincidence of changing circumstances and self-change, as Marx pointed out in his "Theses on Feuerbach," (1976) one would not want to – and indeed could not – carry out the necessary attempt to change oneself to realize one's own happiness as an individual act (1976). Instead, one would realize that this is only possible when started in a group that has set itself the same goal of changing society – which we could term a culture of movement.

The enquiry into the conduct of life seems to be formulated more appropriately when *conduct of life* is translated into what is waiting to be changed: the *production of life* itself. This offers the possibility of naming the involved actors, to apprehend it as a collaborative process and identify happiness and freedom as the goal of self-determination, and take them up politically without disregarding the entanglement of personalities in the old conditions.

References

Goffman, E. (1963). *Stigma: Notes on the management of spoiled identity*. New York: Simon & Schuster.

Gramsci, A. (1971). *Selections from the prison notebooks* (Q. Hoare & G. Nowell Smith, Trans.). New York: International Publishers.

Haug, F. (1992). *Beyond female masochism: Memory-work and politics* (R. Livingstone, Trans.). London: Verso.

Haug, F. (1999). *Vorlesungen zur Einführung in die Erinnerungsarbeit*. Hamburg: Argument.

Haug, F. (2011). *Die Vier-in-einem-Perspektive: Politik von Frauen für eine neue Linke*. Hamburg: Argument.

Haug, F. et al. (1999). *Female sexualization: A collective work of memory* (E. Carter, Trans.). London: Verso.

Haug, W. F., Haug, F. & Jehle, P. (Eds.). (2010). *Historisch-kritischen Wörterbuch des Marxismus*, Vol. 7/2. Hamburg: Argument.

Hyle, A., Ewing, M. S., Montgomery, D. & Kaufman, J. S. (Eds.). (2008). *Dissecting the mundane: International perspectives on memory-work*. Lanham, MD: University Press of America.

Kollontai, A. (1977). *Die neue Moral und die Arbeiterklasse*. Münster: Verlag Frauenpolitik. (Original work published 1920)

Marx, K. (1976). Theses on Feuerbach. In *Collected works* (Vol. 5). London: Lawrence & Wishart (Original work published 1848).

Weiss, P. (2005). *The aesthetics of resistance: Vol. 1. A Novel* (J. Neugroschel, Trans.). Durham, ND: Duke University Press. (Original work published 1975)

13
COLLABORATIVE RESEARCH WITH CHILDREN

Exploring Contradictory Conditions of the Conduct of Everyday Life

Dorte Kousholt

This chapter takes as its point of departure the methodological challenge of exploring the interconnections of subjective and structural aspects of persons conducting their everyday life in and across social practices. My concern is how research can develop knowledge about common problems and social life conditions from the personal experiences of people living their lives in a complex world. There is an increasing awareness that we need knowledge about how problems appear and are embedded in the everyday lives of people in order to develop relevant psychological science and professional interventions (e.g., Hodgetts & Stolte, 2013; Hodgetts et al., 2015, chap. 6 in this volume). Lack of such knowledge often leads to problems becoming abstract and individualized (Højholt, 2015, chap. 7 in this volume; Motzkau & Schraube, 2015). Therefore, a significant methodological question is how to arrange research processes that produce knowledge about everyday personal engagements, efforts and concerns related to participation in social activities and matters at stake in different practices. This is fundamentally related to the theoretical question of conceptualizing the interconnection between subjective and structural aspects of everyday life.

Drawing on research on the everyday life of children and families, I will address possible implications of understanding and aiming to organize research collaboration that enables exploration of and critical reflection on contradictory life conditions in and across social practices. I argue that this calls for continuously de-centering researchers' perspectives on research questions, designs and methods, reflecting how they are relevant for the people we involve in research, as well as open-ended, varied and flexible research processes. In continuation of this, I discuss what I term cross-contextual methodology as entangled processes of following persons' conduct of life across contexts and developing knowledge about social practices from different perspectives and positions. Specific research practices cannot serve as recipes – and the examples explored here do not aim to define, nor confine, how to do research into children's conduct of everyday life. Rather, I see a need for discussions of how the theoretical approach informs the research design and researcher's participation in the investigated practices; in that respect, the chapter can hopefully facilitate methodological reflections.

In the chapter, I draw on examples from two projects: The first addressed children's everyday lives across home and day care institution and everyday practices in families; another project explored children's communities across special school and regular school arrangements. Both projects involved participant observations in the various contexts of the children's lives and interviews with parents and relevant professionals. A recurring aspect of these research projects was that I developed my research position to be able to collaborate with children on exploring their everyday lives across different life contexts, following transitions and shifts together with the children.

Conduct of Everyday Life as Problematic

Everyday life often refers to the mundane and ordinary aspect of life – everyday practicalities and processes that are often taken for granted or dismissed in science (Karlekin-Fishman, 2013, p. 714). Therefore, turning to the everyday lives of people has been associated with critique and resistance, and concern with everyday life has spurred a long tradition of critical ethnographic research (e.g., Hall & Jefferson, 1975/2006; Smith, 1987, 2006; Willis, 1977; see also Karlekin-Fishman, 2013 for an overview). Across this diverse tradition, there is a common, although far from homogeneous, ambition to learn about social and structural problems by exploring the personal stories and struggles of the everyday lives of people. Continuing this debate, and in order to explicate my approach, I take inspiration from research traditions engaged with conceptualizing the active effort of people living their everyday lives in a common world.

From a sociological and psychological background, respectively, Dorothy Smith and Klaus Holzkamp share the aim of developing science as a critique of dominant ideological interests. Additionally, they share the ambition of developing methodology that enables researchers to explore the interconnection of everyday subjective experience and societal structural relations. They contribute to establishing a research approach that takes people's perspectives on living their lives in a social world as the analytic starting point (see also Roth, 2008).

Smith is a leading scholar in the development of Institutional Ethnography as a methodology to link the everyday world of experience and the larger social structure. She argues for establishing an approach to "the everyday world as problematic" (the title of her book from 1987), and draws on an approach based on historical materialism, suggesting that we begin with investigating actual, daily social relations between individuals (1987, p. 98). Furthermore, she argues that our inquiry begin "from the standpoint of the subject" – an embodied subject located in a particular setting as a starting point for analyses of "ruling relations" (ibid., p. 105). Smith uses this term to "bring into view the intersection of the institutions organizing and regulating society with their gender subtexts and bases in a gender division of labor" (ibid., p. 3). The concept of ruling relations designates a complex of organized practices that transcend local settings and carry and accomplish organization and control (see also Devault, 2006; Devault & McKoy, 2006, p. 17).

When the aim is to develop knowledge about structural relations and institutional practices from the vantage point of the everyday lives of subjects, I see some problems regarding the conceptualization of the relation between the local everyday experiences of people and extra-local ruling relations: My concern is to avoid ending up in a rather static understanding of subjects governed "behind their backs" by structural relations, and the associated risk of "de-subjectifying" the people involved in the research (Doran, 1993). Hence, I find it important that social structures are investigated in their meanings to the persons who participate in, and thereby reproduce and change, them. Persons act collectively in relation to their life conditions and transform them in that process. Linking particular personal perspectives to existing power structures cannot replace the analysis of the meanings of structural arrangement for personal experiences, participation and relations (Dreier, 2008, p. 291).

From the vantage point of psychology, Holzkamp suggests the concept of *conduct of everyday life* as a means to analyzing mediating links between socio-structural characteristics and subjective meanings and action possibilities (see Jurczyk et al., 2015, chap. 2 in this volume, for the background in sociological research of the "Munich group"). Following Leontiev, Holzkamp (1987) points to what he terms a dominating problem in psychological theorizing: that the individuals' actions are assumed to be direct causes or effects of certain isolated features of the external world (see also 2013b, p. 255). Holzkamp proposes the concept of conduct of life as an answer to a fundamental critique of the "worldlessness" of psychological research formed in the image of natural science (Holzkamp, 2013b; Osterkamp & Schraube, 2013, p. 4). The concept of conduct of everyday life enables us to address *how* people live their everyday lives. Focus is directed to the *active, creative processes* of arranging and organizing life in relation to various (sometimes conflicting) demands from different contexts and, in relation to this, the personal *reasons* people have for participating in and across contexts in certain ways (Dreier, 2008, 2011; Holzkamp, 2013b). Recent theoretical work employing the concept in research with children has emphasized and expanded on the collective nature of conduct of everyday life (Chimirri, 2014; Højholt & Kousholt, forthcoming; Juhl, 2014, forthcoming; Kousholt, 2011). Conduct of life is fundamentally a social process – persons take part in social practices with common matters at stake, and in doing so create conditions for one another. Thus, personal conduct of life cannot be understood isolated from the conduct of the lives of others. In that way, the concept of conduct of life directs the exploration toward how persons, in social interplay, actively deal with and transform their life conditions while living their lives every day together with other persons.

Conducting one's life entails prioritizing and dealing with different demands and engagements and this implies *exploring* conditions and action possibilities working to achieve influence on relevant life conditions in collaboration with others (Højholt & Kousholt, forthcoming). To unfold this collective transformative aspect of conduct of life, I take up Smith's articulations of the activities people perform every day as "work" (1987, pp. 161ff.). As formulated by institutional ethnographer Marie Campbell, "the idea is to tap into people's expertise in the conduct of their everyday lives – their 'work'" (2006, p. 92). The term work is significant to underline that conduct of life is an *active accomplishment* – it is *work* we do every day. The concept has a dual meaning, which is appropriate here: "work" can also be used in the meaning of "how things work." This directs our attention toward *ongoing transformative processes* – making things work requires continuous resolution of contradictions and conflicts (Axel, 2002). In that way, the concept of conduct of life turns our attention to the processes and challenges involved in living our daily lives – we might say that the concept establishes life as "conflictual," in the sense that living our lives in and across complex and contradictory practices cannot be unambiguously resolved or arranged by forming a personal synthesis or harmonious connections (Dreier, 1997, 2008). Human lives and social cooperation are inherently conflictual (Axel, 2002, 2011; Holland & Lave, 2001; Lave, 2011). Consequently, the focus of the research shifts from single (separate) individuals to "*distributed subjects* who participate in cooperative activity by *relating productively to their conditions of life*" (Axel, 2002, p. 204).

I have argued that directing research to the "conduct of life as problematic" provides opportunities to build knowledge about structural aspects of people's lives with a starting point in participation and social interplay in and across concrete situations and contexts, and analyze this in terms of meanings to the persons involved. I will now take this a step further and explicate how the theoretical foundation of a conceptualization of persons' conduct of everyday life in conflictual social practice is linked to an understanding of research as collaboration on developing knowledge about common problems.

Research as Collaboration on Exploring Common Problems

In continuation of the materialist approach found in the work of both Smith and Holzkamp, production of knowledge is seen as embedded in social practices. The rooting in a "philosophy of practical activity – of 'praxis'" (Bernstein, 1971), encompasses a break with philosophical standpoints according to which valid knowledge (and science) must be purified from subjective and concrete circumstances, and that this is enabled by the researcher's distance from social life – what can be termed the "scholastic position" (Jensen, 2001). In contrast, a philosophy of praxis claims that scientific knowledge is achieved through systematically analyzing the concrete and variable circumstances (ibid.; Jensen, 1999). In this approach, knowledge is understood as related to being involved in the world, engaged in and drawing experience from particular matters. In that sense, research is a process of learning through participation in practice (Dreier, 2008; Lave, 2011).

Research and scientific knowledge are embedded in political arrangements and complex relations of power (Danziger, 1990; Nissen, 2012). Uffe Juul Jensen argues that exceeding the abstract and universal concept of knowledge that follows the "the scholastic position" entails organizing the relation between theory and practice differently than in the forms that have been prevalent in modern society (2001, p. 205). Hereby, Jensen points out that the confrontation with "the scholastic point of view" is not only a matter of understanding the relationship between theory and practice differently but, in a more far-reaching perspective, a matter of reorganizing the practical relationship between researchers and the people they involve in research. In continuation of this approach, research is conceptualized as a collaborative practice.

Along similar lines, Smith points to the fact that in order to develop a critical ethnographic practice, it is not enough to change, for example, methods of interviewing; rather, it is about exploring "methods of thinking" that will organize our inquiry and writing so as "to preserve the presence of actual subjects while exploring and explicating the relations in which our everyday worlds are embedded" (Smith, 1987, p. 111). She argues that beginning with the standpoint of people entails regarding the researcher and those observed as inhabiting the world on the same basis, and breaking with an objectifying practice in sociology (ibid.). Like Smith, Holzkamp (2013a, 2013b) argues for the necessity of taking the standpoint of the subject in research – that persons should not be interpreted "from a standpoint outside" (see also Motzkau & Schraube, 2015). Still, there seems to be a significant difference between Smith's and Holzkamp's position in terms of how the research relations are considered: in what way is the development of knowledge about the relation between subjective experience and structural condition to take place? Smith stresses that we "cannot rely upon them [what women tell us] for an understanding of the relations that shape and determine the everyday" (1987, p. 110). Smith suggests instead that it is the task of the social scientist to investigate these relations. Such formulations seem to (re)install a hierarchical distance between the researcher and "the subjects that are to be interpreted." I will argue that analyzing how structural relations co-produce our everyday experience can also be a collaborative enterprise in research. To explicate the relationship between the researcher and the people he or she involves in the research project, I draw on Holzkamp's term *co-researcher* (2013b). Holzkamp emphasizes that in order to gain the most relevant and rich knowledge about, and valid insight into, people's everyday lives, we must understand and arrange research processes on the basis of a standpoint regarding intersubjectivity. He describes the research relation as a "subject–subject relation in which neither person can turn the other to an object of scientific questions" (Holzkamp, 2013b, p. 307).

Regarding research with children, the term co-researcher requires some clarification: the concept is used in childhood research to emphasize the ambition of engaging children in research through participatory methods (e.g., Alderson, 2000; Christensen & James, 2000; Kellet, 2005; Mayall, 1994). The discussions focus on how to involve children in research and make the research process accessible for children's contributions and influence – and how to empower children as "active researchers" (Kellet, 2005). This childhood research tradition (as formulated by, e.g., James, Jenks & Prout, 1998) has provided valuable insights into possibilities and challenges in relation to engaging children in research, and it can inspire researchers to develop relevant methods when engaging with children. However, the term co-researcher, as used in this chapter, is a methodological standpoint regarding understanding and arranging research relations on the basis of intersubjectivity and collaboration (see Højholt & Kousholt's (2013) account of practice research). Discussions about what kind of involvement at which steps of a research project makes children "real" co-researchers are in this context beside the point. Conceptualizing the participants in research as co-researchers is fundamentally a *theoretical standpoint*, resting on the understanding of persons as active subjects in their own lives. To live our lives we must *explore* our life conditions and how to develop influence on matters important to us in our different life contexts (Højholt & Kousholt, forthcoming). The researcher can, for a period of time, take part in, contribute to and maybe intensify such exploration.

One aspect of this is how we conceive of the relation between the researcher and those involved in the research. Another aspect is what is considered to be the "content" of the research. Within the practice research tradition, the subject matter of the research can be seen as "common problems in a common world." In that way, the focus of the research is not "other people's problems," but what can be learned about problems in social practice by engaging with persons who have different perspectives, positions and engagements in relation to the matter in question (including the researcher). Surely, sometimes the different perspectives on what constitutes the problems can diverge to a degree that problems are not recognized as common or shared. Investigating the basis of the *formulation of the problems* can therefore be an important step in the research process (Højholt & Kousholt, 2014). The problems and research questions will most often be posed differently by researcher and co-researchers and be relevant in different ways and for different reasons. It is not the same things that different children, parents, childcare professionals and researchers will be interested in and concerned about. Furthermore, the researcher's and co-researcher's positions in relation to investigating the problems will be different; nevertheless, their different concerns can be *analyzed as related* – different aspects of a "common matter." In the following, I will address the question of how to arrange the conditions for the research process in ways that make it possible to collaborate on mutual relevant matters – or learn about shared problems.

An "Old Lady" among "the Wild Boys"

It follows from the argument previously in the chapter that the quality of the knowledge produced is linked to finding a way to cooperate on and investigate common matters. Sometimes, this involves a great amount of work – shared relevance and interests are not something given, but something that evolves (and, maybe, changes) during the research process. To illustrate this, I will present some experiences from spending time in a day care institution, trying to get a sense of what this particular context was like seen from the children's perspectives. However, not all children were eager to participate in this exploration at the beginning of the project. A group of boys were often talked about as "the wild boys" and they generated a great deal of frustration among the adults and other children. Some of the boys' immediate opposition to girls and adults worked as a barrier to getting to know them. One particular boy, Mattias, was very explicit in "turning me down" when I approached him and the other boys. He threw sand at me and discouraged me, saying "don't go there," pointing to "the boys' place in the playground." By calling me "an old lady," he clearly distanced himself from me in terms of both age and gender. My focus was the children's perspectives, and therefore I could not explore the issue of "the wild boys" without getting to know these particular boys' perspectives on everyday life in the day care institution. Therefore, I persistently, although still respectfully, approached the boys – sometimes just sitting a few meters away, openly watching their activities. After some time, the boys discovered that I did not interfere in their activities, not even when they occasionally broke the rules of the day care institution. Gradually, I was granted a legitimate position in the boys' community and invited to play with them. Mattias ended up deciding that I was "good enough" – as he explained to the other boys, thereby supporting my presence in their activities. It was necessary to experiment with the research position and work with my way of participating – for example, to witness the boys breaking rules without intervening or showing my discomfort during fights where they seemed to really hurt each other in a manner that did not jeopardize our relationship. I tried to learn ways of interacting from the children that put me on "equal terms." Since the children often criticized and disapproved of each other's actions, I could enter an established practice of negotiating "what is accepted or allowed." In a way, I placed myself in the "apprentice position" in relation to the children (Lave, 2011; Mandell, 1991). My relationship with the children developed in a more mutual direction, and toward a "research relation," as both parties became committed to the explorative character of the relationship (Holzkamp, 2013b, pp. 307ff.). In their own way, the boys recognized our relationship as having a "scientific agenda" – they allowed me to observe their secret activities – "she can come in, she needs to write," as Mattias explained to another boy who did not want "girls" in the room. The occasional writing I did in my notebook was one of the visible features of my position as a researcher.

The problems in the day care institution were formulated and played out in ways that produced divisions and antagonism (between the adults and the boys, and between the boys and the girls), and exploring a shared problem with the boys as well as the professionals meant working to understand and overcome these divisions. In that way, the example illustrates how the position of the researcher will be constituted in relation to how problems are formulated and negotiated in the particular practices in which the researcher engages. Investigating the boys' perspectives, and sharing reflections with the day care professionals, gradually established a research practice that allowed for critical reflection on how the problems in the day care institution were experienced from different perspectives, and how these perspectives were connected to each other and could be understood as different aspects of a common problem regarding possibilities for participation in, influence on and insight into each other's (divergent) experiences in the day care institution.

The research provided insight into how the boys' conflicts and oppositional positions were produced in relation to the spatial and structural arrangements of the day care institution, where the boys' activities were referred to/placed in the far end of the playground or in the "pillow room" – far from the adult presence and gaze. It also demonstrated how this became interrelated with the understanding of boys as more wild and aggressive by nature, and of gender largely being something innate, which we can try to adjust or contain, but not change (see also Haavind, 2003). Such understandings contributed to reproducing the divide between the girls, the adults and the boys, and established barriers in relation to investigating what was going on in the boys' community. Overall, this contributed to feelings of powerlessness among the adults (and girls) in relation to dealing with the boys' "wildness" (the analysis is unfolded in Kousholt, 2008, 2011).

Furthermore, the research process provided knowledge about how the boys were concerned with arranging activities that would be fun and challenging, which often meant that they sought to push the boundaries of their own capabilities and those of each other. "Acting wild" constituted both possibilities and constraints in the boys' community: the physical play and fights were part of the joint activities and thus part of the fun; however, it is not fun getting hurt, quarreling with your friends, or even losing friendships (as the conflicts often resulted in threats of "not being friends any more"). The research provided insight into the boys' different ways of taking part and contributing in joint activities, and revealed that their conflicts had very different meanings for the involved parties. In that way, the research contributed to breaking with the categorization of "wild boys" as a homogeneous group with the same characteristics. The boys had different possibilities in relation to handling the conflicts and influencing joint activities. Moreover, the boys' interplay, as well as the categorization of "wild boys," influenced how they could conduct their lives across the day care institution and their families – since their parents experienced the boys and their conflicts differently and thus understood and supported their boys in different ways. One outcome of the research collaboration was that the day care professionals arranged meetings with all the boys' parents, where they shared experiences and planned joint activities to support the children's communities in the day care institution.

Overall, the conflicts between and around the boys can be understood as an aspect of the problem of how to arrange this particular practice. Day care institutions in Denmark are developed as part of a political endeavor to make it possible for mothers to join the labor force as well as securing "the right development" for the children (Grumløse, 2014). How the day care institutions should be arranged, how best to support the development of the children (e.g., through "free play" or structured activities) is an ongoing debate with continuous disagreements between politicians, professional and parents (see also Højholt, 2008, regarding the dualisms in understandings of children's development). One recent outcome is the implementation of the nursery curriculum and a shift in focus to adult-initiated, structured activities and learning.

Developing research as collaboration involves continuously reflecting on how the researcher's problem interrelates with the children's experiences – what they perceive as relevant issues and problems in their lives (Chimirri, 2014). The researcher's position is not stable but rather developed and adjusted as part of the research collaboration. The collaboration between researcher and co-researchers can give rise to confusion and uncertainty on both sides, since the researcher is traditionally considered to be an uninvolved expert – often an expert who is given power to evaluate or judge what is taking place in practice. In the example above, it was important several times to explicate and discuss with the staff the researcher's reasons and intent behind specific ways of participating. In the beginning, the day care professionals were unsure of how to react, so as not to "disturb the research," while, at the same time, being puzzled about the researcher's ways of taking part (e.g., not intervening in the children's conflicts and not taking breaks together with the staff). Such aspects, as well as the questions and curiosity of the researcher, were regularly discussed at meetings between the researcher and the professionals. The researcher's position in the investigated practice is, in some respect, new and "unknown" and can therefore, in the beginning, be experienced as rather strange and unsettling to the people who usually take part in the particular practice – as well as to the researcher her/himself. In the process of getting acquainted and finding a suitable way of conducting the research, researcher, children and professionals develop their ways of relating to each other, their ways of participating and consequently their knowledge of the particular practice.

When research is collaborative and dialogic, the research process needs to be open-ended and flexible. The researcher should be able to become inspired and develop focus in order to explore different aspects of the issue. Therefore, the research design and process cannot be planned on an abstract basis and in detail in advance; it needs to be adjusted and developed locally in relation to the parties involved and the conditions and opportunities of the collaboration. This does not indicate an accidental or arbitrary development of the design or research position. The step-by-step selections and choices regarding how to develop the research position, who to follow and talk to and what issues to explore next, must be linked to the research questions and collaborative possibilities. In some respects, this is a more vulnerable research position that requires support from fellow researchers and co-researchers, as well as continuous reflection on the implications for the people involved in the research.

There are various ways of getting involved and different ways of participating in the research process. The children and parents are involved through their interplay and dialog with the researcher and the interests they share in relation to the research questions (e.g., what is important for the children in the day care institution?). Some of the professionals are also involved in meetings, where the organization of the research and the initial analyses are discussed. Children and parents will (to a certain extent) use the interplay and dialog with the researcher in their ongoing exploration of their lives and action possibilities. The professionals can (sometimes) use the knowledge and curiosity generated by the research process in their efforts to deal with problems they experience in their work. The research project will be part of the researchers' and co-researchers' everyday lives in different ways, and the results will be considered and put to use in different practices.

Research as Participation in and Across Practices

In order to conduct our lives, we need to move between different practices, which entails that we need to *arrange transitions*. Moving between different contexts often entails changing both place and "matter" (e.g., from work to family). Such movements indicate transitions between different societal arrangements and are both structurally arranged and something that we must find our personal way of dealing with. Persons need to attend to connections (including what we might "leave behind") and arrange in relation to the differences between practices. In that way, transitions can highlight differences between practices and the work persons must do to move between and connect them – which also means leaving and entering contexts. Following transitions as part of research can provide knowledge of both personal conduct of life and structurally mediated constraints and connections between social practices.

When I use the terminology "to follow the children," I am pointing to children's actual movements in and between different contexts. In addition, it connotes being curious and attentive to the children's participation and engagements. Inspired by Tim Ingold, this can be expressed as *walking attentively* alongside the children, paying attention to what happens on the way (Ingold, 2013, 2015, chap. 4 in this volume). Ingold points to "walking" as an alternative to the conventional model of education, which is about instilling knowledge *in* the minds of the learners. Walking takes the learner *out* into the world, and "holding to the trail calls for continual attention" (Ingold, 2015, chap. 4 in this volume, p. 99). Although Ingold discusses a quite different issue than this chapter, I find his attention to walking, and thus movement as well as presence and awareness "on the road," inspiring when reflecting upon following children as part of research. In this sense, following implies the researcher walking alongside the children, paying attention to what happens on the way, being led by the children's activities and engagements – what seems to matter to them. The analogy of walking together can point to the mutual interplay between the researcher and co-researchers (an aspect that may seem missing in the term "following"). Walking together implies coordinating steps and directionality, and sharing experiences. The research situations are made possible as the researcher and co-researchers are mutually integrating one another in their conduct of life (Holzkamp, 2013b, p. 307) – and part of our concerns, engagements and interests intertwine for a shorter or longer period of time.

I will exemplify some points in relation to the discussions above by returning to the research project that included participatory observation in a day care institution.

As mentioned, the main focus of the project was children's everyday lives across day care institution and home. As part of exploring this topic, I followed six children in "24-hour observations" (the methodology and design are discussed in more detail in Kousholt, 2006). The 24-hour observations entailed following the children in the day care institution, and on a particular day being picked up with them by their parents – spending the afternoon with the family, sleeping, waking up, and getting ready for the day care institution again. The insights into these 24-hour cycles of day care institution–home–day care institution, experiencing shifts and transitions together with the children, provided new perspectives on their everyday lives in the day care institution and their families as well. They expanded my understanding of how children combine and connect their different contexts in different ways. These experiences highlighted how children participate in and negotiate the linking of the different contexts in their lives, and how conflicts between parents and children could be understood as related to "joining" their shared conduct of life – the parents' and children's transitions are different, and (part of their) engagement and concerns are related to the parts of their everyday lives when they are away from one another. Additionally, the transitions I shared with the children led me to focus on the apparently small everyday stuff related to children's effort to link practices and engagement (e.g., bringing certain toys or objects to the day care institution that were crucial for their participation in the children's communities, and how it could be difficult for the adults to gain insight into the significance of this). This shed light on how children's possibilities for participation are created across their different life contexts, and how social interplay and conflicts among children in their day care institutions influence relations and interplay between parents and children at home. It also provided a critical view on understandings of family practices as isolated from other contexts and expanded my understanding of parents' possibilities as formed by children's lives across contexts and cooperation with other adults and professionals about the child (Kousholt, 2008, 2011).

Establishing a research position that enabled me to follow children in and across different practices provided embodied experiences of what it could be like to be a child in that particular place as well as how to make this particular transition. My experiences became a point of departure for reflections on what was taking place, and children's positions and possibilities, in and across such particular contexts. As Okely (1992) has pointed out, the research process is not only an "intellectual" exploration, let alone a collection of data untouched by the researcher's personal standpoints and presence. The experience of spending time with the children at home in their families was very different and formed by the way the children involved me in their family life. Some of the children seemed to regard me mostly as their playmate and we spent most of the time in their room playing and talking, whereas in other families, I spent the majority of the time together with the whole family, for example, helping to prepare dinner or watching TV.

Timothy Diamond reflects on the use of participant observation in institutional ethnography, describing the process of observation as a "sensual activity" in order to stress that part of the empirical material is the researcher's feelings of some of the stuff taking place in practice (Diamond, 2006, p. 56). He writes that "putting one's body on the line as part of the research seems to give rise to discovery *in* one's body of relevant data" (ibid., p. 59). My interest is not the researcher's feelings as data as such, but rather how that which the researcher senses and experiences can be used as a starting point for analyses on how various situations can be experienced from different perspectives and guide the development of an intersubjective understanding.

In a subject-scientific approach, *emotionality* – as a moment of human agency – is seen as "a specific form of assessing the subjective relevance of actual possibilities of living and acting in given circumstances" (Holzkamp, 2013a, p. 22). This is a critique of the notion of emotions as isolated inner processes. It is a common aspect of our lives that emotions can "set us on track" of exploring contradictions in our lives and guide our evaluation of action possibilities. Addressing the research process as participation is to stress that emotionality is just as much part of, and not to be separated from, the researcher's engagement in practice. The researcher's experiences can provide opportunities for increased sensitivity to understand the children's situation (Thorne, 1993). Examples of this may refer to situations where following children evoked embarrassment or shame – for instance, when being told off, caught in activities one is not sure are "allowed," or experiencing bewilderment, not being able to find one's way around or figure out what is going on. Emotions that are often referred to as "childish" can often be more adequately understood as linked to children's positions in specific contexts. It is, in this sense, a perspective on emotions associated with participating in and assessing action possibilities in social practices (cf. Holzkamp-Osterkamp, 1991).

In ethnographic work, it is a common warning to researchers not to "go native" – that is, to get so immersed in the field that they become unable to maintain the analytical distance (Hammersley & Atkinson, 1989). Critical discussions of the conventional scientific notion of the distant observer, as well how to balance closeness and distance – being able to get close enough to develop rich and valid knowledge, but not so close that the researcher loses the analytical or critical stance toward the field – is central in the ethnographic tradition. The challenge in relation to such discussions is to overcome the tendency to dichotomize between, and thus separate, involvement and scientific knowledge.

As discussed earlier in the chapter, considering the relations between the researcher and co-researchers in the context of intersubjective understanding entails leaving the researcher's privileged position to individually produce scientific knowledge "from an outsider perspective" (Holzkamp, 2013b, p. 316). Holzkamp links scientific knowledge to an "epistemic distance" – that is, "a not (yet) knowing about the world" (ibid., p. 316). To take this argument a step further, we might say that developing scientific knowledge is not a question of the researcher's distance from the research object, but an approach regarding "not yet knowing" that necessitates involvement and shared reflections and curiosity. In that way, the mutual involvement and exchange related to a shared matter is the prerequisite for the research situation. When research is conceptualized on the basis of an understanding of intersubjectivity, the researcher and co-researchers can share and exchange explorations of, and reflections on, the world and thus engage in analytic endeavors together. This does not imply that researchers and co-researchers have the same interest or possibilities to analyze a given matter. (This is also related to the discussion earlier about how the research collaboration has different meanings to researchers and co-researchers.) The researcher's *involved* and *varied* participation in different practices opens up possibilities to analyze personal dilemmas in relation to structural conditions – and thereby learn about common challenges.

Following "Taxi Children": Learning from Personal Dilemmas Concerning Common Challenges

I have described that following the transitions across different institutional arrangements provides an embodied experience of conducting one's life across these particular contexts. This knowledge can be developed and substantiated through exploration of social practice from different positions and perspectives. This has to do with anchoring the researcher's experiences in an understanding of complex and conflictual social practice. Following children's conduct of life across contexts must not lead to a representation of the child's individualized trajectory detached from social practices. Following children's participation and transitions provides an opportunity to learn from their personal ways of taking part in and linking different social practices where different matters are at stake. To expand on this, I will turn to one last example from the research project about children's communities in after-school institutions that involved following some boys' transition between special school and after-school center (see also Kousholt, 2012). The boys in question were placed in a special school due to social problems and conflicts in their regular school class. However, due to an intention of giving the children opportunities to maintain relationships in their regular school, and thereby support their (re)inclusion in the regular school system, they still went to the regular after-school center.

Following these boys included research situations of running to the taxi after a day at the special school together with Paul – who was taken in a taxi to his after-school center located at his former regular school – and getting out of the taxi in an empty school yard, trying to find out "where are my old classmates?," "what are they up to and who can I play with?" Following Paul in the after-school center revealed his efforts related to, and difficulties with, finding his way into the diverse communities of children in the after-school center, and how this raised issues of belonging for him that were easily overlooked by the adults around him. The transfer between special school and regular after-school center is a noticeable change of socio-material place – the special school is a small confined area with few children and structured, adult-supervised activities, while the after-school center is a large area with several workshops, many activities to choose between and few adults; therefore, the children are expected to organize themselves and seek help when necessary.

Following these boys' "special" transitions by taxi raised issues about how children use each other in transitions between different contexts, working on continuing and changing communities as part of linking their activities and engagement in each place. This attention, and the ambition to understand personal challenges linked to common problems at stake in social practices, spurred the researcher to follow the other children's transitions to the after-school center. Thus, I followed the boys' old classmates at the end of their school day, being picked up by a pedagogue who would talk about "which workshops are open today," and "what you have signed up for," walking alongside the children crossing the school yard to the after-school center together in small groups, chatting about what to do, changing plans and arranging play activities together, while walking to the after-school center together.

The contrast of these transitions helped to understand specific challenges in children's lives in light of, or connected to, a broader knowledge of common dilemmas in the children's social interplay in school and at the after-school center, and how children arrange their lives across these contexts – and use each other in the process. Through knowledge about *common dilemmas and conflicts* in children's lives, I came to understand individual children's specific difficulties and challenges in a new way (Højholt, 2011). This expanded knowledge about how children conduct their lives in and across these particular practices provided other perspectives on what constitutes the problem: From individualized categorizations of some boys' "behavioral problems" to focus on difficult conditions in relation to a common challenge of navigating the multiple, changeable communities in the after-school center and linking friendship and activities in personal, relevant ways.

The structural arrangement of these boys' school day (transferring from a special school to a regular after-school center) can be understood in relation to a national agenda of inclusion. How the school system is to manage the political ambition of inclusion is a highly topical debate in Denmark. Discussions as well as practices regarding inclusion are fraught with paradoxes and disagreements concerning how children's problems are to be understood (Morin, 2008; Røn Larsen, 2012). The example illustrates that processes of both exclusion and inclusion are integral in the practice of the school, as well as the children's communities, and interventions directed at including children in school are carried out in, and become part of, such contradictory conditions. Situated analyses of some boys' personal dilemmas in transferring between special school and regular school arrangements, and struggling to take part and maintaining a sense of belonging, in connection with analyses of social conditions and challenges in children's school lives, opens up possibilities to consider *common contradictions* in the structural organization of the school. Obtaining situated knowledge about possibilities for participation, personal concerns and struggles – as well as insight into social *conflicts*, how they affect us differently, and how we deal with them based on *unequal* possibilities for influencing them – can produce knowledge about common challenges and thereby also critiques of constrained life conditions and unequally structured social possibilities (Højholt, 2015, chap. 7 in this volume).

Summing Up: Developing Knowledge about Contradictory Life Conditions

The concept of conduct of everyday life sets us on track of investigating connections between structural life conditions and personal ways of experiencing and dealing with such life conditions. If we are to analyze connections between life conditions and personal reasons and meanings, we need to intensify our attention – and questions – to the complex and contradictory *life conditions* and (unequal) possibilities for *influencing* and *changing* them.

This entails that we need to arrange cooperation between research and practice in ways that inspire open and mutual exploration of contradictions in practice and support joint exploration of how to change problematic conditions. In relation to this, it is significant to democratize the research process and make room for the contribution of the people involved. A part of the research process is to work on how to arrange conditions for the participation of co-researchers, and thereby the conditions for collaboration. Arranging research as collaboration implies *de-centering* the perspective on the research project – reflecting how the research can become part of, and relevant to, the co-researchers' everyday lives, and how research processes can be arranged and developed to make it relevant for co-researchers to participate with their perspectives and knowledge (Hodgetts et al., chap. 6 in this volume). In that way, research can strengthen investigations of connections between personal dilemmas and social conflicts, and thereby supports an exploration of issues of personal as well as common relevance. In what ways that can be realized will, of course, vary with the problems explored and the people involved in the research projects.

De-centering the perspective on research is, in that respect, also about exploring critically how problems are presented from different perspectives. In that way, researchers' participation in, and collaboration in relation to, investigating social conflicts from different perspectives and positions can generate critical reflection on different positions and possibilities for influence and contributions in practice. The researcher can learn about particular practices by participating from different positions (sometimes crossing established positions and demarcations between positions). Studying practices from different positions and perspectives – for example, talking to adults, children and various professionals – provides opportunities to learn about how problems and conflicts look very different from different perspectives, and thereby to analyze what is at stake in a given situation by *relating* the different perspectives to different positions and possibilities for influencing what is going on – and how these *differences are connected in a shared (contradictory) practice*, related to a common problem. Through this practice, research can provide insight into the complex, heterogeneous and conflictual aspects of social practices, exploring various first-person perspectives, and investigating and relating different positions and perspectives. The concepts of conduct of everyday life in conflictual social practice direct our analytical attention to such *connections* between personal dilemmas in reciprocal relations to social problems and common contradictions in social practices.

The examples above have opened up for discussing personal problems and dilemmas as intertwined with, and aspects of, common social problems. Therefore, we can gain knowledge about common problems, and their structural and social basis, by exploring in collaboration – researchers and co-researchers – personal perspectives on problems and dilemmas, how they are experienced and dealt with and how they are related to contradictory life conditions. Such exploration can contribute to a critical perspective on constrained life conditions. In that way, going "close to" or deeper into a complex social situation from different perspectives and positions is also to go beyond it and broaden the perspective, exploring how this situation is part of structures of social practice. The examples have illustrated that such analyses can take their point of departure in social situations and the different meanings they have to the participants.

References

Alderson, P. (2000). Children as researchers: The effects of participation rights on research methodology. In P. Christensen & A. James (Eds.), *Research with children: Perspectives and practices* (pp. 241–257). London: Falmer Press.

Axel, E. (2002). *Regulation as productive tool use: Participatory observation in the control room of a district heating system*. Roskilde: Roskilde University Press.

Axel, E. (2011). Conflictual cooperation. *Nordic Psychology, 63*(4), 56–78.

Bernstein, R. (1971). *Praxis and action: Contemporary philosophies of human activity*. Philadelphia, PA: University of Pennsylvania Press.

Campbell, M. L. (2006). Institutional ethnography and experience as data. In D. E. Smith (Ed.), *Institutional ethnography as practice* (pp. 91–108). Lanham, MD: Rowman & Littlefield.

Chimirri, N. A. (2014). *Investigating media artifacts with children: Conceptualizing a collaborative exploration of the sociomaterial conduct of everyday life*. Unpublished doctoral dissertation, Roskilde University, Denmark.

Christensen, P. & James, A. (2000). *Research with children: Perspectives and practices*. London: Falmer Press.

Danziger, K. (1990). *Constructing the subject*. New York: Cambridge University Press.

Devault, M. (2006). Introduction: What is institutional ethnography? *Social problems, 53*(3), 294–298.

Devault, M. & McKoy, L. (2006). Institutional ethnography: Using interviews to investigate ruling relations. In D. E. Smith (Ed.), *Institutional ethnography as practice* (pp. 15–44). Lanham, MD: Rowman & Littlefield.

Diamond, T. (2006). "Where did you get the fur coat, Fern?" Participant observation in institutional ethnography. In D. E. Smith (Ed.), *Institutional ethnography as practice* (pp. 45–64). Lanham, MD: Rowman & Littlefield.

Doran, C. (1993). The everyday world is problematic: Ideology and recursion in Dorothy Smith's micro-sociology. *Canadian Journal of Sociology*, 43–63.

Dreier, O. (1997). *Subjectivity and social practice*. Aarhus: Aarhus University Press.

Dreier, O. (2008). *Psychotherapy in everyday life*. Cambridge: Cambridge University Press.

Dreier, O. (2011). Personality and the conduct of everyday life. *Nordic Psychology, 63*(2), 4–23.

Grumløse, S. P. (2014). *Den gode barndom – dansk familiepolitik 1960–2010 og forståelsen af småbarnets gode liv* [The good childhood: Danish family politic and the understanding of the good life for the small child]. Doctoral dissertation, Department of Psychology and Educational Studies, Roskilde University, Denmark.

Haavind, H. (2003). Masculinity by rule-breaking. Cultural contestations in the transitional move from being a child to being a young male. *NORA, Nordic Journal of Feminist and Gender Research, 11*(2), 89–100.

Hall, S. & Jefferson, T. (2006). *Resistance through rituals: Youth cultures in post-war Britain.* London: Routledge. (Original work published 1975)

Hammersley, M. & Atkinson, P. (1989). *Ethnography: Principles in practice.* London: Routledge.

Hodgetts, D. & Stolte, O. (2013). Everyday life. In T. Teo (Ed.), *Encyclopedia of critical psychology.* New York: Springer.

Højholt, C. (2008). Participation in communities: Living and learning across different contexts. *ARECE – Australian Research in Early Childhood Education, 15*(1), 1–12.

Højholt, C. (2011). Cooperation between professionals in educational psychology: Children's specific problems are connected to general problems in relation to taking part. In H. Daniels & M. Hedegaard (Eds.), *Vygotsky and special needs education: Rethinking support for children and schools* (pp. 67–86). London: Continuum Press.

Højholt, C. & Kousholt, D. (2013). Practice research. In T. Teo (Ed.), *Encyclopedia of critical psychology.* New York: Springer

Højholt, C. & Kousholt, D. (2014). Participant observation of children's communities: Exploring subjective aspects of social practice. *Qualitative Research in Psychology, 11,* 316–334.

Højholt, C. & Kousholt, D. (forthcoming). Children participating and developing agency in and across various social practices. In M. Fleer & B. van Oers (Eds.), *International handbook on early childhood education.* Dordrecht: Springer.

Holland, D. & Lave, J. (2001). *History in person: Enduring struggles, contentious practice, intimate identities.* Santa Fe, NM: School of American Research Press.

Holzkamp, K. (1987). Critical psychology and overcoming of scientific indeterminacy in psychological theorizing. *Perspectives in Personality, 2,* 93–123.

Holzkamp, K. (2013a). Basic concepts of critical psychology. In E. Schraube & U. Osterkamp (Eds.), *Psychology from the standpoint of the subject: Selected writings of Klaus Holzkamp* (pp. 19–27). Basingstoke: Palgrave Macmillan.

Holzkamp, K. (2013b). Psychology: Social self-understanding on the reasons for action in the conduct of everyday life. In E. Schraube & U. Osterkamp (Eds.), *Psychology from the standpoint of the subject: Selected writings of Klaus Holzkamp* (pp. 233–341). Basingstoke: Palgrave Macmillan.

Holzkamp-Osterkamp, U. (1991). Emotions, cognitions, and action potence. In C. Tolman & W. Maiers (Eds.), *Critical psychology: Contributions to an historical science of the subject.* New York: Cambridge University Press.

Ingold, T. (2013). The maze and the labyrinth: Walking and the education of attention. In C. Morrison-Bell et al. (Eds.), *Walk-on: From Richard Long to Janet Cardiff* (pp. 7–11). Sunderland: Art Editions North.

James, A., Jenks, C. & Prout, A. (1998). *Theorizing childhood.* Cambridge: Polity Press.

Jensen, U. J. (1999). Categories in activity theory: Marx's philosophy just-in-time. In S. Chaiklin, M. Hedegaard & U. J. Jensen (Eds.), *Activity theory and social practice: Cultural-historical approaches* (pp. 79–99). Aarhus: Aarhus University Press.

Jensen, U. J. (2001). Mellem social praksis og skolastisk fornuft [Between social practice and scholastic rationality]. In J. Myrup (Eds.), *Temaer i nyere fransk filosofi* [Issues in recent French philosophy] (pp. 195–218). Aarhus: Philosophia.

Juhl, P. (2014). *På sporet af det gode børneliv: Samfundets bekymring og børns perspektiver i hverdagslivet* [On the trail of the good child life: Societies' concern and children's perspectives in everyday life]. Roskilde: Roskilde University.

Juhl, P. (forthcoming). Toddlers collaboratively explore possibilities for actions across contexts: Developing the concept conduct of everyday life in relation to young children. In

Dialogue and debate in the making of theoretical psychology: Proceedings of 15th Biennial conference of The International Society for Theoretical Psychology, Santiago, Chile, May 3–7, 2013.

Karlekin-Fishman, D. (2013). Sociology of everyday life. *Current Sociology*, 61, 7–14.

Kellet, M. (2005). Children as active researchers: A new research paradigm for the 21st century? (ESRC National Centre for Research Methods, NCRM Methods Review Papers, NCRM/003, Centre for Childhood, Development and Learning). Milton Keynes: Open University.

Kousholt, D. (2006). *Familieliv fra et børneperspektiv: Fællesskaber i børns liv* [Family life from children's perspectives: Communities in children's lives]. Doctoral dissertation, Roskilde University, Denmark.

Kousholt, D. (2008). The everyday life of children across early childhood institution and the family. *Australian Research in Early Childhood Education*, 15(1), 13–25.

Kousholt, D. (2011). Researching family through the everyday lives of children across home and day care in Denmark. *Ethos*, 39(1), 98–114.

Kousholt, D. (2012). Børnefællesskaber og udsatte positioner i SFO: Inklusion og fritidspædagogik [Children's communities and exposed positions in leisure time institutions: Inclusion and leisure time pedagogy]. In P. Hviid & C. Højholt (Eds.), *Fritidspædagogik og børneliv* [Leisure time pedagogy and childrens' lives] (pp. 192–214). Copenhagen: Hans Reitzel.

Lave, J. (2011). *Apprenticeship in critical ethnographic practice*. Chicago, IL: University of Chicago Press.

Mandell, N. (1991). The least-adult role in studying children. In F. C. Waksler (Ed.), *Studying the social worlds of children: Sociological readings* (pp. 161–178). London: Falmer Press.

Mayall, B. (Ed.). (1994). *Children's childhoods: Observed and experienced*. London: Falmer Press.

Morin, A. (2008). Learning together: A child perspective on educational arrangements of special education. *ARECE – Australian Research in Early Childhood Education*, 15, 27–38.

Motzkau, J. & Schraube, E. (2015). Kritische Psychologie: Psychology from the standpoint of the subject. In I. Parker (Ed.), *Handbook of critical psychology* (pp. 280–289). London: Routledge.

Nissen, M. (2012). *The subjectivity of participation: Articulating social work practice with youth in Copenhagen*. Basingstoke: Palgrave Macmillan.

Okely, J. (1992). Anthropology and autobiography: Participatory experience and embodied knowledge. In J. Okely & H. Callaway (Eds.), *Anthropology and autobiography* (pp. 1–28). New York: Routledge.

Osterkamp, U. & Schraube, E. (2013). Klaus Holzkamp and the development of psychology from the standpoint of the subject. In E. Schraube & U. Osterkamp (Eds.), *Psychology from the standpoint of the subject: Selected writings of Klaus Holzkamp* (pp. 1–18). Basingstoke: Palgrave Macmillan.

Røn Larsen, M. (2012). A paradox of inclusion: Administrative procedures and children's perspectives on difficulties in school. In M. Hedegaard, K. Aronsson, C. Højholt & O. S. Ulvik (Eds.), *Children, childhood, and everyday life: Children's perspectives* (pp. 143–160). New York: Information Age Publishing.

Roth, W. M. (2008). Klaus Holzkamp in the Americas: A personal account. *Journal für Psychologie*, 2, special issue on Holzkamp's *Grundlegung der Psychologie. Nach 25 Jahren*. Retrieved from www.journal-fuer-psychologie.de/index.php/jfp/article/view/178.

Smith, D. E. (1987). *The everyday world as problematic: A feminist sociology*. Boston, MA: Northeastern University Press.

Smith, D. E. (Ed.). (2006). *Institutional ethnography as practice*. Lanham, MD: Rowman & Littlefield.

Thorne, B. (1993). *Gender play: Girls and boys in school*. Buckingham: Open University Press.

Willis, P. (1977). *Learning to labour: How working class kids get working class jobs*. Farnborough: Saxon House.

INDEX

Action problem – learning problem 212
aboriginals 107
abstract conceptualization of everyday life 145–7
abstractness of psychological knowledge and theory 3
academic life 66–6, 115, 117
action theory 52
actor-victim debate 228
Adorno, Theodor W. 10–11, 164–8, 172
after-school centers 253–4
agency, human 8, 11, 107, 125, 146, 151, 158, 170, 190, 194, 209, 216, 229, 236, 252; *see also* "generalized agency"
airline pilots 50–1
alienation, conditions of 164
American psychology 115–16
Arnett, Jeffrey J. 115
Axel, Erik 244

Barnes, M. 148
de Beauvoir, Simone 237
Benjamin, Walter 101, 229
Bird, Kate 149–50
Bolte, Karl Martin 52
Bortoft, Henri 105
Bourdieu, Pierre 10, 71, 117, 211
Brecht, Bertolt 27–8, 190
"businessification" of life conduct 57
Butler, Judith 10, 115, 118
Butler, M. 79

Caffentzis, George 11, 200; *author of Chapter 9*
Campbell, Marie 244

Camus, Albert 113
capitalism 112–13, 176–86, 193, 195, 198, 200
care institutions 247–51
care for oneself 58
care work 40, 197–200
Chaiklin, Seth 146
Chakrabarty, Dipesh 114–15, 120
children's everyday life 10, 145–50, 241–54; conflict involved in 152–7
children's health and wellbeing 197–8
Chile 199
Chimirri, Niklas A. 121, 152, 243
class relations between debtors and creditors 180–4
coherence in everyday life 22–3
"Coleman's bathtub" model 52
collaborative research 245, 249, 253, 255
Colombia 199
Colvin Clark, Ruth 222
"common sense" 229–30, 233
"commons" 198–201
communities of practice 214
conduct of everyday life: and action theory 52; business-like 55, 57; as the consequence of situational decisions and pragmatic arrangements 47; crisis of 58; boundary with "actual life" 95–6; challenges and opportunities for 56–9; concept of 1–6, 9–12, 35–6, 45, 67–70, 72–3, 243–4, 255; cyclicality of 92–6; development of 152; in different social spheres 45–6, 49; in East Germany 43–4; embodiment of 111–21; failure

of 57; familial 53–5; guiding principles for 44–50; implications for critical psychology 15–32; non-deterministic sociation of 47–8; optimization of 57–9; patterns in 37–43; personal 113–14, 151–2; rationalization of 57; "relative autonomy" in 89–92; seen as a collective process 50–1, 146, 152, 243; seen as the individual's active construction and effort 46–7, 151; seen as the individual's system of action 46; seen as problematic 242–4; seen as rules for decision-making 52; seen as a system *sui generis* 48–50; self-contained logic of the system 47; sociological approaches to 68–72, 80–4, 91–2, 115; standpoint of the subject on 79–88, 91–2; by students 205; success of 58; in traditional psychology and psychoanalysis 72–9
conflict in everyday life 7, 53, 145–6, 244; involving children 152–7; *societal* and *political* 159–60
consumerism and the consumer society 179–80
contexts for social practice 18–19, 152
co-operative learning 216
"co-researcher" relationships 80, 84–5, 249–55; involving children in 245–6
countertransference 76
credit 178, 182
credit unions 183–4
critical analyses 159
critical psychology 3–4, 8–10, 16, 24, 26, 86, 111–14, 118, 120, 168–9, 172, 174, 237
cross-contextual methodology 241

Danziger, Kurt 114
Deaux, Kay 136
Debord, Guy 179
debt 176–90; class dimension of 180–4; and everyday life 177–80; politics of 187; *profit debt* and *use-value debt* 178–82, 185; *wage debt* and *pension debt* 182–3
debt alienation 184–7
debt economy and debt society 11, 176, 180, 188
debt-objects 184–5
debtors' movement 187–90
Deleuze, Gilles 105–6
Demszky von der Hagen, Alma 51
Denmark 146–7, 248, 254
dependence on others 29
depression 196–7
Derry, Jan 206

detective novels 51
dialogue 121
Diamond, Timothy 251–2
Dickens, Charles 105–6
digital technology 11–12, 205–6, 217, 220–3
Dilthey, Wilhelm 113
distributed learning 208
"division of labor of the person" 35
domestic work 193–6, 199–200
Dozier, C. 148
Dreier, Ole vii, 4, 8–9, 28, 79; *author of Chapter 1*
Dupont, Søren 219

education of attention 99, 104
education, different senses of the word 100, 103, 108
e-learning 222
emotionality 252
Engels, Friedrich 168, 193
"entreployees" 55–6
epistemic distance 252
ethnography 127, 141, 242, 251–2
everyday life: central significance of 2; conflictual nature of 7; cyclical organization of 5; seen as permanent crisis 195–8; seen as a social process 18–20, 125, 152; understood in theoretical terms 227; varying characterizations of 124–5, 140; *see also* conduct of everyday life
"everydayness" 69, 92–3, 126, 192, 195
experience 2, 4–7, 16, 23, 31, 37, 40, 86, 89, 100, 108, 114, 125, 140, 152, 160, 185, 193, 206, 210, 214, 219, 227, 233–236, 242–245
experimental psychology 73–5, 78
experimental reality 3, 74, 77
"extraordinary everydayness" (Fitzpatrick) 126

family background, influence of 147–8
family life 23, 53–5
family responsibilities 38, 42, 51, 57
family therapy 23
fascism 165–7
Federici, Silvia vii, 11; *author of Chapter 10*
Female Sexualization project 226, 230
feminism 11, 116, 119, 192–4
flexibilization of work 55
Flexibilized Employment and the Organization of the Conduct of Life in Individuals project 35, 68–9, 80–4, 87–92, 96

"fluidity of learning and teaching" 214–217, 220
formative influences on people's lives 45
Fortunati, Leopolda 197, 200
Foucault, Michel 90, 118
Four-in-One Perspective project 12, 226, 238
Frankfurt School of critical theory 113
Freire, Paulo 121
Freud, Sigmund 75–9

Gadamer, Hans-Georg 121
gardens and gardening 134–7, 140–1, 199
gender, performance of 118
gender relations 229; equalization of 42, 57
"generalized agency" 86, 169–73
German Democratic Republic 43–4
German Reunification 37
German Youth Institute 54
Gibson, James 104
Giddens, Anthony 35
globalization 116, 197
Goffman, Erving 230
"going native" 252
Gramsci, Antonio 12, 226–33
grand theories 112
Greig, Andrew 99–100, 109

Habermas, Jürgen 24
habit 117
habitus 71, 111, 115–20
Hacking, Ian 114
Harris, Cheryl I. 119
Haug, Frigga vii, 12, 29, 210, 214, 238; author of Chapter 12
Hedegaard, Mariane 146
Hegel, Georg Wilhelm Friedrich 112
Heiden, Mathias 58–9
Heine, Steven J. 115
Henrich, Joseph 115
hermeneutics 113
Hochschild, Arlie R. 22
Hodgetts, Darrin vii, 8, 10; co-author of Chapter 6
Højholt, Charlotte vii, 10, 19, 146, 158, 213, 241, 244, 246, 254; author of Chapter 7, co-author of Introduction and co-editor
Holzkamp, Klaus vii, 4, 9–10, 15, 17, 23–4, 34, 49–50, 65–6, 68, 89–90, 94, 111–21, 151, 169–75, 206, 208, 211–16, 242–5, 252; author of Chapter 3
homelessness 124–133, 136
Hooks, K. 148
Huchler, Norbert 50–1

imagination, power of 105
imprisonment 94–5
inclusive education 254
indigenous people 137
individualization of life conduct 41
inequality, 159; causes and consequences of 121
inferential statistics 73
Ingold, Tim vii, 9–10, 213, 250; author of Chapter 4
interest payments 181–2, 187
intergenerational transmission of disadvantage 147–50, 158

James, William 117
Japanese culture 210
Jensen, Uffe Juul 146, 245
Jones, Sian 137
journalists, everyday life of 37–8
judging others 173
Jurczyk, Karin vii, 5, 9, 17, 51, 71, 81–3; co-author of Chapter 2
Jürgens, Kerstin 53, 58–9

Karp, J. 148–9
King, Pita vii, 8, 10
"knowledge interest" in psychology and sociology 81, 85–8, 91
Kollontai, Alexandra 237, 239
Kousholt, Dorte vii, 12, 53; author of Chapter 13
Kudera, W. 71, 82

labor, new forms of 55–6
labyrinths, analogies with 99–108
"landscapes of despair" 128, 137–8
Lange, Andreas 51
language, politics of 233
Latour, Bruno 134
Lave, Jean 7, 79, 146, 209–11, 244
learning: *active*, *relational* and *contextual* 207; *affinitive* and *definitive* phases of 213, 221, 223; *defensive* and *expansive* 212–15, 220–3; goal-directed 213; *intentional* and *accidental/incidental* 211–14; *internalization* model of 207–8; in relation to teaching 208, 211, 214–16, 222; loop 211; theorized from the standpoint of learning subjects 211–14, 217–20; *transfer* model of 207–8, 216–17; *see also* action problem – learning problem; co-operative learning; fluidity of learning and teaching; participatory learning
learning processes 205–17

Lefebvre, Henri 2, 128, 134, 176–9, 192–4
Leon, Donna 51
life conduct *see* conduct of everyday life
"lifestyle" concept 71
"linguistic particularities" 234–5
Linton, Simi 115
Lizardo, Omar 117
local practices 27–8
local theories 112–13
Lorenzer, Alfred 76–7
love, lack of 167

MacCaig, Norman 99
McDermott, Ray 154
McIntosh, Peggy 10, 119–20
MacLean, Nancy 195
Mankell, Henning 51
Māori society and culture 10, 124–42
Marcuse, Herbert 229
Markward, M. 148
Markward, N. 148
Martin, Jack 114
Marvakis, Athanasios viii, 11; *co–author of Chapter 11*
Marx, Karl (and Marxism) 11, 44, 85, 112–15, 168, 170, 172, 176–85, 192–3, 238–40
Masschelein, Jan 103–4, 107–8
massive open online courses (MOOCs) 205
Matchar, Emily 196
Mayer, Richard 222
mazes, analogies with 99–103, 106–8
meaning 7, 157, 173, 209, 243; *see also* social meaning
meaning, construction of 233
meaning-reason analyses 92
Mehan, Hugh 85, 157
memory-work process 226–40; anticipatory 239–40; origins of 227–8
Mexico 178
modernization, tendencies of 41–3
mortality 95
Munich University Collaborative Research Center 35, 68, 333; *see also* Flexibilized Employment and the Organization of the Conduct of Life in Individuals

neoliberalism 29, 195, 197, 200
Ngāti Whātua 126–31, 137
Noble, David 223
Norenzayan, Ara 115

objectivity and objective research 15, 80
Occupy movement 187–9
Okely, Judith 251

Osterkamp, Ute viii, 10–11, 24, 229; *author of Chapter 8*

parental influence 148–9
Paretsky, Sara 51
participant observation 242, 250–1
participatory learning 217–20
participatory nature of personhood 20, 24
participatory research 250–3
Passeron, Jean-Claude 211
payday loans 183
pension debt 182–3
performativity 111, 115–20
personal arrangements 21–2
personal reasons, concept of 157, 160
personality, construction of 231–2
Peru 199
phenomenology 113
"plane of immanence" (Deleuze) 105
political conflicts 147, 159
"poor pedagogy" 99, 108
postcolonial theory 114–15
poverty 150
praxis, philosophy of 244
privilege, concept of 111, 115–20
problem-oriented project work 219–20
"problem shifting" 235
psychoanalysis 72–80, 84, 113, 167
psychological research, methodology of 127–8, 141–2, 146–7, 243
psychology: indigenous 115–16; individualistic orientation of 4, 84; standpoint of the subject 85, 170, 173–4; subject matter of 1–5, 9, 15–17, 72, 77–80, 113–15
psychotherapy 25
punctuality 118–19

quality of life, improvement of 90
quasi-employees 56
quasi-experimental design 74

reason discourse 85–89, 94, 115–117, 172
reflection 25; *see also* self-reflection
reflexivity 114–15, 120
Rerrich, Maria S. 17, 40, 53, 71, 81–3
research process 246–55
researcher – co-researcher 8, 80, 84–85, 245–250, 252–255; *see also* "co-researcher" relationships
Rolling Jubilee (RJ) 189–90
Roskilde University (RU) 206, 217–20
routines of everyday life 20–1, 41, 69–70, 94
Rua, Mohi viii, 8, 10; *co-author of Chapter 6*
Rubinstein, Sergey L. 214

sales assistants 40, 53
Saltaris, C. 148–9
Sarte, Jean-Paul 186
Schatzki, Ted R. 27
Schier, Michaela 51
school life 19, 107, 154–5, 158–60
Schraube, Ernst viii, 11, 16, 112, 128, 206, 240, 245; *co-author of Introduction and Chapter 11 and co-editor*
scientific knowledge 244, 252
scientific language 87, 172
scientific procedure 73
scientific thinking 167–8
self-evident facts 85–6
self-reflection 172, 232
"self-reproduction of the person" (Heiden and Jürgens) 58
self-understanding 9, 23–6, 30, 85–7, 90, 146, 152, 159, 173
Serbin, L. 148–9
Shaffer, A. 148–9
shift workers, life conduct of 39
Simmel, Georg 125
situated activity and situated subjects 16, 19, 25–6
situated analyses 159–60
"situated inequality" 10, 158–9
situated learning theory 206–9
situational life conduct 41
Situationists 176–7, 179, 192
Smith, Dorothy 26, 242–5
social bonding 199
social conditions 48, 146–51, 171
social conflicts 146–7, 150–2, 157, 160; and personal conduct of life 151–2
social epistemologies 115–16
social inequalities 147–51
social meanings 157, 209–10;; *see also* meaning
social mechanisms 52
social policy 146, 149
social practice 150–4, 157, 159–60, 206, 209, 244, 246, 253, 256; conflictual 146; participation in 18–21; of science 25; understanding of 23
social problems: different perspectives on 255–6; intertwined with personal issues 255
social psychology 3, 141
social reality 165, 210
sociation 51
societal nature of human beings 112
sociology 72–3, 80–4, 91–2, 115; of the conduct of everyday life 50; subject-oriented 35

Soviet Union 126
special schools 153, 253–4
strategic life conduct 41
structural arrangements 26–7
student loans 188–9
students' organization of their lives 65–6, 205
subalternity 238–8
subjectivity 16, 50, 114–15, 169–74; denial of 172, 174; of learners 208, 211; turn to the subject 2, 166
Sugarman, Jeff 114
systems theory 44
Szymenderski, Peggy 51

"teaching–learning short circuit" (Holzkamp) 65, 208
Teo, Thomas viii, 10; *author of Chapter 5*
Te Whetu, Tiniwai viii, 8, 10; *co-author of Chapter 6*
text dissection 234
traditional life conduct 41
transference 76
transitions between different societal arrangements 250, 253–4

United Nations 194
"universal human being" 116–17
use-value 178–82, 185

Vetter, Hans-Rolf 68
Vico, Giambattista 112
virtual classrooms 222
visual perception 104
Voß, Günter viii, 5, 9, 51–2, 58, 69–72, 82, 92; *co-author of Chapter 2*
Vygotsky, Lev S. 232

wage debt 182–3
walking, analogies with 99–108, 250
"wayfaring" 103
Weber, Max 15, 35, 41, 44, 55, 81
Weihrich, Margit viii, 5, 9, 51–2; *co-author of Chapter 2*
Weiß, Cornelia 58
Weiss, Peter 238
Wenger, Etienne 209–10
Wertsch, James 4
"Western educated, industrialized, rich and democratic" (WEIRD) societies 115–16
whiteness 119
Winner, Langdon 203, 221, 223
Wolf, Christa 229
women's employment 38–43, 57

Women's Liberation 193–4
women's movement 228
women's work 193–5
work–life boundary 57
"workification" of everyday life 42–3, 58

"working customers" 56
World Bank 178
Wundt, Wilhelm 4, 68

Zibechi, Raúl 198–9